The Early Roman Empire in the West

edited by

Thomas Blagg
and Martin Millett

Printed in Great Britain and published by
Oxbow Books
Park End Place, Oxford, OX1 1HN

© Oxbow Books and the individual authors 1990

ISBN 0 946897 22 0

This book is available from booksellers or direct from
Oxbow Books, Park End Place, Oxford OX1 1HN
(Phone: 0-865-241249; Fax: 0-865-794449)
Payment may be made be credit card

Contents

Contents

List of Contributors

Thomas Blagg	School of Continuing Education, University of Kent, Canterbury
J. H. F. Bloemers	Albert Egges van Giffen Instituut voor Prae- en Protohistorie, Universiteit van Amsterdam
Jonathan C. Edmondson	Department of History, University of Sheffield
J. F. Drinkwater	Department of History, York University, Ontario
Michael Gechter	Rheinisches Amt für Bodendenkmalpflege, Bonn
Colin Haselgrove	Department of Archaeology, University of Durham
Simon Keay	Department of Archaeology, University of Southampton
Anthony King	Department of History, King Alfred's College, Winchester
Jürgen Kunow	Rheinisches Amt für Bodendenkmalpflege, Bonn
Nicola Mackie	Late of Department of Classics, University of Aberdeen
Martin Millett	Department of Archaeology, University of Durham
Nicholas Purcell	St John's College, Oxford
Richard Reece	Institute of Archaeology, University College London
S. D. Trow	Historic Buildings and Monuments Commission, London

Fig. 1.1. The growth of the Roman west to AD 14.

1. Introduction

by Thomas Blagg and Martin Millett

Over recent years there has been an increasing interest in the issues surrounding the nature of the Roman Empire, and particularly in the manner of its expansion and its successful control of diverse and extensive territories. This interest has generated many new data, from field survey, from large-scale excavations, and from the study of artefacts – especially those (such as wine-amphorae) which provide evidence for posing and attempting to answer questions of general economic and social importance. Furthermore, a dissatisfaction with traditional approaches and explanations has generated debate among ancient historians and archaeologists, which has drawn on models derived from such other disciplines as anthropology and theoretical economics. This renewal of interest in Roman archaeology is paralleled by a new awareness of the value of historical periods for the development of archaeological methodology. In 1968 D. L. Clarke wrote "work in text-aided archaeology will increasingly provide vital experiments in which purely archaeological data may be controlled by documentary data, bearing in mind the inherent biases of both". Roman archaeology has fruitfully fulfilled this prediction. The papers presented here illustrate this point by demonstrating the use of a variety of approaches which should be of interest to archaeologists outside the usual realms of Roman archaeology.

One particular area of interest and fruitful research has been the study of the interaction between Roman and native peoples and ideas in the formative years of the western Roman provinces. We thought it would be useful to bring together some of those who have been working recently on those subjects. Initially, this was to be for a conference, which was held at the University of Kent at Canterbury, 27-29 March 1987. We also believed that a book on the theme of the early Roman Empire in the West would be timely, and this volume is the result. From the start we aimed to produce not just a collection of conference papers, but a coherent volume, and we hope that it will seem so. The contributions are based on those which were given at the conference, but most of them have been largely rewritten for publication.

The subject matter is very large, and within the intended scope of the volume one could not hope to be comprehensive, either in geographical coverage or in the range of topics. We intended that it should be a volume of essays for debate, which would be primarily thematic in their basic approach, but would collectively give a reasonably even coverage of the western European regions within the period from the initial Roman presence, whenever that happened to be, up to the end of the first century AD.

We asked our contributors to address one or more of the following themes: the nature of the military presence and the rapidity of conquest and subsequent demilitarization; the extent and nature of the integration of native societies within the Empire; the rates of urban development, of the development of trade and external contacts, and of that of agriculture, both before and after Roman invasion. These themes are present in all the contributions in varying proportions and combinations, and for the arrangement of the chapters of the book, a simpler scheme was required. According to the common or comparable elements they contained, the chapters seemed to us to fall into four main sections. The resulting arrangement is in part thematic and, rather by coincidence, in part geographic: it so happpened, for example, that those papers in which urban development seemed the main common factor were also all concerned with the Hispanic provinces. There are also overlaps between the sections: thus, there are papers in sections other than that on urban development (III) which deal with the subject amongst other matters. Nevertheless, it seemed useful to group the papers as we have done, so that in the editorial preface to each section we could draw attention to the complementary, or in some cases contrasting, aspects of the authors' treatment of their subjects and the themes which they have in common. In introducing the volume as a whole, it remains for us to indicate some of the main points and areas of interest which have emerged.

Ideas about what the Roman Empire was, and about the process conveniently described as Romanization, will be found in all the papers, not just those in Section I which have those concepts as their main concerns. Common to many of them is an interest in observing not only the consequences of Roman conquest for the native peoples, for good or bad (Drinkwater) but also those peoples' own rôles in the processes, active and passive. Thus, for Millett, Romanization is a two-way process, and for Edmondson, it is not "a cultural matrix imposed on a native by Rome". Haselgrove's observation that it represents "the aggregate outcome of processes operating at an essentially local level, people by people" is a reminder of the complexity of regional variation which may be obscured by generalized interpretations. It is also a reminder of the fundamentally archaeological nature of this approach, since the evidence itself is the aggregate of essentially local excavations and field surveys, region by region.

This is relevant, first, to the study of the conquest and the initial responsiveness of native populations to Roman ideas. One way of looking at this in recent years has been through application of the concepts of world-systems theories related to colonial imperialism, in particular those which contrast activities at, and relationships between, the core and the periphery of a system. Bloemers uses this approach in formulating his examination of the factors which encouraged, or discouraged, the development of urban settlement in Lower Germany. Kunow, by contrast, is concerned with explaining the non-Romanization of Germany east of the Rhine, and he applies Galtung's model of imperialism (1972), which is basically that the more developed the social system of the periphery, the easier it is to occupy and integrate. Kunow's argument is that Rome did not conquer the Germans because it lacked the sort of links with the German nobility which it had with the more socially developed élite of Gaul. Much therefore depends on the nature of the local élite, and we will revert to that point shortly.

In some cases, however, relative differences in the rate of Romanization depended directly on military and political factors operating at the centre of the system. As several contributors remark, the initiatives of Augustus were of critical importance in the development of the Gaulish and Spanish provinces, in relation to local governmental organization, the laying out of road systems, the creation of new cities, and the making of censuses for purposes of taxation. The relationship of taxation to the development of the Roman economy and of Roman trade has been the subject of much recent debate among historians. Keith Hopkins' thesis (1980), that the economy of the relatively unsophisticated peripheral regions was stimulated to surplus production, and thus to increased trade, by the need to pay imposed Roman taxes, is followed in several of the chapters, though doubted by Millett. Relevant here is the extent and rôle of native coin use, which seems to have been more stimulating to markets in Tarraconensis (Keay) than in Belgic Gaul (Haselgrove). The agricultural infrastructure of the economy, or rather, of local economies, whether coin-using or not, must be seen as fundamental in explaining variations in the rate of Romanization, and in particular, associated changes (or otherwise) in the pattern of settlement. Within both Lusitania (Edmondson) and Britain (Trow) there was considerable diversity of response, notably in what happened to hill-fort settlements. Direct Roman intervention accounts for some of the changes, for example the resettlement of Gallo-Romans round Nijmegen (Bloemers) or the establishment of the Ubii in their new colony at Cologne (Gechter).

There would appear to be a general consensus, despite the last point, that in general Rome was much more laissez-faire in its government than more recent colonial empires. Indeed, it did not have the bureaucratic apparatus to sustain widespread central inter-ventionism, or even the degree of formulated policy and effective control that has often been assumed. Nevertheless, as King points out, in discussing religion, the Druids were suppressed, and the imperial cult was promoted, and both must be seen as official policy.

Such official acts could only in part account for the Romanization of native culture which is manifest in other apsects of religion, e.g. the adaption of native religious cults to Roman iconographic and architectural forms, and in the adoption of the Latin language, to which several contributors call attention. What Ramsay MacMullen (1982) has called the Roman epigraphic habit was not acquired uniformly: the Hispanic provinces were much more articulate than those in the north-west in that respect, though the reasons for this need more investigation.

As with the initial reception of Roman conquest, so with Roman culture, much of the answer seems to lie with the local élites. In the centuriation of the Po valley (Purcell), the inscriptions which call attention to urban munificence in Spain (Mackie), or Gaulish and British houses with courtyards and reception rooms (Blagg), we see the adoption of the "mentalité" of the Roman élite class in new surroundings. The cooperation of local native élites was essential to the government, stability and duration of the Empire. This could only be ensured because Roman material culture provided them with means of maintaining or enhancing the prestige of their own positions. As Trow points out, that process was already operating before the Roman conquest of Britain (as indeed was the case in other areas), and also, it was open to change, since the more widespread the Roman cultural trait became, so proportionately did its prestige value diminish. It must also be noted that the élite may seem significant because it is archaeologically "visible", more so than the great mass of the population, who are also historically inaudible most of the time.

The relationship between archaeological and written sources, and the nature of historical archaeology, are illuminated in several contributions. Too often, in a historically documented period, the function of the archaeologist has been perceived by some as limited to investigating those areas which the written sources do not reach. Others, considering that the historical sources have long been known and are not going to increase significantly, see archaeology as the only key to new knowledge and understanding. There is truth in both views, but each neglects the value of the combination of resources. Archacological evidence can correct bias or omission in written sources, e.g. in what Strabo said about Lusitania, and modern historians' deductions from it (Edmondson); it can amplify them, e.g. on the aftermath of the Second Punic War in Spain (Keay); or it can conflict with them, as in relation to Druidic Gaulish religion (King). It provides means of testing propositions based on written sources, as Kunow illustrates for the Limesvorland in Lower Germany. New questions can be asked of the written sources from the archaeological standpoints of topography and material culture, as Purcell does in considering how the Romans themselves perceived their landscape. The main point to emerge, however, relates to and provokes questions rather than answers. For example, there is much new evidence from intensive field surveys in the past decade, the results of which are important components of several chapters (Bloemers, Keay, Kunow). Haselgrove asks, however, whether these projects are delivering the information sought, and whether we are asking the right questions of it, i.e. questions which it is capable of answering. Reece, who believes that the combination of historical and archaeological evidence results only in confusion, reminds us that, while we try to explain our evidence within the context of the Roman Empire, it could be part of larger patterns of events which had little to do with the Empire as such.

As we wrote above, we intended that the contributions to this book should represent the new discoveries, and the debate in ideas and interpretations, which have made the early Roman Empire in the west a subject of particular interest in recent years. While, in this introduction, we have tried to select and integrate some of the common elements with which the book's contributors have been concerned, it seems appropriate to conclude it on the note of archaeological and historical enquiry in the discussion just summarized.

References

Clark, D. L. 1968: *Analytical Archaeology*, London

Galtung, J. 1972: 'Eine struckturelle Theorie des Imperialismus', *Imperialismus und strukturelle Gewalt. Analysen über abhängige Reproduktion*, (ed. D. Senghaas)

Hopkins, K. 1980: 'Taxes and trade in the Roman Empire', *J. Roman Stud.* 70, 101-25

MacMullen, R. 1982: 'The Epigraphic Habit in the Roman Empire", *American Journal of Philology* 103, 233-46

Section I

Concepts of Empire and Romanization

It is an essential first stage in studying the development of the western provinces of the Roman Empire to examine the perceptions of what that Empire was, and what we understand by the process of its Romanization. The papers in this section approach these matters from three contrasting standpoints.

Purcell investigates how the Romans themselves saw their Empire, given that their concepts of geography and landscape evolved without any idea of the accurate topographical map-making and -reading which are basic to our own comprehension of spatial relationships. He illustrates this mainly from Cisalpine Gaul, where Roman roads and the centuriation of land were part of a political reorganization of the landscape. This was a display of power, but it also illustrates the Romans' underlying conceptualization, their commitment to creating a new productivity, and the foundation of means of communication, and thus cohesion, with Rome and between previously unconnected areas.

Reece, by contrast, is concerned with the fundamental problem of defining a point from which to view 'Romanization' in objective terms; to judge how far the assimilations were consequences of Roman conquest, or otherwise the results of wider processes of change operating within the geographical area of which the Roman Empire happened to be part. The Roman historian or archaeologist may identify with a Rome-centred perception of what happened in the Empire, but this is merely one of the relative positions from which to attempt to interpret the observable changes in material culture. The theory of relativity emphasises the uncertainties inherent in such interpretations.

Millett's concern with the application of archaeological evidence to questions of Romanization is more pragmatic. He sees Romanization as a two-way process, and emphasises that Roman imperialism depended administratively on the adaptability of local élites. Contrary to the common assumption, he would see the army's presence as an obstacle to Romanization, in inhibiting local self-administration, and he suggests that Augustan reforms in administration and taxation encourages the more rapid development seen in the archaeological evidence during the Principate when compared with the Republic. Native élites adopted Roman forms of material culture to maintain their social prestige. This view of cultural assimilation contrasts with those of Wallerstein (1971) and his followers which envisages Rome as a 'World-system' of planned economic exploitation.

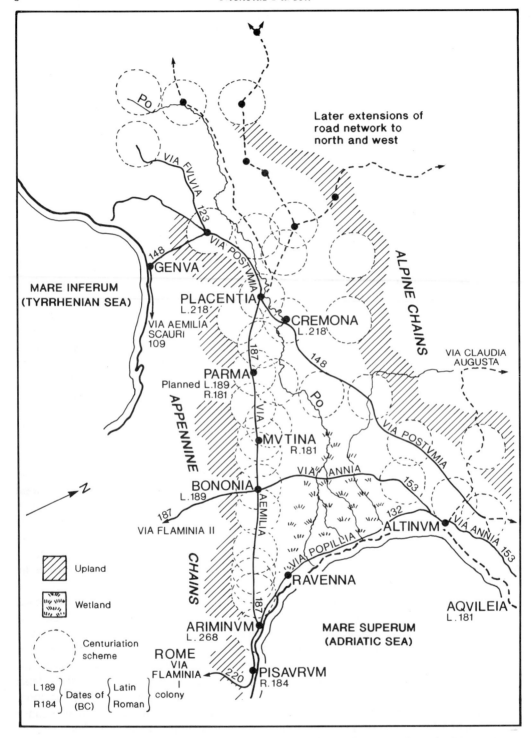

Fig. 2.1. Cisalpine Gaul. Second century BC and earlier coloniae and roads. Rings are territoria with centuriation.

2. The Creation of Provincial Landscape: the Roman Impact on Cisalpine Gaul[1]

by Nicholas Purcell

Se yonder, loo, the Galaxie
Which men clepeth the Milky Wey
For hit ys whit (and somme, parfey
Kallen hyt Watlynge Strete)
Geoffrey Chaucer, *The House of Fame* II, 936-9

Introduction

In the year AD 75, the imperial legate of Syria, M. Ulpius Traianus, supervising detachments of four legions and twenty auxiliary cohorts, was responsible for the building of a canal on the river Orontes above Antioch, in the name of the emperor Vespasian and his sons Titus and Domitian (Van Berchem 1983). The place was christened *Dipotamia*, Two Rivers; the new canal, three miles long, is described as 'channelling the river', *fluminis ductus*. The project included a series of bridges; and inscriptions, on great stone markers like the milestones of imperial Roman roads, make emphatic the ultimate imperial responsibility and the great size of the military workforce involved. It is the recent publication of one of these which informs us for the first time about the project. Two aspects of this undertaking are of particular importance. First, the construction is clearly conceived of as being analogous to the building of a great military road, *viae munitio*; the 'milestones' and the military labour, as well as the language used, make that clear. Second, the harnessing of the great river Orontes is stressed: the power of the emperor, his legate and Rome over the dominant element in the landscape of Syria is demonstrated by the naming of the place (a new, equal, Orontes has been called into existence) and by the phrase *fluminis ductus* (which immediately brings to mind the great artificial rivers, *aquarum ductus*, aqueducts, which demonstrated Roman control over nature in the water supply so showily provided for the cities of the Empire[2]).

Traianus it probably was also under whose auspices the road network of central Anatolia and the Cappadocian frontier was greatly extended; his son was thus enabled, as emperor, to create a single planned network of roads from Trebizond on the Black Sea through Syria and the new province of Arabia to the Gulf of Aqaba and the Red Sea. Trajan equally is the builder of the Via Traiana in Apulia and of the Danube bridge and ship-canal at the Iron Gates, the emperor to whom the younger Pliny proposed the Bithynian canal scheme, who removed whole hills of rock for his building schemes at Tarracina and Rome, marking the height of what he had removed in the latter case with his celebrated column, and who formed safe harbours where no natural port existed at Ostia, Ancona, Tarracina and Centumcellae. His adopted son in turn bridged the Tyne and linked the work with a defensive system as his father did on the Danube, the greatest monument to military piecework from the Roman period, Hadrian's Wall, spanning a province from estuary to estuary, like a highway but more monumental.[3] These three generations of Roman rulers represent the acme of responses to the physical circumstances of provinces, east or west, which we associate with the high Empire. While these examples may indeed be supereminent in scale, what I hope to show in this paper is that they are not novel in conception, but rather are grander versions of forms of imperial behaviour which the Romans evolved in the middle Republic, and which can be seen very clearly in action in Cisalpine Gaul in the period of three hundred years which separated the First Punic War from the conquest of Britain by Claudius. These forms of behaviour are so proverbially Roman that they can escape the searching enquiry, why did the Romans do this kind of thing? Not from some genetic ability at engineering, nor by accident. The reasons which I advance for this continuity of response are connected closely with the Romans' conceptualization of geography and landscape and their view of what effect they could have on them.

Geography has often been emphasized in discussions of Roman imperialism. It has been said that geographical ignorance led the Romans to overreach themselves in northern Europe in the time of Augustus (Brunt 1963, 175); in the previous period a close association of Roman imperialism with Greek geography has been perceived, and Polybius, Poseidonius, Caesar's *Commentarii* and Strabo examined from this point of view (eg. Nicolet 1978, 887-90; compare Nicolet 1988 and the suggestion of Lind 1986). At least one important recent discussion (Harris 1984, 22-3) prefers to consider the actual behaviour of the Romans in making and implementing military and diplomatic decisions, regarding the geographical question as something of a side-issue. This is perhaps because the geographical case has hitherto usually been expressed in too limited terms. In particular, scholars have taken for granted the thought-world of easy, habitual map-literacy. It is hard for us properly to conceive of ancient geographical ignorance, which is a wholly different ignorance from that expressed by the words *terra incognita* on the maps of the late medieval and early modern periods. We must expunge the Voyages of Discovery from our way of thinking if we are to begin to understand how the Romans saw 'new' lands.

One of the first consequences should be that we are cautious about saying, colloquially, and comfortably enough for the thought-world of today, that the Romans 'conquered an area'. Roman imperial behaviour will not be understood until we can say what 'conquest', 'annexation', 'subjugation', 'acquisition' meant in actuality: and, equally important, *what were the proper objects* of these various processes.[4] Ethnic terms for races or peoples, political terms for kingdoms or states, are common objects: geographical ones are not. The 'regional' names of the Roman provinces as they develop are much more closely related to the ethnic or the political than to pure geography – Cyrenaica, Bithynia; kingdoms: Galatia, Numidia; the collectivity of those peoples. Once this has been accepted, however, we can turn to the real instances of geographical understanding, and attempt to assess the much less common, but highly significant, occasions on which the power of Rome was expressed in relation to the landscape of the world.

Rome's empire remained 'cellular' until at least the third century AD – a great mass of individual units whose only common matrix was relationship to Rome, though that could take many different forms. The formation of piecemeal relationships with thousands of cellular entities is reflected in the language of Roman imperialism described above, with its emphasis on the social or political unit. This underdeveloped administration (compare Garnsey and Saller 1987, 20-40) was the inevitable response of a city-state whose magistracies, like those of almost all ancient communities, had, as I have argued elsewhere (Purcell 1985), only three basic models for executive government: the judge's verdict, the slaveowner's command, the officer's order. Nor could more be expected in a world of slow and haphazard communication between ruled and ruler: the randomness of administrative decision-making and the passivity of those in charge have been established by the work of Fergus Millar (especially 1977). Against this background, however, the historian has to set the deliberately grand gestures of Rome in the provinces and in Italy, like the examples from the late first and early second century with which this *Introduction* opened. The Romans did not have the help of concepts like 'Iberian peninsula' or 'North German Plain'. But their roads and frontier systems at least span distances of hundreds of miles; some, at least, of their decisions embraced thousands of communities rather than single cellular entities. An investigation into the Romans' attitude to geographical space should illuminate how this became possible, and also clarify the nature of the boundary zone between core and periphery in the Empire, which is the subject of other papers in this volume, and of the difference between the two. It should also help understand the decisions taken by the Romans and their impact on their subjects and the nature of the process which we usually know as 'Romanization'.

Cisalpine Gaul is an excellent case in relation to which we can pose questions about Roman definitions of and responses to the natural and human landscapes, because both forms of landscape are relatively distinct and unusual there. It is a crucial example of Roman imperial experience, in which the various *mentalités* of imperial control, whether more 'social' or more 'military' (and perhaps we should aim to weaken that dichotomy) can be examined. The main focus of discussion of second century Roman 'imperialism', it has been said, 'ought to be Spain and more importantly still, North Italy' since here the Romans displayed 'a consistent and unremitting combination of imperialism, militarism, expansionism and colonialism' (Millar 1984, 1). This study hopes to help show why that is true, and to analyse in greater depth the behaviour described in that quotation with those four forceful abstract nouns.

Conquest and the definition of space[5]
The Mediterranean world is very big, and the intuitive capacity of the human senses for regions is small. This is a truism which armchair historians need to recall constantly. Valley succeeds valley, plain plain and hill hill beyond hope of easy recall, and no ancient map ever even attempts to set forth the pattern of microregions into which the land divided (Janni 1984). Cisalpine Gaul was one of the largest readily perceptible regions in the Mediterranean basin; it was defined for any observer by the impressive sweep of the snowy Alps, and scarcely less so by the prominence of the Po, a watercourse of unmistakeable superiority at least between its juntion with the Tanarus and its mouth (Harris 1989). But notions of how this readily comprehended place abutted on the Danube lands, or the labyrinth of Alpine valleys, or even the tangled glens of the Ligurian and Umbrian Appennines, are not to be taken for granted. To put it simply: how would a Roman who fought in the armies which defeated Pyrrhus think of the journey from the Tyrrhenian Sea through the Po valley to the Adriatic? And how would the consuls who led those armies think of it? Neither soldier nor general had ever seen a topographical map of Northern Italy.

There are, I think, five possible answers apart from total ignorance. If the individual had done such a journey, which is perhaps not likely, or had spoken to people who had, it is possible that a parrot-fashion route-account of ascent, descent, ford, forest, spring and col could describe the journey from sea to sea. Combined, or separate, could be the 'view' notion just described; the curve of the Alps, the great hollow of the low plain, seen perhaps from the high pasture of the Appennines (thus, interestingly, Strabo (5, 1, 1) on Cisalpina as a 'gulf': the language is the coastal vocabulary of *periplous*). Experience direct or indirect could tell of the characteristic climate, soil, environment of Cisalpina – but that is not any help in relating it to the Ligurian coastlands. Knowledge of the nearest places to which Romans went might produce a sense of Cisalpina being the next place, the land of the Gauls, a zone of danger and alienness: for the Romans had since the beginning of the fourth century been justifiably nervous of Gallic power (*I Galli in Italia* 1979).[6]

But there is a fifth possibility which is perhaps more interesting. During the fifth century BC Greek thinkers had evolved new ways of thinking about space. On the small scale urban morphology seems to have attracted theoretical attention from Hippodamus of Miletus; it remains controversial whether or not he was also concerned with surveying and the division of rural space. On a larger scale however, this is the period of origin of what might be called a 'geometric' perception of the layout, on a very large scale, of the world in general. These investigations, most familiar to us in the attention paid by Herodotus (II 33-4) to the overarching symmetries of river, sea and landmass, did not conduce to topographical accuracy: the small scale irregularities might indeed spoil the order and system of the grand design. But during the fourth century the framework could be employed as the backdrop to increasingly self-conscious 'explorations' linked with political and military events in west and east. In the west the researches and presentations of Timaeus of Tauromenium were the culmination of the process. As the Romans began to insert themselves into the wider Hellenic world of the late fourth and early third century, his work was new and influential. Can we observe any possible reflection of the ways of thinking of this Greek tradition in Roman behaviour in the third century, the time when Rome began to have contact with Cisalpine Gaul?[7]

What we should be looking for are signs of a consciousness of the whole Italian peninsula as a single entity. There are indeed actions by Rome which suggest a new confidence in disposing for a wider region than ever before in an integrated way. The decisive point of contact with Cisalpine Gaul (despite earlier presence on the Adriatic coast) was the foundation of Ariminum in 268 BC. The striking thing is that this seems to be part of a concerted strategy which included the simultaneous foundation of Beneventum in the southern sphere of Roman activity. Ariminum, moreover, was the first in a sequence of twelve new-style more powerful higher status Latin *coloniae* (Salmon 1970, 92-4 cf. Salmon 1982) which seem to have replaced the old strategy of founding new rural *tribus* piecemeal. All this appears against the background of a new confident style of dividing land (which is considered below, pp. 15-19), building networks of treaties (in the north, for example, with Sarsina and Ravenna; cf. Luraschi 1979) and moving populations around wholesale, above all at Falerii and Volsinii. It would not be unreasonable to suppose that novel attitudes accompanied these novel forms of activity, and to associate these attitudes with cultural developments in the Hellenic world.[8] But it would be a mistake to see too early an ability on the part of the Romans to grasp the complex approaches to space which underlay their later military and governmental behaviour. If there is a new view of peninsular Italy, and it is true, as we shall see, that much of the repertoire of Roman imperialism has its roots in the late fourth and early third century, we still do not need to go farther than the needs of short term security in explaining it. Indeed the recent work of Arthur Eckstein (1987) takes the view that relatively uncoordinated responses to a highly dangerous Celtic threat lay behind Roman policy until the second quarter of the second century, a view which tallies very well with the evolution of Roman thinking suggested here.

The geographical view of this early period is likely to have emphasized the Po (sources in Chevallier 1980, 8-11), and probably the Alpine chain, so immediately visible to the traveller.

But the latter is oddly late in appearing (in the early to mid second century; Chevallier 1980, 39-40) and that it then does so in the context of the commonplace of the defences of Italy suggests that, somewhat paradoxically, Hannibal's famous crossing may have done much to establish the Alps as a barrier (contra, eg. Salmon 1982). The tradition on the Po (Chevallier 1989, 78-98) puts it in the context of the simplified 'grand design' approach of the 'geometric' world view with its schematic coincidences – it rises appropriately from the highest peak of the Alps, and has a miraculous underground section like the Nile: it is second only to the Danube among the glreat rivers of Europe (Strabo 4, 6, 5). Some of this goes back, no doubt, to Timaeus (Grilli 1979), who improved on his predecessors' views of the Adriatic coast too (Janni 1984, 96-7); but Polybius in the mid second century found a great deal in Timaeus to disagree with in his turn, and gives us (II, 14, 6; 15, 9-10) what has been called the beginning of a scientific understanding of Cisalpina (Chevallier 1980, 11); part, perhaps one should rather say, of a new way of looking at the world to be associated with Roman conquest (a way which was to have a rich sequence of descendants in later Roman attitudes to 'frontier rivers', cf. p. 22 below). Before that conditions hardly encouraged more.

Not only was Cisalpina the home of the terribly alien Gauls, but it was also far from ethnically homogeneous or isolated. The Gauls retained frequent social links across the Alps through which there was continuous movement (Tizzoni 1981, cf. Eckstein 1987, 12-13); note the exodus of the Boii in 191. The settlements of the coastal wetlands were in close contact with the primarily Hellenic economic and cultural world; some of the settlements of the central plain retained social and even political traces of contacts with Etruscan and Umbrian culture from beyond the Appennines; peoples like the Veneti were of different origin altogether and preserved fertile links across the Julian Alps with central Europe to the north-west (Ridgway and Ridgway 1979, 419-487, Dyson 1985, 46-7). The fusion of these various elements produced a fertile and quickly-changing society, as rich in potential as Gaul or southern Britain before the Roman conquest. If the Gauls were alien, they were not to be perceived as savages.[9]

It is important not to retroject, from the prevailing view of the imperial period, a model for Roman/alien contacts which includes too steep a cultural gradient between the two. Cisalpine Gaul was for the Romans of the third and second century a new and, to some extent, strange place; it was on the edge of the zones in which their decisions usually had force; it was vulnerable to the hostility of its neighbours who were more remote from the usual channels of Roman intervention. But to call it a 'frontier province' entails a vision of Roman power spreading into the world like ripples on a still pond which did not occur to observers in the Republic (if ever). Places with which the Romans were involved were everywhere liable to aggression: each theatre of operations had its own character and its own relationship to the City. Cisalpina was just one among dozens of such theatres. The notion of 'frontier', moreover, suggests perceived cultural backwardness; Cisalpina could not be regarded as different from Samnium or Baetica in this respect when compared with the Roman homeland. In fact part of what distinguished Cisalpina was its wealth and cultural potential. This is perhaps the principal difficulty with Steven Dyson's recent and original study *The Creation of the Roman Frontier* (Dyson 1985); it involves the marginalization and barbarization of the region through transposing from the Empire the language of 'Roman frontier commanders' and their attitude to 'thinly populated zones' (p.63) or 'underused Celtic land' (p.24), and above all, the notion of 'buffers' (eg. p. 51).[10] All Roman interests needed to be protected; the non-Roman in the world was vast, indescribable and undifferentiated; there was no place before the late Republic for the type of relationship with a particular foreign power which makes it desirable to form a third entity as a buffer in between. Rome's boundaries were changing, not in place only, but in kind, constantly; too simple a notion of frontiers obscures how Rome actually developed new types of edge to the areas of her concerns over the centuries.[11]

For the Romans of the first half of the third century the strip of coastal plain south of Ariminum was The Gallic Territory, *ager Gallicus*. From 268 Ariminum had its own city territory, beyond which came the land of allied Ravenna. Where and what was the 'frontier'? The Romans crossed it for ever, decisively, in the ferocious Gallic War of 225-2, a sudden increase in the order of magnitude of their involvement in the area, whether it is seen as the result of Gallic belligerence and Roman fear (Eckstein 1987, 12-18) or simply as nakedly aggressive (Harris 1979, 197-200). The numerous peoples of the Boii were obliterated and the Insubrians humiliated. Now many Romans and their allies had first-hand experience of Cisalpine Gaul.

The practical topographical experience in question is less important than two other steps. C. Flaminius, as consul in 223 BC, or more probably as censor in 220 BC (Wiseman 1970, 143), built the great road that bears his name, the Via Flaminia, from Rome to Ariminum; and in 218, 160 miles into the heart of Cisalpina, the two large Latin *coloniae* of Cremona and Placentia were established. Both moves speak of new ambitions in the region; indeed they should probably be seen as closely associated. The nature of the association and the wider significance of road-building and of the land allotment which accompanied the foundation of a *colonia*, form the subjects of the two sections which follow.

The road and the conquered landscape

Pietro Janni (1984) has investigated the dependence of the geographical conceptions of the ancients on the idea of the itinerary. The Roman control of large areas of land entailed some conception of geographical space, and it is not surprising, therefore, that this control is intimately associated with the itinerary in its most developed form – the built road.

The prehistory of the long-distance Roman road is obscure; it has no obvious Greek antecedents, though the Royal Road of the Persians, a defining backbone for their domain, may be cited as a precursor. The Via Appia of 312 BC, linking Rome with its first substantial new area of involvement at a distance (Frederiksen 1984, 214-5), is the spectacular pioneer of the genre, though we should be careful about not retrojecting the solidity or magnificence of the developed road architecture of the imperial period or the various extensions of the practice which may be dated during the next century (Wiseman 1970).[12] The Via Flaminia and the Via Appia, if not quite unique in the simple fact of their existence as named roads, were alone in the imaginative panache and audacious scale involved in linking Rome with an important settlement days' journey away. Even if they were only systematized tracks, with some grand sections and fords, the *mentalité* which they reveal is one of informed confidence and grand ambition. Informed confidence: but the making permanent and making Roman of the itinerary is itself a way of ensuring the permanence of the information which is power. 'Rome to Capua' and 'Rome to Ariminum' now become *Roman* geographical concepts. We are dealing with what Janni (1984) has called 'the conquest of the second dimension'.

The first Roman roads, unsurprisingly, radiate from Rome. The first not to do so is still, however, an extension of a radius; the Via Aemilia, the great highway which in 187 BC joined the head of the Via Flaminia at Ariminum with the two forty year old *coloniae* in the heart of Cisalpina (Chevallier 1983, 8). An Augustan restoration gives a possible glimpse of how this road was viewed, however, as an ingredient in a topography dominated by the river-routes; an inscription records the rebuilding of 2 BC as extending not from Ariminum to Placentia, but to the river Trebia (*CIL* XI 8103; for rivers as conceptual boundaries, cf. p. 22 below). A second Via Flaminia of 187 BC initiated, to the best of our knowledge, the long-lasting Roman strategy of boxing in the regions between radial roads; crossing the Appennines to Bononia from Roman Etruria it symbolized the subjugation of the mountains which had thus been encircled with a cordon of Roman control.[13] M. Lepidus who built the Via Aemilia is commemorated also in the town of Rhegium Lepidi, some half way along its course. It is striking that he chose the name of the town which was thought of as the other extreme of Italy, but the nuance of the selection is not clear. In this foundation, in the novel strategy of the second Via Flaminia, and in the deliberately impressive straightness of the Via Aemilia (the first secure instance of this well-known geometric display) there are perhaps signs of innovation in the exhibition of power.[14] But the underlying sense of geography remains that of the third century; these are still the Romans for whom the world is so parochial that the Adriatic is the Upper and the Tyrrhenian the Lower Sea (attested in Plautus *Menaechmi* and in a context of 178 BC by Livy 41, 1, 3). But a further change is visible during the second quarter of the second century.

The roads hitherto had been essentially radii from Rome, Roman Cisalpina a protrusion of Roman influence linked with Rome umbilically. While the umbilical metaphor always remains significant, in this period there is a decisively novel change. It seems that there is another change in the geographical outlook of the Roman élite, one which can be fitted into other such developments, as we shall see in the following section. The change involves viewing the world as a series of geometric spaces which can be crossed from one to another by journeys which fit them together into a coherent network. The journey, here as so often, precedes the road, and in 171 we see a pivotal moment when the consul C. Cassius Longinus sets off from Aquileia not just to fight the neighbouring peoples but with the spectacular aim of marching all the way to the other Roman sphere of concern in Macedonia (Livy 43, 1, 5-10). The plan is met with a revealing mixture of hostility and incredulity. It is, however, the beginning of a long tradition. As far as we can see, the moment when it is first crystallised in the road-network is the building of the Via Postumia in 148 BC, from Genua on the Tyrrhenian to Aquileia on the Adriatic Seas, a project the geographical significance of which comes out in the early milestone (*ILLRP* 52) describing the Genua-Cremona section (it is interesting to find Cremona stressed, as the hub of Roman Cisalpina, cf. Strabo 5, 1, 11). Postumius is consciously leaving his mark and Rome's on the the whole of northern Italy. The same idea is strikingly expressed later in the language of the trophy of Augustus commemorating the conquest of the Alps 'from the Upper Sea to the Lower' (Pliny *NH* III 136-7, cf. *CIL* V 7817).[15]

The geometric layout of the lands is measured, expresed and controlled by the celebration of the itineraries across them. The formation of such axes becomes a familiar aspect of Roman attitudes to the empire, almost to the point of being a doctrine. It is these routes which give shape and definition to the world, so that by the second quarter of the first century BC Lucretius can compare them to the putative bounds of the universe itself; unlike the Roman World, he implies, in fact the infinite cosmos is not controlled by such a pattern of communications: 'the whole of existence is bounded by no zone of roads' (I, 958-9). Generals express their achievements in terms of distances traversed: so C. Sempronius Tuditanus in

129 BC expressed his conquest of Istria on the base of his statue at Aquileia with the simple phrase 'From Aquileia to the River Titius, one thousand stadia' (Pliny, *NH* 3, 129, cf. *ILLRP* 334-5). He thought in stadia (units of some 185 m), but the Romans were engaged in inventing the mile, or at least its systematic use (since numbered milestones go back, in very small quantities, to the early third century: *ILLRP* 448-9 (cf. Hirschfeld 1907)). By Polybius' time the distance from Apulia to Sena Gallica had been 'marked out in miles' (Strabo 6, 3, 10 = Polybius 34, 11, 8), and milestones were a conspicuous and relatively novel feature of C. Gracchus' spectacular Rome-centred overhaul of the Italian road-network (Plutarch, 28 something of a *locus classicus* for the complex *mentalités* behind Roman road-building). The welding together of existing routes into great highways in the provinces followed, the Via Egnatia across Macedonia being the most impressive case (Polybius seems to have commented on its length in miles, and to have terminated the reckoning at the great river Hebrus – Strabo 7, 5, 9); the Via Domitia through Narbonensis into Spain is a further example (Polybius 3, 39, 8, explaining in this context the Roman practice of road measurement in some detail).[16] Such routeways came to define some of the commands of the late Republic, as has been shown for Cilicia, which was a geographical concept centred on the road from Asia through the Cilician and Syrian Gates to Antioch (Syme 1939).

It was at the emphatic mountain crossing of the Via Domitia in the Pyrenees that Pompey placed his trophy commemorating the conquest of 876 towns 'from the Alps to the outer edge of Spain' in 72 BC, a precursor of Augustus' Alpine monument quoted above. That recording his Eastern victories eleven years later took the genre to new extremes: he claimed the conquest of 1.2 million people (not areas, we note) 'from the Sea of Azov to the Red Sea'. The idea of conquest from sea to sea, which began at least with the Via Postumia, is developed (as Peter Wiseman has pointed out – 1987b) in the Augustan and imperial ideologies of the empire stretching from sunrise to sunset, that is (sometimes explicitly) from Ocean to Ocean[17]. The monuments set up at the end of their *itinera* by generals who reached (or crossed) Ocean reflect this (below p. 22). The generals of Augustus in particular made considerable efforts to join and unite areas of the outer world with *itinera* between outstanding geographical pivots. These were, in the more successful instances, turned into properly built *viae*, like that which Agrippa had built from Narbonensis to the Ocean on the shore of the Channel (for the world view of the Augustan Age above all Nicolet 1988). The pattern of these *itinera* lies behind the boundary routes of the early Empire like the Fosse Way and their more elaborate successors. Popular responses to the imperial messages embodied in these make their connexion clear; the long road itinerary, from Gades on the Ocean to Rome, and via the older Via Aemilia route, of the Vicarello goblets (Dilke 1985, 122-3) and the representation of Hadrian's Wall on the Rudge Cup are statements in the same language. These frontiers were of course called *limites*, and to interpret that term correctly we need to turn to a quite different aspect of Roman landscape control; although many points of contact between the aspects will become apparent.

Parcelling up the world.

A glimpse of how a roadless and mapless age might respond to the achievement of crossing the landscape with long-distance roads may be had from the lines of Chaucer quoted at the beginning of the paper. Other societies have used the notion of path or route for describing the Milky Way; it is striking to see the name of a great Roman road applied to the bar which splits the night sky.

In fact – and by coincidence – Roman religion also served to associate the layout of the sky with that of the land. The closest of connections bound the line of the augurs' sight and the measurements of the land surveyor and roadbuilder. Rome's earliest coherent street, the Sacred Way, coincides with the view from the augurs' observation post on the Capitol towards the distant Mons Albanus (Coarelli 1983, 97-118). The same technical terms refer to divisions of the space of ground and sky (Dilke 1971, 32-5, 86f.). Until recently such practices were either regarded as immemorial, because obscure, or imported, because exotic. Modern work on Roman religion has tended away from such responses, and is more inclined to accept continuous evolution and change in religious observances, in time with the dramatic changes which took place in Roman culture and society (North 1976). Instead of saying 'the Romans in the late Republic, turning to serious land-surveying, naturally invested it with the rigmarole of an arcane and ancient religion', we should say 'Roman religion responded to the changing view of the world made possible through the opportunity of dividing up space in new ways, and grew with the new cultural forms to produce a coherent system'.

There is a fairly obvious connexion between the visual impression of a region traversed by a line of sight, as discussed above (p. 9), and the extension of such a line as a marked route on the ground to prolong the region defined beyond the limits of vision, and that link has its place, as in the case of the Sacred Way, in the religious system. But lines of sight across the sky also define areas by bounding them, and that too had its correlate on earth in Roman thought. The division of the land into a regular chequerboard of squares by routes parallel and perpendicular to a main axis was again both a feature of administrative practice and an aspect of the religious system. Its effect on the landscape is the system of land-division which we know as centuriation.[18]

It is now possible to make use of the close association of centuriation with religion not, as previous generations did, to argue that it suggests an immemorially ancient origin for this sort of land division, or that it derived from the practice of the Etruscans, but to reason that it reflects the preoccupations and *mentalités*, if not of a much wider segment of the *populus Romanus*, at least of the inner circle of the Roman élite; that it is intimately connected with the structures of power and with the whole range of ways in which those who managed the Roman state conceived of their *imperium* in the world.[19] Some rules of property must go back to the earliest society of Rome; they are irrecoverable, but no doubt are the usual casual, haphazard net of responses to complex needs, fluid, flexible and adaptable. This is not at all what centuriation is like. Centuriation represents a radical and essentially political attitude to landscape and its use; this and its close links with power are reflected in its place in the religious framework of the state. The nature of the ideology concerned needs further examination.

The period of origins is not at all clear; some steps may have been taken during the fifth and early fourth centuries when Rome formed new rural units (the second-generation *tribus*), set up the early *coloniae* and made various intricate arrangements with some of her neighbours.[20] But by the end of the fourth century the dividing up of the part of the fertile plain of north Campania known as the Ager Falernus suggests that the Romans were prepared to use an approach to whole landscapes which has affinities with the practice of some of the Greek cities of southern Italy (the best known is Metapontum). In the Ager Falernus it seems that the early arrangements were rapidly replaced by the different system which became standard, using exact squares instead of elongated rectangles, and emphasizing central axes at the expense of others (Vallat 1983). It seems natural to associate in some way this revolutionary step with the construction in 312 of Rome's first great long-distance road through the heart of the area (compare the use of the new system at Tarracina, also on the Via Appia). The division of Sabinum after 290, where no such road was certainly involved, seems to have been more like the older, more Hellenic, precedents (for other early systems, Castagnoli 1985b). We observe M. Curius Dentatus the conqueror of this territory making interesting play with the fact that he had conquered inhabitants *and* taken their land (*vir. ill.* 33, 1-3); he was also the author of a spectacular landscape-changing drainage project (Cicero, *Att.* 4, 15, 5) and, like Ap. Claudius, the builder of a great aqueduct (Frontinus *Aq.* I, 6; *vir. ill.* 33, 9).[21] Note the connexion between Flaminius' road and his plan to redistribute the *ager Gallicus* (Eckstein 1987, 10-12; Chevallier 1983, 7). Centuriation and highway-planning are, as we shall see, intimately linked (Clavel-Lévêque 1987, 14).

We may pass over the obscure history of centuriation proper until the period when it is triumphantly and massively applied to Cisalpine Gaul, in the wake of the Gallic War of 225-2 and of the further wars against Gaul and Ligurian at the start of the second century. The large *coloniae* of Cremona and Placentia (218) and their reinforcement (191) and the settlement of Aquileia (181) are the key dates: (though the chronology is very hard to fix – Chevallier 1983, 41): it is clear too that some centuriation along its route predates the construction of the Via Aemilia in 187.[22] The end result is clear from the Map (Fig. 2.1); Cisalpine Gaul became a largely centuriated landscape. What can we say of why?

First, doing this to a landscape is a spectacular display of the conqueror's power. Although some environments are more tractable than others for centuriation, the amenability of the terrain does not determine this response (thus Gabba 1983 against Hinrichs 1967). Much more important is the wish to punish and repress. The major instances of centuriation are a catalogue of Rome's discomfitures: Campania, Cisalpine Gaul, Carthage's territory, the lower valley of the Rhone.[23] While there were no doubt other factors at work – the reduplication and consolidation through repetition of the Roman social and political system is one that has been rightly stressed (Gabba 1983b; Frederiksen 1976) – this was among the most significant.

The display of power worked at various levels. We have already discussed how such divisions conceptually integrate and enclose whole regions. They impose a Roman set of measures and units of division (Vallat 1983b). They are also associated with an impressive infrastructure, the roads themselves, fords, causeways, bridges, cuttings, dykes and so on, which change the face of nature: such modifications were the sign of kingly power which could be thought to trespass on the sphere of the divine (Purcell 1987a); compare the description of C. Gracchus' roadbuilding at Plutarch *Gr.* 28. The foundation of *coloniae* and the building of arterial roads went hand in hand; we see that clearly in the middle Republic in Cisalpina, and it is still visible in the provinces in the imperial period. The Via Sebaste and Augustus' colonial foundations in Pisidia are a case in point (French 1980, 707). Centuriation also presupposes a social and economic system. The former inhabitants remain, demoted, humiliated and dependent (Gabba 1983a and b; Chevallier 1983, 75-7). The new units impose Roman legal practice, to maintain communications and access from the *limites* into the centre of the *centuriae* (Capogrossi Colognesi 1983). A new labour-intensive economy depends on these communications and on the newly oppressed work-force of the former inhabitants; its purpose is to provide the new local Roman central place with what it needs, and beyond that to contribute to the well being of Roman consumption in general. But behind it all the motive force is not simple braggart grandiloquence. The aim is the maintenance of a dynamic of growing power (not unlike the motive force in the empires of the Fertile Cresent in the first half of the first millenium BC: collect and deploy in order that you can go on collecting and deploying; if it works, your power grows) through the accumulation of available resources. This is not just some abstract greed (for the need to produce a more subtle model than crude 'greedy' exploitation, Millett, below Chapter 4). The resources clearly include the natural wealth of the region, both physical and as collected by its earlier inhabitants, but also the inhabitants and their descendants, the human resource of manpower.[24] While the inferiority of the conquered can not be doubted, it nonetheless is of a kind which presupposes their future inclusion, or that of their posterity.

Cisalpine Gaul illustrates these points well; it is indeed the case-study on which some of them were based. Emilio Gabba has explored the retention and future role of the previous populations (1983a and b). The control of populations was visible from the start, in the obliteration of the social system of the Boii, in the forcible removal of the Ligurians, in the banning of the new Gallic settlers near Aquileia, in the whole policy of *attributio* which ran on into the first century AD. The pattern of incorporation is beyond our scope here; the remarkable *structure*, running from the fifth century BC to the third AD, of the gradual and measured differential inclusion of fighting men and their élite officers into the Roman system is quite well understood, and need only be mentioned here as a concomitant of the other long-lived *mentalités* and behaviour-patterns which this article does discuss.[25] For the other side of exploitation of resources, the best example of the importance of already accumulated wealth is from Transalpine Gaul, the treasure of Tolosa (Strabo 4, 1, 13; Dio fr. 90); but we notice that the Romans were impressed by the loot of gold and silver in Nasica's triumph of 191 BC (Livy 36, 40), and the gold-mines of Cisalpina were already producing for Rome by 143, during the most creative period of Roman organization in the region (Pliny *NH* 3, 138; 33, 78).[26] Polybius' account of the gold-mines near Aquileia, quoted by Strabo (4, 6, 12) reminds us of how close was the link between mineral wealth and accumulated treasure. In this sense the alleged effect on gold prices throughout Italy (they fell by a third) of the exploitation of the source is of particular interest.

In agriculture, the emphasis we would expect on the move along the spectrum that leads towards the cash-crop away from subsistence is to be found prominently in the mid-second century account of Polybius (*H* 17, 11-12). While he allows that the land has great virtue of its own, the particular merits he describes are not those of a part of the world enjoying a primordial Edenlike abundance. They are the product of good management and recent change which has given local agriculture new standards – wheat prices are low, other prices are fixed and a great variety of important crops is produced with success so that the surplus may be distributed throughout Italy.[27] These are the intended virtues of the centuriated landsacpe, in which every settler is meant to have the opportunity of being part of the new intensification of agriculture, assisted by the labour of former owners or of the more readily available slave, or by less successful neighbours. The *colonus* is not intended to be a 'peasant', but a progressive farmer, like the former master of the freedmen praised by the epitaph of Forum Livii (*CIL* XI 600), who show *pietas* and *fides*, feed themselves and look after any thing that is theirs – in the interests of their patron, a former military tribune. The stone must be more or less Augustan in date, from the period when Strabo, perhaps echoing Poseidonius, gives an expanded but similar narration of the prosperity of Cisalpina (5, 4-12). Not that we should see Cisalpina as of a wholly different quality from that of other centuriated parts of Italy (*pace*

Gabba 1983, 24, who sees the exploitation of the area as a breakthrough from the impoverished south); the system had been evolved in superproductive Campania, where the boundary walls, *maceriae*, which lined the *limites*, gave the agriculture the air of market-gardening, so intensive was it (Pagano 1983, 226).[28]

In Cisalpina many of the *limites* were bordered by *fossae*, which helped improve production as needed through both drainage and irrigation. They were part of the hydraulic control of the environment which formed a large part of its impressiveness as 'man-made landscape', and like the roads, both local and arterial, they assisted the new economy by helping communications, at least in the larger cases. Pliny emphasizes the role of the *fossae et flumina*, and Strabo by chance gives the detail of one such project (5, 1, 11): the control of Trebia and Po above Parma. He explicitly stresses both communications and agriculture. This scheme was no doubt one among many. Place names and casual allusions tell us of a Fossa Clodia, and the early Empire added a Fossa Augusta and Fossa Flavia (Chevallier 1980, 88-94; Bosio 1967). A recent study has played down the economic importance of the waterways of Cisalpina (Harris 1989). If this is right, then it is on the rôle of rivers in communications and in the symbolic landscape that the explanation of their prominence in Polybius, Strabo and Pliny must fall. Hence, for the coastal zone, cults like that of Neptunus Augustus at Hadria (Buchi 1984, 70-7).

We should conclude this section by putting all these Cisalpine examples into their historical context. The Romans were much preoccupied with the ideology of centuriation during the first half of the second century. The probable division of the whole Ager Campanus in 165 was the most spectacular case: a large centuriation was laid out, aligned almost exactly on the points of the compass, a real consummation of agrimensorial art (the recently discovered centuriation of the Pomptine marshes (Cancellieri 1985) shows a similarly doctrinaire lack of topographical concern and may belong to the same context: here the parallel with Cisalpina is maintained through the great drainage schemes of M. Cornelius Cethegus (Livy *Per.* 46) which may be linked with this division. The whole was recorded on a plan – a notable piece of intellectual history, as it is one of the first on record at Rome, which was displayed in the Hall of Freedom at Rome where the censors' headquarters was (Granius Licinianus 9-10). The choice of location helps insert the division in the whole range of steps for maximising public revenue in which the magistrates, and especially the censors, became involved over the period: the receipt of the gains from the new management of Italy. The whole pattern was part of the articulation of Roman power, growing as it was from decade to decade, which brings us round again to the natural associations such attitudes had with the state religion. Livy quotes a pair of highly revealing instances of the way in which the Romans were forming new notions of space (cf. Janni 1984, 130-4). In 181 the seas off Italy were divided into two commands, and we are lucky enough to hear how the matter was conceptualized. These two fragments of the *imperium* were held to be separated by a notional line bisecting the Sorrentine peninsula. The word for the line comes, hardly surprisingly, but very gratifyingly, straight from the thought world of the augur and the *agrimensor*: it is *cardo* (40, 18). In 178 naval operations in the Adriatic likewise made Ancona the *cardo* of their sphere of reference (41, 1, 3).

Not that all this ideology was the uncontroversial *communis opinio* of the Roman upper class. We should not, however, be seeking to identify a few major packages of policy and preference among the *primores viri*, and still less to attribute any such coherent value-systems to particular political groupings. The history of the period has been bedevilled by this: political historians who have only glimpses of the ideas approved by politicians have been forced to make those ideas the whole foundation of their analysis of political dissension, or give up. But opponents agreed and allies differed over the most fundamental ideological questions, and the historian must be content with sketching networks of ideas that belong in proximity to each other, without having the pleasure of attributing them as wholes to groups, let alone to individuals. Aspects of the centuriation ideology can be associated with both the elder Cato and the Gracchi, but to assert that is not to make them politically like-minded! The problem is, of course, similar with the related question of 'imperial policy', where differing responses to the needs of empire fit into value-systems which can not easily be mapped on to the everyday discourse of Roman politics.

The triumph of the ideology of centuriation in the early second century should be linked, for reasons which should now be clear, with the changing attitude to the idea of geographical space in Italy and beyond it, which lies behind the revolutionary expansion of the long-distance road-system towards the middle of the century. The small example of the maritime commands illustrates the application of the thought-world to the widening horizons of Roman power in the Mediterranean. The combination of imperial history and world geography in the writing of Polybius, a Greek intellectual brought to Rome as a result of the process of imperial growth, is vitally important: and it is in Polybius that we find the noteworthy prominence of Cisalpina in his account of the Gallic War in Book II.[29] Still more revealing is the work of the elder Cato, known for his public opposition to Greek cultural influence, but responding in truth to the new intellectual climate which owed much to the world outside Italy. His pioneering attempts to give Rome an indigenous intellectual literature included the famous treatise on agriculture, the agriculture of intensified cash-crop production. He also produced the historical work *Origines*, in which he attempted to account for the past and present of the communities of Italy, Roman and non-Roman. The work reflected a conception of the unity of the whole peninsula, an idea of the land of Italy, bounded by the Alps; and included the whole of Cisalpina at some length.[30] Here too the overlap of the affairs of Italy with the affairs of the empire was apparent, it seems: Cato reflected on the annihilation of the 112 subdivisions of the Boii (Pliny *NH* III, 116), an episode far from irrelevant to Rome's decisions fifty years later (though we cannot tell if his view was more Calgacus' on the subjugation of Britain in Tacitus or the 'I have forbidden the Nasamones to exist' of Suetonius' Domitian). Finally, this is the age of the addition of exact topographical recording of landscape to the wider conceptions of geography – represented by cadastral mapping of centuriation (Dilke 1971, 316), which added the detail to the conceptual *mainmise* on the landscape already represented on the larger scale by the Roman long-distance road.

There are more concrete aspects of the value system too. We have suggested that it stands for a productive, flexible, intensificatory agriculture, and how that can be linked with the management of Italy for the benefit of the *populus Romanus* apparent in the new *vectigalia* and the other censorial initiatives of the time. It is indeed the agriculture of Cato; for centuriation entails the recapitulation of a social order which produces farmers on the Catonian scale alongside the infrastructure of the smaller *coloni*. It is an agriculture which is in many ways the antithesis of Ti. Gracchus' awful vision on the road to Numantia, hostile to the accumulation of huge conglomerations of land, intensive rather than extensive, demanding the care, skill and attention of the farmer. It is a system of production which can help provide the wherewithal, in various senses, for the life of the growing *plebs urbana*, a system characteristic of an Italy centred on Rome, as was emphasized and indeed fostered by the road-building programme of C. Gracchus.[31] But one of its best expressions survives by accident. The man, unfortunately anonymous, who built the great road from Capua to Rhegium on the Strait of Messina – a geographically-conceived point-to-point project if ever there was one –in the later second century, records on the inscription from Polla in Lucania (*ILLRP* 454) that, in addition to the construction of the road with all its monumental structures, and as part of the same scheme, he ensured (where he could, on public land) that pastoralists should make way for arable cultivators. The simple phrase stands for a whole way of thought.

From Republic to Empire

The sources are barely able to sustain our narrative over the period from the decisive developments in Roman policy which produced a kind of 'constructive imperialism' where before there had been only –merited or unmerited – fear, to the full Italianization achieved by the early Empire. On the institutional level there is a continuous modification of the rights and statuses of local communities in both Cisalpina and Transalpina. There were still campaigns, like those of Crassus in the 90's, which had as their offshoots new urban foundations (in this case Forum Licinii in the foothills of the Alps, Poggiani Keller 1986). A Roman magistrate might be called upon to solve boundary disputes (as between Ateste and Vicetia in 136 BC, *ILLRP* 477) or to rule on the management of the resources of the environment (as with the summer pastures of the Appennines above Genoa in the famous Sententia Minuciorum of 117 BC, *ILLRP* 517). Many of the settlements in this region called *Fora* owe more to the encouragement by prominent Romans, whether magistrates or not, of local economic centres, than they do to major institutional strategies (Brunt 1971, appendix 12). The rights of the indigenous ethnic units against the newer communities became clearer, and out of the consciousness of ethnicities of authors such as Cato there gradually came a general practice for the management of such social entities which, by the time it was applied in Gallia Comata and beyond, had become the policy which is often referred to as 'cantonal'. The division of the large mountain and hill territory of Appennine Velleia into equipollent *pagi* named after local toponyms or Roman deities, though undatable, clearly belongs in this context (Frederiksen 1976, 346-8). No overall policy or plan need be postulated here, but the gradual production of zones, great or small, of institutional homogeneity, was to be a vital precedent for the wide upgrading of city-statuses in Caesar's Baetica, and the management of large tracts of the Julio-Claudian provinces. In fact the most sweeping changes were damaging, the confiscations and redistributions of the Second Triumvirate, which provoked the famous reactions of Virgil's *Eclogues* I and X. But here Rome's rulers were applying the ancient techniques of centuriation and landscape-formation to a region which was already in important ways culturally homogeneous with their own world.[32]

This social development is still more difficult to trace, and is bedevilled by a polar viewpoint which sees only the stand-off between metropolitan Romans and stereotyped Gauls. The material culture of Roman settlers in the late third and early second centuries was consciously different from that of the local peoples, and the famous terracotta reliefs of Civita Alba suggest that it had a hostile orientation towards them (Eckstein 1987, 67 and 157). But the culture in question was not unique to Rome – it was rather that of the Hellenizing and prosperous city life of the whole of the central part of the peninsula. By the time that the age of Cicero is drawing to an end that culture is largely a phenonemon of the past, and is no longer an identifier of ruler or ruled. The reactions of the local inhabitants to it (Tizzoni 1981) reflect an indirect emulation – in the acquisition of the epigraphic habit but in local forms, or of the increased use of coinage, but not necessarily Roman. The cultural boundaries were fluid, diverse and complex.

Tracing them is another matter. The researcher familiar with the recent exponential growth in archaeological material from peninsular Italy or the north-west provinces must remember that the synthesis of the Cisalpine material is still somewhat less advanced (Rossignani 1981, 22f). 'Gallic' artefacts scarcely prove separate residual Gallic existence, as recent work has vigorously argued (Luraschi 1980). The simpler antagonistic models have given way to the notion of assimilation, or better, to the idea that a continuum of society and culture came to unite the various peoples of the region, for all that particular localities could retain distinctive characteristics of their own. The integrative process was subtle, working through the institutional forms which we have been considering, tying the descendants of the native population into the more and more refined Roman institutional framework, like the *vernae* of Vicetia in the epigraphic record, whom Gabba (14), surely rightly, sees as this sort of subordinate group.[33] What the conquered had to offer, in the short or long run, was themselves as a demographic resource for Rome's further wars, and it was clearly preferable for a slow amelioration of status in return for service to integrate Gaul with Italian over the generations than for the victorious Romans to maintain a kind of apartheid by military might. Thus in the words of a recent author 'Cisalpine Gaul became the first province to be populated entirely with Roman citizens'.[34]

So the coercion which brought about the subjugation of Cisalpina, after the initial battles, is located not, in the way in which it would be in other conqueror-states, in garrisoning and military repression, but in the instrumentation of the policies examined in the earlier sections, which entail the subordination of the natives as the conquerors organize the landscape in accordance with their geographical preconceptions. Very simply, the Roman perception of the place to be conquered and the process of conquest are so closely related as to be aspects of the same *mentalité*, and there is no need to disjoin them or seek more elaborate explanation.

The geographical particularities of Cisalpina, as perceived by the Romans, are intimately related to the history of its inclusion in the Roman world, and remain a potent ingredient in the formation of its later culture. It had the good or bad fortune to be what Auden called a 'definite place', with the strongest personal identity, an instantly recognizable physiogonomy in its remarkable fertility, its encircling mountains, the extraordinary net of waterways, river, lake and coastal wetland.[35] The geographical perceptions which had moulded the region's history were not simple notions of bald topography, but a response to landscape, and the emphatic presence of the landscape in the cultural life of the élites of Roman Cisalpina is the consequence. Catullus' Sirmio (Wiseman 1987) and the landscape of the Eclogues, the *villegiatura* of the lakes in the younger Pliny or of the Altinate shore in Martial are part of the same interaction which was visible even in the early days of the Roman presence in the Po valley.

This phenomenon is the more noticeable since it was not created equally in other places, even where a striking landscape and a remarkable history combined with a local prosperity – there is no literature of the Alban Hills. Campania, however, does offer a striking parallel. Here too the intricate process of accommodation with Rome had taken the form of a long evolution of landscape forms, in a place of the most unusual physical characteristics; and the end of the process was a still more particular social and cultural milieu. Rome's rulers understood how to make use of such settings, as is hardly surprising since their forebears had done much to form them. So the unstable, fissured rocks of the volcanic craters provided the idea and location for Agrippa's spectacular tunnels; so, to take a more extreme example, the Gulf of Baiae provided the backdrop for the overwrought displays of the emperor Gaius.[36] The parallel occasion in Cisalpina is the little-known spectacle provided by the emperor Claudius when, returning victorious from the geographical triumph of the subjugation of Britain, staying in Ravenna, he staged a ceremonial entry into the mouth of the Po in a monstrous floating palace (Pliny *NH* 3, 16, 120, cf. Poggiani Keller 1986, 119-120). The conqueror of land and sea was celebrating his mastery of both in the ideal place, where they were strangely intertwined and where the river which defined the whole region debouched.

The triumphal procession from Britain which thus made its entry into Ravenna was no doubt commemorated like the actual triumph at Rome itself by some sort of a *monumentum*. The *iter* of the journey itself is a monument of a kind; the connexion between the road and the journey along it is an obvious one. Three such physical memorials may be cited in this case: the Porta Aurea, much of which still survives at Ravenna (Tosi 1986, 466-8); the great lighthouse which Claudius gave the city (*NH* 36, 83); and the road, the Via Claudia Augusta, which joined this region to the Danube across the Alps (Venturi 1985, 273). The associations of each make it a strong contender to be associated with Claudius' *reditus* (formal return from war) through the city (Walser 1980, 438-26). Arches and gates, traditionally associated with the triumphal procession at Rome, mark several cases of the end of the length of a great road traversed by a returning general, or generally symbolic of the power of Rome: they are particularly found where they can also be a seamark, and embellish a transhipment like that of Claudius. Trajan's arch at Ancona and the possible *quadrifrons* at Richborough come to mind. More purely land-oriented is the terminal arch of the Via Flaminia at Ariminum, commemorating Augustus' refounding of the road.[37] Other upstanding objects could serve, like the terminal markers of the Via Appia at Brundisium, or the *statua* which concluded the Via Annia at the Straits of Messina (above p. 20); or altars, like those on the farthest coast of Spain (Syme 1969) or Drusus' on the Albis (Potter 1987) or lighthouses, the best of both worlds, with perpetual fire and lofty height. The lighthouses at Corunna, Dover and Boulogne are clear examples of the lighthouse as route-end monument.[38] The Via Claudia Augusta commemorates the journey of Claudius' father Drusus across the Alps, and it seems extremely likely that it represents the actual route, adopted out of *pietas*, of Claudius' British return. The milestones place it in precisely the context which we have been examining: 'from Altinum to the Danube' and, better, 'from the Po to the Danube',[39] that is 'from the second river of Europe to the greatest' (cf. p. 9 above). The emperor's achievement is described in the language of geometric geography as we saw it deployed in the second century BC; and the achievement itself takes the form of a response to the world of nature, a dialogue with the landscape in the language of power.

All this should perhaps make us a little cautious of using the language of administrative policy or practical utilitarianism in our discussion of Roman imperialism. We have seen the place of rivers in defining the landscape of Cisalpina, as boundaries and as foci and as characteristic wonders. That should remain in our minds as we think of the nature of the Danube frontier or ask what role Augustus intended for the Elbe. It is a poet of that age who glosses '*res componere gestas, terrarumque situs et flumina dicere*' (Horace *Ep.* II, 1, 251f. 'piecing together the narrative of history, stating the lie of the land and position of the rivers'). Traianus at Antioch and the whole tradition of ostentatious waterworks going back to Herodotus may be closer to what the Romans actually thought about the landscapes of the fringes of the developed empire than analyses of their defence strategies in peripheral regions. No doubt there were jumps in scale between Appius Claudius Caecus' road and the great 'geographical' roads of the second century, and between them and Pompey's claim to have subdued the whole East from the Sea of Azov to the Red Sea, and between that grandiloquence and the actual formation of a *limes* from Trebizond to Aqaba: but there is also much that is common to all the stages. And the display of the power of the conqueror to grasp the landscape, human and physical, and change it, is what is essential to Roman imperialism; not greed, or a nebulous expansionism, or an imperial mission, least of all that of cultural Romanization. Manlius Vulso crossed the Po in 218 BC and Claudius Caesar the River of Ocean in AD 43; in both the environments thus reached their successors won renown by 'creating the semblance of what Nature had denied.' And Agricola's famous baths and schools in remote Britain are as far from a mission to Romanize the unacculturated barbarian as Traianus' canal or the centuriation of Placentia.[40]

Notes:

1   I should like to thank the audience and organizers of the Conference at the University of Kent for their remarks about the first version of this paper. Its scope is deliberately broad, and I have tried to keep documentation to a minimum; many of the subjects touched upon are the subject of vigorous debate, and this sketch of a personal view can of course not do them full justice. The comments of the editors and of Andrew Lintott, Fergus Millar and Peter Wiseman have also been of very great help.

2   By coincidence, a second inscription from Antioch shows another canal on the Orontes built under Traianus, this time with corvée labour from the city: the *dioryx gnaphikos*, or Fullers' Canal. We may perhaps assume other projects with regard to the subjugation of the river which are as yet unattested (Van Berchem 1985; Feissel 1985). The status of the Orontes as a 'wonder of Nature' (Strabo 16, 2, 7) should be taken into account; for the control of natural waterways as a sign of the true ruler Strabo 16, 1, 9-11; Purcell 1987a, 192-3; cf. also note 12 below.

3   For these building-projects and their nuance, Purcell 1987a.

4   Lintott 1981 is an excellent example of what can be achieved – in this case with the institutional terminology of *imperium* and *provincia*.

5   The underlying ideas of what follows come from modern work on the cognitive aspects of human attitudes to space: see in particular Downs and Stea 1973 and 1977; for the ancient world Janni 1984.

6   For pre-Roman Cisalpina also Tizzoni 1981.

7   The geometric conceptions should be clearly distinguished from itineraries, another category which was gaining sophistication during the fourth century (Janni 1984, on Scylax and Sherk 1974 on the influence of Alexander's journeys). This mode of thought may not be irrelevant to the fourth century genesis of the Via Appia. For geometric approaches to the geography of Cisalpine Gaul, Strabo 5, 1, 2.

8   The consul of 268 was the second of his family with the eloquent Greek cognomen *Sophus*: he dedicated a temple to Tellus, the Earth, in which, at least two centuries later, there were Greek-style maps of Italy (Varro *RR* 1, 2, 1). These have been taken as mid third century (Wiseman 1986, cf. Dilke 1985, 39), and at the very least show a thematic link between the notion of Tellus and Italian geography. If we understood its circumstances and date better, the establishment of the *colonia* at Saena Gallica about 290 BC might be fitted better into this scheme; see Eckstein 1987, 5, n.6, with the suggestion that Gallic/Samnite cooperation might underlie any concertion of Roman response in north east and central Italy.

9   For a good account of the culture of the Gauls in Italy, the exhibition catalogue *I Galli in Italia*
        1978.

10   Compare the language of 'civilized Romans versus the barbarians' in Toynbee 1965 II, 253 'a
        regression of civilization had preceded the Romans' own foward movement'...'it is unquestionable
        that the advent of the Gauls was a set-back for civilization in the Po basin'. But even Toynbee
        admits (256) that Cisalpina was 'far from being a savage wilderness infested...by a horde of
        savages'.

11   It is clear however that the region was not equally densely populated, and there were more open
        areas in the north-west (Negroni Catacchio 1978).

12   Road-building itself is of course much earlier, and quite elaborate; for Etruscan roads in S. Etruria,
        Potter 1979 fig. 21 and pp. 79-83, a clear contrast to the network established in the second
        century. The ancient Via Latina, the earliest routeway between Rome and Campania, should be
        regarded as a concatenation of these local tracks. It would, however, be interesting to know at
        what date the Capua Gate of Rome was built and named (the walls are fourth century but not
        precisely dated, and there may have been an earlier similar enceinte (Coarelli 1982). The
        development of the district around the gate seems to coincide however with the buidling of the
        Via Appia (Purcell 1987b). Note also how the first aqueducts, the Aquae Appia and Anio Vetus
        (cf. p. 16 above with n.22) date to the same period.

13   For these roads Wiseman 1970 (1987), Chevallier (1983) 8. Note also a further Via Aemilia of
        175 tying Aquileia in on another radius.

14   A characteristic which has long been the most obvious feature of many Roman road systems.
        But we perhaps too often attribute straightness to the pursuit of efficiency, which it does not in
        fact usually serve, any more than it does economy. Breathtaking geometry and ruthless shaping
        of nature are the only explanations, in the pursuit of the display of power. This underlies the
        'aesthetic' appreciation of Plutarch for Gaius Gracchus' work: cf. n.31. The association of
        R(h)egium with the homonymous Greek city seems more plausible than the reasons for reading
        it as 'Royal' (settlement): Ewins 1952; Brunt 1971, 574.

15   'Network roads': the Viae Annia (153) and Popillia (132) replaced waterborne communications
        along the Venetian litoral (the account of Wiseman 1964 should be accepted), and the Via Aemilia
        Scauri of 107 improved communications in the Ligurian area. Problems remained at that end of
        the Postumia; it remained far easier to approach Cisalpina from Rome via the Aemilia (Wiseman
        1970, 134: note also the itinerary of the Vicarello goblets, Dilke 1985, 122) and the Genua end
        of the Postumia should be seen as a grand geographical claim rather than as a route of great
        utility, for the first forty years of its existence at any rate. Hence the implausibility of Toynbee's
        view (1966, II, 284) that the Postumia was a *'chemin de ronde'* inside a sub-Alpine frontier.

16   It is very likely that the Kings of Macedon had improved the route later taken by the Via Egnatia.
        For Roman road-building in a province recently created from a kingdom, compare M. Aquillius
        in Asia 129-6 BC (French 1980): *ILLRP* 455-6.

17   See Sallust, *Cat.* 36.4; cf. Cicero *ND* II, 164; Pliny *NH* II, 242; Ovid, *Pont.* I, 4, 29f. For Ocean
        to Ocean Plutard, *Crassus* 16, 2; Catullus 11, 3; Sallust *Hist.* I, 11, 17.

18   What follows must be once again a hasty survey of an increasingly technical subject. The best
        recent accounts of centuriation are in the catalogues *Misurare la terra*; especially the general
        volume *Centuriazione e coloni nel mondo romano*, 1983. Two further volumes describe cases in
        Cisalpine Gaul: *Il caso modenese*, 1983 for the centuriation of 183 BC in Mutina, and *Il caso
        mantovano*, 1984 for the centuriation of 281 BC in Cremona and the great division of the territory
        of Mantua in 40 BC which affected the ancestral property of the poet Virgil. On the whole subject
        the volume cited under Vallat 1983b is of particular importance. See also Chevallier 1983, 31-80.

19   Against the immemorial origins of centuriation, Gabba 1983a and b.

20   For early centuriations, postulated and/or attested, Castagnoli 1985a and b; 1981; Clavel-Lévêque 1987.

21   The correspondence would be complete if a road-building project of Dentatus in Sabinum can be deduced from the emendation via Curia in Dionysius of Halicarnassus I, 14,4.

22   Tacitus, *Hist.* III 34 on the colonization of Cremona, with an interesting logic: it is *precisely because (igitur)* it was intended as a bulwark for Rome in the region that it was populous, sited for communications and agricultural production, and (most importantly) *benefited from the closest contact and intermarriage with the indigenous peoples.* For the more positive aspects of the subordination of the native population to the new Roman system, see also the discussion below p. 17. For the site of Aquileia, Fabbri 1979; Dyson 1985, 73-4, the senate's debate about the nature of the *colonia* and the site combine to suggest that the centuriation was the main *raison d'être* of the foundation: although the routes across the Alps and into Istria may have played some part at this stage, the strategic considerations are overemphasized by Dyson 1985, 73-4 (for the later ambitions of Longinus and Tuditanus, above p. 13-14).

23   See Clavel-Lévêque 1987.

24   Stressing the importance of Cisalpine manpower in the Second Punic War Eckstein 1987; for its rapid deployment Toynbee 1965, II, 272-3.

25   Rossignani 1981, 228 n.17 (recent finds at Cremona) for the architecture and decoration of the Roman settlements. Note also, on the political urbanization of the second century, Gabba 1976.

26   It is worth remembering that the growing tendency of the Roman state to exact dues of various kinds extracted gain from the redistribution of goods. We should not suggest that any of the attitudes and policies discussed in this paper had the objective of furthering trade as such. But the centuriation ideology and the surplus it involved naturally did no harm to existing patterns of redistribution, northwards from Aquileia, west through Genua, south-east down the Adriatic: and these effects were exploited (a *portorium Aquileiense* existed by 69 BC, Cicero *Font.* 1,2). See Bandelli 1985 for the Dalmatian coast and its rapid development as part of such networks during the first century BC; Panciera 1976 for the Alpine routes; Bandelli 1983 for the early phases of the economy of Aquileia.

27   For the productiveness of Gallic agriculture, see *I Galli in Italia*; Gabba 1983b, 42; Chevallier 1983, 232-49. It remains very uncertain how far the agriculture produced a surplus for redistribution elsewhere (Harris 1979). I am inclined to think that it did not on any significant scale, but the case cannot be proven.

28   Some justification is needed for this view of the agriculture of Cisalpine Gaul. The idea that the land-allotment system is capable of making use of the labour of the old owners, (for the repetition in *coloniae* of Roman social hierarchies, Gabba 1983 and Frederiksen 1976), the poorer settlers, and slaves, is developed from the treatments of Gabba 1976 and 1983. A contrast has been drawn between the local consumption of Cisalpina and the cash-crop 'plantation-agriculture' of the south (eg. De Neeve 1984, 92, 112). But if Gabba is right, the cash-crop producers of the south may have been able to lock in to a similar system, which accords with recent views of the complexity of Italian farming systems (eg. Spurr 1983); and the economic isolation of the north is not what Polybius implies, and goes against the evidence for the wine-trade (Tchernia 1986, 129-35, Baldacci III and Dressel 6 amphorae; 185, *spionia* grape). The plantation of the Sasernae, whose treatise was the second on agriculture in Latin, was at Dertona (Kolendo 1973). For older accounts of the subject Chilver 1941, 129-44; Brunt 1971, 172-84. On the agriculture of centuriation see also De Neeve 1984, 130-45; Keppie 1983.

29   For Polybius' researches with the help of Scipio Aemilianus, Pliny *NH* 5, 1, 9. On the development of these tendencies in the Augustan period, see now Nicolet 1988.

30   For Cato's intellectual setting Toynbee 1965, II ch. 15; Astin 1978, ch. 8.

31   The aesthetics of the straightness of Gaius' roads is emphasized by Plutarch, and that the distances were emphasized by the large-scale use of regular milestones (83); *CGr* 7). For the combination

of road-building and allotments note also the example of Flaminius (n. 13 above). For the Polla stone see Wiseman 1970 (1987), dating the project to 130-28 and attributing it to T. Annius Rufus. The Gracchan moment is certainly appropriate for the interpretation favoured here: see also Hinrichs 1967.

32   Dyson 1985 is good on the cities of Transpadana, although he is inclined to blend second with first century experience. See also Poggiani Keller. The main foundations, with accompanying centuriation, are Dertona and Eporedia to the west. For the triumviral settlements Keppie 1983.

33   The excellent work of Giorgio Luraschi (1979; 1980) should be emphasized in this context.

34   The question of the enfranchisement of Cisalpina has long been extremely vexed (Ewins 1957; Millar 1977, 398-403; Luraschi 1980) and of course can not be covered in detail in this discussion.

35   Note the description of the coastal zone in Servius (ad Georg. I, 262) 'for the greater part of the Veneto is so rich in rivers that all exchange is carried out in boats; Ravenna and Altinum are typical – hunting, fowling and agriculture alike are practical for boats'. For the wetlands see Traina 1983 and 1988; for their natural wonder Strabo 5, 1, 5.

36   This line is developed to some extent in Ch. 14 of Frederiksen 1984. Note that the Agrippan tunnels are one of the few wonders indicated on the Peutinger Table, a possible descendant of Agrippa's world map: cf. Wiseman 1987b.

37   Ariminum, *ILS* 84, 'via Flaminia et reliqueis celeberrimeis Italiae vieis...muniteis'. Note the Augustan *colonia* have; Keppie 1983, 187. Ancona; Lepper 1969, 256 (this piece discusses also Trajan's mid point arch for the Via Appia Traiana at Beneventum). For the Tiberian arch for Germanicus on Mt. Amanus as E. frontier of the Empire, Potter 1987. Note also the Ianus Augustus at Cordoba, centre of the road-system of Baetica, Smallwood 1967, 333. Note the imperial embarkation-point as a concept in Strabo (*naustathmos*), 4, 1, 9, cf. 4, 3, 3.

38   For such monuments (*horoi cheirocmetoi* Strabo 3, 5, 6 with a general discussion of their geographical significance) Syme 1969, the case of Spain: for lighthouses in particular Hutter 1978. See also the lighthouse of Caepio at the mouth of the Baetis, a significant location (Strabo 3, 1, 9); perhaps to be attributed to Q. Servilius Cn. f. Caepio who governed Further Spain in 140-39 BC, in which case the example would be interestingly early.

39   The milestones are respectively *CIL* V 8002 and *ILS* 208, Smallwood 1967, no. 328, Levick 1985 no. 98. See also Chevallier 1983, 11. For imperial *itinera* cf. Millar 1982.

40   The quotation is Tacitus, *Ann.* XV 42. Purcell 1987a examines some of these reactions to the landscape in a domestic context.

References

Astin, A. E. 1978 *Cato the Censor*, Oxford

Bandelli, Gino 1983 'Per una storia della classe dirigente di Aquileia repubblicana', in *Les 'bourgeoisies' municipales italiennes aux IIe et Ier siècles av.J.C.*

Bandelli, Gino 1985 'La presenza italica nell'Adriatico orientale in età repubblicana', in *Aquileia, la Dalmazia e l'Illirico*, 1985 (= *Antichità Altoadriatiche* XXVI), 59-84

Bosio, Luciano 1967 'I problemi portuali della frangia lagunare veneta nell'antichità', *Venetia* I, 11-96

Brunt, P. A. 1963 review of Hans D. Meyer, *Die Aussenpolitik des Augustus und die augusteische Dichtung*, 1961, *J. Roman Stud.* 53, 170-6

Brunt, P. A. 1963 *Italian Manpower*, Oxford

Buchi, E. 1984 '*I quattuorviri iure dicundo* di Adria e il culto del dio Nettuno', *Epigraphica* 46, 65-89

Buonopane, A. 1986 review of Traina 1983, *Riv. Fil.* 114, 224

Calzolari, Mauro 1984 *Carta degli insediamenti di età romana nella, Bassa Modenese*, Modena

Capogrossi Colognesi, Luigi 1983 'Le servitù di passaggio e l'organizzazione del territorio romano in età repubblica', in *Misurare la terra, centuriazione e coloni nel mondo romano. Città, agricoltura, commercio; materiali da Roma e dal suburbio* 1983, 28-32

Castagnoli, Ferdinando 1983 'Resti di divisioni agrarie nel territorio del odierno Lazio', in *Misurare la terra...*, 38-40

Castagnoli, Ferdinando 1985-6 'Sulle più antiche divisioni agrarie romane', *Atti Acc. Lincei* 39, 241-58

Cancellieri, M. 1985 'Pianura pontina' in *Misurare la terra...*, 44-8

Chevallier, R. 1959 'Rome et l'Italie du Nord', *REL* 37, 132-50

Chevallier, R. 1980 *La romanisation de la Celtique du Po*, I, Paris

Chevallier, R. 1983 *La romanisation de la Celtique du Po*, II, Paris

Chilver, G. E. R. 1941 *Cisalpine Gaul*, Oxford

Clavel-Lévêque, M. 1987 'Questions de méthode et approches comparatives: cadastres et histoire', in G. Chouquer *et al.* (eds.) *Structures agraires en Italie centro-méridionale*, Rome (= *Coll. Ec. Fr. Rome* 100), 3-57

Coarelli, Filippo 1982 in I. Dondera and P. Pensabene (eds.) *Roma repubblicana fra il 509 e il 270 a.C.*, 22 Rome

Coarelli, Filippo 1983 *Il Foro Romano, I, periodo arcaico*, Rome

De Neeve, P. W. 1984 *Colonus: private farm-tenancy in Roman Italy during the Republic and Early Principate*, Amsterdam

Dilke, O. A. W. 1971 *The Roman Land Surveyors*, Newton Abbot

Dilke, O. A. W. 1974 'Archaeological and epigraphic evidence of Roman Land Surveys', *Aufstieg und Niedergang der Römischen Welt* II,I, 564-92

Dilke, O. A. W. 1985 *Greek and Roman Maps*, London

Downs, R. M. and Stea, D. 1973 *Image and Environment. Cognitive mapping and spatial behaviour*

Downs, R. M. and Stea, D. 1977 *Maps in mind. Reflections on cognitive mapping*

Dyson, S. L. 1985 *The Creation of the Roman Frontier*, Princeton

Eckstein, A. M. 1987 *Senate and general; individual decision-making and Roman foreign relations 264-194 BC*, Berkeley

Ewins, U. 1952 'The early colonization of Cisalpine Gaul', *Papers of the British School at Rome* 20, 54-70

Fabbri, Paolo 1979 'L'aspetto fisico del territorio di Aquileia', in *Il territorio di Aquileia nel 'antichità'* (= *Antichita Altoadriatiche* XV)

Feissel, D. 1985 'Deux listes de quartiers d'Antioche astraints au creusement d'un canal (73-4 ap. J.-C.)', *Syria* 62, 75-103

Frederiksen M. W. 1976 'Changes in the patterns of settlement' in P. Zanker (ed.), *Hellenismus in Mittelitalien*, Gottingen 341-55

Frederiksen, M. W. 1984 *Campania* (ed. N. Purcell), London

French, D. H. 1980 'The Roman Road System of Asia Minor', *Aufstelg und Niedergang der römischen Welt* II, 7, 2, 707-29

Garnsey, P. and Saller, R. 1987 *The Roman Empire, Economy, Society and Culture*, London

Gabba, Emilio 1976 in P. Zanker (ed.), *Hellenismus in Mittelitalien*, Gottingen

Gabba, Emilio 1983a 'Per la storia della società romana tardo-repubblicana', *Opus* I, 373-87

Gabba, Emilio 1983b 'Strutture sociali e politica romana in Italia nel IIs. a.C.', in *Les 'bourgeoisies' municipales italiennes aux IIe et I siècles av. J.C.*, 41-5

Grilli, Alberto 1979 '*Il territorio di Aquileia nei geografi*', in *Il territorio di Aquileia nell 'antichità'* (= *Antichità Altoadriatiche* XV)

Harris, W. V. 1979 *War and Imperialism in Republican Rome*, Oxford

Harris, W. V. (ed.) 1984 *The Imperialism of Mid-republican Rome*, Rome

Harris, W.V. 1989 'Trade and the River Po: a problem in the economic history of the Roman Empire', in J.-F. Bergier (ed.) *Montagnes, fleures, forêts dans l'histoire: barrieres ou lignes de convergence*, 123-33

Hinrichs, Focke Tannen 1967 'Der römische Strassenbau zur Zeit der Gracchen', *Historia* 16, 162-76

Hinrichs, Focke Tannen 1974 *Die Geschichte der gromatischen Institutionen*, Wiesbaden

Hirschfeld, O. 1907 'Die römischen Meilensteine', *Kleine Schriften* (1913), XLIV

Hoyos, B. 1976 'Roman strategy in the Cisalpina 224-22 and 203-191 BC' *Antichthon* 10, 44-55

Hutter, S. 1978 'Der antike Leuchtturm von La Coruña, *Antike-Welt* 9, 2, 33-48

I Galli in Italia Exhibition Catalogue (ed.) Paola Santoro, 1979

Janni, Pietro 1984 *La mappa e il periplo, cartografia antica e spazio odologico*, Rome

Keppie, L. 1983 *Colonization and veteran settlement in Italy 47-14 BC*, London

Kolendo, Jerzy 1973 *Le traité d'agronomie des Saserna*, (= *Archiwum Filologiczne* XXIX), Wroclaw

Lepper, F. A. 1969, review of F. J. Hassel, *Der Trajansbogen in Benevent; ein Bauwerk des römisches Senates*, Mainz, 1966, *J. Roman Stud.* 59, 250-1

Levick, Barbara M. 1985 *The government of the Roman Empire, a sourcebook*, London

Lind, 1986 'The idea of the Republic and the foundations of Roman political liberty', in C. Deroux (ed.), *Studies in Latin literature and Roman history*, IV, 44-108, Brussels

Lintott, A. 1981 'What was the imperium Romanum? *Greece and Rome* 28, 53-7

Luraschi, Giorgio 1979 *Foedus, ius Latii, civitas*, Pavia

Luraschi, Giorgio 1980 'La romanizzazione della Transpadana: questioni di metodo', *Studi in onore di Ferrante Rittatore Vonwiller*, II, Como, 207-17

McDonald, A.H. 1974 'The Roman conquest of Cisalpine Gaul (201-191 BC)', *Antichthon* 8, 44-53

Marcotte, D. 1987, review of Janni 1984, *Latomus* 46, 234

Millar, F. G. B. 1977 *The Emperor in the Roman World*, London

Millar, F. G. B. 1982 'Emperors, frontiers and foreign relations, 31 BC-AD 378', *Britannia* 13, 1-23

Millar, F. G. B. 1984 'The political character of the classical Roman Republic, 200-151 BC', *J. Roman Stud.* 74, 1-19

Negroni Catacchio, Nuccia 1978, in *I Galli in Italia*, 76-80

Nicolet, Claude 1978 'L' "imperialisme" romain', C. Nicolet (ed.), *Rome et la conquête du monde Méditerranéen*, Paris 883-920

Nicolet, Claude, 1988 *L'inventaire du monde: géographie et politique aux origines de l'Empire romain*, Paris

North, J. A. 1976 'Conservatism and change in Roman religion' *Papers of the British School at Rome* 44, 1-12

Pagano, Mario 1983 'Un nuovo termine della centuriazione dell' *ager Campanus*', in *Misurare la terra 1983: centuriazione e coloni nel mondo romano*, Modena, 231-4

Panciera, Silvio 1976 'Strade e commerci tra Aquileia e le regione Alpine', *Antichità Altoadriatiche* IX, 153-72

Peyre, C. 1979 *La Cisalpine Gaulloise du IIIe au Ier siècle av. J.-C.* (= Etudes d'histoire et d'archéologie I), Paris

Poggiani Keller, R. (ed.) 1986 *Bergamo dalle origini all'altomedievo*, Modena

Potter, D. S. 1987 'The *Tabula Siarensis*, Tiberius, the Senate, and the Eastern boundary of the Roman Empire, *ZPE* 69, 268-76

Potter, T. W. 1979 *The Changing Landscape of South Etruria*, London

Purcell, N. 1985 'The Arts of Government' J. Boardman, J. Griffin and O. Murray (eds.) *The Oxford History of the Classical World*, Oxford, Chapter 23

Purcell, N. 1987a 'Town in country and country in town', (ed.) E. MacDougall, *The Roman Villa Garden*, Washington

Purcell, N. 1987b 'Tomb and Suburb', (eds.) H. von Delsberg and P. Zanker, *Römische Gräberstrassen*, Munich

Ridgway, D and F. R. (eds.) 1979 *Italy before the Romans*, London

Rossignani, Maria Pia 1981 'Problemi aperti relativi all' età romana', (eds.) A. Piccoli and P. Gasperini *Primo convegno archeologico regionale, Museo archeologico Cavriana, Ati*, Brescia

Salmon, E. T. 1970 *Roman Colonisation during the Republic*, London

Salmon, E. T. 1981 *The Making of Roman Italy*, London

Sherk, R. K. 1974 'Roman geographical exploration and military maps', *Aufstieg und Niedergang der römischen Welt* II, 1, 534-63

Smallwood, E. M. (ed.) 1967 *Inscriptions illustrating the reigns of Gaius, Claudius and Nero*, Cambridge

Spurr, S. 1983 *Arable Cultivation in Roman Italy*, London

Susini, G. C. 1965 'Aspects de la romanisation cispadane, chute et survivance des Celts, *CRAI*, 143-63

Syme, R. 1939 'Observations on the province of Cilicia', in *Anatolian Studies presented to W. H. Buckler*, 239-332 (= *Roman Papers*, Oxford, 1979, no. 10)

Syme, R. 1969 'A governor of Tarraconensis', *Epigr. Stud.* 8, 125-33 (= *Roman Papers*, Oxford, 1979, no. 54)

Tagliaferri, Amelio 1986 *Coloni e legionari romani nel Friuli Celtico*, Pordenone

Tchernia, A. 1986 *Le vin de l'Italie romaine*, Rome

Tizzoni, M. 1981 'La seconda età del ferro', (eds.) A. Piccoli and P. Gasperini, *Primo convegno archeologico regionale Museo archeologico Cavriana, Atti*, Brescia, 211-24

Tosi, G. 1986 'La porta Aurea di Ravenna e un disegno de Andrea Palladio', *R M* 93, 425-70

Toynbee, A. 1966 *Hannibal's Legacy*, Oxford

Traina, Giusto 1983 *Le Valle Grandi Veronesi in età romana*, Pisa

Traina, Giusto 1988 *Paludi e bonifiche del mondo antico*, Rome

Van Berchem, D. 1983 'Une inscription flavienne du Musée d'Antioche', *Museum Helveticum* 40, 186-96

Van Berchem, D. 1985 'le port de Sélencie de Piérie et l'infrastructure logistigne des guerres parthiques', *Bonner Jahrbücher*. 185, 47-87

Vallat, Jean Pierre 1983 'Studio di un catasto nell' *ager Falernus*', in *Misurare la terra...*, 227-30

Vallat, Jean Pierre 1983b '*Ager publicus*, colonie et territoire agraire en Campanie du nord a l'époque républicaine', (ed.) M. Clavel-Lévêque *Cadastres et éspace rurale, Table Ronde, Besançon*, Paris. 187-98

Venturi, E. 1985 'La politica edilizia di Claudio a Rome e in Italia', *RStAnt*. 15, 257-77

Walser, G. 1980 'Die Strassenban-Tätigkeit von Kaiser Claudius', *Historia* 29, 438-62

Wiseman, P. 1969 (1987) 'Viae Anniae again', *Papers of the British School at Rome* 37, 82-91 (= *Roman Papers*, Liverpool, 1987, 116-25)

Wiseman, P. 1970 (1987) 'Roman Republican road-building' *Papers of the British School at Rome* 38, 122-52 (= *Roman Papers*, Liverpool, 1987, 126-56).

Wiseman, P. 1986 'Monuments and the Roman annalists', (eds.) I. Moxon, J. Smart and T. Woodman, *Past perspectives, studies in Greek and Roman historical writing*, 87-100

Wiseman, P. 1987b 'Julius Caesar and the Hereford World Map', *History Today*, November 1987, 53-7

3. Romanization: a point of view

by Richard Reece

The conference on Romanization tempted me to discuss the application of the theory of relativity to archaeology. The fact that I find it a temptation rather than an opportunity puts me firmly in the backward looking brigade at odds with those who are reacting against the evils, as they see them, of the classical, enlightenment, scientific method, of positivism and of fact-bound number-crunching. Yet I refuse to be classified with quite that ease. The conflict, I think, comes from the general failure, in both camps, to recognize the dual nature of archaeology, or perhaps better, the study of the past. There is the study of the litter that the past has left, and there is the attempt to say what the litter, once reduced to order, means. However devoted the interpreters they still arrange their data; they still dig stratigraphically, they still draw their pots, and they still measure the depth of their post-holes. To this extent I think they still rely on the old scientific method and they might even admit as much in the right company.

Disaster strikes when the old scientific method is applied to interpretation for it seems quite clear to many people, whether scientific or interpretative, that interpretation of materials from the past and understanding the past are not elements of the physical or biological sciences and therefore cannot share their methods. Analogies with ideas such as 'uncertainty' in atomic physics may well be useful as warnings of how to interpret, but I find them of little inspiration for the gathering and manipulation of material. Thus one group, when talking about interpretation, may rightly remember how physicists have been shown that at the sub-atomic level they must talk in probabilities rather than certainties. The material addict will point out that the flight of a bullet is better judged by Newton's Laws of Motion, if you want to avoid it, than by Heisenberg's Uncertainty Principle or Schroedinger's attempt at solving the wave equation.

If there is a message in all this it is to the effect that the limits of certainty or the degrees of certainty in any observation or interpretation ought to be carefully examined and firmly understood and remembered. But to bring in the idea of relativity is to take a step deeper, for it tells us not simply that matters will look different from different points of view, but that ostensibly objective judgements made from different vantage points will be absolutely different. Thus time, and the measurement of time, will vary according to the circumstances of the measurer, however objective he may be.

When we come to the question of Romanization, or interaction between Roman and Native, then there is more to the problem than simply warning the observer that what to the Roman was an advance of civilization into the depths of Celtic depravity, and therefore not only good but self-evidently so, looked to the British or Belgae or the Gauls in general like self-seeking expansion with the sole motive of authoritarian greed. Once the process under discussion has been isolated and defined then it can be interpreted from any point of view in the knowledge of partiality, but this does not allow us to analyse what was happening, only to describe it. Thus the process of homogenization evident in the sequence of material culture in the first century BC and the first century AD in the area between the Mediterranean and the North Sea can be described accurately once the basic tenets of approach have been set out. There is an Italian material culture of, say, 300 BC whose most obvious attributes can be defined. By use of these attributes this set of material which makes up Roman material culture can be separated off from other similar cultures, Greek and Iberian, and this can be used to define Roman-ness. At the other end of the scale will be the material culture assemblage of Britain in 300 BC which will be substantially different though there will be a very small number of similarities with Rome. The process of Romanization can be monitored as traits from one cultural assemblage enter another and the result in AD 300 will be a cultural assemblage both in Rome and Britain which is more alike than were the assemblages of 300 BC, but perhaps with more differences between dates than between places. In other words not only will both ends have changed, but the mixture itself will have changed so that comparisons will only be valid when made geographically at roughly the same time rather than chronologically in the same area.

So I perservere with this old fashioned approach which will strike dismay into the hearts of forward-looking archaeologists who hoped that such material sterility had been left behind, not because I want to hurt them, but simply because I want some objective material observations, or facts, before I begin to try to interpret them. I have no illusions about the relevance of these 'facts' to the societies under study. I agree completely when it is pointed out to me that the proportion of 'A' ware to 'B' ware, which I am using as an index of cultural homogeneity, was something which the society under study never knew about, never cared about, and would not have cared if it had known. I am interested in this proportion simply as a material fixed point against which interpretations can be evaluated. If the site in question is in Switzerland, and 'A' ware comes from Italy and 'B' ware from the Baltic, and the predominance swings from 80% 'B' ware in 100 BC to 80% 'A' ware in AD 100 any discussion of influence, routes, political influence and so on must at least be consonant with the 'fact'. My aim is to build up a supply of these facts so that we can test all the ideas produced on the process of Romanization or assimilation, or merely cultural homogenization, eliminate some and strengthen others. The two processes, of providing factual base-points, and producing interpretations, are very different; while I insist that material facts have to be assembled and tested by the methods of old-fashioned classical science, I see that these guide-lines are of little use in formulating ideas and interpretations, and I fully acknowledge that this second process is an interesting approach to making sense of the litter left from the past.

These first two steps seem to me fairly well defined and straightfoward. We need a compilation of material to spark off ideas and to limit the number and scope of explanations so that we have some measure of our nearness to reality. Then we need to produce ideas in order to try to build consistent pictures of what we each think happened in the past and to inform new excavations and compilations of material with lines of reasoning and fruitful areas of material research. So far we are on the lines of traditional archaeology and ancient history; the point which I find difficult to grasp and therefore shall find difficult to put across is the problem of standing outside our chosen ethnic or political or religious viewpoint to try to see the events, material and ideas generated in some sort of overall pattern. Thus I want to get further away from the process of Romanization or whatever we call it than just to assimilate both the Roman and the native point of view. I also want to be able to look from the outside on to the whole Roman process to try to see whether, as most Ancient Historians would assume, the process that we are studying is the intentional movement of a conquering power into areas of previous resistance or barbarism, or whether the Roman machine is simply part of an overall process that can be identified which is being speeded up by the machine.

Part of what I think is a glimmer of light comes from the remarkable paper by Willy Groenman-van Waateringe (1980) in which she says something that can be interpreted as 'The Romans conquered the part of the North West that had already been predigested for them, but failed miserably in those parts that were not predigested for conquest'. I must emphasize that this is what I got out of it, not what she necessarily put into it; to those who agree the credit should be hers, to those who disagree the disfavour mine. A second ray of light comes in the process of assimilation between Roman and British, or Roman and Gaulish material culture that had been going on for several decades before the troops arrived to hasten the process. I want to avoid posing another great IF of history, but would Britain in the fourth century AD have been very different if a military conquest had not taken place? The answer seems to be an obvious yes: Britain in the fourth century was irredeemably Romanized. What then about the fifth century? This is at once a more difficult and therefore more interesting problem, for to all intents and purposes Britain by the middle of the fifth century seems to be de-Romanized.

This raises a whole host of problems which are so far divorced from material study that they are rarely discussed. They are also problems which cannot be glimpsed without stepping outside conventional period boundaries; Romanists will therefore never be aware of them if they are well behaved. If we divide the Romanization of Britain into a super-structure such as language, administration, law, taxation and money, and a sub-structure such as ploughing, milking of cows, building of barns and cottages, forging of rakes and decorating with enamel, then do the two structures move into harmony with the Mediterranean world in the same way and at the same rate and for the same reasons, or are the two parts separate? If, as I strongly suspect, the two parts are separate, and Romanization and harmony are far greater and more obvious only in the super-structure, then what are the changes in the sub-structure, and how far are they congruent with political boundaries and monetary systems? Or, on the contrary, are they better aligned with the processes which affect the whole of North West Europe in the millennium from 500 BC to AD 500 without respect of Imperial boundaries or constraints?

This is the point at which relativity comes in because the observer has to stand somewhere in order to see around him and his point of stance may well affect the ideas that he creates. Thus the Romanist stands inside the empire and looks out; he is aware of neither uniformity or diversity outside the frontier except in as far as the outside affects the inside. To ask someone with this point of view whether the process of empire is part of a wider series of events in which Italians got caught up is pointless. Firstly he will not have the knowledge to answer, and secondly, if he is tarred with the historical brush, he will have the view point of the Italians around whom the rest of the world revolved. The archaeologist outside the empire is separated from his fellow non-Romanist by thousands of miles, except for his immediate neighbours, and for over half the Roman world, there is no outside. From the North Sea, round the Iberian peninsula and probably across the whole sweep of Saharan Africa as far as Ethiopia any outsiders are sandwiched between Romans and the elements and are few in numbers. Older civilizations to the East pose a different question so that it is only by the time that we come to the Black Sea and continue round to the Baltic that there is the opportunity for the Mediterranean world to react with other similar or less developed cultures. Any standpoint within Europe is fraught with problems because it was either part of the Roman world, or part of the barbarian world, either was affected by Rome, or can not be seen to be so. Yet even on the European fringes there must have been a wave effect from the frontiers of the empire rippling outwards. Thus the process which includes the Romanization of north western

Europe cannot be judged by comparison with a chosen null point in western Europe where there is supposed to be no Romanizing effect. There is no point in judging what happened in Britain against what happened in, say, Denmark because it looks very likely either that Romanization was having a ripple effect on Denmark, or else that contemporary changes there are part of some wider set of changes of which Romanization is only a part. It is no good going to the other extreme and trying to judge, for example the rate of material change in western Europe in the first to third centuries AD against a standard of what happened in China because that is part of a different interlocking system of parts with only very superficial known links to the West. The rate of change in China is presumably dictated by the processes of the time in China.

All this makes assumptions which, when stated explicitly, seem to be on the following lines. The inhabited world is split up into several different areas, and an area can be very roughly defined by the ease of communication within it. Thus the American continent and Europe have until recently had very little ease of communication and inevitably formed different areas. The Sahara ensures that the northern part of Africa communicated in the past very little with the south, but the northern part can communicate easily by sea and land with western Europe and this produces southern Africa as one unit and the Mediterranean littoral and western Europe as another unit. This is the unit which the Roman empire developed, but it was only ever a part of the potential unit. I think I see how to study the Roman part of this unit, how to study the different non-Roman parts of the unit, and even how to study the interaction between the two, but what I find difficult even to express and visualize is the possibility that the unit works on its own processes of which the Roman empire may well be an involuntary part. And the problem that I am trying to express is what to judge Romanization and other unit processes against, because anything inside the unit is invalid *because* it is inside the unit, and anything outside is invalid because it is part of another unit.

I am hopeful that if we can take The Unit as something stretching from the Urals and Caucasus to the Sahara and the Atlantic and North Sea then the only fuzzy entity or entities are those processes about which I seem to be so concerned. What, just as an example, might these be? I am thinking of processes such as movement of population or ideas from outside the unit, which must by definition be rare; or processes of nucleation of settlement or dispersion of settlement, or perhaps the processes which cause either of these things whatever they might be; the bonds which might be getting stronger or weaker between ethnic groups or linguistic groups, or even religious groups, for none of these need coincide with the Roman empire and could have over-riding effects. Though I am reasonably well informed about burial customs inside the Roman empire and note a change from inhumation to cremation as part of a pre-Romanization process in England, I do not know what is happening on a wider front. In this position of ignorance I must leave the change in burial custom out of any list of 'Romanization processes' because the Roman empire and the non-Roman areas might all be going through a unit process with leaders and laggers, but all due to some unit change. We would then see this change as one of precocious Romanization simply because unit changes would tend to happen, perhaps, first or last in the more or less developed areas in the unit. I do not know whether this is possibly true of the whole unit, I do not know what might be causing such a unit (to a western European one could easily say a 'global') change, and I have no idea whether, if some of my basic worries are sound, burial rite is something which obeys unit demands or political demands or ethnic demands.

Perhaps my basic worry on relativity will stand another repetition. I am so unsure about all these things because I do not know where to take as my fixed point, out of the danger of change, against which to judge what is happening in the unit, the Roman empire or whatever. Anywhere inside the Empire is no good because it is part of the change, and this applies to anywhere in the unit. Any site in the unit is subject to just the changes that are under investigation so it cannot be taken as a fixed point. On the other hand a site in another unit is likely to be irrelevant because it is part of a different system with different processes going on at different rates. This is why I started off with my mention of relativity, which might have sounded pretentious, because this seems to me exactly the problem which the discussion over time and the speed of light faces, crudely put in the disagreement between the crew of the space-craft and the people back home over how long it was since they went away.

But do nit-picking worries like this matter to the archaeologist? If he or she is concerned only with material and its classification then the answer is probably NO. But if the archaeologist goes on to interpret the material studied then the point which is the subject of my present mental confusion will make its presence felt if things are thought through far enough. If interpretation is period bounded and politically insulated then my worries will not be felt. Whatever happens in Britain between AD 1 and 100 is the result of the expansion of the Roman Empire, and there need be no more said. But if a comparative study of four regions in North West Europe is undertaken for the first century BC and the first century AD, and two of those areas turn into Roman provinces, and two do not, the whole subject and idea of Romanization might have to be radically changed. And the problem that would follow all the way through would be the point of stability against which different sorts and rates of change can be measured. What will be needed will be a point from which to have a view, and hence my title and my concern.

References

Groenman-van Waateringe, W. 1980 'Urbanization and the North-West frontier of the Roman Empire', *Roman Frontier Studies* 1979, (eds.) Hanson, W. S., and Keppie, L. J. F., Oxford: B. A. R., 1037-1044

4. Romanization: historical issues and archaeological interpretation

by Martin Millett

Over the past few years there has been an increased interest amongst both ancient historians and archaeologists in the perennial issues of Roman imperialism and Romanization. This interest coincides with a questioning of our own imperial past, particularly amongst those of the first generation to have grown up in the post imperial age. The important historical issues raised are first, the nature of Roman imperialism, its motives and methods, and secondly the nature of the processes of social change which we call Romanization. The purpose of this paper is to survey these issues and evaluate their relationship to the archaeological evidence.

There has been much important discussion by ancient historians about the nature of Roman imperialism. This discussion is of importance to archaeologists because it has called into question some of the fundamental, although unspoken, assumptions upon which many current archaeological interpretations are based. Garnsey and Whittaker (1978, 1-5) have summarized the debate, distinguishing several different views of the motivation for Roman expansion. These range from the development of Polybius' purposive view summarized in the quote (1.63.9) 'it was perfectly natural that by training themselves in such vast and formidable enterprises, the Romans should have acquired the courage to aim at world dominion and also fulfilled their aim', to the idea that the acquisition of an empire was an accidental result of a series of factors beyond the control of contemporaries. This view led Garnsey and Whittaker (1978, note 4) to recall J.R. Seeley's remark that the British acquired their empire 'in a fit of absence of mind'.

A more circumscribed variant of the same view is the doctrine of 'defensive imperialism' which interprets the acquisition of territory as a consequnce of a series of entirely defensive acts. This may be attacked because it does not fully reconcile the clear expansionist interests of the ruling oligarchy with the collective interests of the state, which were claimed by contemporaries to be defensive.

Dispute over the rôle of the oligarchy in initiating and in benefitting from territorial expansion, particularly in the late republic, has generated enlivened debate especially over the extent of any economic motivation. Badian (1968, 16-17) follows the traditional view that Roman imperialism should be viewed in terms of 'politics, strategy, social ethos and even psychology' dismissing the concept of any specifically economic motivation (Badian 1968, 16-28). Beard and Crawford (1985, 74-5) also stress the pressures for expansion which resulted from the structure of the socio-political system in Rome. Harris (1979, 54-104) has strongly challenged the underemphasis on the desire for economic gain by those involved in Rome's territorial expansion, pointing out that plunder and slaves were economically vital to the élite and their acquisition cannot be separated from the social and political competition character- istic of Roman society since the participants cannot have been unaware of the tangible economic benefits of expansion. In this sense it can be suggested that 'the ever-increasing need for warfare in the acquisition of personal riches, glory and clients amongst a competitive élite...was bound to produce an empire' (Garnsey and Whittaker 1978, 5).

The ramifications of these issues have recently been explored in discussions of the structural consequences of imperial expansion for the members of Roman society (Hopkins, 1978; Beard and Crawford 1985). These have increased our awareness of the social, economic and historical context of Rome's expansion in both the Republic and Principate highlighting a series of issues to which archaeology can contribute. Whichever view of imperialism one takes it is certain that the processes were not simple and clear cut, as they were bound up with a fundamental series of internal stresses and pressures which nevertheless resulted in the emergence of a remarkable empire. As Loewenstein has put it (1973, 380): 'it may be one of the miracles of the history of government that the Principate succeeded, at least for the first two centuries, in ruling its far-flung realm by the only feasible device: the regime proceeded from the simple fact of military occupation by the erstwhile conqueror, transforming it to a varying degree, into areas of local administration centrally directed by the Roman Imperial institutions and policies'.

Roman archaeologists, rather than ancient historians, have been slow to realise the implications of these ideas so they have rarely put them into practice by developing the field strategies capable of generating the new and critically valuable data which might clarify the issues concerned. Romanists have rather taken the view put simply for Britain by Sellar and Yeatman (1975, 11) that 'The Roman Conquest was, however, a *Good Thing*, since the Britons were only natives at the time'.

This has been disadvantageous to the discipline, as Roman archaeology has a major contribution to make both to the resolution of the specific historical issues and in contributing to broader debates in the social sciences. One of its major values lies in the possibility of comparing its results with information independently derived from the ancient sources, thus providing a valuable testing ground for ideas developed elsewhere. It is particularly unfortunate that Romanists have not addressed these more general issues as 'prehistorians and medievalists alike seem to take the view that the Roman empire constituted a great commercial organization, the administration of the empire directing and promoting the economic exploitation of the provinces. Nothing could be further from the truth' (Mann 1982). Thus Hingley (1981) and Hodges (1982) have both taken this view, developing the idea that the Empire can be viewed as an instance of a 'World-Empire System' as described by Wallerstein (1974) – that is an administered system of economic exploitation. Hodges, for instance, has stated 'we cannot deny that the ubiquitous market principle was a force planned by the Romans in their bid to articulate the Iron Age Economies on a new scale' (1982, 6).

Such a view is almost wholly at variance with the evidence which suggests first that the economic exploitation which did take place was not heavily directed and secondly that the net result of the flow of taxation was to move money from the centre of the Empire towards the peripheral provinces where the army was concentrated (Hopkins 1980) – the exact opposite of the model proposed (eg. Hingley 1981). This misfit should not blind us to to the potential contribution that these broad approaches can make to our understanding by forcing us to attempt to grasp the processes at work, and encouraging us to compare these with the patterns found in other pre-industrial societies.

Many of the issues raised in this debate are however beyond the scope of archaeological analysis alone, and it is the contribution of archaeology which I believe to be of the greatest importance at present. The issue of why the Roman Empire came into being is beyond the archaeological evidence but the more pedestrian issues of how (descriptively) the Empire grew and functioned are issues which we can address, in the process providing information not available from other sources. These issues are central to any discussion of Romanization, by which I mean the study of the two way process of acculturation within the Roman provinces.

The concept of acculturation is itself important as it removes us from the one-sided view of Romanization, encouraged by the entirely Roman textual evidence, which has dominated the literature on the subject. Thus it is often suggested that Rome brought a missionary zeal leading her to 'Romanize' the inhabitants of the annexed territories. The view has often been based on the Tacitean statement (*Agricola* 21) that Agricola 'gave private encouragement and official assistance to the building of temples, public squares and houses' which is taken to imply a policy of Romanization with the construction of a whole new social system in addition to the physical buildings of the towns (Millett 1990).

This view has recently been countered in the Dutch literature which has presented a far more balanced discussion of the process of acculturation by drawing on allied disciplines within the social sciences for interpretative insights (eg. Brandt and Slofstra 1983). This has led to more emphasis on the nature and organization of the native societies incorporated into the Empire. This new emphasis has great importance, and deserves to be emulated elsewhere, as the nature of the society which emerges after Romanization owes as much to the native as to the Roman ingredient. This point has often be lost in previous studies, in part as a result of the partisan nature of the ancient sources which limits their value for the understanding of native societies. Thus, for instance, Tacitus wrote 'who the first inhabitants of Britain were is open to question: one must remember we are dealing with barbarians' (*Agricola* 11). The resulting tendency has often been mistakenly to see native societies as comparatively primitive and uniform in character. Archaeology is demonstrating their variability and promises to provide far more information on the different ways in which the varying native societies were incorporated into the Empire (Gechter this volume).

The vital element in understanding and assessing the dominant British view of Romanization lies in removing the debate from one based on a prevailing pro-imperialist attitude to another which takes a more neutral view of the available evidence and in particular tries to assess the cultural changes, in relation to both the historical debate about the nature of Roman imperialism and our knowledge of the structure of the Empire.

Whether or not we accept a view of Roman imperialism as motivated by accident or design Roman administration has a series of clear characteristics (Loewenstein 1973). These include an essentially loose centralizing structure which, from the Augustan period to the third century, allowed the cities a very large measure of self-government within prescribed limits. Incorporation thus involved a process of encouraging the native aristocracies to identify their interests with those of Rome. This was based on the republican tradition of avoiding any excessive administrative commitments which would have resulted from any highly centralized system of direct rule (Badian 1968, 77-78). The net effect of this method of administration was to keep the levels of taxation low, and maintain a remarkably small public service, at least until the Diocletianic reforms (Garnsey and Saller 1987, 20-42).

Against this background one must question more closely any idea that Rome had any real policy of Romanizing its conquered territories beyond ensuring an efficient administration without burdening herself with a heavy cost of either military occupation or direct administration. In this context we should note that Garnsey (1978, 253) has argued that the education of Britons (Tacitus *Agricola* 21) was solely aimed at making British chieftains and their sons identify with Roman interests, thereby encouraging them to fulfill their administrative rôle. We should also perhaps further question whether there was a distinction between such 'education' and the holding of heirs hostage to ensure parental loyalty. Any suggestion of a more comprehensive Romanization policy must present some cogent justification for its existence which takes account of the otherwise apparently *laissez-faire* attitude of Rome to her provinces.

Against this non-interventionist background, we need to develop an explanation of the acculturation of the provinces which made them appear more Roman. This needs to take more notice of the native side of the equation than has hitherto been normal. Absence of detailed information about pre-Roman native society is the most important single problem confronting archaeology in most of the areas of the western provinces, especially around the Mediterranean where our knowledge of social structures and settlement patterns is at best patchy.

A general model of Romanization is thus required, but it is important that this is based on our understanding of the core rather than the peripheries of the Empire. Such a model can be proposed tentatively, although it must be subject to substantial modification: it is presented as a stimulus to further research, rather than as an end in itself.

1)   Given that Rome's main aim was to administer through the native élite, she worked through the native communities which where treated *as* city states whether they had this sophisticated organization, or one based on a tribal system which could be treated as such.

2)   This meant that after conquest, the army was moved forward and civil administration established as early as possible through agreement – the *lex provincia* – imposed by Rome on the native élites.

3)   This settlement gave the élite power to govern provided that it was exercised in broad accordance with Roman principles within a Roman style constitution which provided *inter alia* for taxation to be passed to the Roman administration.

4)   The aristocracy involved in the administrative system thus did not need to be forced to become Romanized as the maintenance of their power within society was sufficient incentive in itself (Millett 1990):

       a)   within society their social position was reinforced by its identification with the external power (and force) of Rome.

       b)   This enhanced the desire of the élite to use the symbols of *Romanitas* by emulating Roman material culture. This will have set them apart from the remainder of society and provided a mechanism for the maintenance of their power within society, providing status indicators such that 'competition for honour proved as effective as compulsion' (Tacitus *Agricola* 21).

5)   Progressive emulation of this symbolism further down the social hierarchy was self-generating encouraging others in society to aspire to things Roman, thereby spreading the culture.

This model generally envisages Romanization as a result of accidents of social and power structures rather than deliberate actions. As such it is complementary to the similar views on the nature of Roman imperialism already discussed.

Provided we understand that this process can use abstract as well as material elements (eg. language and style) it provides a useful interpretative framework in which the motor for Romanization can be seen as internally driven, rather than externally imposed. This has the great advantage that it does not require the postulation of Roman intervention which is neither widely attested nor to be expected within the imperial framework as presently understood. Several qualifications and clarifications to the model are however necessary to make it more generally applicable both geographically and temporally.

First the adoption of native aristocracies was clearly more straightfoward and comprehensive in areas which had a previous tradition of urbanism and developed central authority. Indeed, we may suggest that (except in the East where Rome came up against a developed and powerful rival in the form of Parthia) the limits to Roman expansion were determined broadly by the presence of social systems which were adaptable to the Roman administrative system.

In those areas without a developed social hierarchy we need to know more certainly how the administration coped with occupation and the establishment of civil administration. It has often been thought that Rome established urban communities both by plantation and the deliberate fostering of the type of social system needed. Although there are clearly areas, like Lower Germany, where such action took place, we may perhaps doubt that such social engineering was really as widespread as has sometimes been suggested or that it can have had more than a marginal effect on social evolution.

It is also often suggested that the military presence in some areas stimulated the development of the institutions necessary for self-government. This presents a series of problems as any sustained period of direct rule would have usurped the function and power of any incipient native élite, and therefore seems likely to have damaged the chances of subsequent self-government. The idea of military government also presents a series of difficulties (Millett 1984) so it is *a priori* more likely that a rapid transition to native civilian rule was favoured. Given the gradual cessation of Roman expansion during the Principate, and the resulting longer periods of military presence on the frontiers, the problem of establishing self-government in frontier areas may have been compounded. Whatever the solution, it is certain that the areas of long term military occupation were exceptional, and should not be used as the principal model to apply to the more substantial areas where the military presence was more transitory.

The success of the administrative system in identifying the interests of the native élite with those of Rome is best illustrated by the remarkably low incidence of native revolts in the conquered territories. This is reinforced by an examination of the causes of these revolts which demonstrates that most are the result of internal social stresses generated by incorporation rather than by any sustained resistance to Roman repression (Dyson 1975).

Of more general significance for the model is the difficulty in interpreting the differences in the rates of Romanization in the incorporated provinces, with a general pattern apparently showing a slower emergence of Roman institutions in the provinces annexed in the Republic in comparison with those incorporated later. This seems entirely contrary to the predicted patterns, since the societies incorporated earlier seem to have been the more developed. Much information concerning this vital problem of the speed of Romanization has still to be collated from the archaeological sources, and it is here that archaeology perhaps has the greatest single contribution to make.

In the absence of detailed information it seems worthwhile suggesting that the developing structure of provincial government had an important influence on the nature of this process. In these terms it is possible to see a major structural distinction in administration between the Republic and Principate. The incorporation of annexed land in the Republic led to large scale, not to say unbridled, economic exploitation by the Roman élite both through removal of the spoils of war and subsequently the expropriations of taxation by the *publicani* on their own behalf as well as that of the Roman state. The net effect of this may have been to increase economic activity (in Spain for instance) but it seems that this process had only a limited centralizing effect on the native societies as it was essentially stimulated by external activity. This contrasts with the ideas frequently discussed recently where trade contacts between peripheral societies and core areas have been seen as a stimulus to centralization within them (eg. Nash 1978). This is perhaps surprising as the Late Republican period when economic exploitation of the provinces was unbridled best fits the exploitative economic system described in such core-periphery models (eg. Hingley 1981).

We may see this delay in Romanization in the development of towns in the three Gauls, which does not appear to take place for a generation or so after the conquest (Wightman 1985). The same slow start to urbanism also seems apparent in Spain, at least away from the previously urbanized areas. Both these observations are surprising in terms of the model, especially as Roman government was essentially city based.

The provinces incorporated in the Principate seem to have become centralized far more rapidly, and to have generated more Romanized institutions comparatively quickly. This Romanization also affects the older provinces from the beginning of the Principate with a rash of new civic buildings in Italy, Spain and Gaul from the Augustan period (Ward-Perkins 1970, 1-4). Although this in part reflects a shift in the architectural *milieu* at Rome, we must view this change itself as significant in the process we are observing.

The whole pattern may be explained by Augustus' alterations in the administrative system crystallizing major changes which had a twofold effect, first generating local administrative centralization and secondly weakening the hold of the *publicani*, thereby ameliorating the effects of the excessive zeal of the tax gatherers, and leaving more money in circulation to be accumulated by the local élites who subsequently used it to invest in their own cities. The centralizing effect of the new administrative system resulted from the collection of taxes through the cities in the Imperial Provinces. This will have both enhanced the rôles of the cities as economic and social centres, since the focal tax gathering functions will have multiplied the effect by increasing their marketing and administrative rôles. This will also have benefitted the controlling élites who are unlikely not to have benefitted financially from their control of taxation and marketing. The process may thus have acted as a stimulus to urbanism and Romanization, changing the trajectory of the established provinces and preparing for new indigenous development in the newly acquired territories. It is therefore paradoxical that these changes to the administrative system increase the misfit between the Roman system and that described in Wallerstein's 'world system', as direct economic exploitation of the peripheries by the core seems to have been trimmed during the Augustan period.

These ideas suggest some of the mechanisms by which Romanization may have occurred. They are not themselves an end, but are designed as a series of ideas to stimulate the collection of new data and the enhancement of the rôle of archaeology by moving it to address questions not answerable from the texts. For this to happen the collected data urgently need to be collated and focussed on specific issues. If I may, I should like to codify some of the essential questions which we presently need to address:

1   What was the nature of the military presence in each territory, and how rapid was the conquest and subsequent demilitarization?
2   How quickly and in what ways were native societies integrated into the Empire?
3   How urbanized was the territory before conquest and how was this trajectory changed in speed and intensity following annexation?
4   How is the intensity and direction of trade and exchange affected by incorporation into the Empire?
5   Is the development of agriculture and rural settlement affected by incorporation into the Empire?

Acknowledgements:

I would like to thank Simon James and Tony King for reading and commenting upon this paper. I remain responsible for any errors.

References:

Badian, E. 1968 *Roman Imperialism in the late Republic*, New York: Cornell paperback (second edition)

Beard, M. and Crawford, M. 1985 *Rome in the late Republic*, London: Duckworth

Brandt, R. and Slofstra, J. 1983 *Roman and Native in the Low Countries*, Oxford: BAR

Dyson, S.L. 1975 'Native revolt patterns in the Roman Empire' in, H. Temporini (ed.) *Aufstieg und Niedergang der Römischen Welt II.3*, Berlin: W. de Gruyter, 138-75

Garnsey, P.D.A. 1978 'Rome's African Empire under the Principate' in, Garnsey, P.D.A. and Whittaker, C.R. (eds.) *Imperialism in the Ancient World*, Cambridge University Press, 223-54

Garnsey, P. D. A. and Saller, R. 1987 *The Roman Empire: Economy, Society and Culture*, London: Duckworth

Garnsey, P.D.A. and Whittaker, C.R. 1978 'Introduction' in, Garnsey, P.D.A. and Whittaker, C.R. (eds.) *Imperialism in the Ancient World*, Cambridge University Press, 1-6

Harris, W.V. 1979 *War and Imperialism in Republican Rome, 327-70 BC*, Oxford: Clarendon Press

Hingley, R. 1981 'Roman Britain: the structure of Roman Imperialism and the consequences of Imperialism on the development of a peripheral province' in, Miles, D. (ed.) *The Romano-British Countryside*, Oxford: BAR, 17-52

Hodges, R. 1982 *Dark Age Economics: the origins of towns and trade AD 600-1000*, London: Duckworth

Hopkins, K. 1978 *Conquerors and Slaves*, Cambridge University Press

Hopkins, K. 1980 'Taxes and trade in the Roman Empire 200 B.C. – A.D. 400' *J. Roman Stud. 70*, 101-25

Loewenstein, K. 1973 *The Governance of Rome*, The Hague: M. Nijhoff

Mann, J. C. 1965 'City foundations in Gaul and Britain' in, Jarrett, M. and Dobson, B. (eds.) *Britain and Rome: essays presented to Eric Birley*, Kendal: Titus Wilson, 109-113

Mann, J.C. 1982 Unpublished paper on Roman Imperialism read to research seminar, Durham University

Millett, M. 1984 'Forts and the origins of towns' in, Blagg, T.F.C. and King, A.C. (eds.) *Military and Civilian in Roman Britain*, Oxford: BAR, 65-74

Millett, M. 1990 *The Romanization of Britain: an essay in archaeological interpretation*, Cambridge University Press

Nash, D. 1978 'Territory and state formation in Central Gaul' in, Green, D., Haselgrove, C. and Spriggs, M. (eds.) *Social Organization and Settlement*, Oxford: B.A.R., 455-76

Sellar, W.C. and Yeatman, R.J. 1975 *1066 and all that*, London: Methuen paperback

Wallerstein, 1974 *The Modern World System: capitalist agriculture and the origin of the European world economy in the sixteenth century*, London: Academic Press

Ward-Perkins, J.B. 1970 'From Republic to Empire: reflections on the early Provincial architecture of the Roman West' *J. Roman Stud. 60*, 1-19

Wightman, E.M. 1985 *Gallia Belgica*, London: Batsford

Section II
Initial Contacts and Acculturation:
The Northern Provinces

The papers in this section are concerned with the north-western provinces: Belgic Gaul, Lower Germany and Britain. These regions were on the periphery of the Roman world, and were perceived so by the Romans themselves. Within them, Celtic-speaking peoples were suddenly brought into direct contact with the Romans as the result of Julius Caesar's campaigns in the 50s BC. Their experience was in contrast with that of Hispania (Section III), where generally there was rather more familiarity with Greco-Roman culture. In the north-west, it might be expected that initial contact and acculturation was closely connected with the act of Roman conquest or the subsequent threat of it (even if in Britain it was not to happen for nearly a century after Caesar's expeditions), as well as the effects of selective exposure to Roman material culture.

Despite the above attempt at generalization, it is clear from all the papers in this section that Haselgrove is right to emphasise the importance of attention to the differing histories of acculturation of different groups and regions. For this reason, a Roman province may be too large as a suitable area for analysis. One problem is in deciding whether archaeological evidence for change (eg. coinage, wine amphorae, settlements) is to be interpreted as Romanization, or the result of other long-term processes (a possibility which Reece also considers). That is affected by the quality of the archaeology, but also by the appropriateness of the questions asked of the evidence: whether for example it can be used to define the territories of the Gaulish *civitates*. Haselgrove uses the Aisne valley as a testing ground for these ideas.

The evidence for settlement nucleation which he discusses indicates the 'core' communities through which those further on the periphery experienced Roman acculturation at one remove. The core-periphery model, and the interpretation of changes in settlement type and settlement pattern in relation to contact with the Romans, are also prominent in Bloemers' chapter on Lower Germany, a relatively underdeveloped region in 50 BC. He contrasts Nijmegen with the Batavian tribal area around it: the former he interprets as an urban settlement planted in a territory which, to judge from the different artefact types, had little contact with it, such contact as there was being focused on the native élite, for military reasons: the Batavians provided crack troops, and were consequently left immune from taxation.

Kunow is led to examine a different aspect of Rhineland settlement by noting the results of field survey which show increasing Germanic occupation of the east bank of the Rhine from the mid-first century AD. This is not an area kept empty for strategic reasons as historians had deduced from Tacitus. Applying Galtung's model of imperialism, he argues that the Romans failed to 'build a bridgehead' to the German periphery (and assimilate it), because social institutions were insufficiently developed for the necessary response. Only in the northern part of the *Vorfeld* were relations of clientship successfully established.

A powerful noble élite would seem to be a requisite of the social development envisaged by such explanatory models. The case of the Ubii, examined by Gechter, appears to be an exception. They lacked a nobility, but nevertheless were loyal allies of Rome, perhaps because they needed Rome's protection. New evidence from Neuss and Bonn indicates that native settlements had preceded the building of the forts; Cologne, however, appears to have been newly founded as an urban centre for the *civitas*.

Trow, in discussing Britain, is concerned with very similar matters to those discussed by Haselgrove and Bloemers. Before the Roman conquest, the south-east is distinguished from the rest of Britain by the degree to which imported Roman goods were used to display social differences, mainly through an etiquette involving exotic food, drink and tableware. The economic significance of this as potential evidence for more extensive trading relations is problematic. There is an economic reorientation after the conquest, for which Trow sees the army, and the introduction of coinage for army pay, as the catalyst. The goods previously imported became more common, and so the élite turned to villa architecture (further discussed by Blagg below) to continue the demonstration of its prestige. Urban development, and its connexion with native *oppida*, is complex: some of the latter (eg. Bagendon) may have been aristocratic estate centres rather than truly urban settlements. here (as in northern Gaul) is a contrast with the nature of urbanization in the Spanish provinces (Section III).

5. The Romanization of Belgic Gaul: some archaeological perspectives

Colin Haselgrove

Introduction

Like most empires before her, Rome generally sought to rule newly conquered peoples through the existing native élites, backed by her own imposed administrative and military structures as these had evolved through two centuries of near-continuous expansion under the later Republic. Nowhere evokes the first stage of this process more vividly than Belgic Gaul, and Hirtius' account of how, in 51BC,

> "Caesar in Belgio cum hiemaret, unum illud propositum habebat continere in amicitia *civitates*, nulli spem aut causam dare armorum ... itaque honorifice *civitates* appellando, principes maximis praemiis adficiendo, nulla onera nova iniungendo, defessam tot adversis proeliis Galliam condicione parendi meliore facile in pace continuit"
> *(Commentariorum de Bello Gallico (BG) VIII, 49).[1]*

On this occasion, the short-term military consideration that lenient treatment of the native élites would lessen the likelihood of rebellion in his rear probably weighed rather more with Caesar, about to make his bid for supreme political power, than creating a framework for the future Roman province. Even so, the episode, following a relatively brutal war of conquest, goes far to explain the achievement which sets the Roman Empire apart from those which went before: Rome's outstanding success in retaining the possessions which her military prowess brought her (Mann 1986). In ensuring the continuing cooperation and paramountcy of the Gaulish élites, Caesar was in fact acting very much in accordance with what gradually became standard Roman practice everywhere. The same is true of the treaties by which he vested his loyal Gaulish allies with increased lands and population (eg. BG. VI, 4; VIII, 6).

The successful development of the new Gaulish provinces was further assisted by the underlying similarities between the social and political ties which held the indigenous groups together (eg. BG. I, 4, 18; VI, 12), and the patron-client relationships of the Roman world (Crumley 1987). Whether or not in Gaul such ties entailed the same rights, duties, privileges and obligations as Roman custom, they were clearly sufficiently similar to be described and exploited as such. Accordingly, granting of Roman citizenship to native leaders and linking their self-interests directly to those of the Julio-Claudian house by making them its clients (Drinkwater 1983) was another obvious way of using the existing social structure to ensure the continuing loyalty of the élite. The relatively rapid take-up of Roman culture and language by the class who owed their continued position to the Roman alliance, in Belgic Gaul (Haselgrove 1987) and elsewhere in the western Empire, is thus hardly surprising. In turn, gradual emulation of élite behaviour by other sections of the population, especially the upwardly mobile elements, provided the motor for the more widespread changes in architectural fashion and material culture which we conceive of as Romanization. This transformation was thus effectively locally-driven rather than expressing any conscious policy from the centre (M. Millett, this volume), so the outcome inevitably varied in form and degree from one people to another, according to circumstances and history. Therein also lies its interest.

The Romanization of Belgic Gaul in particular and the nature of developments there during the first centuries BC and AD has seen much recent discussion, most notably by Wightman in her brilliant study of the province (1985), and in earlier work (eg. Wightman 1971; 1975; 1978). In the area of the province which was subsequently detached as Germania Inferior, a similar approach which gives due weight both to the indigenous population and to Roman innovations has been followed by Dutch (eg. Bloemers 1983; 1988; this volume; Roymans 1983; Willems 1984) and German scholars (eg. Gechter and Kunow 1986; this volume). I myself have recently argued that various features of the archaeological record of Belgic Gaul in the later first century BC are best explained by Roman rule at this crucial period being *de facto* largely through pro-Roman native factions, and by the difficulties these clients may nevertheless have experienced in maintaining their position even with Roman backing (Haselgrove 1987, 113-121).

Building on the foundation offered by these studies, we can therefore take stock of the directions which research might now take. Three questions appear fundamental. The first is methodological and concerns the choice of the province as the conventional scale of analysis for much archaeological analysis of Romanization. Is this the scale most appropriate to our understanding of the processes at work? A second, related question must be whether current archaeological fieldwork is delivering the information we require, and what indeed are our expectations of archaeological evidence? Thirdly, and allied to this, are the questions posed of the material sufficiently realistic, ie. are they potentially answerable, or should we be addressing different problems? Here I shall discuss these issues specifically in relation to Belgic Gaul, but they are clearly of relevance to most of the western Empire.

Romanization: scale of analysis and the Iron Age background

According to the model outlined above and elswhere (Haselgrove 1987; Millett this volume), Romanization however uniform the eventual outcome was in material terms – represents the aggregate outcome of processes operating essentially at a local level, people by people. Even within a single province, the form and degree of change varied between different groups and regions, depending on the socio-political organization and cultural complexity of the con-quered peoples, differing histories of pre-Conquest acculturation, the circumstances that impelled a Roman take-over, the potential of different areas for agricultural and industrial intensification and wealth accumulation, and so on. A similar point has recently been made by Burnham (1986) in criticizing the application of monocausal explanations to the growth of small towns in Roman Britain. Analysis at a provincial level conflates too many different trends, thereby disguising underlying patterns and processes wherein may lie the explanation for the development of particular sites or groups of sites. Provinces are, of course, a valid and interesting level of analysis for asking certain questions, and to compare, but this supposes that their internal heterogeneity has first been characterized and comprehended, as in Gechter and Kunow's (1986) contrasting of developments within the differing natural environments of the middle Rhineland or in Willem's (1984) study of the Batavi.

In Belgic Gaul, the necessity of approaching the whole through its constituent parts is at its most acute, given the sheer size and diversity of the province. Moreover, both textual and archaeological evidence suggest that there were considerable variations in the social and political organization of the different later Iron Age communities inhabiting the area, and indeed in their level of exposure to the Roman world prior to the Conquest. Thus, although

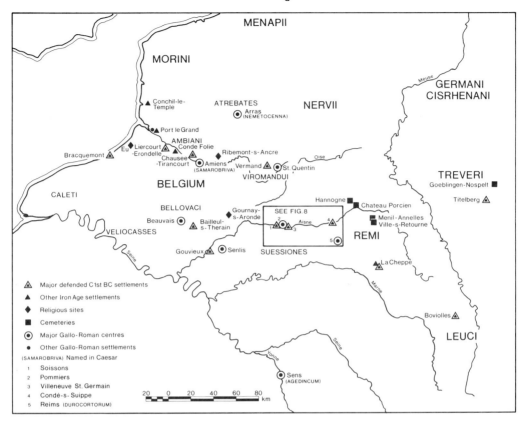

Fig 5.1. Belgic Gaul, showing the principal peoples and sites mentioned in the text.

Caesar no doubt elaborated some political and ethnic distinctions in his Commentaries purely to serve his own ends in Rome, other variations in his narrative and terminology relating to settlement and society (Buchsenschutz and Ralston 1986) suggest a considerable degree of cultural and social heterogeneity even within the major regions. Thus, although Caesar treats the Belgae as a separate people with their own distinctive language, customs and laws (BG., 1,1), only part of the population which lived between the Rhine, the Seine, and the Marne, actually gave itself this name (Hawkes 1968). The territory occupied by these groups, which Caesar calls 'Belgium', coincides roughly with the historic regions of Picardy and Upper Normandy (fig. 5.1).

This grouping may well have its origins in the hegemony which Nash (1984) deduces that the communities of the Somme region exercised over their neighbours at a slightly earlier period. Although the gold coin evidence suggests that by the mid first century BC the focus of power had shifted to the north-east of the Paris basin, the inhabitants of this 'Belgium' clearly had some capacity for common action in the face of the Roman advance (BG. II, 4), even perhaps to the extent of adopting uniform currency measures (Scheers 1977). However, as in all Caesar's passages which imply a measure of centralization or a permanent leadership, we must not forget that we are dealing with societies in a period of high stress. Temporary war leaders may well have been appointed to unify larger groupings, but their power may have been as short-lived as the crisis that brought them to prominence (Collis 1987), outward appearances masking a reality of fragmented, competing groupings.

Outside 'Belgium' we find several other important groups which are differentiated on a variety of grounds; Caesar's allies, the Remi (BG. II, 3 etc), the Nervii and Celtic-speaking Treveri both of whom laid claim to Germanic ancestry (Tacitus, *Germania* 28), and a variety of smaller units referred to collectively as the Germani Cisrhenani, who seem to have been migrants from across the lower Rhine, rather like the Ubii resettled by Agrippa on the western bank in the later first century BC (Wightman 1985). Cross-cutting these are further distinctions introduced by Caesar, even if he himself attached no obvious significance to them (Hachmann 1976). In connection with 'Belgium' and the Remi he speaks of heavily fortified settlements called oppida, apparently resembling sites elsewhere in Gaul, whereas the Nervii and coastal groups such as the Morini and Menapii did not, when in danger, take refuge in fortified settlements, but in swamps, fens or forests (BG. II, 28; III, 28-9, etc). Even if he had no clear notion of their social and political structures, Caesar's differentiating the Morini and Eburones as *barbari*, or the Nervii, who would not allow the importation of wine or other luxuries (BG. II, 15) as a *gens* and *homines feri* (BG. V, 34; VI, 36) is likely to be significant (Haselgrove 1987; Roymans 1983).

At face value, these attributes suggest decentralized political conditions and a dispersed settlement pattern in Belgic Gaul different to those in central Gaul, where it is frequently argued that communities such as the Aedui, the Arverni and the Bituriges had achieved political statehood and were already urbanized before the Roman Conquest (eg. Crumley 1987; Nash 1976). However, the archaeological and numismatic evidence leaves little doubt that it would be wrong to extend this characterization to the whole of Belgic Gaul. As Caesar himself recognized, it properly applied only to the coastal and marshland communities in the extreme north, where the settlement pattern is very different. 'Belgium' proper contains several major fortified sites, such as Bailleul-sur-Therain, Bracquemont, La Chaussée-Tirancourt, Gouvieux, Liercourt-Erondelle and Pommiers (Buchsenschutz 1984). Their intensity of occupation, while not always fully determined, is not conspicuously different from that associated with the earlier stages of the fortifications further to the south, such as modern excavations are now revealing at Mont Beuvray (Peyre *et al.* 1987). Other undoubtedly important late Iron Age centres are the Titelberg with its succession of regularly laid-out timber buildings (Metzler and Weiller 1973; Rowlett *et al.* 1976) and Boviolles, in the territories of the Treveri and the Leuci respectively.

An orthogonal layout and dense occupation are also features of a second group of complex sites occupying low-lying locations on the southern fringes of Belgic Gaul: Villeneuve St Germain and Condé-sur-Suippe in the Aisne Valley (Demoule and Ilett 1985), La Cheppe, and probably Reims (Neiss 1984), Durocortorum of the Remi, where Caesar convened a Gallic council in 53 BC (BG. VI, 44). However, some supposedly important places mentioned by Caesar have as yet no certain archaeological substance, eg. Samarobriva of the Ambiani, where he convened a Gallic council in 54 BC and wintered in 54-3 BC (BG. V, 24, 47, 53) or Bratuspantium of the Bellovaci (BG. II, 13). Roman Amiens was a new foundation of the late first century BC (Bayard and Massy 1983). Since both Samarobriva ('the Somme crossing') and Nemetocenna ('the forest') – Caesar's winter-quarters in Atrebatic territory in

51-50 BC (BG. VIII, 46) – refer to general topography (Wightman 1985), the names may well have been transposed from earlier settlements in the vicinity.

The coin evidence presents a complementary picture to the major fortified settlements (Haselgrove 1988). Most northern coastal communities had no coinage until a late date (Roymans and van der Sanden 1980) or only used coins imported from elsewhere in Belgic Gaul. Gold was the only metal used in two of the principal circulation areas, in 'Belgium' and in what became Treveran territory, prior to the mid first century BC, apart from a few distinctive thin silver issues found in Picardy (Scheers 1977). All these coinages are uninscribed and neither the silver, nor the few bronze series with possible pre-Caesarian origins can be related to particular gold types. Inscribed struck base metal issues, here as elsewhere, are primarily a post-Conquest phenomenon, continuing to circulate, often in enormous volumes and over long distances (eg. Reding 1972). Later on, during the Augustan period, they were quite possibly used alongside actual high-value Roman issues, as the Roman monetary system and denominational structure gradually closed its hold over the province (Crawford 1985).

In the Champagne chalklands and further south-east in the territory of the Leuci, coinage development followed a different path, with extensive uninscribed potin (cast bronze) coinages achieving widespread circulation there in the early first century BC. This was essentially an extension of the core area of early potin production, focused on the agriculturally-rich plains of eastern-central Gaul (Haselgrove 1988). These potin coinages were arguably issued to meet similar functions to precious metal coinage by authorities lacking the requisite resources. However, the scale of the finds at many nucleated settlements, eg. Basel-Gasfabrik (Berger and Furger-Gunti 1981) and Condé-sur-Suippe (Massy 1983), leaves little doubt that once in circulation, potin rapidly acquired uses in everyday transactions which resulted in its frequent loss.

Apart from the Aedui, the core area of early potin use embraced the territories of the Sequani (the predecessors of the Remi as the other paramount community of Gaul; BG. VI, 12) and the Lingones, together with the Helvetii immediately to the south-east. These three peoples were, it seems, initially included in Belgica on strategic grounds (Wightman 1985) and later detached when Germania Superior was created (Drinkwater 1983). All three peoples are also included by Nash (1976) in her zone of inferred state formation in central Gaul, the Sequani and the Helvetii certainly, the Lingones probably. Here, further discussion will be mainly directed to the part of the eventual province which is now northern France, which more nearly coincides with Caesar's idea of Belgica. But it is important to note that at its furthest extent, Belgica seems to have embraced a spectrum of political complexity ranging from the genuinely acephalous communities of the coastal zone, through more hierarchical regionally-organized groups, but nevertheless still competitive and relatively unstable in their behaviour patterns, as in 'Belgium' – chiefdom societies in anthropological parlance (eg. Earle 1987) – to the putative fully-formed states in the extreme south of the province. Alongside this trend of increasing political centralization from north to south, we can also discern other consistent trends, of greater settlement complexity and sophistication of money use, the closer we come towards the boundaries of the Roman world at the time of Caesar's intervention in Gallia Comata in 58 BC.

The same trend is apparent in the penetration of Roman ideas and goods before the mid first century BC. The primary evidence of contact is afforded by pre-Caesarian burials such as Hannogne and Chateau Porcien in the Aisne Valley region (Flouest and Stead 1977) and

by the familiar map (fig. 5.2) showing the findspots of Republican Dressel 1 wine amphorae
(Fitzpatrick 1985). Even allowing for the biases which Fitzpatrick discusses, the overall
distribution apparently bears out Caesar's observation that being farthest removed from the
Roman province, Belgic Gaul (ie. the more northerly parts of the province) was least often
visited by merchants with luxuries for sale (BG. I, 1) and his various references to groups
on either side of the Rhine, such as the Nervii, who would not admit merchants
(Buchsenschutz and Ralston 1987).

The significance of the material along the southern fringes of Belgic Gaul is less easy to
assess. Many of the later Dressel 1B amphora finds are presumably post-Conquest arrivals,
when the volume of imports rose markedly (Haselgrove forthcoming a). Far fewer sites yield
the earlier Dressel 1A amphora type – only the Titelberg and one other site in Treveran
territory, for example, have this form. Even where larger numbers of finds occur, as in the
north-east of the Paris Basin and in Champagne, there is nothing to compare with the massive
quantities from sites to the south such as Basel Gasfabrik, Mont Beuvray or Chalons-sur-Saône
where 24000 amphorae were dredged from the River Saône (Tchernia 1983). Similarly, only
three sites in Belgic Gaul have yielded Campanian ware – the Titelberg, Condé-sur-Suippe,
and Villeneuve St Germain – whereas these finewares are common on sites nearer the original
Roman province (eg. Nash 1976). Nor does the manner in which the Remi placed themselves
at Caesar's service in 57 BC suggest that their previous relations with Rome were direct
(BG. II, 3), although their favourable disposition could have been of longer standing. However,
after the Conquest, the quantity and range of imports reaching Belgica rapidly widened to
include Spanish amphorae alongside Italian (Fitzpatrick 1985), central Gaulish micaceous
wares and Arretine. Amiens indeed, has the third largest collection of Arretine stamps north
of the Alps (Massy 1980), although whether this indicates a military phase or belongs to the
earliest urbanization is arguable (Walthew 1982).

The bulk of the contact between even the southern fringes of Belgic Gaul and the Roman
world was probably indirect, both in the pre-Conquest period and in the following decades
(Haselgrove 1987). Certainly, the decreasing number of imports found to the north of central
Gaul is most easily interpreted as prestige trade mediated by the halo of more developed
polities there, rather than as direct commercial trade with the original Roman province in
southern Gaul (Buchsenschutz and Ralston 1987). Even so, these processes probably
contributed to the enhanced degree of centralization apparent in this zone and along the
southern fringes of Belgic Gaul, compared to further north. The key question, however, is
what effects these differences had when these communities came to be reorganized as city
states on Roman lines.

In northern Belgica, the *civitates* created during the Augustan census and reorganization
of Gaul in and following 27 BC must have been essentially artificial (cf. Wightman 1985).
Elsewhere we can be fairly sure of the existence of more permanently established élites with
whom Rome could deal. As noted above, readily assimilable principles of social reproduction
certainly existed in Roman and Gaulish society, the question is rather how fully were the
latter elaborated and integrated in larger structures which the Roman administration could use
as a basis of *civitas* organization? How stable was élite control? How frequently was power
transferred, and between whom? Over what size of territories was it exercised? What was the
cultural, ethnic or geographical basis of the various identity groups that so perceived
themselves, or were recognized as such by others? How stable or shifting were these groupings
and the boundaries between them? The increased emphasis on large fortified sites in the late

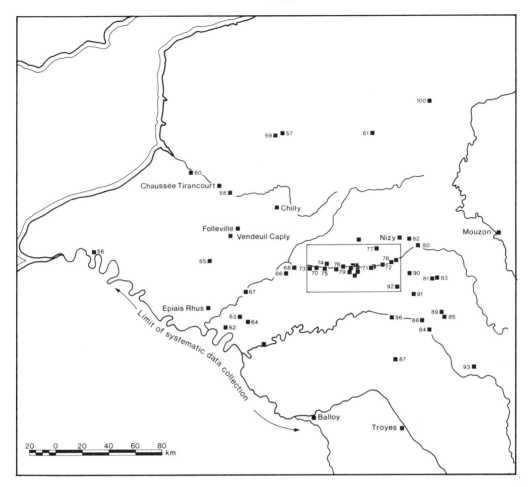

Fig 5.2. Findspots of Dressel 1 wine amphorae in Belgic Gaul (after Fitzpatrick 1985, with additions).

La Tène period in Belgic Gaul is widely held to indicate an upsurge in warfare at this time (eg. Hachmann 1976). Equally, what was the degree of social and economic differentiation of these groupings? And in particular, to what extent did the complexity of the communities of southern Belgic Gaul approach that of their more southerly neighbours, presenting fully-formed territorial entities which could be taken over or adapted as self-governing units largely as they stood?

Recent opinion is significantly more cautious about the degree of political complexity and urbanization achieved even in central Gaul prior to 50 BC. Woolf (1988) has recently reassessed the probable level of differentiation, integration and organizational capacity of the communities inhabiting this region. On none of these criteria, he concludes, can the case for political statehood made by Nash (eg. 1976) and Crumley (eg. 1987) be maintained from the archaeological and textual evidence, although the degree of organization in the late Iron Age is certainly greater than at an earlier period. The preparation undertaken by the Helvetii prior to their attempted migration is a case in point (Champion 1980). The coin evidence presents a comparable picture, also indicating an intensified trend to centralized political authority and increasing monetization of local economies, but stopping short of demonstrating state control (Haselgrove 1988). Similarly, use of the term 'urbanized' seriously overstates the position that we can demonstrate for the late Iron Age by archaeological means (Ralston 1984). Even at the leading fortified sites, the principal developments belong to the post-Conquest period (Collis 1984). Those open sites like Aulnat, Basel-Gasfabrik, Levroux and Roanne which do demonstrate settlement nucleation by the late second century BC (Colin 1984) fall well short of the criteria demanded of urban centres. If anything, sites like Condé-sur-Suippe in the Aisne Valley or La Cheppe – where an open settlement at Camp de Mourmelon (Chossenot 1987) could be contemporary with the fortified Camp d'Attila 3 km away – in Champagne, appear more sophisticated. However, on the current chronology, these postdate the open settlement horizon further south (Colin 1984), while at the Aisne Valley sites, the regularity of the layout (eg. Demoule and Ilett 1985) implies implantation in special circumstances.

Beyond these points, however, there is broad agreement. The areas of greatest economic and political development in the late Iron Age were focused on the best agricultural land which is provided by the plains of eastern-central Gaul (Woolf 1988, fig. 3). This region shows the earliest signs of increased settlement nucleation and more sophisticated money-use, and by the mid first century BC, it had been extensively opened up to Roman trade. The more populous areas of southern Belgic Gaul seem to participate in the same general trend, albeit to a lesser degree. But even the most highly organized of these late Iron Age communities were probably little more than islands of greater complexity and population density, only loosely held together by ties of alliance and paramountcy, and physically separated from each other by large upland expanses and other sparsely populated boundary zones.[2] Some groups were thus in a real sense ecologically circumscribed and defined (Nash 1978; Woolf 1988). Those core communities distinguished themselves as named identity groups, but the boundaries between them were probably neither immediate nor stable (Crumley 1987). Rather, although they economically and numerically dominated the smaller groupings around them, these latter were probably only loosely attached to them as clients, as with those of the Aedui or the Arverni (BG. VII, 75), or were effectively outside their control altogether (Woolf 1988). As Caesar had most of his dealings with the more important peoples, these smaller groupings are often unrecorded, as the pagus Catuslo attested by an inscription from the sanctuary at Bois L'Abbé, Eu (Mangard 1982).

Similarly, in 27 BC it was to these same larger and richer peoples, who by then had also developed more recognizably central place settlements, that Augustus turned in transposing the Roman concept of a *civitas* (Mann 1960) to Gaul. In the process, Augustus distorted the model, first to accommodate the greater scale of these core territories (Woolf 1988), and secondly through expediently attaching thinly populated areas to these 'core' peoples on geographical grounds or because of non-viability as separate units, and thirdly by ratifying the *de facto* incorporation of lesser peoples, made clients by the Caesarian settlement (cf. BG. VIII, 6). This then is one possible explanation of the unusually large *civitas* territories that are characteristic of Gaul (Mann 1960).

Archaeological perspectives 1: recent research and settlement continuity

The crucial formative period for the Romanization of Belgic Gaul was undoubtedly that between Caesar's campaigns and the early first century AD when the Roman garrison became permanently established along the Rhine frontier (eg. Gechter 1979) with its long-term economic consequences for the development of both regions (Hopkins 1980). The period is, however, only intermittently documented. In outline, Gallia Comata was left largely to its own devices until 40 BC when it was taken over by Octavian. He successively devoted his attention first to military requirements, appointing Agrippa, his leading commander, to his first governorship in 39 BC, when he proceeded to organize the road communications, then from 27 BC (as Augustus) to creating the administrative and legal basis of what now became three separate provinces, and finally, from 16 BC, to finding a solution to the German question (Drinkwater 1983). So much is reasonably certain. But for more information, we must then turn to archaeology "for the most consistent picture of the actual society in the course of its adaptation" (Wightman 1985, 44).

What can archaeology add? Archaeology, it is true, starts from the data provided by individual excavated sites. It is not, however, particularly well-equipped to transform this kind of information into histories of 'events and individuals' in the sense of Braudel (1972) – such as Caesar's narrative provides. Rather, archaeology synthesizes its knowledge of a mass of specific events, such as filling a pit, building a house or abandoning a site, and observations as to date, location, quantity, type, etc, to infer more general cultural patterns and processes. Owing to the partial nature of archaeological data, the resultant economic and social perspectives are much more akin to Braudel's histories of 'groups and groupings' and 'of the very long term' – seen in the relations of a population with its environment (1972, 20-1).

Not so much should we be addressing questions which are not answerable from textual evidence (Millett, this volume), as selecting from them the most worthwhile questions which are answerable from archaeological data. In Braudel's terminology, the Romanization processes most amenable to archaeological study will be those relating to 'groups and groupings'. However, providing the overall picture of variation through time and between regions is first ascertained, it may then be possible to link certain kinds of changes to particular historical causes and thus bring these two types of knowledge more meaningfully together (Wightman 1985). If this is to happen, the different kinds of change need to be more precisely defined than at present. It also presupposes that the right kinds of archaeological data are, or already have been, collected.

Much harm continues to be done by the failure to distinguish rigorously between those changes set in motion by the Conquest and those which merely represent an intensification of already existing trends. I have already noted how in terms of trade, the material Romanization of Belgic Gaul was a long-drawn out process with origins in the late second century BC. Against this, the actual military conquest hardly registers archaeologically, apart from its impact on coin production and hoarding (Haselgrove 1984). Conversely, largely because they are recorded, the revolts in the seventy years following the Conquest (eg. Dyson 1975) tend to be overemphasised and were actually relatively few. Pre-Conquest warfare, by contrast, was probably endemic (there may well be substance in Caesar's claim that the Belgae were continuously at war with the trans-Rhenine Germans), but generally went unrecorded. How often, too, were so-called revolts actually purely local disputes sparked off by causes which had little to do with Roman oppression?

In Britain, faunal assemblages at sites in close contact with the Continent show that dietary preferences were already being set along partially Romanized lines amongst the Iron Age élite (King 1984). The same is true of wine consumption. In both Britain and Gaul, such imports probably contributed to the evolution of a structure better capable of supporting Roman colonisation, by fostering pro-Roman attitudes and consolidating the power of those élites with access to imports and stimulating economic intensification to produce the reciprocal exports (Haselgrove 1987). This whole process of 'pre-Romanization' helped set the limits on successful Roman expansionism (cf. Groenman van Waateringe 1980). In Belgic Gaul, Caesar's intervention undoubtedly speeded up these changes, compressing into a few years shifts that might otherwise have taken a generation (Wightman 1985). But in Britain these processes ran a further course, which undoubtedly contributed to the relatively high level of monetary development and political centralization there by the time of Claudius' invasion (Haselgrove 1988).

The problems mentioned above are compounded by the tendency to attribute to Romanization changes which had little or nothing to do with the Conquest. Often this is due to incomplete evidence or poor dating. It is now clear that a much more significant phase of agricultural innovation in Britain occurred during the later first millennium BC, the Conquest merely adding a range of exotica. While the Roman period certainly saw more effective utilization, and probably some intensification and expansion too, the change is one of degree not kind (Jones 1981). This is almost certainly the case in Belgic Gaul too, although detailed evidence is still required. Many other processes, which originated earlier, such as settlement expansion, probably only become apparent in the Roman period, owing to the greater visibility of the material culture and of the sites. More difficult still to evaluate are changes which occurred in the Roman period in reaction to conditions that began to form earlier: the processes of the 'very long term' (Braudel 1972) such as climatic change, soil degradation or population increase whose effects are cumulative and not felt by individuals or even generations until particular circumstances, such as a series of failed harvests, eventually trigger off an irreversible change, such as the abandonment of upland settlements. Such questions of the 'very long term' deserve consideration alongside those posed by Martin Millett elsewhere in this volume, if our analysis is to be a balanced one.

A number of other difficulties are purely archaeological. These include the relative crudeness of the archaeological timescale and the false conclusions to which this can lead; and the uncertain reliability of much of the older data. Even where plentiful, this was rarely collected systematically with regard to the questions of interest today. The uneven distribution of the archaeological material is also a major problem, systematically underrepresenting certain places and phenomena. Even for such an obvious category as Iron Age hillforts, new examples are still discovered almost yearly in areas of intensive work such as the Ardennes and the Hunsrück-Eifel (Wightman 1985, 18).

We also need to beware of the still widespread attitude that patient accumulation of new evidence, coupled to new analytical techniques and some new interpretation, will in itself eventually overcome these difficulties and bring us closer to understanding Romanization processes. I doubt this is so and propose to examine it further, using the information on later Iron Age and early Roman sites reported in Gallia between 1970-85.[3] As Wightman (1985, 101) reminds us, one question where an archaeological contribution is essential – and can be expected – is the basic interplay between continuity and change in the settlement pattern in the century or so on either side of the Conquest and the ensuing Augustan reorganization. In short, were the same sites occupied? Did the settlement types change? Did the overall pattern of siting and exploitation change significantly and if so, how suddenly? Above all, when did the major changes occur and does the pattern vary between regions?

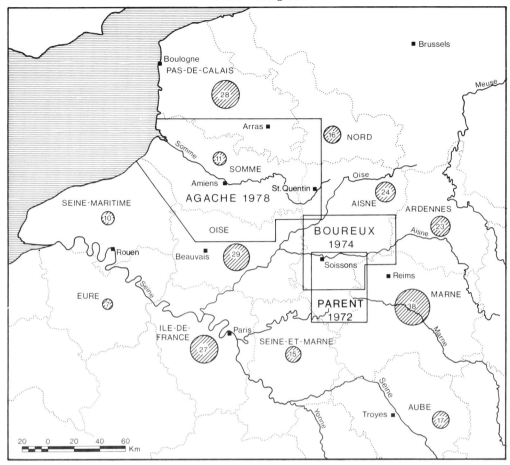

Fig 5.3. Northern France: areas of intensive survey and numbers of excavations on sites of the first centuries BC-AD reported in Gallia 1970-85, by Département.

The pattern of recent archaeological activity in northern France is undeniably variable (fig. 5.3). On the Picardy chalklands, Agache's (1978) internationally acclaimed aerial surveys have transformed our knowledge of the distribution and density of indigenous farmsteads and Gallo-Roman villas alike. Boureux's (1974) work, in the Aisne Valley has had similar results, reporting site densities around one per square kilometre along the gravel terraces of the river Aisne. Outside these areas, however, a similar depth of coverage is lacking. Systematic ground survey has been even more restricted, an exception being the work of Parent (1972). Although primarily concerned with earlier periods, fieldwork in a 15km radius around Fère-en-Tardenois added 32 Gallo-Roman sites to only 17 known previously, an increase of nearly 200%; a total of 182 Iron Age and Gallo-Roman sites are recorded within his overall study area (Parent 1972). An intensive field survey recently begun in the Aisne Valley (Haselgrove 1989) has so far recorded a density of over 2 Gallo-Roman sites or concentrations per square kilometre walked. Over large areas then, known sites can form only a small proportion of the total, inhibiting discussion of many aspects of settlement pattern and continuity until the rest of northern France has been sampled by comparable ground and aerial surveys.

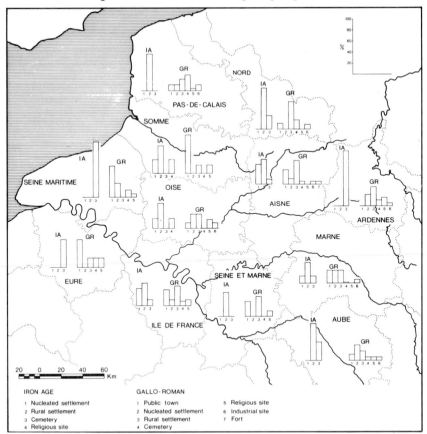

Fig 5.4. Northern France: proportions of excavations on different types of Iron Age and Gallo-Roman sites with occupation of the first centuries BC-AD as reported in Gallia 1970-85, by Département.

Similar imbalances are found with the excavated sites occupied in the first centuries BC and AD (fig. 5.3 above). The overall pattern is dominated by the menace of gravel extraction along the river terraces of the Paris Basin, particularly the Aisne, the Oise and the Marne. With a few exceptions, eg. the late La Tène site at Conchil-le-Temple, Pas-de-Calais (Leman-Delerive and Piningre 1981), extensively excavated rural settlements are confined to this zone. The lack of follow-up to Agache's work in Somme is especially marked. Sites have generally been excavated either on too small a scale to resolve basic problems, eg. Condé-Folie (where a Roman style building with associated late Iron Age pottery lies obliquely across the partition of a typical Iron Age rectilinear enclosure), or not at all, eg. Port-le-Grand (where another Iron Age type enclosure is situated very close to a courtyard villa) (Agache 1978). The average number of sites of all types excavated by modern methods is only 20 per Départment, many under far from ideal conditions. The limitations of our database for late Iron Age to Gallo-Roman settlement continuity are obvious.

Breaking the figures down according to the number of recorded excavations on different types of Iron Age and Gallo-Roman site reinforces these biases (fig. 5.4). In some areas such as Upper Normandy, the only excavated late Iron Age sites of known character are funerary.

In Ardennes, too, settlement evidence is needed to complement the important cemeteries at Menil-Annelles and Ville-sur-Retourne (Flouest and Stead 1979). Elsewhere, the position is reversed, although there are still disproportionately few excavations on rural sites compared to nucleated settlements, Iron Age as well as Roman. And while modern excavations are transforming our knowledge of religious sites such as Bois l'Abbé, Eu, Gournay-sur-Aronde and Ribemont-sur-Ancre, providing crucial information on the changing ideologies and ritual practices of the transitional period (Brunaux 1986; Roymans 1988), remarkably few early military sites have been excavated anywhere. Overall, then, the pattern of modern excavation is far too variable for the same basic questions to be answered with equal validity from one region to the next, nor does it leave us grounds for much optimism that if we wait long enough, the right sort of data will eventually turn up. If this is to happen, an overall guiding strategy, harnessing regional studies to common aims, is needed (cf. Van Es 1983). Otherwise, the patterns which emerge, especially at a provincial level, are likely to be misleading, however plausible they may seem on the surface.

Nevertheless, on the assumption that the recently excavated sites provide a reasonably representative sample, we may persist in examining settlement continuity during the first centuries BC and AD. The sites are divided into two non-exclusive groupings, those with Iron Age occupation and those with Gallo-Roman occupation (some sites thus appear in both sets). The question of continuity is framed as follows (fig. 5.5): when, if at all, were sites of the former group abandoned, and when were sites in the latter group first occupied? Although there is no overwhelming trend, some interesting points emerge. Taking the 'Gallo-Roman' group first, the proportion of sites founded between *c.* AD 25-100 is consistently high (between 50 and 80% for all but one Département), confirming that the later first century AD was a period of particular building activity throughout Belgica (over half of all villas appear to have been built then; Wightman 1985, 105). Many of these sites were apparently new foundations and the total number of establishments probably increased as well. However, we should not overlook the potential bias imparted by this phase being longer and the material being more readily dated, compared to the earlier sites.

Secondly, the overall degree of continuity into the post-Conquest era appears to be small, although detailed case studies would be required to establish whether major or only minor shifts in settlement location and territories were involved. Both groups of sites suggest that the period *c.* 70-25 BC was one of very considerable change. More Gallo-Roman sites seem to start at this period than either continue from earlier periods, or were founded in the succeeding Augustan age. Yet on the urban evidence, the latter era is often held as a key period of settlement shift (eg. Wightman 1985, 48, 75). Conversely, the proportion of later Iron Age sites abandoned between *c.* 70-25 BC is also consistently high. However, without more detailed evidence, we must not assume that these changes were due solely to the historical events of the Conquest; there could be other reasons for instability. This particular discontinuity needs viewing in a longer-term perspective of Iron Age settlement development, enabling us to assess the normal rhythms of site continuity and change in the preceding centuries. The pattern also needs breaking down to see what happens with different categories of sites, such as nucleated and single-unit settlements and cemeteries.

Archaeological perspectives 2: population and polity
From questions on which archaeology should have some input, I shall turn briefly to two

matters regarded as fairly intractable: population density and the basis of the Augustan *civitas* boundaries. Several areas show increased numbers of sites in the late Iron Age, eg. the Aisne Valley (Demoule and Ilett 1985). However, it is not realistic to argue a general population increase from this evidence, given the greater ease of discovery of late La Tène settlements as enclosure cropmarks and the more robust and readily diagnostic ceramics of this period compared to earlier. Absolute population densities which use Caesar's figures are similarly guesswork. Even where they supposedly derive from the Helvetii's own register (BG. I, 29), the size of their territory is hypothetical. However, most estimates of the average population densities of different Gaulish groups, based on their fighting strengths given by Caesar, fall within a range of 10-20 individuals per square kilometre, depending on whether a multiplier of 1:4 (as for the Helvetii) or 1:5 is used for the ratio of warriors to the rest of the population. This order of magnitude is commensurate with what is known for Medieval Europe (eg. Pounds 1973).

More information may perhaps be gleaned from the relative strengths of the warrior contingents which the Belgic peoples contributed to their confederate army in 57 BC and to the relief army which Vercingetorix summoned to Alesia in 52 BC (BG. II, 4; VII, 75). Rather than relying on the accuracy of the specific accounts given by Caesar, the standard deviation can be employed as a measure of significant differences. Using Thiessen polygons to predict their territories,[4] we can then investigate for which peoples Caesar's figures suggest a population density either significantly above or below the mean values for all 11 groups in 57 BC and all 12 in 52 BC.

We lack information on two important peoples, the Remi and the Treveri, and only seven peoples are common to both sets of figures. Even so, the two maps present some interesting comparisons (fig. 5.6). First, the highest densities are consistently found in the north-east of the Paris basin. Secondly, this zone is surrounded (where we have information) by lower than average densities, especially to the north and west. The Menapii in the northern coastlands are unsurprisingly also below the average. Thirdly, the Atrebates and the Morini are consistently within the average band, as were the Nervii in 57 BC. In 52 BC, however, this latter group is included among those who were very significantly below the mean.

Several explanations are possible. Caesar could easily have exaggerated the fighting strength of the Bellovaci and the Suessiones, two of his more formidable opponents. This seems less probable, however, for the Parisii. The north-east of the Paris basin is one of the richest agricultural areas in France and supported notably high population densities in the fourteenth century AD (Pounds 1973, figs. 6:2, 6:6). This therefore, could well be true of the first century BC. By contrast, a population well below the mean is not unlikely in the chalk areas inhabited by the Ambiani, the Veliocasses and the other groups. If so, the high site densities recorded by Agache (1978) should eventually be surpassed in the area north-east of Paris, which the number of sites now known on the river terraces makes increasingly likely. Alternatively, since the figures used are Caesar's, but the territorial boundaries are probably closer to those finalised in the Augustan reorganization, stronger groups such as the Bellovaci may have lost clients and lands to their weaker neighbours in the meantime – as implied by the creation of the *civitas* of the Silvanectes. If their 'zone of influence' was originally much larger, and the neighbouring territories rather smaller, their population densities will be reciprocally distorted, the former upwards, the latter downwards. It is tempting to suggest that the downturn in the status of the Nervii bears out the very high casualties which Caesar claims to have inflicted on them in 57 BC (BG. II, 28).

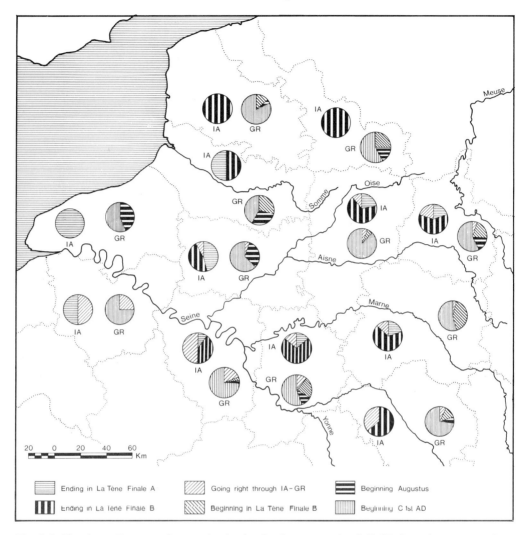

Fig 5.5. Northern France: site continuity in the first centuries BC-AD based on excavations reported in Gallia 1970-85; (1) as proportions of Iron Age sites; (2) as proportions of Gallo-Roman sites, by Département.

The archaeological ideal of analysing Romanization in the longer timescale of 'groups and groupings' is in practice difficult to implement. Study of spatial variation in later Iron Age material culture assemblages in northern France has yet to proceed much beyond the definition of major regional differences (eg. Duval 1976; 1984). Focussing on the peoples we know from later boundaries imposed by Rome will inevitably cross-cut some significant pre-existing divisions in society and arguments from coin distributions are, in practice, almost circular (Haselgrove 1988). One possible approach to the underlying rationality of the Roman administrative decisions is to compare the 'known' *civitas* boundaries with those predicted under certain conditions, by extending an earlier analysis of the Low Countries frontier zone

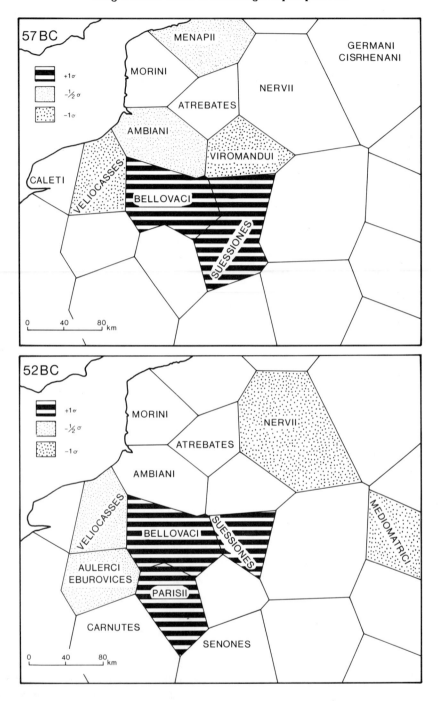

Fig 5.6. Inferred relative population densities in parts of Belgic Gaul in 57 and 52 BC based on figures given by Caesar (BG. II, 4; VII, 75); data for named groups only.

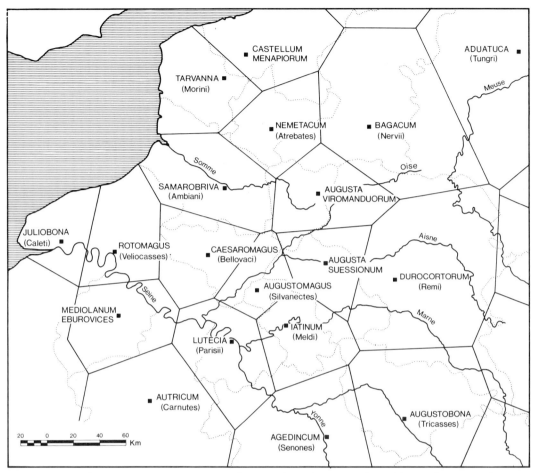

Fig 5.7. Northern France: comparison of civitas boundaries predicted from Thiessen polygons (after Bloemers, 1983, extended) and reconstructed from late Roman diocese boundaries (after Rice-Holmes, 1911).

(Bloemers 1983) and tracing a Thiessen polygon around the administrative focus of each *civitas* to define its 'sphere of influence'. In Belgic Gaul, the 'known' boundaries, as inferred from the pre-1792 diocesan territories, are, of course, widely assumed to be mainly artificial Roman impositions (Nash 1978; Rice-Holmes 1911; above).

The results of this exercise show a very reasonable goodness of fit (fig. 5.7). As expected, the fit is particularly strong in the areas inhabited by groups whose level of political integration was manifestly weak, such as the Morini and the Menapii (cf. Roymans, 1983). Equally, the *civitates* of 'Belgium' are noticeably smaller than their neighbours to the south and east. This suggests that we may indeed be dealing with the leading sub-units of a wider cultural or ethnic grouping, with some capacity for common action at this higher level of inclusion. The persistence of these subdivisions even into the modern Département boundaries is striking – the Ambiani, for example, coincide almost exactly with Somme (cf. fig. 5.2 above), the Bellovaci and Silvanectes together with Oise, and so on.[5] It may therefore be worth exploring whether natural geography, through its influence on regional settlement patterns, was a major factor in the emergence of basic group identities in 'Belgium'.

Significant disagreements between 'expected' and the 'observed' territories are relatively few. The over-representation of the Nervii at the expense of the artificially created *civitas* Tungrorum may be linked to the Roman resettlement of the left-bank Germans. Their territory also included a large expanse of the inhospitable Ardennes. Similarly, the vesting of the loyal Remi with extra clients and lands at the end of the Gallic War must explain their enormous, but still under-represented, territory. A reason for the over-representation of some smaller groups, eg. the Silvanectes or the Viromandui, is harder to give, but must reside in the mode and chronology of territorial allocation.

The close correspondence between the hypothetical polygons and the actual boundaries implies that the location of the administrative centres, rather than the territories of the eponymous groups, was the main determinant in the formation of the *civitates*. What determined the *civitas* to which the population of a particular area belonged was the nearest administrative centre. This makes sense. The city in the Roman world was the *civitas* (Mann 1960), and its citizens derived their identity from this rather than from the territory they inhabited. At the time of the Augustan reorganization, the eventual physical centres of the different *civitates* varied considerably in form. Some were still-occupied native centres, like Vermand which was later replaced by a completely new foundation at St Quentin a few kilometres away. Some, like Reims, were possibly Conquest period foundations. Others were or had been important military sites, eg. Agedincum and Samarobriva, the latter also apparently a native focus of importance, though not necessarily a major settlement. All these sites were almost certainly in some way focal to the élite control and administration of the communities with which they came to be identified. Their frequently asymmetrical location within the *civitas* suggests that it is from their relative spacing that the territorial boundaries followed. If it had been the other way around, one would expect the locations selected for the administrative foci to have been more central to the territories.

There are two possible explanations for the *civitates* with territories much smaller than the settlement geography predicts. Some, like the Silvanectes, may be secondary creations, detached from their larger neighbours, the Bellovaci, after the first stages of the Augustan reorganization had already been completed. Others were presumably formerly independent peoples, like the Suessiones, who were temporarily placed under the control of the Remi, losing dependents and land in the process, and only now made responsible for their own affairs. The association of Augustus placenames with several of these smaller *civitates*, as at Senlis, St Quentin and Soissons, is a further indication that there was more than one stage in the organization of the Belgic *civitates*. Although both St Quentin and Soissons are apparently successors to nearby Iron Age sites (one of which was itself a Noviodunum), their wholly Romanized names contrast markedly with the public towns of probable primary *civitates* which are either wholly native or belong to an early stage of the Roman occupation, like Beauvais (Caesaromagus).

Conclusions: Romanization in the Aisne Valley, a case study

The Aisne Valley region of southern Picardy has already been mentioned several times due to the intensity of recent archaeological work there, both aerial survey (Boureux 1974) and large-scale rescue excavations on the river gravels (Demoule and Ilett 1985), including those on the remarkable late La Tène nucleated settlements at Condé-sur-Suippe and Villeneuve St Germain. The area is largely agricultural today and spans the geological transition from the rolling chalklands of Champagne in the east to the limestone plateau and river valleys of the Paris basin in the west (fig. 5.8). The "Limon" soils of the plateau are more fertile but also much harder than those of the valley bottoms. Archaeologically, the area effectively provides a transect *c.* 50 x 25 km running between the central places (Iron Age and Roman) of the *civitates* of the Remi and the Suessiones, with their initially contrasting attitudes to Rome (BG. II, 4). Excavations on rural sites, including the author's on an Iron Age and Gallo-Roman establishment at Beaurieux, Les Grèves (Haselgrove, forthcoming b) and intensive fieldwalking are now offsetting the earlier bias to the major centres and the river gravels, permitting the relationships between different components of the settlement pattern to be assessed: urban and rural; Iron Age and Roman; valley, slope and plateau. The area is thus well placed for evaluating some of the questions about Romanization set out elsewhere (Millett, this volume).

One controversial subject is the chronology of the later phase of the late La Tène period in the region. There is disagreement over the dating of virtually every category of evidence which would normally be helpful, eg. bronze coinage, fibulae, etc. (cf. Buchsenschutz 1981) and crucially, whether or not their appearance pre-dates Caesar's intervention (eg. Debord 1984; Fleury 1986). In fact, notwithstanding the numismatist's arguments (eg. Scheers 1977), the excavations at Condé-sur-Suippe leave little doubt that potin coinage had achieved widespread circulation in the region by the earlier first century BC (cf. Massy 1983), with the implications this has for the rest of the dating. The view adopted here is that the final phase of the late La Tène period – defined by the appearance *inter alia* of the Dressel 1B Italian amphora form, high quality wheelmade pottery and certain fibula types (eg. the Almgren 65, Spoonbow and Arched forms; Fleury 1986) – most probably occupies the period *c.* 75/65 –30/20 BC, when Arretine and the first North French Gallo-Belgic wares appear. Sites with this material may therefore pre-date Caesar, but precise dating will have to await seriation studies of the settlement finds.

Roman military presence in the region may be disposed of rapidly. The large legionary fortress at Mauchamp, situated opposite Condé-sur-Suippe, thought Caesarian by Napoleon III, has *claviculae* at the entrances, pointing to a later date. There are, however, also surface finds of Dressel 1B amphorae from the site. The successive Tiberian and Flavian forts at Arlaines just west of Soissons are plausibly linked to the revolts of AD 21 and 69 (Wightman 1985). Otherwise we are reduced to seeking Roman military installations in the orthogonal layout of the implanted valley-bottom sites such as Villeneuve St Germain (Debord 1982) or the quartering of troops in existing native fortifications (cf. Todd 1985), as Caesar certainly did (BG. VIII, 5). One possible candidate is the promontory fort at Pommiers, near Soissons, where vast quantities of Italian Dressel 1B, and also probably Spanish, amphorae are present. The Liercourt-Erondelle cropmarks (Agache 1978) suggest an annexe as an alternative interpretation of the external features, which Vauvillé (1903-4) claimed as Caesarian siegeworks (cf. BG. II, 12).

At Reims, the recently excavated timber buildings of later first century BC date aligned on the street grid (Neiss 1985) have a rather military appearance, postdating an earlier, probably mid first century BC, occupation attested by pits and wells. It is still uncertain to which phase the earliest fortification relates. This is a sub-oval ditched enclosure of *c.* 110 ha extent of first century BC date (Neiss 1984) and itself apparently integrated with the main Trier and Lyons roads. Reims could therefore represent either a Roman fortress or another orthogonally laid-out native settlement like Condé-sur-Suippe and Villeneuve. But there is as yet no firm evidence for military activity at Reims and we must avoid invoking a hypothetical military presence in native fortifications as a stimulus to post-Conquest urbanization (cf. Wightman 1977). At Reims, the streets associated with the early timber buildings were transformed into roads and regularly remetalled from the early first century AD onwards and there was also a slight change in orientation. A second massive ditched enclosure, which predates the mid first century AD (Neiss 1984) is presumably linked to the status of the Remi as a *civitas foederata*.

The large valley-bottom settlements at Condé-sur-Suippe and Villeneuve are widely taken to signify the development of a more complex and hierarchial settlement pattern in the first century BC and thus a genuine step toward urbanization (Demoule and Ilett 1985; Fleury 1986). Their strict orthogonal layouts and functional division into living areas, workshops and agricultural zones reflects a high level of organization. Productive activities attested include metalworking and minting (Debord 1982) and the preparation of skins and pelts of wild animals (Meniel 1987). The high proportion of pig, a feature of late Iron Age faunal assemblages in Belgic Gaul (Meniel 1987; cf. King 1984) has been linked to the well attested export of Gallic salted pork to Italy (Strabo, Geography IV, 4, 3; cf. Demoule and Ilett 1985). Both sites were consuming large quantities of Roman imports. Recent work on the Villeneuve amphorae (Devos 1986) even suggests the possibility of identifying particular consignments and following their fate within the settlement. Neither site, however, was long-lived, although the most recent excavations at Condé-sur-Suippe have revealed a shadowy second phase restricted to part of the site (P.Pion, pers. comm.). Even so, the total period of occupation is unlikely to have been much more than a generation. Both sites, in some sense, must represent implanted settlements on open land, arguably amounting to little more than the concentration of a series of activities previously dispersed across the landscape into a new, organized and spatially confined setting. The degree of zoning need not differ greatly from that apparent in extended late Hallstatt – early La Tène agglomerations such as Berry-au-Bac, le Vieux Tordoir, which subsequently disappeared.

The relationship of the valley bottom sites to late La Tène plateau fortifications such as Pommiers and St Thomas is complicated by our limited knowledge of the latter sites, derived largely from older excavations. Debord (1984) has suggested that Villeneuve represents an intermediate, post-Conquest stage in a move down from Pommiers to the new foundation of Augusta Suessionum (Soissons), but there are indications of a more complex relationship. Villeneuve St Germain may begin rather earlier than Debord allows, possibly even before the Conquest, while there is certainly later first century BC material from Pommiers and the recent excavations by URA 12 suggest two distinct phases of activity (P.Brun, pers. comm.). The nineteenth century excavation plan of Pommiers suggests that the excavator, Vauvillé (1903-4) followed a series of linear features, which were almost certainly ditches forming a cruciform arrangement similar to that at Villeneuve (eg. Debord 1984). If so, this implies a comparable spatial organisation and a further link between the two sites. Most of the coins from the Pommiers ditches are inscribed struck bronzes, some of which are certainly post-Conquest (eg. Scheers 1977, 153), suggesting a relatively late date for their infilling – later, in fact, than the equivalent cruciform arrangement at Villeneuve. The question thus becomes not so much whether Villeneuve and Pommiers overlap, but rather for how long, which began the earlier, and what was the nature of the post-Conquest occupation of Pommiers, which has Augustan material, whereas Villeneuve was certainly abandoned by *c.*

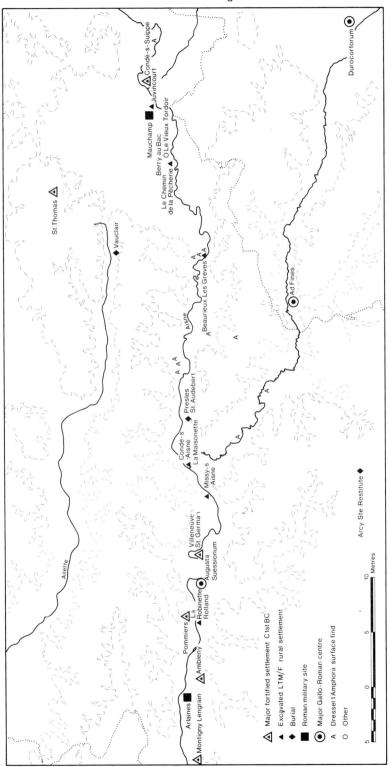

Fig 5.8. The Aisne Valley region, showing the principal sites mentioned in the text.

30 BC. There is no way of knowing whether there were links between St Thomas and Condé-sur-Suippe, 13 km apart, or between the abandonment of the latter site (otherwise known as Vieux-Reims) and the foundation of Reims 20 km to the south of it.

Demoule and Ilett's (1985) view that there was only a limited (re)occupation of the limestone plateau in the late Iron Age, linked to the foundation of defended sites like Pommiers, and that full exploitation of the plateau soils did not occur until the Gallo-Roman period, increasingly needs qualification. Recent fieldwalking implies that this process was underway by the later Iron Age (Haselgrove, 1989). Indeed given favourable climatic conditions and the availability of a mature iron technology and suitable crop species (cf. Jones 1981), the strong, fertile soils of the plateau were surely being exploited by this period, even if the settlements themselves avoided the exposed plateau top (as they do today) in favour of the more sheltered plateau margins and slope locations. Overall, however, the rural settlement record of the first century BC is essentially one of discontinuity. Most sites occupied early in the later Iron Age appear to be open settlements, eg. Berry-au-Bac, Le Chemin de la Pêcherie and Juvincourt, whereas large rectilinear ditched enclosures are a prominent feature of sites established in the closing stages of late La Tène, eg. at Condé-sur-Aisne, La Maisonette and Missy-sur-Aisne, Les Gardots.

At Beaurieux, Les Grèves, an earlier open settlement was succeeded, in or soon after the mid first century BC, by a large rectilinear ditched enclosure, probably following a short interruption. Several large timber buildings, sited close to the enclosure ditch, were grouped around a central space in a manner which strikingly anticipates the great courtyard villas of the Somme (cf. Agache 1978; Blagg, this volume). The internal organization of the enclosure at Missy-sur-Aisne may well have been similar (Haselgrove, forthcoming b), suggesting that an ordered layout was as much a feature of rural sites of the period, as of the large nucleated settlements. Between the open and enclosed settlement phases, the Beaurieux faunal assemblage shows a shift from pig to greater emphasis on cattle and sheep. The (earlier) Condé-sur-Suippe and (later) Villeneuve faunal assemblages change similarly in emphasis (cf. Meniel 1987), so the shift may well be chronological. Late in the first century BC, the rectilinear enclosure at Beaurieux was remodelled and reduced in size, apparently as part of a wider landscape reorganization.

The evidence such as we have suggests considerable instability in the first century BC settlement pattern, evinced both by the short-lived fortified nucleations and by the rural sites, some of which were abandoned for good, some reoccupied after a short break and still others, completely new foundations. These latter share with the major sites their organized layouts. Two of these certainly, and Pommiers and Reims possibly, look like implanted settlements, and the lack of any indications to the contrary, such as evidence of more gradual growth, is striking. Overall, a 'crisis' model, such as Collis' (1985, 83-5) of settlement centralization during a period of sustained military or socio-economic stress, offers a far better fit to this data, than the more conventional model of an evolving settlement hierarchy. This view would link the foundation of the fortified settlements such as Villeneuve St Germain to the abandonment of many of the rural settlements during a period of sustained crisis, the population subsequently dispersing back to the land when this was over, or moving to other nucleated settlements that replaced them. The Roman invasion alone cannot have sparked off this process in the Aisne Valley, since Condé-sur-Suippe at least was founded well before this date. Subsequently, it may, however, have contributed in one of two ways. By prolonging the period of stress, Caesar's intervention may have laid the foundation for more fundamental changes in the settlement pattern, and a move to greater nucleation. Conversely, the *pax Romana* may have made its mark by bringing the emergency to a close and thus enabling what was by inclination still an essentially rural population to return to their lands sooner than would otherwise have been the case.

The increase in the range and quantity of Roman goods reaching the region in the later first century BC has already been discussed (cf. Haselgrove 1987). This influx (along with warrior service in Roman rather than native armies and increasingly making and receiving payments in Romanized coin) was presumably the major Roman impact on most of the Belgic populations until well into the first century AD. In some ways, burials such as Presles St Audebert, like those at Goeblingen-Nospelt (Thill 1967), demonstrate just how quickly the Belgic élites did become integrated into Roman ways, but in other respects no more than continue pre-Conquest trends. The nature of the coinage did evolve rapidly, but this is exceptional (Haselgrove 1984). Several other changes probably had little or nothing to do with the Conquest. This should not surprise us. Rome's aim was to rule newly conquered peoples with the minimum of effort, not to Romanize them; if it had been, she would surely have gone about it rather differently.

Notes

1   "During the winter which he spent in Belgic Gaul Caesar made it his single aim to keep the tribes loyal, and to see that none had any pretext for revolt or any hope of profiting by it...so he made their condition of subjection more tolerable by addressing the tribal governments in complimentary terms, refraining from the imposition of any fresh burdens, and bestowing rich presents upon the principal citizens. By these means it was easy to induce a people exhausted by so many defeats to live at peace." (Translation Handford, 1951, 260).

2   This argument need not be taken as far as eg. Demangem (1905). He envisaged all the Belgic peoples inhabiting circumscribed areas separated from each other by dense forests, one group – the Morini – actually dwelling within them. It is, however, probably true that the areas of the most fertile soils exploitable with the climate and technology of the time will have supported appreciably larger populations than the rest. Caesar's figures for the settlements and population of the Helvetii (BG. I, 5, 29), who were circumscribed by mountains on all sides, and Iron Age settlement evidence elsewhere suggest this was equally true of the rich agricultural plains of eastern and central Gaul, eg. in the Auvergne plain compared to the surrounding uplands, which as today will have been more sparsely populated (Woolf, 1988).

3   The figures included in *Gallia*, although reasonably comprehensive, are not complete. The compilations are non-standard and not all the relevant sites are necessarily reported. In addition, some sites have had to be omitted here as there was insufficient information about their precise date, while some multi-period sites with first centuries BC-AD occupation which fell within the remit of the Direction des Antiquités Préhistoriques will have been reported in *Gallia Préhistorique*, which was not consulted. In most cases, however, there is no reason why the excavations reported in *Gallia* should not be fairly representative of the overall pattern of excavations in each Département.

4   An analysis using *civitas* boundaries derived from the pre-1792 Diocesan boundaries gives a virtually identical result. The Meldi are included with the Suessiones for 57 BC, but not for 52 BC, as they are generally believed to have gained their independence in the intervening years, following the Roman defeat of their paramounts (eg. Scheers, 1977).

5   Further examples are the Suessiones and the Viromandui (Aisne), the Atrebates and the Morini (Pas-de-Calais), the Caleti and the Veliocasses (Seine-Maritime) and the Aulerci Eburovices (Eure).

Bibliography

Agache, R. 1978 *La Somme Pré-Romaine et Romaine*. Amiens.

Bayard, D. and Massy, J-L. 1983 *Amiens romain*. (Rev. Archéol. de Picardie Num. Spéc.) Amiens.

Berger, L. and Furger-Gunti, A. 1981 'Les sites de l'usine à gaz et de la colline de la cathédrale à Bâle' in O. Buchsenschutz (ed.) *Les structures d'habitat à l'âge du fer en Europe temperée*, 173-86. Paris.

Bloemers, J.H.F. 1983 'Acculturation in the Rhine/Meuse basin in the Roman period: a preliminary survey' in Brandt and Slofstra (eds.) 1983, 159-209.

Bloemers, J.H.G. 1988 'Periphery in pre- and protohistory: structure and process in the Rhine-Meuse basin between *c*. 600 BC and 500 AD' in Jones *et al.* (eds.) 1988, 11-35.

Boureux, M. 1974. *Prospections aériennes dans l'Aisne en 1974: Laonnois, Soissonais et Tardenois*. Laon.

Brandt, R. and Slofstra, J. (eds.) 1983 *Roman and native in the Low Countries* (Brit. Archaeol. Rep. S184). Oxford.

Braudel, F. 1972. *The Mediterranean and the mediterranean world in the age of Philip II*. London.

Brunaux, J-L. 1986 *Les Gaulois: sanctuaires et rites*. Paris.

Buchsenschutz, O. 1981 'L'apport des habitats à l'étude chronologique du premier siècle avant JC' in *L'Age du Fer en France septentrionale* (Mém. Soc. Archéol. Champenoise 2): 331-8.

Buchsenschutz, O. 1984 *Structures d'habitats et fortifications de l'âge du Fer en France septentrionale* (Mem. Soc. Préhist. Française 18).

Buchsenschutz, O. and Ralston, I.B.M. 1986 'En relisant la Guerre des Gaules', *Rev. Aquitania Suppl.1*, 383-7.

Buchsenschutz, O. and Ralston, I.B.M. 1987 'Reflexions sur l'économie de la Gaule d'après César et les données archéologiques' in *Mélanges offerts au docteur J-B Colbert de Beaulieu*. Paris.

Burnham, B. 1986 'The origins of Romano-British small towns' *Oxford J. Archaeol. 5 (2)*, 185-203.

Champion, T.C. 1980 'Mass migration in later prehistoric Europe' in P.Sorbom (ed.) *Transport, technology and social change*, 32-42. Stockholm.

Chossenot, M. 1987 'Contribution à l'étude des monnaies Gauloises; les fouilles de la Cheppe, Camp de Mourmelon (Marne) in J-L.Brunaux and K.Gruel (eds.) *Monnaies découvertes en fouilles* (Dossiers de Protohistoire 1), 55-62. Paris.

Colin, A. 1984 'Préliminaires à une étude chronologique des oppida au premier siècle avant JC' in *Recherche sur la naissance de l'urbanisation au premier siècle avant JC dans le Centre de la France*, 154-168. Paris.

Collis, J. 1985 *Oppida: Earliest towns north of the Alps*. Sheffield.

Collis, J. 1987 'Celtic Europe before the Romans' in J.Wacher (ed.) *The Roman World*, 15-37. London.

Crawford, M. 1985 *Coinage and money under the Roman Republic*. London.

Crumley, C. 1987 'Celtic settlement before the Conquest: the dialectics of landscape and power' in C.Crumley and W.Marquardt (eds.) *Regional dynamics: Burgundian landscapes in historical perspective*, 403-429. New York.

Debord, J. 1982 'Premier bilan de huit années de fouilles à Villeneuve St.Germain (Aisne)' *Rev. Archéol. de Picardie* (No. Spécial Vallée de l'Aisne), 213-264.

Debord, J. 1984 'Les origines gauloises de Soissons: oscillation d'un site urbain' *Rev. Archéol. de Picardie 3-4*, 27-40.

Demangem, A. 1905 *La Picardie*. Paris.

Devos, M-F. 1986 Essai d'analyse spatiale à partir de l'étude des amphores d'un site de la Tène tardive: Villeneuve St Germain (Aisne, France). (Mémoire de DEA, Université de Paris X).

Demoule, J-P. and Ilett, M. 1985. 'First millennium settlement and society in northern France: a case study from the Aisne Valley' in T.C.Champion and J.V.S. Megaw (eds.) *Settlement and Society: aspects of West European prehistory in the first millennium BC*, 193-221. Leicester.

Drinkwater, J.F. 1983 *Roman Gaul*. London.

Duval, A. 1976 'Aspects de La Tène moyenne dans le Bassin Parisien' *Bull. Soc. Préhist. Française 73*, 457-84.

Duval, A. 1984 'Regional groups in Western France, in Macready and Thompson (eds.) 1984, 78-91.

Dyson, S. 1975 'Native revolt patterns in the Roman Empire' *A.N.R.W. II*, 3, 138-75.

Earle, T.K. 1987 'Chiefdoms in archaeological and ethnohistorical perspective' *Ann. Rev. Anthropol. 16*, 279-308.

Fitzpatrick, A.P. 1985 'The distribution of Dressel 1 amphorae in north-west Europe' *Oxford J. Archaeol. 4 (3)*, 305-340.

Fleury, B. 1986 'Late Iron Age chronology in the light of new material from the Aisne Valley (Northern France)' *Bull. Inst. Archaeol. Lond. 23*, 29-46.

Flouest, J-L. and Stead, I.M. 1977 'Une tombe de la Tène III à Hannogne, Ardennes' *Mém. Soc. Agric. Comm. Sci. Arts Marne 92*, 55-72.

Flouest, J-L. and Stead, I.M. 1979 *Iron Age cemeteries in Champagne: the third interim report*. (Brit. Mus. Occ. Paper 6). London.

Gechter, M. 1979 'Die Anfänge des Niedergermanischen Limes' *Bonner Jahrbücher 179*, 1-129.

Gechter, M. and Kunow, J. 1986 'Zur ländlichen Besiedlung des Rheinlandes im römischer Zeit' *Bonner Jahrbücher 186*, 377-396.

Groenman van Waateringe, W. 1980 'Urbanisation and the north-west frontier of the Roman Empire' in W.S.Hanson and L.J.F.Keppie (eds.) *Roman Frontier Studies 1979* (Brit. Archaeol. Rep. S 71), 1037-1044.

Hachmann, R. 1976 'The problem of the Belgae seen from the Continent' *Bull. Inst. Archaeol. Lond. 13*, 117-137.

Handford, S.A. 1951 *Caesar: the conquest of Gaul*. Penguin translation, London.

Haselgrove, C.C. 1984 'Warfare and its aftermath as reflected in the precious metal coinage of Belgic Gaul' *Oxford J. Archaeol. 3*, 81-105.

Haselgrove, C.C. 1987 'Culture process on the periphery: Belgic Gaul and Rome during the late Republic and early Empire' in M.Rowlands, M.Larsen and K.Kristiansen (eds.) *Centre and Periphery in the ancient world*, 104-124. Cambridge.

Haselgrove, C.C. 1988 'Coinage and complexity: archaeological analysis of socio-political change in Britain and non-Mediterranean Gaul during the later Iron Age' in D.Blair Gibson and M.Geselowitz (eds.) *Tribe and polity in late prehistoric Europe*, 69-96. New York.

Haselgrove, C.C. 1989 'Fieldwork in the Aisne Valley 1988', *Archaeol. Reports Univ. Durham and Newcastle 12*, 21-28. Durham.

Haselgrove, C.C. forthcoming (a) 'The Aisne Valley and the Mediterranean during the La Tène Iron Age', in A. Duval *et al.* (eds.), *Vix et l'Age du fer*, Paris.

Haselgrove, C.C. forthcoming (b) 'Later Iron Age settlement in the Aisne Valley: some current problems and hypotheses', in *Actes du XIIe colloque de l'AFEAF, tenu à Quimper*.

Hawkes, C.F.C. 1968 'New thoughts on the Belgae' *Antiquity 42*, 6-16.

Hopkins, K. 1980 'Taxes and trade in the Roman Empire (200 BC – AD 400)' *J.Roman Studies 70*, 101-125.

Jones, M.K. 1981 'The development of crop husbandry' in M.Jones and G.Dimbleby (eds.) *The environment of man* (Brit. Archaeol. Rep. 87), 95-127. Oxford.

Jones, R.F.J., Bloemers, J.H.F., Dyson, S.L. and Biddle, M. (eds.) *First millennium papers* (Brit. Archaeol. Rep. S401). Oxford.

King, A. 1984 'Animal bones and the dietary identity of military and civilian groups in Roman Britain, Germany and Gaul' in T.F.C.Blagg and A.C.King (eds.) *Military and civilian in Roman Britain* (Brit. Archaeol. Rep. 136), 187-217. Oxford.

Leman-Delerive,G. and Piningre, J-F. 1981 'Les structures d'habitat du deuxième âge du Fer de Conchil-le-Temple (Pas de Calais). Premiers resultats' *Mém. Soc. Archéol. Champénoise 2*, 319-330.

Macready, S. and Thompson, F.H. 1984 *Cross-channel trade between Gaul and Britain in the pre-Roman Iron Age* (Soc. Antiq. Lond. Occ. Paper (N.S.) 4). London.

Mangard, M. 1982 'L'inscription dédicatoire du theâtre du Bois L'Abbé à Eu (Seine Maritime)' *Gallia 40*, 35-51.

Mann, J.C. 1960 'Civitas: another myth' *Antiquity 34*, 222-223.

Mann, M. 1986 *The sources of social power, vol I*. Cambridge.

Massy, J-L. 1980 'Les origines d'Amiens. Essai de chronologie d'après les découvertes de céramiques arétines' *Cahiers Archéol. de Picardie 7*, 115-136.

Massy, J-L. 1983 'Informations archéologiques: Circonscription de Picardie' *Gallia 41*, 231-261.

Meniel, P. 1987 *Chasse et élevage chez les Gaulois*. Paris.

Metzler, J. and Weiller, R. 1977 'Beiträge zur Archäologie des Titelbergs' *Publ. de la Section Historique de l'Institut du Grand Duché de Luxembourg 91*, 17-187. Luxembourg.

Nash, D. 1976 'The growth of urban society in France' in B.Cunliffe and T.Rowley (eds.) *Oppida: the beginnings of urbanisation in barbarian Europe* (Brit. Archaeol. Rep. S 11), 95-133. Oxford.

Nash, D. 1978 'Territory and state-formation in Central Gaul in D.Green, C.Haselgrove and M.Spriggs (eds.) *Social organisation and settlement* (Brit. Archaeol. Rep. S 47), 455-475. Oxford.

Nash, D. 1984 'The basis of contact between Britain and Gaul in the late pre-Roman Iron Age', in Macready and Thompson (eds.) 1984, 92-107.

Neiss, R. 1984 'La structure urbaine de Reims antique et son évolution du Ier au IIIe siècle ap. JC' *Rev. Archéol. de Picardie 3-4*, 171-191.

Neiss, R. 1985 'Informations archéologiques: Circonscription de Champagne-Ardennes' *Gallia 43*, 357-374.

Parent, R. 1972. 'Le peuplement préhistorique entre la Marne et l'Aisne (2)' *Travaux de l'Institut d'Art Préhistorique 14*, Université de Toulouse-le-Mirail.

Peyre, C *et al.* 1987 'Les fouilles du Mont Beuvray: rapport biennal 1984-1985' *Rev. Archéol de l'Est et du Centre Est 38* (3-4), 285-300.

Pounds, N.J.G. 1973 *An historical geography of Europe 450BC- AD 1330*. Cambridge.

Ralston, I.B.M. 1984 'Les caractères de l'habitat à la Tène III: les structures urbaines et leurs correspondances avec les entités politiques' in *Recherche sur la naissance de l'urbanisation au Ier siècle avant JC dans le Centre de la France*, 169-198. Paris.

Reding, L. 1972 *Les monnaies gauloises du Titelberg:* Luxembourg.

Rice-Holmes, T. 1911 *Caesar's conquest of Gaul*. Oxford.

Rowlett, R.M., Thomas, H.L., Sander-Jorgensen Rowlett, E,. and Stout, S.D. 1972 'Stratified Iron Age house floors on the Titelberg, Luxembourg' *J.Field Archaeol. 9*, 301-12.

Roymans, N. 1983 'The north Belgic tribes in the first century BC: a historical-anthropological perspective' in Brandt and Slofstra (eds.) 1983, 43-69.

Roymans, N. 1988 'Religion and society in late Iron Age northern Gaul' in Jones *et al.* (eds.) 1988, 55-71.

Roymans, N. and van der Sanden, W. 1980 'Celtic coins from the Netherlands and their archaeological context' *BROB 30*, 173-254.

Scheers, S. 1977 *Traité de numismatique celtique II: la Gaule Belgique*. Paris.

Thill, G. 1967 '*Ausgrabungen bei Goeblingen-Nospelt*' Hémecht, 18, 483-91.

Todd, M. 1985 'Oppida and the Roman army. A review of recent evidence' *Oxford J. Archaeol. 4 (2)*, 187-199.

Tchernia, A. 1983 'Italian wine in Gaul at the end of the Republic' in P.Garnsey, K.Hopkins, C.R.Whittaker (eds.) *Trade in the ancient economy*, 87-104. London.

Van Es, W.A. 1983 'Introduction' in Brandt and Slofstra (eds.) 1983, 1-10.

Vauvillé, O. 1903-4 'L'enceinte de Pommiers' *Bull. Soc. Archéol. Hist. Sci. de Soissons (Sér. 3) 12*, 321-361.

Walthew, C.V. 1982 'Early Roman town development in Gallia Belgica: a review of some problems' *Oxford J. Archaeol. 1 (2)*, 225-236.

Wightman, E.M. 1970 *Roman Trier and the Treveri*. London.

Wightman, E.M. 1975 'The pattern of rural settlement in Roman Gaul' *A.N.R.W. 2.4*, 584-657. Berlin.

Wightman, E.M. 1977 'Military arrangements, native settlements and related developments in early Roman Gaul' *Helinium 17*, 105-126.

Wightman, E.M. 1985 *Gallia Belgica*. London.

Willems, W. 1984 'Romans and Batavians. A regional study in the Dutch Eastern River area, II' *BROB 34*, 39-331.

Woolf, G. 1988 'Assessing social complexity in the final Iron Age of central France'. Paper given to First Millennium Seminar, Cambridge.

6. Lower Germany: *plura consilio quam vi*
Proto-urban settlement developments and the integration of native society

J.H.F. Bloemers

Introduction

The region I would like to discuss is the delta of the three large rivers of northwestern Europe: the Schelde, the Meuse and the Rhine (Fig. 6.1). I roughly define the limits of this area on the basis of the drainage basin of these rivers, bordered by the Ardennes, the Eifel and the Sauerland, and the North Sea. The Rhine formed from Augustus' reign on formally or informally the border between the Roman empire and Germania libera. The area we are concerned with here can be given structure by tracing hypothetical polygons around the main towns, the *capita*, of the *civitates* south of the Rhine dated to the 2nd century AD. These *civitates* usually coincided with the territories of the main indigenous tribes. Three zones may be distinguished:

1) The borderland south of the Rhine, situated for the most part within the territory of the 2nd century Roman province of Germania Inferior;
2) The *civitates* in the second and third line represented the hinterland and belonged for the most part to the province of Gallia Belgica;
3) The zone north of the Rhine in Free Germany.

At the beginning of the Roman occupation *c.* 50 BC, the majority of the region had a relatively simple socio-economic structure: power and status were based on proven qualities rather than inheritance. Co-operation and unity flowed from kinship ties and consensus. The economic system was primarily geared to subsistence needs and only to a small degree to surplus production, due to the limited political and economical specialization. With the exception of the southern area, administrative and economic centres had not developed. This is partly reflected by the distribution of late-La Tène defended sites, which do not extend north of the line Calais-Tongeren-Cologne.

The Roman government and its army had to adapt their strategy to achieve a lasting subjection of such a poorly developed region. The relations between the army and the native population were determined by the extent to which the latter could supply necessary provisions for the military apparatus. Some of these needs were too organizationally and technologically complex to be produced immediately by the local communities of the Rhine area. Other needs could be more easily and quickly supplied. Finally, the nature of the relations determines whether or not they can be archaeologically recognized. I include lines of communication and information, political alliances, manpower in the form of auxiliary troops, food – to some extent – and certain resources, such as clay and wood, as those provisions and services available in the Rhine zone, which were needed by the army in the initial phases of conquest. Most other provisioning would have necessitated imports, or more or less radical transforma- tions of the local system. Consequently, I believe that the local population of the frontier zone underwent three phases of incorporation: 1) Communication with the élite; 2) mobilization

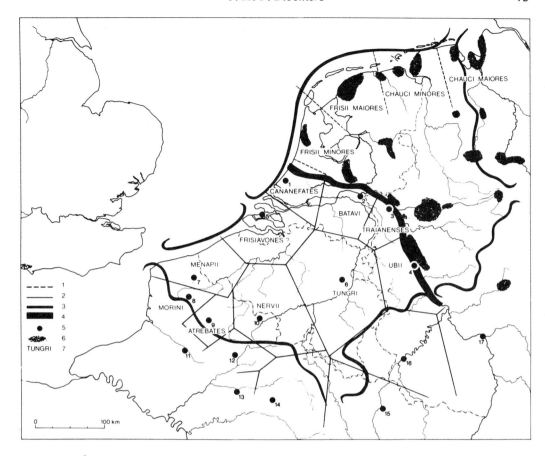

Fig. 6.1. The Delta and hinterland of the Schelde, Meuse, Rhine, Vecht and Eems (first to third century AD).

Legend: 1. boundaries of polygons (uncertain); 2. boundaries of polygons; 3. limits of the research area; 4. frontier of the Empire between *c.* AD. 50 and 400; 5. capitals of *civitates*; 6. concentration of native settlement; 7. tribal names.

Capitals of provinces and *civitates*: 1. Forum Hadriani/Municiplum Aelium, or Aurelium Cannanefatium (Voorburg-Arentsburg); 2. Ulpia Noviomagus Batavorum (Nijmegen); 3. Colonia Ulpia Traiana (Xanten); 4. Colonia Claudia Ara Agrippinensium (Cologne); 5. Ganuenta (?); 6. Atuabuca Tungrorum (Tongeren); 7. Castellum Menapiorum (Cassel); 8. Tarvana (Thérouanne); 9. Nemetacum (Arras); 10. Bagacum (Bavai); 11. Samarobriva (Amiens); 12. Augusta Viromandorum (Saint-Quentin); 13. Augusta Suessionum (Soissons); 14. Durocortorum (Reims); 15. Divodurum (Metz); 16. Colonia Augusta Treverorum (Trier); 17. Mogontiacum (Mainz).

of auxiliary troops by means of contact with the élite; and, 3) incorporation and adaptation of the native political and economic system.

I prefer to look at this incorporation with the help of concepts of world-systems in connection with colonialism and imperialism and expressed in relationships between core and periphery. Two concepts will be mentioned: peripheral imperialism and structural dependency. Peripheral imperialism means imperialistic expansion outside the control of the core and in part caused by factors within the periphery such as collaboration of the local élite, maintenance of peace and order, and high-handed actions taken by core representatives in the periphery.

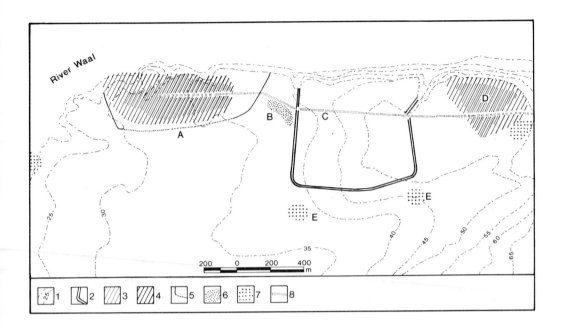

Fig. 6.2. Nijmegen: sites from c. 10 BC-AD 30-70.

Sites: A. proto-urban settlement area; B. cemetery; C. unoccupied area of former legionary camp with still visible ditches; D. occupation at the Kops Plateau; E. various smaller cemeteries.

Legend: 1. contour lines; 2. double ditch around the Augustan legionary camp, an area unoccupied in this period; 3. inhabited area, investigated and/or many finds; 4. inhabited area, not investigated and/or few finds; 5. ditch, certain and hypothetical trajectory; 6. cemetery, investigated and/or many finds; 7. cemetery, not investigated and/or few finds; 8. Roman road.

Expansion of the sphere of influence is not consciously sought, but the result of an unavoidable, but arbitrary process out of control. A structural relation of dependency exists between core and periphery, possibly only through co-operation between the élite in both areas to serve their collective interests: namely, the retention or even extension of their own societal position. Because of the greater social differences in the periphery, this co-operation is in favour of the core-élite. Those of the core and the periphery, not belonging to the élite, however have contrasting social interests.[1]

The Batavian case as a pilot study for one type of contact and urbanization

Research in the tribal area of the well known Batavians illustrates one way of contact between Roman and native, the rôle of military organisation and urbanization and the meaning of the concepts and terms mentioned in the foregoing section. Data and ideas are based on the extensive excavations in the large cluster of Roman sites at Nijmegen, the excavations of some rural settlements and cemeteries and the recent study of archaeological, geological and historical sources concerning the Eastern River Area.

The core of the Batavian tribal area is in a geographical sense identical with the Holocene depositions between the rivers Rhine and Meuse in the centre of the Netherlands now named the Betuwe, a name that must have been derived from the Roman name Batavia. The Batavian *civitas*, the Roman-period administrative unit, has certainly included a large part of the Pleistocene soils in the modern province of North-Brabant south of the river Meuse.

Nijmegen

Nijmegen belongs together with Xanten and Neuss to the main strategic sites established on the left side of the Rhine for the large Augustan and early-Tiberian campaigns to conquer northwest Germany between Rhine and Elbe. Between *c.* 10 BC and AD 30 an area with a length of *c.* two kilometres and a maximum width of 700 metres was the site of at least three different military installations with various functions and chronologies (Fig. 6.2). They give a good idea of the character, duration and the intensity of the Roman presence in this section of the Rhine front during this early phase. To the east we have the 13 hectares large Kops Plateau-site (D), where large-scale excavations started in 1986 and several ditches together with various finds point to the military function of the site. Further to the west lies the immense 42 hectares fortress on the Hunerberg, where two legions or their equivalent could have been garrisoned (C). Finally there is the *c.* 2 hectares Trajanusplein-fort dating from the second and possibly third decade of the first century AD. In my opinion this fort had a consolidating and defensive or at best supporting character, while the large fortress must have functioned as an offensive base. The various sites allow us to reconstruct the course of the main road. Along this road a small cemetery developed east of the Trajanusplein-fort (B) and west of the fort some settlement activities of unknown character took place (within A); potters, at least were probably at work there as is suggested by a clay depot closely dated by pottery and a brooch.

The situation in the next period from AD 30-70, the reigns of Tiberius, Claudius and Nero, is quite different from the previous one. The Kops Plateau-site was still occupied, but it would be unwise to speculate about the character of the settlement in view of the ongoing fieldwork there. The large fortress was no longer in active use, but continued to be reserved for official purposes and remained a topographical element of importance; after the Batavian revolt the Tenth Legion was garrisoned in the eastern part.

Important developments took place to the west. The small Trajanusplein-fort was given up and levelled. Along the western extension of the main road and closer to the river Waal a settlement with a regular lay-out developed. Although only relatively small parts were excavated, buildings seem to have common orientations and frontlines and in this way suggest a pattern in the form of *insulae*. One more or less complete plot showed a rectangular compound surrounded by a palisade and probably secondary roads on two sides (Fig. 6.3). Within the compound were two periods with two buildings of clear provincial-Roman character as shown by their dimensions, division and construction. In other areas again these two periods were found, but in two cases a third phase in stone was on top. Stone-buildings with a pre-Flavian date in the Low Countries are extremely rare. Several wells, probably constructed with wine-barrels, indicate that water supply was organized on a individual basis. A square pit or cellar contained an immense quantity of wine-amphorae Dressel 2-5, which points to the existence of a wine-merchant or an inn. The spectrum of the finds in general includes about 90 percent Roman and Belgic wares, in great quantities and of excellent quality, coins, bronzes, some oil lamps and only 10 percent native hand-made pottery. Such a spectrum in this period in the Lower Rhine area normally would be considered as an indicator of Roman military presence. The two sculptured blocks found in a fourth century ditch may have had a functional relationship with this settlement, depending on their final dating and interpretation. The blocks are part of a column and show a *togatus* laureated by a Victoria and offering on an altar; the inscription on the altar reads as Tiberius Caesar. Exact dating and meaning of the monument are still to be discussed in detail. Contemporary finds from the surrounding area are found in large quantities over *c.* 10 hectares, in smaller portions over 20 hectares. This area seems to be enclosed by a ditch with a more or less asymmetrical shape, which even seems to take into consideration the shape of the former Trajanusplein-fort; the enclosed area has a surface of *c.* 28 hectares and was certainly not completely build up or intensively in use. There are no traces of a wall or palisade.

The picture is completed by the characteristics of the cemetery to the east, which shows its main activity in this period. It covers an area of *c.* 1.5 hectare, where during some 50 years 1500-2000 individuals must have been buried; only about 150 burials were excavated in a regular way. All individuals were cremated and buried in small pits without surrounding features. In most cases the pits contained some grave-goods, mainly consisting of Roman and Belgic wares and sometimes of glass and oil-lamps; native pottery is extremely rare (Fig. 6.4). Some 25 percent of the 73 brooches are rosette-shaped, a type which is considered to be typical for women's dress; compared with military sites this proportion is large. This suggests that women formed an important component of the population, a suggestion which is strenghtened by the presence of some child-burials. Based on a length of use for the cemetery of 50 years and a life-expectancy of 25-30 years the population size can be estimated as averaging 675-1205 individuals.

From these selected data and features it can be concluded that this settlement and cemetery had the following characteristics:

1   The settlement had a mainly civilian function with administrative, trade or market and industrial activities; in this way it represents the future role of the later Batavian *civitas*-capital Ulpia Noviomagus;
2   Size, lay-out and architecture represent Roman scale and style; it is a completely new type of settlement in the Lower Rhine area;
3   The population had a Roman or rather Gallo-Roman origin and must have (been) deliberately settled here;
4   The settlement is to be identified with the pre-Flavian Batavodurum or Oppidum Batavorum mentioned by Ptolemaeus and Tacitus.[2]

The Batavian tribal area

What happens in the same period outside Nijmegen in the native society? Recent work of especially Roymans and Willems has updated and complemented older archaeological and historical data. Based on this evidence I will select four elements, which are crucial for the discussion of one mode of early-Roman contacts: the location of pre-Roman native centres, the presence of Roman imports in native contexts, the foundation of the Gallo-Roman temple at Elst and the recruitment of native auxiliaries in combination with grants of Roman citizenship.

The hierarchical differentiaton of the native settlement system in the area between Rhine and Meuse during the late first century BC is very restricted. However, there are some indications for at least two regional centres of gravity, one in the central part around 's Hertogenbosch and another not far west of Nijmegen. Roymans and van der Sanden have published a remarkable concentration of La Tène brooches, bracelets and swords and especially

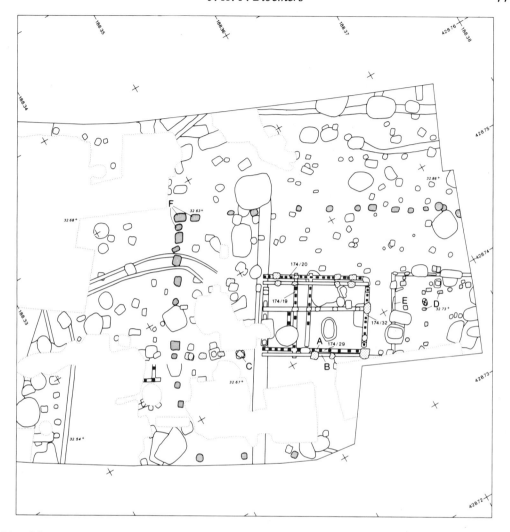

Fig. 6.3. Nijmegen. House and yard within the proto-urban settlement. A, B, C. building with three periods; D, E. building with two periods; F. Palisade.
(Grid intersections at 10m spacing)

Celtic coins, dredged from the river Meuse at Rossum/Lith (Fig. 6.5). The coins of the Lith-type are dated between 50 and 30 BC and are considered to have been a Batavian emission. From a stylistical viewpoint this emission is closely connected with coins of the Mardorf-type in the middle-Rhine area and illustrates Tacitus' story about the Hessic origins of the Batavians. Just south of 's Hertogenbosch we have the well known altar from Ruimel, erected somewhere around AD 50 to Hercules Magusanus by Flavs, the son of Vihirmas who was *summus magistratus* of the *civitas Batavorum*. In the area around Wijchen some 10 kilometres southwest of Nijmegen Willems traced a group of sites which could have been somewhat richer and perhaps larger than normal. This is for example expressed by a striking concentration of late-La Tène glass bracelets. Surprisingly this was not the area where the later

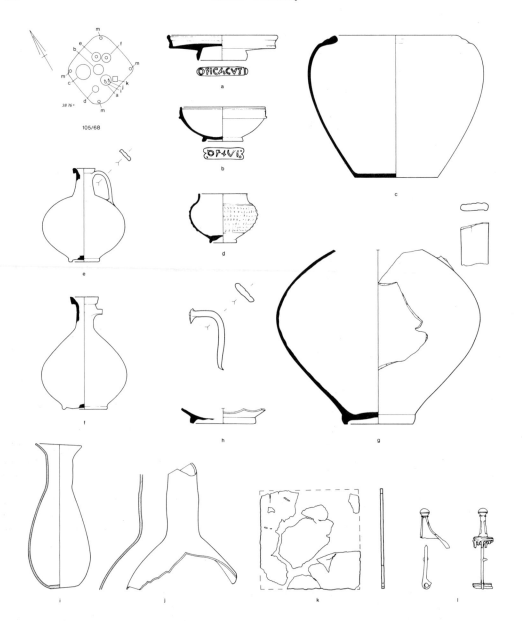

*Fig. 6.4. Nijmegen. Inventory from a grave in the cemetery belonging
to the proto-urban settlement. Scale approximately 1:6.*

capital of the Batavian civitas was founded. That site distinguished itself by the marked
absence of any native occupation at all.

During the same period from 50 BC to AD 70 Roman imports in a native context were far
less numerous than expected, when Willems started his survey in 1978 (Fig. 6.6). From some
142 settlement sites only 8 have imports dated to the Augustan period, 21 imports from the

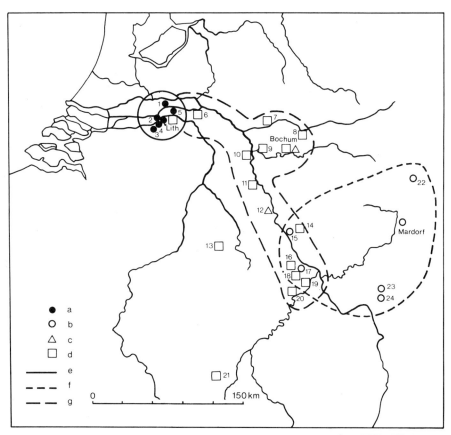

Fig. 6.5. *Distribution of groups of triquetrum coins in the Middle and Lower Rhine basin.*
Legend: a. coin(s) of gold or electrum, including those of the Mardorf group; b. coin(s) of silver, not of the Lith group; c. copper coin(s), the Bochum group; d. distribution area of coins of the Lith group; e. chief distribution area of gold and electrum coins; f. chief distribution area of coins of the Bochum group.
   Sites: 1. IJzendoorn; 2. Rossum/Alem/Maren; 3. Orthen; 4. Kessel; 5. Megen; 6. Nijmegen; 7. Haltern; 8. Oberaden; 9. Mülheim; 10. Bettenkamper Moor; 11. Neuss; 12. Cologne; 13. Siersdorf; 14. Oberpleis; 15. Stieldorf; 16, 17. Andernach; 18. Ochtendung; 19. Cobern; 20. Polch; 21. Titelberg; 22. Kirchberg; 23. Heidetränk-oppidum; 24. Höchst. (After Roymans/van der Sanden 1980)

first half of the first century and 36 from the pre-Flavian era. It can be taken to reflect the increasing availability of Roman artefacts, but generally only one, two or three finds per site are involved, which, compared to that of the contemporaneous proto-urban settlement at Nijmegen, is a completely insignificant quantity. This is incidentally contrasted by the appearance of relatively 'rich' Roman imports in cemeteries, whose native character is illustrated by the circular and rectangular ditches around the graves. In some cases like at Oss, Hatert and Zoelen graves within ditches with larger dimensions than normal contain fine brand new samian ware, expensive glass rib vessels and other complete pottery vessels. This pattern suggests that Roman imports still functioned mainly in the sphere of personal prestige, which archaeologically was expressed in life after death.

There is only one well dated non-military Roman site outside Nijmegen from this period: the Gallo-Roman temple under the church at Elst, just halfway between Nijmegen and Arnhem and consequently made available for archaeological research by war actions during the Battle of Arnhem in September 1944. In Bogaers' opinion the first phase consists of a simple rectangular groundplan and must have been built in stone somewhere around AD 50. This is another exceptionally early use of stone, which is best explained by some sort of official Roman involvement. Some indications were found for the existence of an older occupation of possible native character. The location of the temple probably indicates another regional point of gravity. More important however is, that like the Roman imports in some graves, the earliest clear expression of Roman influence is found in the sphere of symbolisrm and religion.

Finally we have to look at the rôle of the Batavian auxiliaries. Batavians are considered in Roman sources as crack troops, which is confirmed by the simple fact that they contributed in a significant way to the conquest of Britain; since then only the Normans under William the Conqueror managed to repeat this heroic act a millennium later. Around AD 50 nine cohorts, one cavalry unit and one élite corps forming the emperor's bodyguard are mentioned. If one accepts with Alföldy and Bellen that these units at that time already had developed into regular troops, their total strength can be estimated at some 5500 men in permanent service. They had their own commanders and some of them are known to us by their Roman names like Claudius Paulus, Claudius Victor, Julius Briganticus and the most renowned of all, Caius Julius Civilis; they belonged to the élite of their tribe. The Julio-Claudian emperors had granted them Roman citizenship, as is shown by the various *nomina gentilicia*. From this emerges a clear picture of large numbers of warriors involved in increasingly intensive contact with Roman army organization and native leaders gaining prestige on the battlefield and by receiving imperial grants. Contact and prestige were restricted to one segment of the native society in one specific setting: men able to fight.[3]

A provisional explanatory model for the observed data

Comparing the observations made in the cluster of sites at Nijmegen and the native rural area outside during this early-Roman period, the following explanatory points can be made:

1) There is no relationship at all between the location of pre-Roman or early-Roman native centres of gravity and the proto-urban central place of the future tribal capital. The location of the latter seems to be determined by the same factors that ruled the location of military sites: strategical position in view of the geographical and morphological properties of the region. On the other hand this new proto-urban centre did not originate from a military site or its surroundings. Military and civilian settlement were not located on the same site, possibly not even existing at the same time and consequently having no direct economical link. Size, lay-out, function and population indicate that the proto-urban centre must have been a settlement that was deliberately and artificially created, populated with inhabitants coming from the Gallic hinterland. Veterans may have formed part of this population, but they could never have been the prime mover of this development. Their number must have been too low in a phase where the empire was waging wars to expand the frontiers; their age must have been too high to give their best for the development of a booming town, and finally: what about their skills, except for the carpenters, potters, smiths and others experienced in craft or commerce?

2) Interaction between Romans and natives was channelled by contacts with the local élites, aimed at the mobilization of warriors and consequently mainly restricted to the male

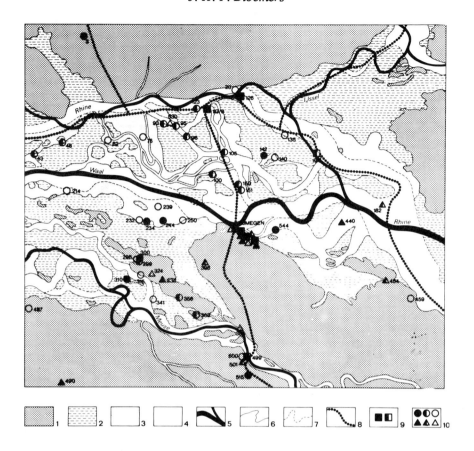

Fig. 6.6. Eastern River area with a reconstruction of the landscape and the river courses during the Late Iron Age and the Roman period and the location of sites with early imports and primary routes (early axes of military activity).

Legend: 1. Pleistocene deposits; 2. flood-basin deposits and peat; 3. bank deposits and pre-Roman channel zone deposits; 4. estimated channel deposits (meander-belts) related to active river branches, major brooks, and some of the small and in part still active fossil channels; 5. present day river channels; 6. boundaries of deposits; 7. reconstructed boundaries of deposits; 8. routes; 9. military settlements, Augustan and IA AD; 10. native settlements (circles) and cemeteries (triangles), Augustan, IA and pre-Flavian. (map width approximately 44km)

segment of native society. This harmonized with social and economic properties of this society. Like many Celtic or Germanic tribes, traditionally, much of the prestige could be earned on the battlefield, and manpower was more easily mobilized and more effective for Roman short term purposes than the low level native agricultural system. Courage and loyalty were honoured with gifts like pottery and glass vessels, grants of Roman citizenship and special arrangements like tax exemption, all gifts which were not too expensive for the Roman state. All this is told to us by Tacitus in his description of the Batavians: "Their distinction persists as the emblem of their ancient alliance with us: they are not insulted, that is, with the exaction of tribute, and there is no tax-farmer to oppress them: immune from burdens and contributions, and set apart for fighting purposes only, they are reserved for war, to be, as it were, our arms and our weapons."

3)   Integration of the native economic system during this early-Roman period must have been very restricted. Native agriculture was certainly not yet geared for substantial surplus production of food and other products of at least minimal quality needed in great quantity by the Roman army. Clear changes in this direction appear only after the Batavian revolt. Apart from that, the administrative and commercial infrastructure with central places was lacking. That was the reason to stimulate the development of a proto-urban settlement in Nijmegen called Batavodurum or Oppidum Batavorum, which must have meant 'town in the land of the Batavians' rather than 'town of the Batavians'. In its early years it must have been supported by the Roman administration.

Parallel developments in other tribal areas of Germania Inferior and Gallia Belgica?

There are indications for similar developments in other tribal areas of Germania inferior and Gallia Belgica, when we look at settlements in Xanten, Tongeren, Cologne, all destined to become the capital of a *civitas*.

Especially Xanten is important in comparison with Nijmegen and its surroundings: it is one of the main military sites for the conquest of Germania libera, it is Nijmegen's most important neighbour on the Rhine front at only 70 kilometres distance and it has been the subject of large-scale systematic research for decades. Without the data from Xanten it would have been more risky to interpret the Nijmegen data, as is done above. On the ice-pushed ridge of the Fürstenberg lies the legionary site *Vetera I*, which was in active use from Augustan times until its destruction by the rebellious Batavians in AD 69. Northwest of it at a distance of 2.5 kilometres the Colonia Ulpia Traiana was founded somewhere around AD 100. Under the Colonia clear indications are found of an older settlement, which is generally called the "Vorgängersiedlung" and has sometimes been interpreted as a native settlement of the regional tribe the Cugerni. Settlement finds cover the central area of the later Colonia west of the Roman road and show three phases of occupation with timber constructions and one in stone. The earliest is dated around 30/40 AD, the second one was burned down in AD 69/70. The sleeper beam construction is normally used during the timber phases. The general lay-out of the building plots is regular and differs only slight from that of the later Colonia. Finds have mainly a Roman or Gallic origin, only a small quantity must be native products; pre-Roman finds are exceptional. Economy seems to have been based on trade and crafts rather than on agriculture. To the north, a short lived early-Tiberian fort is supposed to have existed, to the south various pre-Flavian graves have been discovered. Settlement and military finds cover an area of roughly 30 hectares or even more. Tacitus mentions in his description of the Batavian revolt that not far from the legionary camp a settlement "in modum municipii" existed, which may have been identical with the "Vorgängersiedlung". Oelmann has suggested that the name for this site was Oppidum Cugernorum, Bogaers recently Cibernodurum.

The archaeological data for Cologne are less conclusive, but in several respects the historical data are very useful. From Tacitus' description we know that in AD 14 the Ara Ubiorum, the Oppidum Ubiorum and the two-legion fortress *apud aram Ubiorum* were close to each other. The Ubians were a Germanic tribe originally living on the right bank of the Rhine, but who were allowed to settle on the left bank, perhaps around 38 BC. The Ara Ubiorum was founded at an unknown date before AD 14 and intended to function as the political and religious centre of the Germanic provinces. The Oppidum Ubiorum became the Colonia Claudia Ara

Agrippinensium around AD 50 by intervention of the empress Agrippina, who was born there in AD 15. The fortress was garrisoned by the 1st and the 20th Legions from *c.* AD 10 to 40. Features are extremely scarce which can be exclusively identified with the various sites known from historical sources. A pre-Claudian street grid seems to have the same lay-out as the Colonia. Settlement finds occur over an area of at least 80 hectares and consist of Roman and Gallic products, Roman sculptures and monuments, with no signs of previous native occupation. In the northern part of it a ditch, an earth-timber wall and the *praetorium* point to military activities; within this area the early-Augustan Arretine stamps are found. Later Arretine ware was discovered in the southern part, where the so-called monument of the Ubii and several pottery kilns of Tiberian-Claudian date have also been excavated. The area of 80 hectares is large enough to have accommodated both a two-legion fortress of *c.* 50 hectares to the north and a civilian settlement of *c.* 30 hectares south of it.

Tongeren is the third site chosen for a closer look. It has a strategical position in view of its connection between the Gallic hinterland and the Lower-Rhine front. Various finds from early Augustan times onwards are found over an area of *c.* 80 hectares. Celtic coins seem to concentrate in the southwest, where also a ditch from pre-Flavian or possibly early-Roman date has been excavated. The occupation of the southwest area seems to have ended before the reign of Tiberius and from then on it was used as a burial ground. Only in the eastern part, where a pre-Flavian ditch has also been found, did occupation continue. Under Claudius a regular grid of streets was constructed over an area of *c.* 56 ha. Timber buildings with sleeper beam constructions and foundation trenches with fragments of stone from Claudian date cut Augustan features, but traces of a native pre-Roman occupation have not been discovered. The groundplans differ clearly from what now is known as the typical native farmstead in this region. There are no special indications of the nature of the economic activities in the settlement. Generally, the site is referred to as Atuatuca Tungrorum. Mention should be made of the existence of a 20 hectares-large defended site some 13 kilometres east of Tongeren on the left bank of the river Meuse. The construction of its timber walls is dated by dendrochronology around 31 BC. It is reasonable to suspect that this site represents some sort of gravity point for this region in the late-La Tène period. The dislocation of the proto-urban settlement at Tongeren and even the early-Roman occupation at Maastricht, within view of this site, is remarkable.

The indications of Roman influence or activities in the region around the settlements at Xanten, Cologne and Tongeren have not yet been discussed. This can only be done in a very provisional manner, since data are incomplete and unbalanced. Gechter and Kunow have recently collected the finds from five different environmental units in the Lower-Rhine area between the North-Eifel and the German-Dutch border. All units including that close to Cologne show that Roman imports dated before the middle of the 1st century are extremely rare. Only from that time on do imports greatly increase. For the area round Tongeren with its large number of Roman villas it is generally accepted that Roman imports increase in Flavian times.

The sites discussed have some essential common characteristics, which coincide well with the Nijmegen data:

1   At all sites, indications are found for the development of a large and probable civil settlement, where intensive building activities started about AD 40 or at least during the reign of Claudius.

2   All sites had some sort of military presence of Augustan and sometimes Tiberian date near to the civil settlement. This military presence seems to have stopped before, or at least during, the early phase of the development of the civil settlement.

3   No site has yielded any clear indications for the presence of a native pre-Roman predecessor, and, consequently, the location is discordant with native settlement patterns.

4   All sites have dimensions much larger than the known permanent native settlements in the region; have some sort of regular layout and have, as far as is known, buildings which differ in construction and plan from the known native houses.

5   All sites have large quantities of Roman and Gallo-Roman products.

6   As far as expressed by Roman imports, contacts with the rural areas around these settlements seem to have been very restricted before the middle of the 1st century AD. They increase strongly from then on.

These phenomena suggest an explanation for the period AD 40 to 70 similar to that in the Batavian area: namely, the foundation of an entirely new type of settlement with non-native inhabitants and a very restricted economic interaction between this settlement and the native society; interaction between the Roman administration and native society was mainly focussed on the native élite for alliances and aiming for example at the mobilization of troops.[4]

Some remarks on contacts, integration and colonial cities

To support this sort of interpretation, it is useful to look at contact situations, rate of integration and characteristics of colonial cities in subrecent colonial history.

The combination of a given strategy, eradication, acculturation or equilibrium, with domination in the form of colonialism or imperialism will result in a specific outcome, each with different consequences for the archaeological record (Fig. 6.7). Combinations need not to be mutually exclusive in a geographical or temporal sense. In the discussed situation the colonialism/equilibrium outcome is interesting, where the newly established settlement functions like an enclave inside the native society. This approach represents a low profile strategy, which allows for the most efficient control and exploitation of locations and resources believed important, while indigenous populations are limited in cultural exposure and retain their native values. This is in agreement with the concept of structural dependency. Gradually, especially after the Batavian revolt, the strategy may have shifted to the colonialism/acculturation outcome.

	COLONIALISM (settlers)	IMPERIALISM (no settlers)
ERADICATION- RESETTLEMENT	abrupt cultural change (replacement)	regional 'empty cell'
ACCULTURATION	slow indigenous culture change	slow indigenous change in economics
EQUILIBRIUM (metastable)	settlement enclaves 'two cultures'	indigenous cultural maintenance

Fig. 6.7. A matrix of probable behavioural outcomes in situations of power domination, based upon ethnographic and historical examples. After Horvath 1972 and Bartel 1985.

French neo-marxist anthropologists like Meillassoux have emphasized the concept of "articulation": the foreign intrusive mode of production is combined with the indigenous mode of production rather than replacing it. The native economy is generally based on a kinship mode of production; the foreign one on surplus production in combination with a system of money, markets, tributes and taxes. The intrusive mode becomes gradually dominant by incorporation of the native one. Since this is a gradual process, contacts in an early phase between both systems are so few that it is difficult to trace them archaeologically.

A special topic of research in colonial history is the so-called "colonial city", which has some unique features compared with other urban agglomerations:

1) Power is principally in the hands of a non-indigenous minority;

2) This minority is superior in terms of military, technological and economic resources and, as a result, in social organisation;

3) The colonised majority are racially or ethnically, culturally and religiously different from the colonists.

A selection of some characteristics is of special interest for us: a dualistic economy, which means an economy with connections in two different cultures; existence of an intervening population, a grid-iron planning dictated by foreign models, multiplicity of functions, heterogeneous demographic structure.

Perhaps these analogies can help us in future research on early contacts between natives and Romans. The absolute date of this phase will vary from one Roman province to another. For Lower Germany the reigns of Tiberius and Claudius seem to mark the turning-point. Tacitus' remark on Tiberius' policy for Germany reflects this: "plura consilio quam vi": more with prudence than with force. The same could apply for our own research.[5]

Acknowledgements

I thank Mrs. L.L. Therkorn for correcting the English translation, N. Roymans., W. van der Sanden and W.J.H. Willems for the permission to use their maps and A.M. Nijs and J.H. van Vlierden for preparing Fig. 5.3.

Notes

1   Bloemers 1983; 1988; Roymans 1983; Willems 1984, 197-386.
2   Bloemers 1985 and in prep.; Noviomagus 1979, 17-36; Willems 1984, 73-76 and 83.
3   Bogaers 1955; Roymans/van der Sanden 1980; Willems 1984, 197-239.
4   Xanten: Hinz 1975, 826-839; Rüger 1980, 495; von Detten 1983; Schmidt 1984; Bogaers 1984. Cologne: la Baume 1972; Hellenkemper 1972-1973; Doppelfeld 1975, 718-728 and 732-737; Gechter 1979, 95-97. Tongeren: Vanvinckenroye 1975, 15-29; Mertens 1985, 262-263.
5   Raatgever/Geschiere 1982, 4-8; Bartel 1985; King 1985.

References

Bartel, B., 1985: Comparative historical archaeology and archaeological theory, in: S.L. Dyson (ed.), *Comparative Studies in the Archaeology of Colonialism*, Oxford (British Archaeological Reports, Int. Ser., 233), 8-37.

Baume, P. la, 1972: Das römische Köln, *Bonner Jahrbücher* 172, 271-292.

Bloemers, J.H.F., 1983: Acculturation in the Rhine/Meuse Basin in the Roman Period: a preliminary survey, in: R. Brandt/J.Slofstra (eds.) 1983: *Roman and Native in the Low Countries. Spheres of interaction*, Oxford (British Archaeological Reports, Int. Ser., 184), 159-209.

Bloemers, J.H.F., 1985: Drie basiskaarten voor de bewoning uit de 1ste eeuw na Christus te Nijmegen, in: S. Scheers/E. Scheltens (ed.), *Miscellanea in honorem Josephi Remigii Mertens. I. Topographia Antiqua*, Leuven (Acta Archaeologica Lovaniensia, 24), 39-51. (1987)

Bloemers, J.H.F., 1988: Periphery in pre- and protohistory. Structure and process in the Rhine-Meuse basin between *c.* 600 BC and 500 AD, in: R.F.J. Jones, J.H.F. Bloemers, M. Biddle, S. Dyson (eds.), *First Millennium Papers*, Oxford: BAR.

Bloemers, J.H.F., in prep.: *Excavations at Nijmegen, I*, Amersfoort (Nederlandse Oudheden).

Bogaers, J.E.A.Th., 1955: *De Gallo-Romeinse tempels te Elst in de Over-Betuwe. The Romano-Celtic temples at Elst in the Over-Betuwe District*, Den Haag (Nederlandse Oudheden, 1).

Bogaers, J.E., 1984: Zum Namen des "oppidum Cugernorum", *Naamkunde* 16, 33-39.

Detten, D. von, 1983: Die Strassengrabung CUT Schnitt 80/23-24, in: G.Bauchhenss and G.Hellenkemper Salies (eds.), *Ausgrabungen im Rheinland 1981/1982*, Köln/Bonn, 114-118.

Doppelfeld, O., 1975: Das römische Köln. I. Ubier-Oppidum und Colonia Agrippinensium, in: H. Temporini/W. Haase (eds.), *Aufstieg und Niedergang der römischen Welt. Geschichte und Kultur Roms im Spiegel der neueren Forschung. II.4. Prinzipat*, Berlin/New York, 715-750.

Gechter, M., 1979: Die Anfänge des Niedergermanischen Limes, *Bonner Jahrbücher* 179, 1-138.

Hellenkemper, H., 1972-1973: Oppidum und Legionslager in Köln. Uberlegungen zur frührömischen Topographie, *Kölner Jahrbuch für Ur- und Frühgeschichte* 13, 59-64.

Hinz, H., 1975: Colonia Ulpia Traiana. Die Entwicklung eines römischen Zentralortes am Niederrhein, in: H. Temporini/W. Haase (eds.), *Aufstieg und Niedergang der römischen Welt. Geschichte und Kultur Roms im Spiegel der neueren Forschung. II.4. Prinzipat*, Berlin/New York, 825-869.

King, A.D., 1985: Colonial cities: global pivots of change, in: R.J. Ross and G.J. Telkamp (eds.), *Colonial cities*, Dordrecht/Boston/Lancaster, 7-32.

Mertens, J., 1985: Les débuts de l'urbanisation dans le Nord de la Gaule, *Caesarodunum* 20, 261-280.

Noviomagus 1979: *Noviomagus. Auf den Spuren der Römer in Nijmegen*, Nijmegen.

Raatgever, R. and P. Geschiere 1982: Inleiding. Een eerste verkenning van het werk van Franse marxistische antropologen, in: W. van Binsbergen and P. Geschiere (eds.), *Oude produktiewijzen en binnendringend kapitaélisme. Antropologische verkenningen in Afrika*, 1-23.

Roymans, N., 1983: The North Belgic Tribes in the 1st Century BC: a historical-anthropological Perspective, in: R. Brandt and J. Slofstra (eds.) 1983: *Roman and Native in the Low Countries. Spheres of interaction*, Oxford (British Archaeological Reports, Int. Ser., 184), 43-69.

Roymans, N. and W. van der Sanden 1980: Celtic Coins from the Netherlands and their Archaeological Context, *Berichten van de Rijksdienst voor het Oudheidkundig Bodemonderzoek* 30, 173-254.

Rüger, C.B., 1980: Research on the *limes* of Germania Inferior (German part), 1974-1979, in: W.S.Hanson and L.J.F.Keppie (eds.), *Roman Frontier Studies 1979. Papers Presented to the 12th International Congress of Roman Frontier Studies*, Oxford (British Archaeological Reports, Int. Ser., 71), 495-500.

Schmidt, F.W.V., 1984: Die Grabung im südöstlichen Forumsbereich der Colonia Ulpia Traiana bei Xanten, *Bonner Jahrbücher* 184, 317-326.

Vanvinckenroye, W., 1975: *Tongeren. Romeinse stad*, Tongeren.

Willems, W.J.H., 1984: Romans and Batavians. A Regional Study in the Dutch Eastern River Area, II, *Berichten van de Rijksdienst voor het Oudheidkundig Bodemonderzoek* 34, 39-331.

7. Relations between Roman occupation and the *Limesvorland* in the province of Germania Inferior

by Jürgen Kunow

A more detailed contribution to this theme has already been published (Kunow 1987). In that paper I included further evidence and distribution maps. Here I have provided more extensive treatment of the theoretical background to the successful occupation of Gaul and the attempted but unsuccessful conquest of Germany.

Beginning with the strip of land that extended from Germania Inferior to the east and north-east, this paper will deal with three themes connected with the occupation of our region. First, we will concern ourselves with the *Limesvorland* (the area in front of the *limes*) in the southern area of the province, its significance and development from its beginnings to Late Antiquity. Secondly, we examine in a wider context the different reasons for the successful occupation of Gaul and the failure of the conquest in Germany. Thirdly, we return to the *Limesvorland*, including the zone further north, in what is today the Netherlands, to investigate the question of an attached client zone of dependent German tribes of a type common in Germania Inferior. It is intended to show that these three themes are closely connected.

Military exploitation and native settlement
in the Limesvorland of southern Germania Inferior

Whilst it is known that during the Roman period people settled on the left bank of the Rhine in Lower Germany following large migrations, until recently very little attention has been devoted to the adjacent strip of land on the right bank. One can cite only the work of Kahrstedt (1950, especially p.46) and von Petrikovits (1979, especially p. 238) who have outlined hypotheses for this area and have produced syntheses of the historical evidence. The *Limesvorland* was first described as the 'glacis' by Kahrstedt. This term refers to the original characterization of the right bank of the Lower Rhine by Mommsen (1885, 111), who thought that for Rome this territory 'was like, for instance, the terrain lying under the fort commander's cannons'. Other students like von Petrikovits (1978, 67) have adopted Kahrstedt's terminology. We, however, consider this term to be inappropriate since in early modern defensive terminology 'glacis' suggests a piece of land that is artificially raised and which the attackers must overcome when storming a fortress. If one wanted to speak of a 'glacis' at all in the Roman period, it would be with reference to the earthworks around the military camp, and it would certainly not have been situated in front of the *Limes*.

At the first *Limes* congress, Kahrstedt dealt with the *Limesvorland* on the right bank of the Rhine. As an ancient historian he started mainly from the written sources and attempted to relate them to the archaeological evidence already published by von Uslar (1938). The passage from Tacitus (*Annals* 13, 54) which describes an event on the Lower Rhine in AD 58, played a central rôle in Kahrstedt's argument. At that time, the Frisii were attempting to occupy abandoned estates the use of which was reserved for the military (*...ripae agrosque vacuos et militum usui sepositis insedere...*). They established themselves but were subsequently expelled by imperial decree. Shortly afterwards the Ampsivarii attempted to do the same but with equally little success. It is known that this tribe were on good terms with Rome; their leader was Boiocalus, whose loyalty could be traced right back to the days of Arminius.

Informative in this context is Boiocalus' accusation that despite the modest extent of the land, the military overgrazed it. He spoke of 'wasteland and desertion' (*vastitatem et solitudinem*). From the context of this reference, it is apparent that security requirements were more important than the economic value of these estates. We will return to discuss this further.

Kahrstedt (1950, 41) believed that with the change in Roman policy towards Germania following the defeat of Varus in AD 9, a wider strip ('glacis') of the *Limesvorland* was to be kept free from native settlement. It was not until Vespasian (*c.* AD 70) that the ban was dropped and an increase in settlement permitted. Kahrstedt made further distinctions, defining two areas, one north and one south of the River Lippe, which flows east-west. He recognized that the establishment of this buffer zone did not take place until AD 47 in the area north of the Lippe and could therefore be seen in connexion with Corbulo's campaigns and the retreat to the Rhine frontier.

Obviously, a break in occupation of only twenty-three years can hardly be recognized archaeologically, so the area north of the Lippe, in contrast to that to the south, may be seen as having a continuous sequence of occupation. This problem will be discussed again in relation to the region between the Lippe and the Dutch-German border.

Even if Kahrstedt's geographical distinctions are not used, although not disproved, it is now generally agreed that from the Flavian period the *Limesvorland* was settled by Germanic peoples right to the bank of the Rhine. According to von Petrikovits (1979, 238) the presence of small groups was acceptable, although the settlement of a whole tribe was not. He believed that this was a result of the army's need for exploitable land rather than any concern for security. Such a demand could be fulfilled in the *Vorland* without putting pressure on the provincial population. Both the hypotheses of Kahrstedt and von Petrikovits about the *Limesvorland* on the right bank of the Rhine are models based on historical sources and general considerations. Until now the archaeological evidence has hardly been considered in relation to this problem. For this reason I shall concentrate upon it.

It may come as a surprise that we know of more than 200 Roman findspots in the *Limesvorland*. This clearly demonstrates that the zone was more densely settled during the period than has hitherto been believed, on the basis of Tacitus for instance. The findspots can be divided into two groups, one Roman the other native. The known Roman finds are a result of either:

1. the exploitation and use of natural resources
2. agricultural exploitation
3. the establishment of military training camps

There is no evidence whatsoever for the presence of civilians on these sites. One may add a further category of material, namely objects (such as Roman building materials) which sometimes had a secondary use. Clearly in this case we must also consider individual instances of demolition and transportation of materials across from the left bank of the Rhine. The 21 Roman findspots are all closely associated with the river Rhine, and are all no further that 10 km from it. This area can correctly be called the *Vorland*.

The majority of the known findspots – over 200 – are associated with Germanic settlement. Only settlement sites and cemeteries where continuity of use can be demonstrated have been researched. Hoards and individual finds that cannot be certainly attributed to Germanic activity have been disregarded. These native findspots are also found right up to the Rhine and demonstrate, at best, a very sparsely settled strip behind them. In the south and centre of the study area the low densities of finds can largely be explained in terms of topographical factors (the Bergisches Land and the Sauerland); in the extreme north, beyond the Lippe, and to the east (in Westphalia, outside the study area) we would expect more dense Germanic settlement in front of the sparsely settled strips of land. Additionally, in the north, to the west of the river Ems, large areas of marshland formed a natural barrier which separated the Germanic settlers of the Lower Rhine from the inhabitants of Free Germany (Gechter 1979, 115, fig. 52). The east-west flowing Lippe, however, functioned to open up the Westphalian Basin.

Of the 186 Germanic findspots in the *Limesvorland*, only 107 – scarcely 60% – can be closely dated. This percentage is low as a result of lost pre-War finds. The datable assemblages can be securely assigned to three approximate periods, first century, second-third century, and fourth-fifth century. However, like the majority of sites known from casual finds, the haphazard evidence does not cover the whole period under examination. The following interpretations are therefore based upon only the more reliable information. These limitations are not applicable to this area, the Altkreis Rees, north of the Lippe, where several fieldwalking surveys undertaken in the 1960s give a better picture of site distribution and chronology.

In the *Limesvorland* of southern Germania Inferior 21 first century AD native findspots are known. Three can be accurately dated to the Augustan period; otherwise the finds date to the second half of the first century, the parallels being with the Claudio-Neronian horizon at Hofheim. The pattern suggests that the reasonably sparse pre-Roman occupation is abruptly terminated (Marschall *et al.* 1954; Reichmann, 1979, 218); only a few finds continue into the first century AD. By the middle of that century a gradual reoccupation is seen, and this develops until the end of the century. As there is no evidence for any continuity of settlement or population, this is clearly a result of new immigration.

From the second century AD the picture changes fundamentally. In the middle Empire we have 91 native findspots from an extensive area of the *Limesvorland*. Despite the favourable research conditions scant concentrations are recorded north of the Lippe. In the southern and middle river sections, further Germanic settlements may have been on the preferred land between the lower river terrace and the adjoining hills. Large scale excavations have been undertaken on three sites south of the Lippe, for which, however, there is secure evidence only for second-third century occupation. These sites were the cemeteries of Troisdorf-Sieglar (Joachim 1987) and Leverkusen-Rheindorf (von Uslar 1938, 224), and the mid-Empire settlement of Düsseldorf-Stockum (Rech 1982, 477). At a fourth large excavation near Haffen-Mehr, north of the Lippe, the settlement continued into the succeeding period (Neuffer-Müller 1978, 479).

The distribution map for the Late Antique period shows yet another change. Only 22 findspots are known in contrast with the 91 of the previous phase. The decrease is thus considerable. If we look at the situation north of the Lippe, the recorded invasion is less clear (42 mid-Empire; 19 Late Antique). This situation approximates to the numbers known for the adjoining northern Batavian region (Willems 1986, appendices 3 and 4). The question arises, of whether this bias affecting the north side of the Lippe in the fourth century is explicable by the intensity of research alone. That may be so in part, but it remains striking that the excavations (at Troisdorf-Sieglar, Leverkusen-Rheindorf and Düsseldorf-Stockum) have also produced little Late Antique material. One is forced to conclude that, in the *Vorland* north of the Lippe, there was a greater density of native population even though this represents a reduction on the numbers in the middle Empire. The evidence suggests that along the Lower

Rhine the Chattvarii, a Frankish tribe, took over the settlements of the Tencteri and the Bructeri (Neumann and von Petrikovits 1982, 391).

The changes observed in the *Limesvorland* from the first to fourth century AD are striking, although its value to the Empire is questionable. Was the strip primarily strategic, thus a security zone, or was it more significant for military logistics? The evidence presented above shows that the answer is clear. Germanic settlement was spread uniformly through time, and variations in the intensity of military exploitation caused differences in Roman limitations on Germanic settlement. In the periods of modest native settlement, in the first and fourth-fifth centuries, the need for exploitable land was no greater than that in the mid-Empire. That the army also used the strip for economic purposes is certain, and is attested by casual finds, but there was no exclusive 'military territory' (Rüger 1968, 51; Mócsy 1972, 133; Vittinghoff 1974, 123) along the right bank of the Rhine.

From the beginning, the *Limesvorland* took on a strategic significance; only in this way can the collapse of native settlement in the first century AD be explained. It is sufficiently understood to say that, after the defeat of Varus and the failure of Germanicus' campaigns, the forward development of the Lower Rhine frontier was abruptly curtailed and a supply line (the Rhine) established for the *Limes*. From then onwards, as it was no longer possible to maintain a defence in depth, the *Vorland* must have taken on a greater importance. It was thus sensible not to allow significant native settlement in the area. Sometime towards the end of the first century or at the beginning of the second, a change occurs. We would like to relate this change to Trajanic demilitarization rather than the Vespasianic reorganization of the *Limes* following the Batavian rebellion as Kahrstedt believed (1950, 80; 1952, 46). Trajan, amongst other things, reduced the number of legions on this frontier by half (Gechter 1979, 126). For about 150 years, until the onset of Frankish attacks, the Lower German *Limes* was peaceful. It was as a concession to this situation and as a result of the attractiveness of the Empire that the administration of the *Limesvorland* became less rigid. With the onset of the Frankish invasions, the *Limesvorland* must have regained its strategic importance and consequently was again depopulated.

It follows that the *Vorland* was valued as an integral part of the Empire. The environmental conditions meant that the settlement of Germans in the second-third centuries was more closely linked to the Empire than Free Germany. Presumably the depopulation of the *Limesvorland* in the Late Empire corresponds to resettlement on the left bank – an event not altogether new for the Lower Germanic peoples. The erection of a *prata legionis* boundary, represented by a stone altar at St Augustin-Niedermenden (von Petrikovits 1974, 27), corresponds well with this context, and is of Spanish or Danubian type (Mócsy 1972). It may indicate a clear territorial claim on the *Regio Translimitana* (Kiechle 1962, 171).

Reasons for the differing course of the conquest of the Gauls and Germans

We now turn to interpret the analysis of the *Limesvorland* and apparently digress from the theme to look at the analysis of the geographical area. In only a few years of war against the Gauls, Caesar conquered a vast region up to the Rhine. Despite their great military power his successors, Augustus and Tiberius, could not continue his success by annexing the area on the right bank of the Rhine up to the Elbe as had been planned. The central question is thus, why the operation suceeded in one case but not in the other. Different military strength or eagerness for battle can hardly have been the sole reasons. Rome finally failed on the right

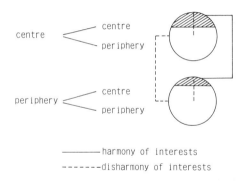

centre
— centre
— periphery

periphery
— centre
— periphery

————— harmony of interests
------- disharmony of interests

Fig. 7.1. The structure of imperialism (according to Galtung 1972).

bank of the Rhine because the prerequisites for occupation were absent. An explanation for this can be found in Galtung's (1972) model of imperialism, which may be as unknown in the English speaking world as it is in German archaeology (for the Dutch version see Bloemers 1983). In the following model (Fig. 7.1) we see an idealized statement of fact, in the style of David Clarke (1972, 2).

Starting from modern colonial/imperialist relations, Galtung has developed theoretical hypotheses about the structure of imperialism that may be applied to the situation in antiquity. Galtung's basic idea is that the centre (the nobility) of the central nation (Italy) must have succeeded in building a bridgehead to the peripheral nations (Gaul and Germany). This connexion must have been well chosen and must without fail have reached the centre of the peripheral nation (the native nobility). Only in this way, in the long term, is the integration (as distinguished from the occupation) of the conquered land at all possible. This bridgehead is so established that the centre of the periphery and the core of the central nation are bound together; their ties being in the interests of mutual harmony. Both are so connected that they rise, decline, and even collapse together. Between the periphery of the central nation and the peripheral nation itself there exist no common interests (but rather a 'disharmony'), as the products of the peripheral nation, for instance, were seen at the core as competition for the central nation's own products (Galtung 1972, especially 37). The application of this model makes the successful Gallic and unsuccessful Germanic occupations understandable. Only with a few German tribes, such as the Marcommani and the Quadi on the Danubian *Limes* (Kólnik 1986), were links successfully forged with the native nobility. In order to understand this, it is necessary to compare the different levels of social development and the different types of social structure within Gallic and Germanic societies. We will begin with the Gauls.

From written sources we know that the Celtic world had a rigid hierarchically structured society (Dobesch 1980, 433 ff.), the top of which comprised the *equitatus* and *principes* of the *nobilitas*. The *auctoritas* of individual leaders was so great that they even minted their own coinage which was also used as a means of payment outside the limits of their own spheres of influence. The installation of a central authority (this expression is used in accordance with Weber (1956, 519) as an 'external compulsory mid-permanent institution') is reflected in its own specific coinage for which the acceptance of authority in special measure is a prerequisite. We can only name the native personalities that have come down to us from

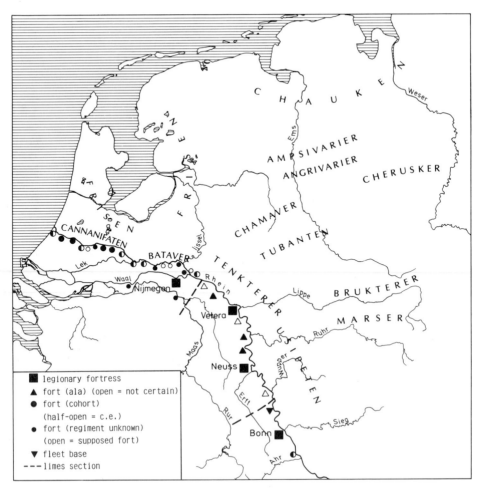

Fig. 7.2. The approximate probable territories of the native German tribes on the right bank of the Rhine in the first century AD with the frontier as it existed under Vespasian.

Caesar, such as Vercingetorix, Orgetorix, Dumnorix, Litavicus, Tasgetius, Divitiacus, Lucterios or Espasnactus, whose own coinages are well known (Forrer 1968, 112 ff; Allen and Nash 1980, 128 ff). Such a high level of society as this was only reached by the Germanic tribes with the coin-minting Franks or Ostrogoths in the sixth century AD (Werner 1954).

The reason that the occupation of Gaul could proceed so quickly was that Caesar found an adversary both socially and economically highly developed, showing a rigid social structure and a population living in proto-urban settlements. Caesar had only to corrupt the native nobility (and annihilate any uncooperative faction), and destroy the *oppida* for the opposition to be broken. However, Caesar found a totally different type of population when he attempted to conquer the Rhine. Here he came upon the Germans, who were in a state of 'ethnogenesis' (Wenskus 1961, 246 ff; 429 ff). Caesar's successors, who wanted to continue his work in the conquest of the Germanic tribes as far as the Elbe, learnt the lesson that has been repeated by colonial powers in modern times, for instance by the Dutch (Fieldhouse 1965, 278 ff) in

Java (with kingship), and Borneo (with headhunters): that the low level of social development that existed among the German tribes when compared directly to the Celts protected them from annexation. Victory over a single tribe or confederation created no long term permanent solution, especially since the tribal seat regularly shifted its position (for example Tacitus *Germania* 33, 36; *Annals* 55ff).

We may also look at Germanic society during this period, in order to describe its essential traits (Wenskus 1961, 272 ff; 305 ff; 339 ff). Of course Tacitus' *Germania* gives even more information about the central authority (such as the *reges*, *principes*, etc.) and social stratification (*nobilitas – servi*); moreover, archaeological research shows that a privileged class was already in existence in the northern Germanic areas in the first century BC. Note for instance the rich chariot burials such as Langaa and Husby (Raddatz 1967) or the complex at Hodde (Hvass 1975) which were clearly set apart from other settlements. On the other hand, it is again striking just how much influence the people themselves had (*Germania*, 11). Quite clearly, the development of central authority differed between the individual tribes: the Chatti (*Germania*, 30), the Marcommani and the Quadi, for example, appear to have been particularly developed (*Germania*, 42). In general, however, the position of central authority within the Germanic tribes does not appear to have gone unchallenged. There appear to have been physical sanctions taken against tribal elements with pretentions towards 'classical' authority, as Tacitus twice mentions (*Germania*, 7, 11). It appears that the Germanic tribes of the first century AD still comprised segmented and acephalous groups (Sigrist 1979). These factions, like the assimilated tribes, were forced into existence by frequent migrations. The development of authority and the rise of central control were frequently successful, but as Langaa and Hodde have shown, this was not exclusively a result of contact with the more developed Celtic and Roman worlds.

One aspect of this can be seen through Galtung's model which suggests that the more developed the social structure of the periphery, the easier it is under normal circumstances to occupy the area. Rome succeeded in establishing a bridgehead to the Germanic nobility, in so far as they existed at all, on only a few occasions. These events emphasize the varied development of the *Limes* as a flexible response to the existing situation in the *Vorfeld*: we are not suggesting that an incorrect evaluation of the situation led to a *volte face*, but rather that the failure was a result of the poorly developed native social stratification. The fact remains that a certain level of development had to be reached not only for a permanent occupation, but also for the ultimately successful integration of the conquered territory. With this theme, we return to the initial subject of our study, the Lower Rhine *Limesvorland*.

The problem of a client zone on the Lower German Limes

Against the background of the previous discussion, we would like to conclude by looking at whether or not the Lower Rhine *Limesvorland* and the area to the east can be seen as a client zone. According to Luttwak (1976, 20 ff.), whose strategic theories have yet to be accepted by German scholars, a structural change from 'hegemonic' to 'territorial' empire developed through the Principate. Such a 'hegemonic' empire, characterized primarily by a client zone extending foward from the frontier with limited responsibility for defence, has been identified by Willems (1986, 223, 230) as existing until the reign of Claudius. Until AD 47, the emperor prohibited the subjugation of the Frisii and Chauci by his provincial governor Cn. Domitius Corbulo and established the Rhine as the frontier instead. Despite these events, which exhibit all the features of a relationship with a client power (which then finally failed), we must ask whether this system really existed everywhere on the Lower German *Limes*.

In the Lower Rhine and the immediate area to the east, Klose (1934, 135 ff.) saw a client relationship – in Galtung's terms – through a bridgehead between Rome and the following German tribes: the Batavi, the Cannanifates, the Frisii, the Chauci, the Bructeri and the Cherusci. The first thing to note is that only a few of the German tribes which occupied the zone with which we are concerned are mentioned. Klose failed to name, for instance, the Usipetes, the Tencteri, the Marsi, the Tubantes, the Chattvarii or the Chamavi in the Lower Rhine area (Fig. 7.2). Theoretically, of course, the poor survival of the historical record may be the reason why no client relationships with the latter tribes are known to us, although their otherwise apparently belligerent relations with Rome makes this unlikely. The possibility of a client zone in the Lower German *limes* is thus ruled out. It remains, however, striking that the north of Germania Inferior, as well as the territory in front of the *limes*, was inhabited by tribes which conducted peaceful relations with Rome over a long period. Here we are dealing with the first four tribes listed by Klose.

In the north the Batavi and Cannanifates were regarded as *gentes foederatae* but were still incorporated into the Empire to a large degree, that is as members of the Empire (Klose 1934, 21, 27). Similarly, the Frisii, who had settled in the east, were also regarded as members of the Empire. This continued not only up to the time of Corbulo's retreat, but at least into the Neronian period, when two representatives of the nobility were awarded rights of Roman citizenship by the Emperor (Tacitus *Annals* 13, 54). Here we would like to see a true client relationship in the *Vorfeld*, without specifying its ultimate lifespan. Since the North Sea coast which was inhabited by the Frisii, lost its military significance in the course of the first century, the task of securing this section of the *limes* was no longer of importance. That the north-eastern neighbours of the Frisii, the Chauci, became clients through conquest in AD 5 is certain. However, after the Romans fell back to the Rhine in AD 47, distance prevented them from maintaining this relationship. So much for the north of Germania Inferior and its *Vorfeld*.

In the southern *Vorfeld*, Klose (1934, 45, 47) regarded only two of the many tribes as clients, the Bructeri and the Cherusci. They are, however, close to being clients in a real sense: in both tribes there were temporary pro-Roman factions which endeavoured to install puppet kings controlled by the Empire. These, ultimately unsuccessful, attempts demonstrate Rome's interest in manipulating the buffer zone in which the Bructeri and the Cherusci remained enemies and could, in the final analysis, be turned against the military. Thus a client zone existed, although only in its preliminary stages of development.

From the above it is clear that the *Limesvorland* displays varying infrastructures. It is hardly surprising that these differences are repeated in the establishment of the *Limes* itself, which was certainly only a reaction to the existing situation: the *Limes* was an indicator of the situation in the *Vorfeld* and vice versa. As is well known, the Lower German frontier demontrates a tripartite build up (the legionary bases are irrelevant in this context):

- the southern sector occupied by cohorts (Remagen to Cologne)
- the middle sector exclusively alae (Cologne to Altkalkar/Rindern)
- the north-west sector exclusively cohorts (Herwen to Valkenburg/Katwijk)

The occupation of the middle sector solely by cavalry shows that it was the most threatened part of the frontier, as is also demonstrated by the Frankish assaults of the third century. In contrast to the north-eastern *Vorfeld*, no client relationship existed with the Germans who were able to establish a buffer zone. The previously mentioned environmental barriers of this sector also, ultimately, proved unsuitable for the defence of the frontier (Gechter 1979). While controls and influence became more difficult in the *Vorland* and in the area occupied on its border, the restrictions were not so stringent that they prevented determined opponents from fulfilling their intentions.

Acknowledgements
This paper was produced at the request of the conference organizers to whom I am grateful for ensuring its translation by Karen Waugh.

References

Alföldy, G. 1968 *Die Hilfstruppen der römischen Provinz Germania inferior*, Düsseldorf (Epigraphische Studien 6)

Allen, D. F. and Nash, D. 1980 *The Coins of the Ancient Celts*, Edinburgh

Bloemers, J. H. F. 1983 *Periferie in Pre- en Protohistorie*, Amsterdam

Clarke, D. L. 1972 'Models and paradigms in contemporary archaeology', *Models in Archaeology* (ed. D. L. Clarke), London, 1-60

Dobesch, G. 1980 *Die Kelten in Osterreich nach den ältesten Berichten der Antike*, Wien

Fieldhouse, D. K. 1966 *The Colonial Empires: a comparative survey from the eighteenth century*, London

Forrer, R. 1968 *Keltische Numismatik der Rhein- und Donaulande*, (second edition), Graz

Galtung, J. 1972 'Eine strukturelle Theorie des Imperialismus', *Imperialismus und strukturelle Gewalt. Analysen über abhängige Reproduktion*, (ed. D. Senghaas, Frankfurt, 19-104)

Gechter, M. 1979 'Die Anfänge des Niedergermanischen Limes', *Bonner Jahrbücher* 179, 1-138

Hvass, S. 1975 'Das eisenzeitliche Dorf bei Hodde, Westjütland', *Acta Archaeologica* 46, 142-58

Joachim, H. E. 1987 'Kaiserzeitlich-germanische und fränkische Brandgräber bei Troisdorf, Rhein-Sieg-Kreis', Rheinische Ausgrabungen 27, 1-39

Kahrstedt, U. 1950 'Methodisches zur Geschichte des Mittel-und Niederrheins zwischen Caesar und Vespasian', *Bonner Jahrbücher* 150, 63-80

Kiechle, F. 1962 'Das Giessener Gräberfeld und die Rolle der Regio Translimitana', *Historia* 11, 171-91

Klose, J. 1934 *Roms Klientel-Randstaaten am Rhein und an der Donau. Beiträge zu ihrer Geschichte und rechtlichen Stellung im 1. und 2. Jahrhundert nach Christus*, Breslau

Kolník, T. 1986 'Römische Stationen im slowakischen Abschnitt des nordpannonischen Limesvorlandes', *Archeologické Rozhledy* 38, 411-34; 467-72

Kunow, J. 1987 'Das *Limesvorland* der südlichen Germania inferior', *Bonner Jahrbücher* 187, 63-78

Kunow, J. 1987a 'Die Militärgeschichte Niedergermaniens', *Die Römer in Nordrhein-Westfalen*, (ed. H.G. Horn), Stuttgart, 27-109

Luttwak, E. N. 1976 *The Grand Strategy of the Roman Empire*, Baltimore

Marschall, A., Narr, K. J. and von Uslar, R. 1954 *Die vor- und frühgeschichtliche Besiedlung des Bergischen Landes*, (Beiheft Bonner Jahrbücher 3), Köln-Graz

Mócsy, A. 1972 'Das Problem der militärischen Territorien im Donauraum', *Acta Antiqua Academiae Scientiarum Hungaricae* 20, 133-68

Mommsen, T. 1885 *Römische Geschichte Bd. 5*, Berlin

Neuffer-Müller, C. 1978 'Die frümittelalterliche Besiedlung von Haffen, Kreis Wesel', *Bonner Jahrbücher* 178, 479-502

Neumann, G. and von Petrikovits, H. 1981 'Chattwarier', *Reallexikon der Germanischen Altertumskunde, Bd. 4*, (Second edition ed. J. Hoops), Berlin and New York, 391-3 von Petrikovits, H. 1974 'Beiträge zur Geschichte des Nieder-germanischen Limes', *Der Nieder-germanische Limes*, (eds. J. E. Bogaers and C. B. Rüger), Köln, 9-29

von Petrikovits, H. 1978 *Die Rheinlande in römischer Zeit*, Düsseldorf

von Petrikovits, H. 1979 'Militärisches Nutzland in den Grenzprovinzen des römischen Reiches', *Actes du VIIe Congrès international d'epigraphieC grecque et latine*, (ed. D.M. Pippidi), Bucuresti, 229-42

Raddatz, K. 1967 *Das Wagengrab der jüngeren vorrömischen Eisenzeit von Husby, Kreis Flensburg*, Neumünster

Reichmann, C. 1979 *Zur Besiedlungsgeschichte des Lippemündungsgebietes während der jüngeren vorrömischen Eisenzeit und der ältesten römischen Kaiserzeit*, Wesel

Rech, M. 1982 'Düsseldorf', *Bonner Jahrbücher* 182, 522-24

Rüger, C. B. 1968 *Germania inferior*, (Beiheft Bonner Jahrbücher 30), Köln-Graz

Sigrist, C. 1979 *Regulierte Anarchie. Untersuchungen zum Fehlen und zur Entstehung politischer Herrschaft in segmentären Gesellschaften Afrikas*, Frankfurt

von Uslar, R. 1938 *Westgermanische Bodenfunde des ersten bis dritten Jahrhunderts nach Christus aus Mittel- und Westdeutschland*, (Germanische Denkmäler der Frühzeit 3), Berlin

Vittinghoff, F. 1974 'Das Problem des "Militärterritoriums" in der vorseverischen Kaiserzeit', *I diritti locali nelle provincie romane con particolare riguardo alle condizioni giuridice del suolo*, (Accademia nazionale dei Lincei 371), Rome, 109-24

Weber, M. 1956 *Wirtschaft und Gesellschaft*, Tübingen

Wenskus, R. 1961 *Stammesbildung und Verfassung: das Werden frühmittelalterlichen gentes*, Köln

Werner, J. 1954 *Waage und Geld in der Merowingerzeit*, München

Willems, W. 1986 *Romans and Batavians. A regional study in the Dutch Eastern River Area*, Amsterdam

8. Early Roman military installations and Ubian settlements in the Lower Rhine

by Michael Gechter

From the mid 50s BC after his rapid initial success in Gaul, and as a result of the Gallic rebellion, Julius Caesar felt compelled to demonstrate Roman power both to the east of the Rhine and also in Britain. He crossed the Rhine in 55 and 53 BC. The crossing most probably took place in the area of the Neuwied Basin (Neuwieder Beckens). This area, on the right bank of the Rhine, was inhabited by the Ubii. The treaty of friendship between the Ubii and Rome, which was to be so important for the Lower Rhineland during the following century, may well already have been in existence at this time (Caesar *DBG IV*, 16.5).

Amongst the most dangerous of Rome's enemies along the Rhine were the Eburones who lived in the loess region between the river and the Maas lowlands, north of the Ardennes and Eifel. In 54-53 BC, one and a half legions wintered close to their tribal capital at Atuatuca. These troops were annihilated by the Eburones under the leadership of their chief Ambiorix. In retaliation, Caesar invaded their territory in 53 BC and slaughtered the Eburonian army, plundered their land, and sold the inhabitants as slaves (Caesar *DBG VI*, 34.8). As a result of this Roman victory, the rebellion in north-east Gaul collapsed and henceforth peace prevailed in the region. Shortly afterwards, however, the revolt under Vercingetorix broke out in central Gaul.

After the annihilation of the Eburones, the situation in the Lower Rhine was as follows. The Treveri lived in the Mosel valley and the uplands of the Eifel and Hunsrück. The Ubii were settled on the right bank of the river in the Middle Rhine and Lahn valley, whilst to their north, around the Cologne Basin, were the Sugambri. Further north, in present day Holland, was the territory of the Usipi and Tencteri. The Menapii were settled in the region of the Rhine-Maas-Schelde Delta. The fertile loess in between, formerly the territory of the Eburones, is usually asserted to have remained unoccupied. In the former territories of the Eburones and Sugambri there is evidence of extensive solitary hillforts being abandoned in the mid first century BC. These included the Alte Burg near Euskirchen-Kreuzweingarten (Eburones) and the defences on the Petersberg near Königswinter, and at Benberg near Cologne (Sugambri – Joachim 1982, 414). In addition, recent excavations have demonstrated a mid first century BC evacuation of the large lowland *oppidum* in the Hambach Forest, which had extended over an area of 200m x 170m and was defended by a rampart and ditch (Göbel and Joachim 1980, 83). Until now these four sites have provided the only known indications of the warlike incidents of 53 BC. We know of no sites dating to the period c. 50-1 BC in this region; only in the mid first century AD is a resettlement evident.

The consolidation of Roman control on the Rhine began after Caesar. It included a restructuring of native settlement, beginning in 38 BC under the governorship of Agrippa with the resettlement of the Ubii in the former Eburonian territory. At the same time the Batavi colonized the area between the Rhine and the Waal. Similarly, west of the Batavi, the present region of south Holland was colonized by the Cannenefates (Pliny *Nat. Hist. IV*, 101-106; Tacitus *Germania*, 29; *Histories* IV, 15).

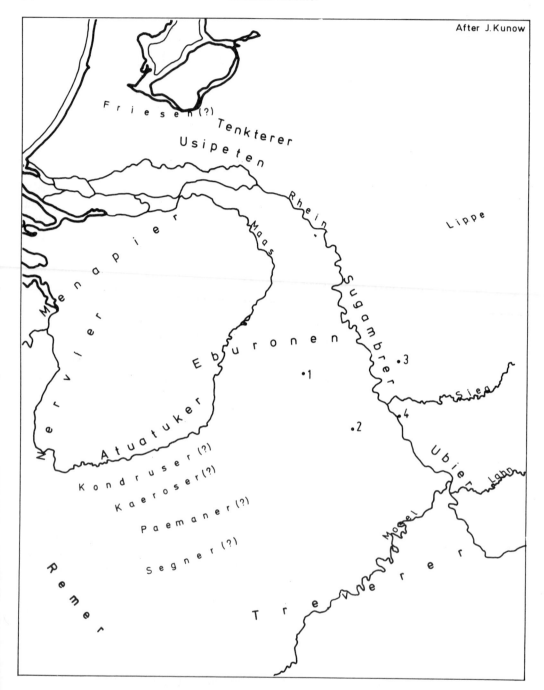

Fig. 8.1. Territories of the native tribes in the Rhineland at the time of Caesar.
Late La Tène oppida: 1. Hambach Forst (Ha 382); 2. Euskirchen-Kreuzweingarten;
3. Bensberg-Moitzfeld; 4. Königswinter-Petersberg.

Caesar's plan to conquer Germany as well as Gaul was revived by Augustus following the suppression of the Pyrenean tribes. Consequently, in 19 BC, the troops no longer needed in Spain were transferred to Belgica. This campaign was hastened with the defeat in 17-16 BC of L. Lollius at the hands of the Sugambri, who had crossed the Rhine. In the summer of 12 BC approximately a third of the whole Roman army assembled on the Rhine for the start of the conquest. Five years later they had taken the conquest of Germany up to the river Elbe.

The Ubii had already entered history as allies of Rome. Indeed they were the only tribe to remain loyal to Rome, even during the revolt of the Batavi. Their tribal capital (Cologne) quickly attained the status of *colonia* and a provincial altar for Germany was also planned here, like that for the Three Gauls at Condate, Lyon (Tacitus *Annals*, 1.57). In contrast to the Batavi, Sugambri, Tungri, Cannenefates and Treveri we know of no Ubian nobility in the first century, and the tribe also provided scarcely any auxiliary troops for the Romans, with only two cohorts known (only one by name). Furthermore, they were the only tribe from the Lower Rhine who provided no cavalry (Alföldy 1968, 73).

Up to and including the Claudian period, we know of the following units from the tribes mentioned:

Batavi: 1 ala, 9 cohorts (Alföldy 1968, 13, 73)
Cannenefates: 1 ala, 1 cohort (Alföldy 1968, 14, 51)
Tungri: 1 *ala*, 4 cohorts (Alföldy 1968, 38 – *ala Frontoniana*; 73)
Treveri: 2 *alae*, (Alföldy 1968, 19 – *ala Indiana*; 37 – *ala Treverorum*)
Sugambri: 4 cohorts (Holder 1980, 324)

This can be interpreted in the following way. The Batavi and Cannenefates contained splinter groups – *stirps regia* – from the Chatti comprising kinship groups who had previously elected the tribal chiefs (Wenskus 1961, 425). As a result of internal quarrelling, these clans migrated. Most of them were on horseback, as shown later by the mustering of mounted units from the Batavi and Cannenefates, although the Chatti themselves lacked such cavalry (Wenskus 1961, 424 citing Tacitus *Germania* 30; *Histories IV*, 12; 17).

The Ubii known to Caesar no longer had a chief. They were dependent on the Suebi and were forced to pay tribute. Caesar referred to them as *principes ac senatus* (*DBG IV*, 11.3). From this we can infer the presence of a tribal leader, hence what was understood as an oligarchic nobility.

On the basis of the above, it is apparent that the Ubii supplied the Roman army with the smallest number of troops of any of the tribes on the Rhine. It thus appears that the stronger the existing nobility, the more troops they provided for the Romans. This is demonstrated by comparing the Batavi with the Ubii. If it is correct to equate the Batavi with the former noble stratum of the Chatti who provided their chief, then the Ubii must be taken to represent exactly the opposite. Finally, looking at this from another angle, it means that the Ubii were resettled by the Romans without their former nobility.

The nobility seems to have been destroyed as a result of battle or through social unrest before their first contact with Rome. The early readiness of the tribe to conclude treaties of protection and mutual assistance with Rome cannot otherwise be explained (Caesar *DBG IV*, 16.5). This must surely have had something to do with the tribe's dependence on the Suebi. It is possible that the Ubian nobility was destroyed in battle with them (Caesar *DBG IV*, 3.4). Nevertheless, the social structure of the tribe must still have been sufficiently pronounced to enable a pact with Rome to have been achieved (Kunow, this volume). It was not however, so developed that any tribal leader was appointed commander of the troops. On the other hand, they were important enough to have attracted the support of the Romans. It is also possible that the Ubii themselves could not survive without aid from Rome. As the Germanic group on the Rhine who intervened on Rome's behalf, they were rewarded commensurately.

In this respect, it would not be surprising if the earliest traces of Roman troops on the Lower Rhine were to be found on Ubian territory. It has been known for a time that a Roman camp existed at Neuss from 16 BC. We now have evidence of a similar camp at Bonn, also in Ubian territory.

Neuss

The earliest camp (A), had an extent of *c.* 250 x 500m and could therefore accommodate half a legion. It lay on the lower terrace of the Rhine between that river, the Erft Valley and a marshy former course of the river Erft (Meertal), thus in a well protected position. Excavations have produced not only the earliest imported Italian pottery dating to around 16 BC, but also native late La Tène pottery. Since similar pottery had not previously been found, these finds were not interpreted as pottery from a native settlement (hitherto unpublished; Gechter 1979, 100).

Bonn

The earliest camp in Bonn lay on a lower terrace protected from high water, between the Rhine and a surrounding marshy former course of the river, again in a protected position. The extent of this camp is uncertain although it does not seem as large as that at Neuss. The latest excavations have revealed evidence of a preceding native settlement – four late La Tène *Grubenhäuser* and a contemporaneous kiln were found. The pottery from the settlement and kiln can be dated to the 30s BC (Gechter 1985, 121). A re-examination of the evidence from the early camp at Bonn, previously interpreted as an auxiliary fort, has shown that there was only a palisade and no ditch. Late La Tène pottery was also found in this area. It therefore seems not to have been a Roman camp (new interpretation previously unpublished, for the site see Gechter 1979, 79). The finds from Bonn can therefore be interpreted as a lowland *oppidum*, located in a geographically very protected area, and founded around 30 BC. In 16 BC, the settlement was occupied by the Roman military.

A similar interpretation should be assumed for Neuss. In both cases we have a native settlement – although at Neuss as yet no physical remains – developing in protected positions on the Rhine. In 16 BC both places were occupied by the military, although the native settlements may well have continued. In 12 BC the military vacated their positions, returning again around the turn of the century. Both these forts on the Lower Rhine almost certainly originated as reconnaissance camps for the projected campaigns of 12 BC. They lay in Ubian territory at an *oppidum* at Bonn, and on something similar at Neuss. This again illustrates the great significance of the Roman-Ubian treaty of friendship, and Rome's confidence in it.

In contrast the true settlement of *oppidum Ubiorum* (Cologne) seems to have been founded later. No pre-Roman pottery has yet been found in the Cologne area (H. G. Hellenkemper, pers. comm.). The early Roman camp there was first established *c.* 5 BC (Gechter 1979, 96). It is significant that this settlement with its native settlement was founded by the Romans. The following points are significant: the position in an open area without any natural protection, but with an offshore island in the river (the harbour). This contrasts directly with the defensive river terrace positions of the earlier sites at Bonn and Neuss.

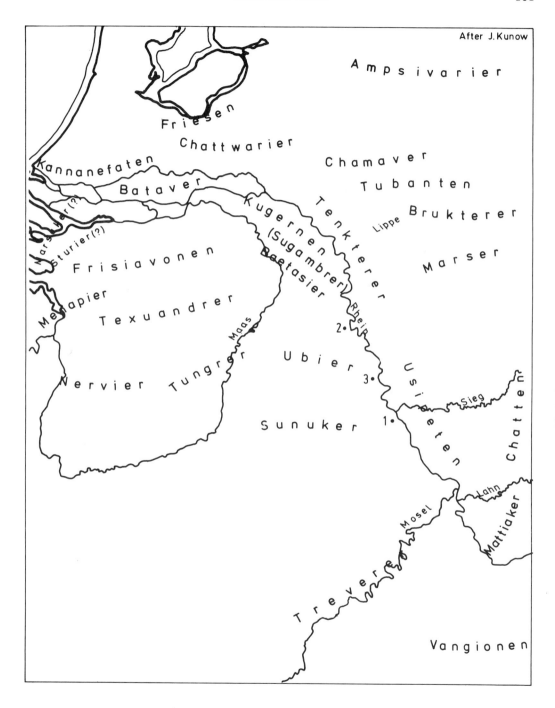

After J.Kunow

Ampsivarier

Friesen

Chattwarier

Chamaver

Tubanten

Kannanefaten

Bataver

Tenkterer

Lippe

Brukterer

Narsier(?)

Sturier(?)

Frisiavonen

Kugernen
(Sugambrer)

Baetasier

Rhein

Marser

Menapier

Texuandrer

Maas

Ubier

2•

Usipeten

Nervier

Tungrer

3•

Sieg

Sunuker

1•

Chatten

Mosel

Lahn

Mattiaker

Treverer

Vangionen

Fig. 8.2. Territories of the native tribes in the Rhineland at the birth of Christ.
1. Bonn; 2. Neuss; 3. Köln.

In conclusion we can see that the Ubii, who were resettled by Agrippa, had a different social structure from the other Germanic tribes on the Rhine. Their former nobility seems to have been absent. They had probably already been deprived of power before Caesar's arrival, through external pressure or internal unrest. The new élite which made a pact with Rome appears to have been made up from a lower nobility or 'merchant class'. In any case, they did not behave in the same way as the upper strata of the other tribes, for example serving as troop commanders. This is also illustrated in the modest number of Ubian units in the pre-Claudian period.

In contrast, the contact with Rome was so strong that the earliest reconnaissance camps for the projected German campaigns were situated in Ubian territory. These places carry un-Roman names (Bonna, Novaesium). To compare with this, the later capital of the Ubii at Cologne bears the artificial name *oppidum Ubiorum*. Here the tradition of native placenames is lacking. Nevertheless, the site was looked upon by Rome as the location for the Altar of Germania. Relatively quickly, *c.* AD 50, it attained the status of colonia. Hence it shows clearly the special treaty relationship that the Ubii had with Rome from the time of Caesar.

Acknowledgement

This paper was translated from the German by Karen Waugh.

References

Alföldy, G. 1968 *Die Hilfstruppen in der römischen Provinz Germania inferior*, Düsseldorf (Epigraphische Studien 6)

Gechter, M. 1979 'Die Anfänge des Niedergermanischen Limes', *Bonner Jahrbücher* 179, 1-138

Gechter, M. 1985 'Ausgrabungen in Bonn in den Jahres 1983/43', *Ausgrabungen im Rheinland 1983/84*, 121-8

Göbel, J. and Joachim, H. E. 1980 'Eine befestigte Spätlatènesiedlung im Hambacher Forst (Hambach 382)', *Ausgrabungen im Rheinland 1979*, 83-5

Holder, P. A. 1980 *Studies in the Auxilia of the Roman Army from Augustus to Trajan*, Oxford

Joachim, H. E. 1982 'Die Ausgrabungen auf dem Petersberg bei Königswinter', *Bonner Jahrbücher* 182, 393-440

Wenskus, R. 1961 *Stammesbildung und Verfassung: das Werden der frühmittelalterlichen gentes*, Köln

9. By the northern shores of Ocean[1]
Some observations on acculturation process at the edge of the Roman world

S. D. Trow

> 'It (Britain) has peoples and kings of peoples, but they are all uncivilized and the further they are from the continent the less they know of other kinds of wealth, being rich only in herds and lands....'
> Pomponius Mela, *De Chorographia* II, 6 (85)

Introduction

Britain is better served than most other provinces of the Roman empire in studies of conquest, colonization and the process of cultural interchange between victor and vanquished. Recent works have addressed these themes either generally (Burnham and Johnson 1979), or more specifically, eg. in terms of military/civilian relations (Blagg and King 1984) or rural development (Miles 1982). In addition, an increasing range of regional studies is becoming available. Against this backdrop, this paper is intended to explore the relationship between the intensity of long-distance trading contacts, the disposition of high status settlements and the growth of urban centres. Although the topics under discussion may seem rather diverse, all three are sensitive indices of the rate and degree of the Romanization of Britain and all lend themselves to techniques of archaeological investigation.

Particular attention will be paid to differential rates of development between south-eastern England and the surrounding zone comprising East Anglia, the Midlands and western England, both before and after the Roman Conquest. That major differences in the nature and organization of native British society existed between these areas has long been recognized and a particularly useful model utilizing the concept of core-periphery relations to explore the divergent but interrelated development of these zones has recently been proposed by Haselgrove (1982 and 1984, 32-3).

The nature, extent and intensity of pre-conquest trade

The transition from Dressel 1A to 1B amphorae and the possible causes of the apparently synchronous increase in the volume of imports entering south-eastern England have been discussed at length (eg. Cunliffe 1982, Fitzpatrick 1985 and Williams 1981) and need not be rehearsed here. Perhaps more significant than the increasing level of wine, oil and sauce importation in the post-Caesarean period is the introduction of a whole series of accessories relating to the *etiquette* of eating and drinking. The demand for a range of ceramic and metal vessels, particularly jugs, cups and strainers, as well as fine tablewares and mortaria (Partridge 1981) suggests that alongside a fondness for wine amongst the British élite, a desire had developed to emulate Roman fashions in the preparation and consumption of food and drink.

To a considerable extent, the presently perceived distribution of these imports is a reflection of the variation in burial practice apparent in pre-conquest Britain (Whimster 1981). Although recent settlement excavation has both increased the range of items attested on domestic sites and augmented the overall distribution, the majority of prestigious imports occur in the accompanied cremation burials of south-eastern England. Archaeologically 'visible' categories of import other than ceramics and amphora-borne commodities include glass vessels, brooches (Bayley and Butcher 1981) and other bronzes (Potter and Trow 1988), worked bone (Greep 1983) and possibly engraved gemstones (Trow 1982a).

Despite these additional sources of evidence, fine ceramics and amphorae, by virtue of their comparatively frequent occurence and post-depositional durability, remain the principal medium for determining trading contacts between pre-conquest Britain and the continent. Of necessity, therefore, it is largely this material which is used as an indication of the rate and extent to which prestigious commodities were becoming available to differing sections of British society.

Recent work has considerably extended the number of findspots of Augusto-Tiberian tablewares both of Gallic and Italian origin. A dense concentration in the Hertfordshire/Essex region, best exemplified by the major assemblages from Braughing (Rigby 1981 and 1988a) and Camulodunum (Hawkes and Hull 1947), is complemented by a more attenuated distribution across the Midlands, West Country and south of the Thames. Augustan material has recently been recognized at Oare and Casterley, Wiltshire; Boxgrove, Sussex (Bedwin and Orton 1984 and Rudling forthcoming); North Cerney, Glos. (Rigby 1988b); Leicester; and Silchester, Hants. (Fulford 1986) although it is only at the last site that material is occurring both in quantity and in unambiguously pre-conquest deposits. Elsewhere the possibility of the post-conquest arrival of old stock, though unlikely, cannot be wholly ruled out.

Within the gross distribution of early Gaulish imports, a particularly early group of material – a range of micaceous platters, jars and flagons originating from Central Gaul – can be discerned (Rigby and Freestone 1986). Examples have been recognized at Baldock, Canterbury, and Leicester and in larger quantities at Silchester, Camulodunum, Braughing and Verulamium as well as in several Welwyn-type burials. That imported finewares were apparently arriving as early as 25 BC begins to provide some insight into the dynamics of the exchange in prestige items affirming the pre-eminence of the Hertfordshire/Essex region and, on the basis of recent evidence, Hampshire. This is reflected not only in the early appearance of these wares but also in terms of the variety of sources of supply and, it could be argued, sheer quantity. Additionally, within these areas, it would appear that ceramic imports were not restricted to major nucleated settlements and were also available on smaller sites, such as Kelvedon, Essex (K. Rodwell 1979) and Owslebury, Hants. (Collis 1970, 257). Beyond the south-east the evidence, although limited, suggests a different pattern of availability. High status centres such as Bagendon/North Cerney and Dorchester-on-Thames appear to receive limited fineware supplies from the Tiberian (possibly Augustan) period onwards. These imports do not seem to have escaped the 'gravitational pull' of the major centres, as smaller farmsteads in the region such as Frocester, Glos., Claydon Pike (Miles and Palmer n.d.) and Barton Court Farm, Oxon. (Miles 1986) do not appear to establish fineware supplies until some time after the conquest.

Although concentrations of imported prestige items reflect the increasing wealth of native centres, the absence of such imports need not indicate a lack of prosperity. Social, political or religious motivations might cause the deliberate exclusion of imported prestige items – Caesar, for example, records that in Gaul the Nervii banned the import of wine and other luxuries, which they believed would impair their courage (*Bell. Gall.* II, 15, 4). In Britain, East Anglia provides an example of an area in which the manifestation of wealth and influence was articulated through insular traditions rather than imported exotica. Generally, the paucity of imports in Suffolk and Norfolk stands in stark contrast to the remarkable concentration of gold-alloy neck-torcs and coin hoards recovered from the area. Similarly, although requiring the mobilization and large-scale consumption of both material and human resources in its construction, the recently excavated conquest period settlement at Thetford, Norfolk (Frere 1983, 308-9: excavator T. Gregory) is impoverished in terms of imported finewares (Rigby pers. comm.)

The comparable absence of imported items in western Britain has recently been addressed by Daphne Nash (1984) who suggests that imported prestige items were necessary to sustain the expansive societies of the south-east because of the inherent instability of their social structure. Amongst the pastorally-based societies of the west prestige, goods were largely an irrelevance. In the light of this suggestion it is worth reiterating the observations of Pomponius Mela (*supra*).

The mechanism for cross-channel exchange remains obscure. By analogy with continental evidence, Haselgrove (1984, 29-30) has highlighted the probability of archaeologically 'visible' colonies of continental traders in pre-conquest Britain. Positive identification of such settlements is still lacking, but the precociously Romanized centre at Braughing-Puckeridge, Hertfordshire is perhaps the foremost candidate amongst known British sites. Excavation at a number of locations within the complex has revealed a series of Augusto-Tiberian deposits which contain items of imported bonework (Greep 1983), glass, bronze toilet implements, iron styli (Potter and Trow, forthcoming) and mortaria as well as the more conventional ceramic and amphora-borne commodities (Partridge, 1981). The site also produced a series of legible graffiti from sealed pre-conquest deposits including an example inscribed 'Graecus' (Partridge 1982a).

On the basis of epigraphic evidence it has been suggested (Middleton 1979) that long-distance bulk trade in Gaul was primarily linked to the demands of the Roman military garrison, with civilian requirements insufficiently developed to sustain large-scale trading activity by Gallic and Mediterranean merchants. This minimalization of the role of continental entrepreneurial activity has important implications for both the mechanics and the intensity of the movement of prestige goods into pre-conquest Britain and suggests that such goods were more likely to arrive in the guise of diplomatic gifts or bribes rather than as freely-traded items. If this is the case, colonies of foreign craftsmen and 'merchants' such as that tentatively proposed at Braughing-Puckeridge would have been subject to a high degree of direct political control. It is therefore no surprise that the Braughing complex has also produced a quantity of British 'coin moulds'.

An appreciation of the true volume of pre-conquest exchange in luxury goods is bedevilled by the absence of published sealed pottery groups quantified in a manner which allows comparisons of the fine pottery supplies between different sites to be drawn. Until detailed ceramic quantification independent of the overall volume/area of the excavation are available, it will not be possible to comment in detail on the incidence of pre-conquest imports either intra- or inter-regionally. Equally importantly, with only a small proportion of the archaeological resource sampled, it has not yet been possible to gain an impression of the *overall* quantity of material entering Britain, although there are indications that the trade in such items may have been sporadic and non-systematic. A detailed study of potters' stamps on Gallo-Belgic pottery by Valerie Rigby has demonstrated the low representation of each die impression within Britain (Rigby 1978, 198-9). This can be interpreted as indicating that Gaulish wares were arriving in small quantities, perhaps as make-weights amongst other traded items, rather than in large batches directly from the production centre. Current figures suggest an even lower quantity of pre-conquest terra sigillata entering Britain (Rigby 1986).

That the wide distribution of ceramic imports signifies the movement of other, archaeologically invisible materials cannot be doubted. The nature of this trade is, of course, unknown but it may well have involved spices and other foodstuffs in organic containers, textiles, livestock and, in addition, the exchange of specialist information and expertise. However, the exchange of information was not inextricably linked to the circulation of prestige goods as Jones (1982) has demonstrated in terms of certain agricultural innovations.

The apparently small quantity of pre-conquest imports penetrating beyond south-eastern and central southern England does serve to illustrate that those areas were in contact, albeit indirectly, with the continent and that we can, therefore, expect to find evidence for the reciprocal mobilization of resources for export. This assumption is supported by Strabo's allusion to the valuable tribute levied on British commerce (*Geog.* II, 5, 8). Although there is no reason to regard it as comprehensive, Strabo's checklist of exports and imports still occupies a central position in any discussion of economic relations with the continent. In his recent analyses of late Iron Age social development in the south-east, Haselgrove (1982 and 1984) stressed the role of the peripheral zone – the tribal lands of the Durotriges, Dobunni, Corieltauvi and Iceni – in the supply of the commodities destined for export. It would appear that native British coinages played little part in the mechanics of this exchange. The tribal issues of the peripheral zone shows little overlap with those of the south-east suggesting that their function concerned the maintenance of intra- rather than inter-tribal social relationships.

The difficulties in recognizing stimulated production of resources for exchange is well illustrated by considering the case of the Dobunni, frequently regarded as the classic 'middlemen' of late Iron Age Britain, controlling access by south-eastern polities to Welsh gold, Forest of Dean iron and Mendip lead and silver. At face value, there would appear to be considerable evidence for large-scale exchange of iron. Iron was specifically mentioned by Strabo amongst his list of exports and Caesar's mention of the British use of *taleae ferreae* as a form of exchange (*Bell. Gall.*, V, 12,4.) has led to the adoption of the term 'currency bars' for the strip-like ingots typical of the later Iron Age. These references are particularly intriguing in the light of the distribution of 'currency bars' which is essentially western and therefore outside Caesar's south-eastern theatre of operations (Allen 1967, figs. 1 and 2). In the absence of any known alternative method for the transportation and exchange of iron it can be suggested that the present distribution pattern reflects the limits of *hoarding* rather than *use* or *exchange* of the bars and, as such, records a difference of cultural attitudes to the storage of wealth between the south-east and areas to the north and west.

Little evidence exists as yet for the pre-conquest extraction of gold and lead deposits in Wales and the west of England. Hengistbury Head appears to have been involved in the refinement of silver (Northover 1987), possibly from lead ores of Mendip origin, and the rapidity with which this resource was utilised under the Romans – lead ingots dated as early as AD 49 – implies a degree of earlier exploitation. The ready availability of silver, illustrated by the copious silver coinages of the Dobunni, Durotriges and Iceni, may hint at exchange patterns amongst the peripheral tribes not readily discernible amongst other categories of evidence. The Dobunni also minted considerable gold issues at least as late as the conquest, suggestive of access to if not control over gold supplies from Wales. Gold, also listed by Strabo, was certainly reaching the south-east in considerable quantities. The enormous coin issues of Cunobelinus and Verica alone represent over 6,000 kg of base gold most of which,

Allen believed, originated from a single ore source (Allen 1975; Allen and Haselgrove 1979). The contemporary diminution of the Icenian gold issues (Allen 1970, 11) implies that the increase was created at the expense of other pre-existing patterns of supply.

Prominent amongst Strabo's list of British exports are several types of farm produce –cattle, hides and corn. Certainly, in terms of agriculture, the late Iron Age witnesses a considerable intensification of agricultural activity. Within the Dobunnic tribal area this is best exemplified by the work of the Oxford Archaeological Unit in the Upper Thames Valley where excavation and aerial survey have demonstrated the development of a highly organized landscape of enclosures, fields and trackways (Jones and Miles 1979). This increased preoccupation with land division is accompanied by the appearance of new types of farming unit such as those at Claydon Pike and Barton Court Farm (Miles 1986) on sites which continue to be occupied into the Roman period. In most respects the century preceding the Roman conquest was more agriculturally innovative than that following (Jones 1981). Whether the intensification of production was stimulated by internal pressures such as an increase in population or through external factors such as the need to create the surplus for export attested by Strabo is uncertain. No doubt the adoption of new farming techniques through the exchange of information and possibly the acquisition of improved breeds was a major factor in the ability to raise levels of productivity.

Continental influences may well be apparent in the sphere of animal husbandry. Anthony King (1984) has drawn attention to the fact that animal bone assemblages from the major nucleated settlements of the south-east demonstrate an essentially Gallic dietary preference towards pig and cattle and away from sheep. It is quite possible that the conscious desire to emulate 'Romanized' eating habits reflected in the importation of wine, sauces and tableware was also influencing the nature of animal husbandry in certain areas.

Trade after the conquest

Measured in terms of access to imported luxury goods, it is apparent that the first decades after the conquest witnessed considerable economic expansion. Several major nucleated settlements appear to have originated or experienced an intensification of activity during the same period. At Camulodunum, those areas sampled by excavation exhibit an increase in industrial activity (Niblett 1985) and demonstrate an increase in material wealth. Further west, at Bagendon, Glos. the majority of the excavated material belongs to the Claudian and Neronian periods and the rate of deposition of coins, brooches, glass vessels and fine pottery vessels increases considerably during the lifetime of the site (See Clifford 1961, 115, 185, 199-200 and 209-10). Newly recognized *oppida*-type settlements at Stonea, Cambs, (Potter and Jackson forthcoming) and Redcliff, Humberside (Crowther 1987) are characterised by a surge of activity in the Claudian and Neronian periods. Interestingly, Bagendon and Redcliff lie close to the rivers Severn and Trent/Humber which may mark a hiatus in the Roman advance (Tacitus *Annals* XII, 31). It seems probable that such sites functioned as 'gateway communities' involved in the channelling of prestige items to areas outside the occupied zone, along pre-existing trade routes. Further advances by the Roman military would have deprived such communities of their raison d'etre and the date of their decline corresponds to such a possibility. A similar involvement with the increased volume of exchange may also have precipitated the rapid growth of the Stanwick, N. Yorks. complex in the years after the Roman invasion of southern Britain (Haselgrove and Turnbull 1983, 1984 and 1987).

The nature of the stimulus provided by the Roman conquest to interprovincial and inter-regional trade has been the subject of recent discussion. Hopkins (1980) has proposed that the imposition of taxation and rents by the Roman state in 'economically unsophisticated regions' would, of necessity, have induced surplus production and thus stimulated the economy and increased the flow of trade. The army in particular has been identified as the major catalyst in the economic reorientation of Britannia, not only as the principal consumer of tax contributions but also through its role as a customer for Romanized imports (Middleton 1979). Additionally, as the most significant source of Roman coinage entering the province, the military is perceived as playing a crucial role in allowing the British economy to articulate with that of Rome (cf. Drinkwater 1983). In contrast, by postulating a relatively low level of tax contribution from Britain and by stressing the likelihood that some form of tribute was already being levied by native élites prior to the conquest, Millett (1984) has questioned the assumption that Roman taxation substantially stimulated the British economy.

Accepting Millett's argument (although see Fulford 1984, 130) an alternative model for the apparent economic upswing must be sought rather than seeking the explanation wholly in terms of the increased demands of taxation and rent. An hypothesis based on the disruption of the existing pattern of social relations can be offered. In the immediate post-conquest period, the newly established provincial administration would have had a vested interest in underpinning the authority of those sections of the native aristocracy favourably disposed to, or at least reconciled to, Roman rule. Despite this, the inevitable post-conquest influx into southern Britain of merchants and traders, even if on a small scale and primarily interested in servicing military requirements (Middleton 1979), would have had a severely disruptive effect on an élite previously dependent on controlling access to prestige goods. By the Neronian period, imported luxury items of a type previously available only to the upper echelons of society were appearing on a wide range of Romano-British settlements (cf. Millett 1980, fig. 23 A-B). It seems probable that the prestige value of such items declined in inverse proportion to their availability. That such a dislocation did take place after the conquest may be signified by the apparently rapid decline in the numbers of those lavishly furnished cremation burials which typify the late Iron Age of central-southern and south-eastern England. The burials which do perpetuate the tradition into the post-conquest period display a marked decrease with time in the variety and intrinsic value of their grave goods (Millett 1987). In addition to these stresses, the opportunity for native aristocrats to establish new clientage relationships *beyond* Britain and the access to professional moneylenders (Dio, LXII, 2, 1) operating outside the existing network of social relationships would have considerably raised the level of economic activity within the province.

Urbanization and the problem of oppida

Attitudes to the degree of urbanization in pre-conquest Britain revolve around the contrasting perceptions of prehistorians and Romano-British archaeologists and their divergent definitions of urban settlement (compare Collis 1979 and Hassall 1979). This non-coincidence of viewpoints has hampered attempts to assess effectively the native contribution to the process of urbanization in Britain.

It is now accepted that some Iron Age hillforts exhibited certain urban characteristics – density of occupation, 'zoning' of activities, proportionately greater industrial and storage capacities than surrounding smaller sites, and a possible administrative role. The decline of hillforts over much of southern England, apparently in favour of more accessible low-lying settlements, has led to the assumption that these later sites were also at the apex of a hierarchy of settlement types and fulfilled a similar range of activities. Unfortunately, the precise status of these so-called *oppida* remains obscure, the term itself posing considerable problems due to its non-systematic usage, both by classical and modern writers (see Saunders 1982). Modern use of the term *oppidum* tends to conflate a variety of site types including major hillforts, defended low-lying sites and open nucleated centres, and the grouping together of morphologically similar sites implies an unproven similarity of function, obscuring regional differences in their nature and development.

The presence or absence of 'defences' particularly clouds the definition of *oppida*. The high-statuus nucleated settlements of southern England include ostensibly undefended sites such as Braughing-Puckeridge, Herts. and Prae Wood/Verulamium as well as the dyke-enclosed complexes at Camulodunum, Chichester and Silchester. By analogy with the latter group, other linear dyke complexes, for example the Oxfordshire Grim's Ditch dyke system, have been defined as *oppida* (Jones and Miles, 1979, 318) although evidence of nucleated or prestigious settlement within the dyke circuit is not yet available. Known linear dyke complexes are largely confined to southern England at present, except for the major site at Stanwick, North Yorkshire. Newly identified candidates for the status of *oppidum* include examples at Ilchester, Somerset (Leach and Thew 1985), Stonea, Cambs. (Potter and Jackson, forthcoming) Gussage Hill, Dorset (Bradley 1984, 153-4), and possibly Dorchester (Sparey Green 1986), although the contrasting nature of these sites further devalues the usefulness of the term. Concentrations of British coins or early imported finewares from several Romano-British towns suggest that other examples await discovery.

During the 1970's analogies with continental, particularly Gallic, sites led to the assumption of a comparable level of urban development for British *oppida* (Cunliffe 1976). Recent assessments (eg Haselgrove 1982, 87, note 7) have been more circumspect, or have stressed the non-urbanized nature of *oppida*:

> 'The largest noble settlements in a warrior society were ... in all likelihood the inflated households of the dominant nobility, attached to their estates, and might take the form of rambling establishments with internal pasturage for sheep, cattle and horses, and space for the accommodation of variable numbers of dependants and visitors.'
>
> *(Nash 1984, 101)*

Although an increasing number of British *oppida* have been sampled by excavation, work has generally been on a small scale in proportion to the overall area of the settlement. In addition, given the undoubted degree of intra-site variability and the non-systematic approach to excavation strategy for this type of monument, it has not been possible adequately to correlate results from different sites. Despite these reservations, excavated evidence has demonstrated attributes common to several sites. The presence of coin flan moulds, for example, implies a possible administrative function. (See Tournaire *et al.* 1982, for distribution with more recent examples from Boxgrove, Sussex (Rudling, forthcoming) and North Cerney, Glos. (Trow, 1988). Note also alternative interpretations of 'coin moulds' (Selwood 1980)). In addition most *oppida* exhibit a propensity for imported glass, ceramics and foodstuffs which quantitatively and/or qualitatively is at a level unequalled by surrounding non-nucleated settlements. The presence of such prestige items confirms the high status intimated by the dyke complexes around several of these sites, although it need not imply a redistributive function.

Those *oppida* surrounded by complex dyke systems were, no doubt, the focus of considerable social obligation but this need not have involved a large and permanently resident community. Unfortunately, the lack of large-scale sampling precludes any possible estimate of the density of population, although the non-systematic excavated sample currently available to us demonstrates considerable variation in the density and character of occupation within British *oppida*. At Camulodunum and Verulamium a combination of excavation, field survey and aerial photography has suggested that functionally discrete foci of settlement were scattered amongst farmland (Dunnett 1975, 15-27 and Saunders 1982) and it is apparent that farming activities played a major part in the role of these *oppida*. The juxtaposition of the Gorhambury enclosure and the Verulamium dyke system indicates a close connection between the industrial and agricultural aspects of this complex. Similarly, the palimpsest of enclosures and droveways in the area around the Gosbecks enclosure (Crummy 1977, fig. 13) denotes intensive involvement with animal management which, on the basis of animal bone evidence, was primarily cattle ranching (cf. Luff 1982).

Although as yet unsupported by excavated evidence, the configuration of the Camulodunum dyke system intimates that the Gosbecks enclosure may represent an early nucleus of occupation or the later formalization/veneration of such a nucleus (Hawkes 1982, 10-11). Development from an earlier, possibly defensive enclosure can be paralleled elsewhere. Excavations at Braughing-Puckeridge have provided a comparable picture of multiple-focus settlement over an area of some 100ha, with an early nucleus in and around an earthwork at Gatesbury (Partridge 1981). In addition to this impression of a rather dispersed settlement pattern, widely spaced sampling of the site has demonstrated that occupation was both transitory and migratory, with various 'foci' flourishing and declining independently (Partridge 1981 and 1982b; Potter and Trow 1988; Stead 1970).

In contrast, recent excavations below the Romano-British forum-basilica at Silchester have revealed a highly organized settlement plan originating as early as the third quarter of the first century BC (Fulford 1986). Within the excavated area activity was apparently organized into *insulae* separated by roadways, although the more typical pattern of dispersed occupation foci is attested by intensive fieldwork on the periphery of the Silchester earthwork complex (Corney 1984). Whether the highly organized nature of the 'core' settlement is unique to Silchester, or whether its singularity reflects the lack of sampling of comparable areas within other 'oppida' is, as yet, unknown. Although large areas have been excavated within Verulamium and Colchester, the earliest deposits were ignored or sampled on a small scale. The large pre-conquest enclosure sealed by the Verulamium forum-basilica illustrates the point. Virtually nothing is known of its extent, internal organization or surrounding features (Frere 1957, 9-10).

From *oppidum* to *urbs*

The inadequacy of our understanding of major Iron Age settlements and, to a large extent, of the pre-Flavian phases of Romano-British towns, makes it difficult to assess adequately the extent of the native contribution to urban development and the processes by which only some of the major *oppida* evolved into Roman towns. Given the pre-existing trend towards nucleated and, in the case of Silchester, highly organized settlements, it seems probable that in the first decades after the conquest urban development on certain sites may have pursued a course that owed as much to native inspiration as to Roman innovation. That native-type 'oppida' should continue to develop or even originate in the immediate post-conquest period should occasion no surprise. Similar processes can be detected in Gaul at Mont Beuvray and Alesia where Romanized building types and materials are adopted although the settlement plan remains firmly Gallic in intent.

At Silchester, for example, it has been suggested that the construction of one of the dyke circuits originates during Cogidubnus' clientage (Boon 1969: although see Rigby and Freestone 1986). More intriguing is the relationship of the putative pre-conquest street 'system' to the later grid. Recently excavated evidence suggests that, at least in the central area, the orientation of the Romano-British *insulae* dates from AD 55/65, allowing over a decade for development on the Iron Age alignment to continue after the conquest (Fulford 1986). It is tempting to suggest that the NNE/SSW alignment of many of the Romano-British buildings, first noted by Aileen Fox (Boon 1974, 47), echoes pre-conquest or Claudio-Neronian boundaries and property divisions surviving the later layout. Unfortunately, the present lack of evidence for early timber buildings within Silchester does not permit the suggestion to be pursued.

The *oppidum* at Bagendon provides an example of developing nucleated settlement in the Claudio-Neronian period unencumbered by direct military involvement or later Romano-British urban development although, as a 'failed' settlement, it cannot be held to be typical of its class. The generally accepted hypothesis for the relationship between Bagendon and Cirencester has been succinctly summarised by Wacher (1975, 30-32): the native *oppidum* originates early in the first century AD and during the Claudian period is policed by a cavalry fort some 5km to the south. By the 60's AD a civilian *vicus* was developing around the fort whilst at the native site activity was declining.

Recent research allows an alternative model for the relationship of both sites to be postulated. Vivienne Swan (1975) has suggested that the occupation levels excavated by Mrs Clifford during the 1950's were Claudio-Neronian in date rather than pre-conquest. Further small-scale excavation has supported this view and demonstrated that the limestone platform excavated by Mrs Clifford is in fact a road constructed in typically Roman fashion and leading through a gap in the linear earthwork system towards the interior of the site (Trow 1982b). The concentration of industrial activities along the principal route into the settlement is one which can be paralleled at other oppida (Collis 1979), for example at early Roman Mont Beuvray. Recent excavation at North Cerney, some 2km north of the Bagendon dyke complex has located a 4ha ditched enclosure which appears to originate rather earlier than the occupation at Bagendon and to be involved in a similar range of high-status activities including the manufacture of gold and silver coin flans (Trow 1988). In the Claudio-Neronian period the enclosure is levelled and during the first century AD a villa building erected. The proximity, contemporaneity and shared functions of the two sites suggests that both are related aspects of a single complex and that the North Cerney site represents the high status nucleus of that complex. The labour involved in the construction of the dykes implies that Bagendon/North Cerney was a focus for the large-scale exercise of social obligation.

Given the evolution of the North Cerney settlement into a Romano-British villa estate, it can be posited that, rather than a major centre of population, the Bagendon complex prior to the conquest represents an aristocratic estate exercising administrative functions. The economic catalyst of the conquest stimulates the initial development of a nucleated settlement at

Bagendon which continues to function, with Roman approval, as an administrative centre. The expanding settlement, devoid of direct Roman influence, develops to a 'native' pattern within a linear dyke system – to all intents and purposes an *oppidum*. Various aspects of the material evidence suggest that the Roman fort at Cirencester might be later in date than is generally accepted, perhaps originating in the Neronian period (Reece 1982; Rigby 1988b). This would account for marked differences in the coarse pottery repertoires of Bagendon and Cirencester (Trow 1988) and the contrasting ratios of native and Roman coins at the two sites (Reece 1979). The establishment of the fort and the development of *canabae* during the Neronian period would have diminished the significance of the Bagendon complex. With the withdrawal of the military *c.* AD 75 the topographically more suitable site at Cirencester was chosen as the administrative centre of the newly-established civitas, being integrated into the developing communications network (Burnham 1986, 193-4) and topographically suited to future expansion. Industrial activity at Bagendon declined rapidly and, with the early erection of a villa building on the site of the North Cerney enclosure, the site once more resumed its role as the centre of a rural estate.

The late development of the Bagendon complex relative to the *oppida* of the south and south-east, together with the eventual erection of a Romanized building at the putative early (?) focus of occupation within that complex provides interesting parallels with the occupation sequence currently being elucidated by excavation at Stanwick (Haselgrove and Turnbull 1983 Fig. 10). A similar pattern of development can be very tentatively proposed for the early villa establishments at Shakenoak and Ditchley, Oxon. which are situated within the poorly understood Grim's Ditch dyke complex. Perhaps significantly, all of these sites failed to develop directly into Romano-British urban centres of any significance.

From aedificium to villa estate

In the face of the greatly increased access to imported goods of the immediate post-conquest period it would have been important for those members, presumably the majority, of the British élite whose authority survived the transition to Roman rule to establish a new medium for conspicuous display. Ideally, this medium would stress not only the status of the individual but also underline his favourable relations with the occupying power. The obvious vehicle for such expression was architectural, particularly amongst a native élite who had already assumed other Gallo-Roman pretensions. The visual impact of this imported style of building, must have been considerable. Although a rectilinear building tradition existed in the south and south-east (W. Rodwell 1978), over the greater part of pre-conquest Britain the dominant architectural type was the roundhouse (eg. Allen *et al.* 1984). The early employment of masonry building techniques, in particular, would have necessitated the involvement of continental craftsmen and would have provided a forceful demonstration of the owner's links to influential patrons (Slofstra 1983).

The pattern of development repeated for many British villa sites is the slow evolution of a 'native-type' farmstead over a century or more prior to the eventual construction of a Romanized dwelling. This gradual increase in material Romanization is generally interpreted as indicative of the steady accumulation of capital through surplus production. In contrast, an increasing number of sites, particularly in southern and eastern England, are now recognized as demonstrating a considerably more compressed development, with the appearance of fully Romanized structures within a generation or so of the conquest (Rodwell and Rodwell 1985,

41-5). The problems of archaeologically ascertaining the nature of villa ownership (Branigan 1982) means that it is uncertain whether the major investment of construction capital implicit in these early structures represents the realization of the considerable assets available to the British élite or the expenditure of foreign capital.

The rapidity with which luxurious Romanized structures began to appear on rural sites contrasts with their development in urban contexts. A public building programme was already underway in several towns during the reign of Nero and appears to have increased in pace and scope in the early Flavian period – a trend usually attributed to the positive intervention of Agricola (*Agricola* 21). Early monuments include the *fora* at Verulamium, Cirencester and Silchester and temples at Colchester, Chichester and Hayling Island. The inscription providing the only evidence for the Chichester temple (*RIB* 91) additionally demonstrates that major public buildings were being erected for the self-aggrandizement of the native aristocracy at an early date. Urban domestic housing, however, showed a far less precocious development (Walthew 1975). The degree of sophistication apparent in the construction and decoration of urban housing does not equal that employed for villa buildings until about the mid second century. Masonry-built domestic structures, for example, are particularly rare in towns before the mid second century even in areas where there is an adequate supply of building stone, as at Cirencester. This retarded development is also apparent in the *coloniae* at Colchester and Gloucester where a more rapid development of Romanized housing might be expected. The contrast between rural and urban developments becomes more pointed because in several instances the early development of villas is closely associated with the growth of urban centres. Around Verulamium, for example, a 'cluster' of villas has been recognized, several of which originate in the pre-conquest period (Frere 1979).

That the construction of luxurious Romanized dwellings in the countryside should precede that in the newly-established towns should occasion no surprise if it is accepted that many or most of these structures were in native hands. A study of Iron Age coin distributions (Collis 1971) and recent cemetery evidence (Millett 1987a) supports the concept of a rurally-based élite and increasing evidence is becoming available that several early villas succeed pre-conquest sites of considerable status. Two recently excavated examples illustrate this point. At Rivenhall, Essex, a substantial masonry structure and a later villa, apparently of Gallo-Roman type, are built on the site of an affluent native farmstead (Rodwell and Rodwell 1985 – although see Millett 1987b). The North Cerney structure noted above (Trow 1988, Trow and James forthcoming) lies within an Iron Age enclosure producing 'coin-mould' fragments. Its elevated and rather exposed location is rather anomalous in terms of normal villa location and is difficult to reconcile other than in terms of direct continuity of ownership.

Together the evidence for high status native precursors for several early British villas and the primacy of prestigious rural domestic architecture over that in towns supports the notion that distribution of these early establishments – largely confined to south-eastern England with a few outliers possibly linked to *oppida*-type complexes – appears to represent the investment of native wealth previously directed towards the acquisition of prestigious Roman imports.

Discussion

Surveying the increasing quantity and quality of data presently available to the archaeologist it would appear that, in material terms at least, the 'Romanization' of southern Britain was achieved with considerable rapidity. It is possible to suggest that, in the early stages of this process of acculturation, three major episodes can be identified.

Firstly, and becoming increasingly understood, is the 'knock-on' effect of Caesar's annexation of the three Gauls. Internal strife within the empire appears to have retarded certain aspects of the Romanization of Gaul (Drinkwater 1983, 19 and 27) and allowed the development of a Gallo-Roman culture with a vigorous native component. It was the activities and aspirations of this hybridized society which were mirrored in the changing mores of pre-conquest Britain. These influences were strongest in central-southern and south-eastern England and may have involved the semi-permanent presence of Roman or Gallic craftsmen and traders. Changes in eating and drinking habits are merely symptomatic of more deep-seated changes in British society in the south-east. Increased political centralisation and a trend towards nucleated settlement may also be attributed to developments in Gaul. Elsewhere in Britain radical differences in social organization may have retarded the pace at which Romanized tastes and manners were adopted.

The second major episode of innovation occurred, inevitably, in the immediate aftermath of the Claudian invasion. Prior to its annexation it seems likely that Britain comprised a market of secondary importance for Gallic and Mediterranean merchants with the main traffic in long-distance trade directed towards the Rhine garrison. Immediately after the conquest, the presence of a standing army in Britain and the availability of a largely unexploited market must have caused an influx of craftsmen, entrepreneurs and usurers to the newly-founded province, with far-reaching consequences for the balances within native society. For the lower echelons of the population conquest meant a (modest?) rise in tribute and a rapid increase in the availability of the type of luxury items previously rare outside south-eastern England and generally restricted to the aristocracy. Amongst a British élite whose wealth was largely based on herd and landholding, the sudden availability of credit and a new tier of patronage would inevitably have created tensions amongst the existing networks of social obligation. In tandem with these stresses the widening availability of those imports previously significant in the maintenance of the élite's prestige would have necessitated the adoption of new forms of display. It is suggested that the principal medium for this display was architectural and that the earliest developments were directed towards public structures in a limited number of urban centres and the aggrandizement of aristocratic *aedificia* by the construction of Romanized dwellings. That the distribution of early villa-buildings is generally restricted to those areas which were in receipt of the greatest quantities of imported luxury items in the pre-conquest period supports the suggestion that the villas are manifestations of the investment of native wealth. This early development of a rural Romanized building tradition contrasts with the pattern in Gaul where the earliest developments appear to have been town-based (Drinkwater 1983, 190).

Existing native nucleated settlements continued to develop, although Roman military dispositions in or near these centres greatly influenced the exact pattern of their evolution both in terms of economic stimulus and surveying and building technique. Simultaneously, in those areas peripheral to the south-east where the development of nucleated settlements was retarded, the stimulus provided by Britain's annexation appears to have initiated the development of certain aristocratic estates into native-type *oppida*. In several cases, for example at Bagendon and Stanwick, these centres flourished briefly but failed to develop directly into major Romano-British centres.

A third major stimulus towards material Romanization appears to have been the movement of the army to more northern positions. Although this process was halted by the Boudican revolt, the failure of this rebellion to become more widespread suggests that many Britons already identified their interests with those of Rome. The fairly piecemeal movement of troops westwards and northwards was accompanied by the creation of self-governing *civitates* whilst the foundation of the *colonia* at Colchester provided a model of planned urban development not previously available. The Flavian period certainly witnessed considerable urban expansion with the creation of several towns and dramatic remodellings of existing developments at, for example, Silchester and Verulamium. This upsurge of development was presumably related to the newly-realized importance of the *civitas* capitals as administrative centres and reflects the involvment of the local élite in their own government. That the British aristocracy were engaged in *aemulatio*, with urban architecture wholeheartedly adopted as the vehicle for conspicuous displays of status, seems to be confirmed by Tacitus' observation that in the governor Agricola's attempts to promote *Romanitas*:

"competition for honour proved as effective as compulsion" – *(Agricola 21)*

That these earliest efforts appear to have been directed towards urban public buildings and rural private dwellings provides an important insight into the disposition of the British aristocracy at this time. Despite their cltose involvment with the promotion of the growth of towns, the British élite were still largely resident on country estates and the predominant influence on the relationship of early villa and town may well have been the distribution of *aedificium* and *oppidum* in the pre-conquest landscape.

Acknowledgements

The writer wishes to thank Ann Clark, Simon James, Martin Millett and Richard Reece for reading and commenting on an earlier draft of this paper. All views expressed remain, of course, the responsibility of the author.

Notes
1   Dionysius Periegetes *Orbis Descriptio* 562.

References

Allen, D. 1967: Iron currency bars in Britain. *Proc. Prehist. Soc.* 11, 307-335.
Allen, D. 1970: The coins of the Iceni. *Britannia* 1, 1-33.
Allen, D. 1975: Cunobelin's Gold. *Britannia* 6, 1-19.
Allen, D. and Haselgrove, C. 1979: The gold coinage of Verica. *Britannia* 10, 1-17.
Allen, T., Miles, D. and Palmer, S. 1984: 'Iron age buildings in the Upper Thames region', in Cunliffe, B. and Miles, D. (eds.) *Aspects of the Iron Age in central southern Britain* (University of Oxford: Committee for Archaeology monograph 2), 89-101.
Bayley, J. and Butcher, S. 1981: Variations in alloy composition of Roman brooches. *Proc. 1980 archaeometry conference, Paris, Revue d' Archaeometrie, supplément*, 24-36.
Bedwin, O. and Orton, C. 1984: The excavation of the eastern terminal of the Devil's Ditch (Chichester Dykes), Boxgrove, West Sussex, 1982. *Sussex Archaeological Collections* 122, 63-74.
Blagg, T.F.C. and King, A.C. (eds.) 1984: *Military and Civilian in Roman Britain: cultural relationships in a frontier province* (Oxford, Brit. Arch. Reps. 136).

Boon, G.C. 1969: Belgic and Roman Silchester: the excavations of 1954-8 with an excursus on the early history of Calleva. *Archaeologia* 102, 1-82.

Boon, G.C. 1974: *Silchester: The Roman town of Calleva*, Newton Abbot.

Bradley, R. 1984: The social foundations of prehistoric Britain (London).

Branigan, K. 1982: Celtic farm to Roman villa in Miles, D. (ed.) *The Romano-British Countryside* (Oxford, Brit. Arch. Reps. 103), 81-96.

Burnham, B.C. 1986: The origins of Romano-British small towns. *Oxford Journal Archaeology* 5, 185-205.

Burnham, B.C. and Johnson H.B. (eds.) 1979: *Invasion and response: the case of Roman Britain* (Oxford, Brit. Arch. Reps. 73)

Clifford, E.M. 1961: *Bagendon: A Belgic oppidum. A record of the excavations 1954-56*, Cambridge.

Collis, J.R. 1970: Excavations at Owslebury, Hants: A second interim report. In *Antiq. J.* 50, pt. 2, 246-262, Oxford.

Collis, J. 1971: Functional and theoretical interpretations of British coinage. *World Archaeology* 3.1, 71-84.

Collis, J. 1979: City and state in pre-Roman Britain. In B. Burnham and H. Johnson (eds.) 1979, 231-240.

Corney, M. 1984: A field survey of the extra-mural region of Silchester. In M. Fulford 1984, *Silchester: excavations on the defences 1974-80* (London, Britannia Monograph Series 5), 239-297.

Crowther, D. 1987: Redcliff, in *Current Archaeology* 104, 284-5.

Crummy, P. 1977: Colchester, fortress and colonia. In *Britannia* 8, 65-107, London.

Cunliffe, B. 1976: The origins of urbanization in Britain. In B.W. Cunliffe and T. Rowley (eds.) *Oppida: the beginnings of urbanization in barbarian Europe* (Brit. Archaeol. Reps. 11, Oxford), 135-161.

Cunliffe, B.W. 1982: Iron Age settlements and pottery 650 BC - 60 AD. In M. Aston and I. Burrow (eds.) 1982, *The Archaeology of Somerset* (Bridgwater).

Drinkwater, J.F. 1983: *Roman Gaul: the three provinces 58 BC-AD 260* (London).

Dunnett, R. 1975: *The Trinovantes* (London.)

Fitzpatrick, A. 1985 : The distribution of Dressel 1 amphorae in north-west Europe. *Oxford Journal of Archaeology 4(3)*, 305-341.

Frere, S.S. 1957: Excavations at Verulamium 1956. *Antiq. J.* 37, 1-15.

Frere, S.S. 1979: Verulamium: urban development and the local region. In B.C. Burnham and H.B. Johnson 1979, 273-280.

Frere, S.S. 1983: Roman Britain in 1982, in *Britannia* 14, 280- 335.

Fulford, M. 1984: Demonstrating Britannia's economic dependence in the first and second centuries. In T. Blagg and A. King (eds.) 1984, 129-142.

Fulford, M. 1986: *Silchester excavation 1986* (privately circulated).

Greep, S.J. 1983: Early import of bone objects to south-east Britain. Note in *Britannia* 14, 259-261.

Haselgrove, C.C. 1982: Wealth, prestige and power: the dynamics of late iron age political centralisation in south-east England. In C. Renfrew and S. Shennan (eds.), *Ranking, resource and exchange: aspects of the archaeology of early European Society* (Cambridge), 79-88.

Haselgrove, C.C. 1984: 'Romanization' before the conquest: Gaulish precedents and British consequences. In Blagg and King 1984, 5-63.

Haselgrove, C.C. and Turnbull, P. 1983: *Stanwick: excavation and research. Interim report 1981-3* (University of Durham Dept. Archaeology, Occ. Paper no. 4).

Haselgrove, C.C. and Turnbull, P. 1984: *Stanwick: excavation and research. Interim report 1984.* (University of Durham Dept. Archaeology, Occ. Paper no. 5).

Haselgrove, C.C. and Turnbull, P. 1987: *Stanwick: excavation and research. Third interim report 1985-6.* (University of Durham Dept. Archaeology, Occ. Paper no. 8).

Hassall, M.W.C. 1979: The impact of Mediterranean urbanism on indigenous nucleated centres. In Burnham, B.C. and Johnson, H.B. *Invasion and response: The case of Roman Britain.* (Brit. Arch. Reps. 73), 241-235, Oxford.

Hawkes, C.F.C. 1982: Colchester before the Romans or who were our Belgae?, *Essex Arch. and History*, 3-14.

Hawkes, C.F.C. and Hull, M.R. 1947: *Camulodunum*. London.

Hopkins, K. 1980: Taxes and trade in the Roman Empire. *J. Roman Studies* 70, 101-125.

Jones, M.K. 1981: The development of crop husbandry. In M.K. Jones and G.W. Dimbleby (eds.) *The environment of man: the Iron Age to the Anglo-Saxon period* (Oxford, Brit. Arch. Reps. 87), 95-127.

Jones, M.K. 1982: Crop production in Roman Britain. In D. Miles (ed.) *The Romano-British Countryside* (Oxford, Brit. Arch. Reps. 103) 97-107.

Jones, M.K. and Miles, D. 1979: Celt and Roman in the Thames Valley: approaches to culture change. B. Burnham and H. Johnson (eds.) 1979, 315-325.

King, A. 1984: Animal bones and the dietary identity of military and civilian groups in Roman Britain, Germany and Gaul. T.F.C. Blagg and A.C. King (eds.) 1984, 187-217.

Leach, P. and Thew, N. 1985: A late Iron Age *oppidum* at Ilchester, Somerset. An interim assessment 1984. (Archive report).

Luff, R.M. 1982: *A zooarchaeological study of the Roman north-western provinces.* (Brit. Arch. Reps. 137), Oxford.

Middleton, P. 1979: 'Army supply in Roman Gaul: an hypothesis for Roman Britain' in Burnham and Johnson 1979, 81-97.

Miles, D. 1982: *Romano-British countryside: Studies in rural settlement and economy.* (Brit. Arch. Reps. 103), Oxford.

Miles, D. (ed.) 1986: *Archaeology at Barton Court Farm, Abingdon, Oxon.* (Oxford Archaeological Unit Rep. 3: CBA Res. Rep. 50).

Miles, D. and Palmer, S. n.d. (1982): *Figures in a landscape: archaeological investigations at Claydon Pike, Fairford/Lechlade, Gloucestershire. Interim report* (Oxford).

Millett, M. 1980: Aspects of Romano-British pottery in west Sussex. *Sussex Archaeological Collections* 118, 57-68.

Millett, M. 1984: 'Forts and the origins of towns: cause or effect?' in Blagg, T.F.C. and King, A.C. (eds.) *Military and Civilian in Roman Britain; cultural relationships in a frontier province* (Brit. Arch. Reps. 136), 65-74.

Millett, M. 1987a: 'An early Roman burial tradition in central southern England' *Oxford Journal of Archaeology* 6(1), 63-8.

Millett, M. 1987b: 'The question of continuity: Rivenhall reviewed'. In *Archaeological Journal* 144, 434-444.

Nash, D. 1984: The basis of contact between Britain and Gaul in the late pre-Roman Iron Age. In S. Macready and H. Thompson 1984, 92-107.

Niblett, R. 1985: *Sheepen: an early Roman industrial site at Camulodunum* (London, CBA Res. Rep. 57).

Northover, P. 1987: Non-ferrous metallurgy in B. Cunliffe 1987 *Hengistbury Head, Dorset. Volume 1: The prehistoric and Roman settlement, 3500 BC - AD 500* (Oxford, Oxford University Committee for Archaeology Monograph no. 13), 186-96.

Partridge, C. 1981: *Skeleton Green* (Britannia Monograph Series 2).

Partridge, C. 1982a: Graffiti from Skeleton Green. Note in *Britannia* 13, 325-6.

Partridge, C. 1982b: Braughing, Wickham Kennels 1982. *Herts. Archaeol.* 8, 1980-82, 40-59.

Potter, T.W. and Jackson, R.P.J. forthcoming: *Excavations at Stonea Cambridgeshire, 1980-85*

Potter, T.W. and Trow S.D. 1988: *Puckeridge-Braughing, Hertfordshire. The Ermine Street Excavations, 1971-72.* (= *Herts. Archaeol.* 10).

Reece, R. 1979: Roman monetary impact. In B. Burnham and H. Johnson (eds.) 1979, 211-217.

Reece, R. 1982: The Roman coins. In J. Wacher and A. McWhirr, *Early Roman occupation at*

Cirencester (Cirencester, Cirencester Excavations I), 86-7.

Rigby, V. 1978: The early Roman finewares. In A. Down *Chichester excavations 3* (Chichester), 190-204.

Rigby, V. 1981: The Gallo-Belgic wares. In C. Partridge 1981, 159-195.

Rigby, V. 1986: Gaulish fine-ware imports in I.M. Stead and V. Rigby 1986, *Baldock* (London, Britannia Monograph 7), 223-234.

Rigby, V. 1988a: The Gallic imports in T.W. Potter and S.D. Trow 1988.

Rigby. V. 1988b: The Gallo-Belgic wares in S.D. Trow 1988.

Rigby, V. and Freestone, I. 1986: The petrology and typology of the earliest identified central Gaulish imports. *Journal of Roman pottery studies* 1, 6,21.

Rodwell, K.A. 1979: Rome and the Trinovantes in B. Burnham and H. Johnson (eds.) 1979, 327-338.

Rodwell, W.J 1978: 'Buildings and settlements in south-east Britain in the late Iron Age', in Cunliffe B. and Rowley, T. (eds.) *Lowland Iron Age communities in Europe* (Brit. Arch. Reps. Supp. Ser. 48), 25-41.

Rodwell, W.J. and Rodwell, K.A. 1985: *Rivenhall: investigations of a villa, church, and village, 1950-1977* (Chelmsford Archaeological Trust Rep. 4: CBA Res. Rep. 55, London).

Rudling, D.R. forthcoming: The excavation of a Romano-British settlement at Ounces Barn, Boxgrove, West Sussex. *Sussex Archaeological Collections*, forthcoming.

Saunders, C. 1982: Some thoughts on the *oppida* at Wheathampstead and Verulamium. *Herts. Archaeol.* 8, 31-39.

Selwood, D.G. 1980: The President's address. In *The Numismatic Chronicle* 140, i-vii.

Slofstra, J. 1983: 'An anthropological approach to the study of romanization processes', in Brandt, R. and Slofstra, J. (eds.) *Roman and Native in the Low Countries* (Brit. Arch. Reps. Supp. Ser. 184), 71-104.

Sparey Green, C. 1986: Earthworks of prehistoric or early Roman date in the Dorchester area. *Proc. Dorset Nat. Hist. and Arch. Soc.* 108, 193-4.

Stead, I.M. 1970: A trial excavation at Braughing, *Herts. Archaeol.* 2, 37-47.

Swan, V. 1975: Oare reconsidered and the origins of Savernake ware in Wiltshire. *Britannia* 6, 37-61.

Tournaire, J., Buchsenschutz, O., Henderson, J. and Collis, J. 1982: Iron age coin moulds from France, *Proc. Prehist. Soc.* 48, 417-35.

Trow, S.D. 1982a: An early intaglio found near Cirencester, Gloucestershire. Note in *Britannia* 13, 322-323.

Trow, S.D. 1982b: Recent work at Bagendon - a brief interim report. In *Glevensis* 16, 26-9.

Trow S.D. 1988: Excavations at Ditches hillfort, North Cerney, Gloucestershire, 1982-1983. In *Trans. Bristol and Glos. Arch. Soc.* 106, 19-85.

Trow, S.D. and James, S. forthcoming: Excavations of a late Iron Age enclosure and Romano-British Building at North Cerney, Gloucestershire, 1984 to 1985.

Wacher, J. 1975: *The towns of Roman Britain* (London).

Walthew, C.V. 1975: 'The town house and the villa house in Roman Britain'. *Britannia* 6, 189-205.

Whimster, R. 1981: *Burial practices in Iron Age Britain* (Brit. Archaeol. Rep. 90, Oxford).

Williams, D.F. 1981 : The Roman amphora trade with late Iron Age Britain. In Howard, H. and Morris, E.L. (eds) *Production and Distribution: a ceramic viewpoint* (Oxford, Brit. Archaeol. Rep. Int. Ser. 120), 123-32.

Section III

Urban Development – Hispania

The city and city-life was one essential component of Roman life, and thus of Romanization in the Provinces. Urbanization is a common factor in the three papers which discuss the Spanish Provinces. Both Keay and Edmondson, on the provinces of Hispania Citerior and Lusitania respectively, are concerned with areas which, though contrasting geographically, both have forms of proto-urban hillfort settlement, and were penetrated to some extent by Mediterranean ideas through Greek and Punic trade and coastal colonization before the Roman conquest. Keay makes the point that the conquest of Hispania from 218 BC onwards began before Rome had evolved an administrative framework for provincial government. The Romans' response to Spain was thus very influential on their administrative approach in other provinces. In Spain, initially, their preoccupation was with the Carthaginians rather than with the Iberians, hence the early fortification of Tarraco as a military base. Keay argues that Roman urbanization and administrative organization were secondary developments, a by-product of economic growth. The imposition of taxes was followed by the development of native coinages, the creation of a market for imported Italian goods, and the growth of local wine production. This market economy stimulated the growth of such new Iberian towns as Gerunda in the early first century BC. Roman-style urbanization followed, under Caesar and Augustus, with the foundation of colonies at Emporion, Tarraco and Barcino, and the reorganization of the coinage on Roman models.

Edmondson develops the point that a prerequisite for urbanization was a prosperous agricultural hinterland, and shows how the physical differences in the three *conventus* of Lusitania led to regional imbalances in cultural development. As a corrective to Strabo's characterization of the whole area as uncivilized, he cites archaeological evidence for Greek acculturation of the *castros*, religious sanctuaries and buildings layout. Archaeology also shows a diversity of responses in the degree to which hillforts developed into fully Romanized towns. He regards these as depending essentially on the native élites rather than on Roman imposition, and concludes with a more detailed comparison of the colony of Augusta Emerita, consciously imitating Rome itself, and the Celtic community of Conimbriga, responding architecturally to its acquisition of Roman status.

The creation of the towns, their provision with buildings and amenities of Roman type, depended essentially on private munificence. The acts of individual benefactors are recorded on inscriptions (in which Spain is notably richer than the provinces to the north). Mackie's examination of this material provides insight into some of the personal motivations and decisions which contributed to the wider patterns of activity and response studied in the previous two papers. She considers the objects of that munificence, and the reasons for recording it epigraphically. The reward, for the individual benefactor, was public esteem; *honor*. The concept probably accompanied the adoption of the Latin in which it was expressed. Mackie explains that the effectiveness of *honor* depended institutionally on the formal existence of the local councils with legal powers to respond to munificence (by voting statues, administering endowments etc.). The 'constructive collaboration' between benefactors and local governmental organizations was a significant factor in the Roman Empire's long survival.

10. Processes in the Development of the Coastal Communities of Hispania Citerior in the Republican Period

by Simon Keay

Introduction

Discussions about Romanization in the Western Empire tend to draw upon historical and archaeological evidence from the provinces of Gaul, the Germanies, Britain and Africa. They focus upon issues pertinent to the character of each area and the 'models' are then applied to areas about which we know rather less. For the Iberian peninsula, this is very unsatisfactory. The Spanish provinces of Citerior and Ulterior were amongst Rome's earliest territorial acquisitions. They were created before Rome had evolved any specific administrative frame-work for its provinces and, thus, provide us with an almost unique opportunity to study the processes of social change which contributed to the emergence of the Augustan provinces of Tarraconensis and Baetica. In areas like Iberia, Rome reacted to local conditions and evolved an administrative framework which was later applied to newly conquered areas. It follows that the Iberian evidence is vital to a clear understanding of Romanization of later western provinces.

During the later third and second centuries BC, the main areas of sustained contact between the Romans and indigenous peoples of Iberia were southern Spain, the east coast and the lower Ebro valley. In this paper, attention is focused on the coast between the Pyrenees and the Ebro valley (Fig. 10.1). Its aim is to study the long-term impact of the Roman conquest and subsequent processes of change amongst the coastal communities of eastern Spain between 218 BC and the very end of the first century BC. Five basic themes will be pursued:

1. That there was no ready-made provincial framework or policy of administration applied to this part of Citerior by the Romans. That which did emerge, however, was a response to local conditions.

2. The effect of a regular system of taxation in stimulating sufficient agricultural surplus amongst the Iberian communities to generate marketable goods.

3. The role of commercialized exchange in breaking-down the Iberian settlement pattern.

4. The importance of events and decisions outside north-eastern Iberia influencing the siting and movement of high-status towns within the Iberian settlement pattern.

5. The decline of the larger Iberian hillforts as centres of prestige, in favour of the development of a hierarchy of high-status Roman towns underscored by social rivalry and expressed in terms of extravagant building programmes.

The character of Iberian settlement along the east coast of Iberia prior to the Roman Conquest

The north-eastern coast of Iberia (Fig. 10.2) has enjoyed a long tradition of contact with the neighbouring cultures of western Europe,[1] and the Mediterranean.[2] This entered a new era around 600 BC, when colonies were founded at Emporion (Empúries) and Rhode (Roses). The former was ideally situated at the headwaters of the Ter and Fluvià, important rivers which provided access through the fertile soils of the Empordà into the Serrelada Transversal

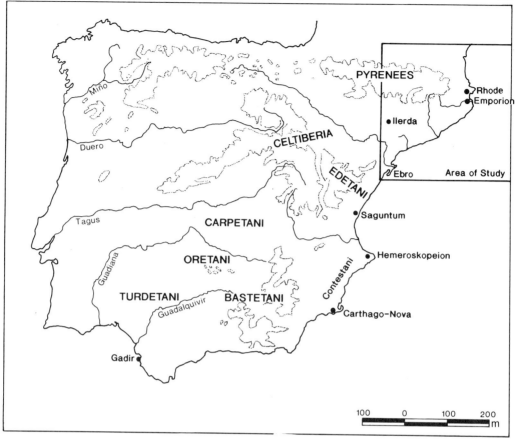

Fig. 10.1. Map of Iberia showing the location of the area discussed in this paper.

at the foothills of the Pyrenees. The colonists, thus, were in a position to tap their immediate agricultural hinterland and relatively close to sources of iron, silver and copper.[3] Rhode was not quite so well-placed, but offered a far more sheltered harbour. After a period from the sixth to later fifth centuries BC, during which their role was restricted to the vicinity of the Empordà, Emporion began to assume a very influential role as a 'port of trade'.[4] Its primary zone of influence was the coastal area between the modern French province of Languedoc in the north, and the Garraf mountains on the south side of the river Llobregat. Settlement at Emporion had spread from a small offshore island (modern Sant Martí d'Empúries) to a sizeable mainland port (the 'Neapolis'), planned in the Greek way, which was distinct from the surrounding Iberian communities. Excavations have revealed a wide variety of imported goods at Emporion, including Attic Black- and Red-Figure pottery, together with pre-Campanian Black-Glaze, Massiliote amphorae, Punic pottery and amphorae. Items such as these were used in exchange transactions with middlemen from Iberian communities.

The exceptional character of Emporion was further defined by the issue of a series of small silver coins between the later fifth and the first half of the third centuries BC,[5] which was then replaced by a larger coin – the silver drachma, which bore the name of the colony and which was probably issued down to as late as the second century BC.[6] This silver coinage never seems to have been used primarily as a medium of exchange. Rhode issued a bronze coinage, and fractions, which were copied by some local communities.

Between the sixth and early fifth centuries BC, the coastal area between the Garraf mountains and the Ebro fell outside Emporion's zone of primary influence. Communities in this zone were influenced by Phoenician traders exploring the lower Ebro valley.[7] The only other focus of Greek influence lay at Hemeroskopeion (Denia), a long way to the south.[8] It was only with the expansion of the influence of Emporion and Hemeroskopeion and the foundation of further Massiliote colonies after the beginning of the fifth century BC, that Greek influence began to prevail upon the area between the Garraf and the Ebro.

The evidence suggests, therefore, that in the area of study, Emporion and Rhode were the main foci for Greek cultural influence from the earlier fifth century BC onwards. There is little evidence for any sustained Italian influence prior to the Roman invasion of 218 BC.

The Iberian peoples of the east coast were strongly influenced by the Greek colonies. The later classical sources inform us about their disposition at about the time of the Roman conquest.[9] The Indiketes were to be found in the vicinity of the colonies while immediately to the south-west lay the Ausetani. In the foothills of the Pyrenees, to the north, were the Cerretani, Bergistani and Lacetani. The Laietani were a coastal people occupying most of the modern province of Barcelona, whilst to the south of the Garraf lay the Cessetani. The Ilercaones encompassed the mouth of the Ebro and the northern part of the modern province of Castelló de la Plana.[10] Broadly speaking, these were coastal peoples shut-off from the hinterland by the peaks of the inner coastal mountain chain, and whose near neighbours to the west were the Ilergetes.

Research in recent years has revealed the existence of a large number of Iberian settlements in this area. The absence of any coordinated research, or survey, precludes discussion of settlement hierarchies or settlement densities. For the purpose of this paper, however, a distinction can be made between larger and rarer 'central-place' settlements and sites of lesser importance. Amongst the Indiketes, examples of the former can be found the great hill-fort of Puig de Sant Andreu (Ullastret) (Fig. 10.3) and Puig Castellar (Pontós).[10] Puig del Castell (Sant Julià de Ràmis) and Mas Castell (Porqueres) lay in the territory of the Ausetani, while Burriac (Cabrera de Mar), Turó d'en Boscà (Badalona), Turó del Vent (Llinas del Vallès) and Puig Castellar (Santa Coloma de Gramenet) were in the territory of the Laietani. Amongst the Cessetani, one might cite Olèrdola (Vilafranca del Penedès), a large Iberian settlement beneath the lower town of Tarragona, the site of El Vilar (Valls) and Santa Ana de Castellvell. The Castellet de Banyoles (Tivissa) overlooked the Ebro in the territory of the Ilercaones. These settlements developed in tandem with the growing influence of the Greek colonies, between the fifth and fourth centuries BC. For the most part, they were situated on defendable promontories, controlling access to good agricultural land, river systems and, ultimately, the coast.

The layout of these settlements was characterized by intensively occupied areas enclosed within monumental stone walls, which often reflected the influence of Greek planning techniques. Houses were simple with no internal decoration or architectural pretensions and were flanked by regularly planned streets. There is no evidence for any public buildings, although small temples have been discovered within the walls of the Puig de Sant Andreu and Burriac.[11] These sites were, thus, important population centres exercising a degree of control over their surrounding territory. They were also centres of craft specialization and exchange. Excavations have uncovered ample evidence for textile manufacture,[12] while one

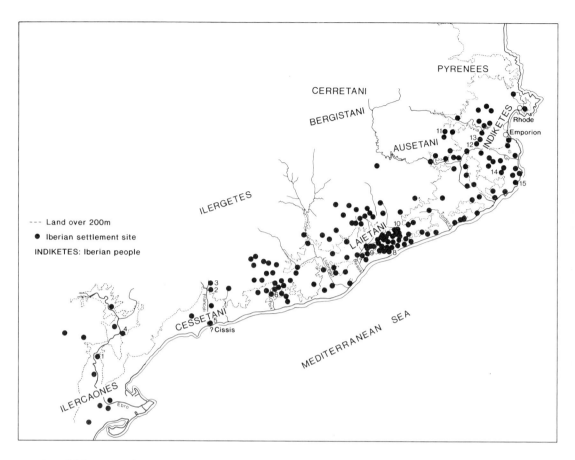

Fig. 10.2. Map showing the distribution of sites in north-eastern Spain prior to the Roman conquest of 218 BC (based upon published sites and compiled largely before 1983).

Numbers refer to sites mentioned in the text: 1. Santa Ana de Castellvell 2. El Vilar 3. Fontscaldes 4. Castellet de Banyoles 5. Tarragona 6. Olèrdola 7. Puig Castellar 8. Burriac 9. Turó d'en Boscà 10. Turó del Vent 11. Mas Castell (Porqueres) 12. Puig del Castell (Sant Julià de Ràmis) 13. Puig Castellar (Pontós) 14. Puig de Sant Andreu (Ullastret) 15. Castell de la Fosca (Palamós).

must assume that much of the metalwork and painted pottery that is so common at these sites was either manufactured at dependant sites close by,[13] or within their walls. There is also evidence that sites like Puig Castellar de Pontós, Puig de Sant Andreu, Mas Castell and Burriac stored large quantities of grain and other foodstuffs produced in the territory under their control.

The sites of lesser importance are far more common and are found in uplands and lowlands throughout the area under study. One area of great density is to be found in the uplands of Laietanian territory, especially in the hinterland of the larger settlements of Burriac and Mas d'en Boscà. These vary from smaller versions of the larger settlement sites – like, for instance,

Castell de la Fosca (Palamós: Fig. 10.4) – to the scatters of Iberian pottery which litter the lowlands in areas of the Tarragonès and Penedès. Recent excavations at one of these small farm sites[14] uncovered storage pits for grain, suggesting that the site was used for storage by farmers prior to the removal of the grain to the neighbouring major settlements at Alorda Park, or Aderró. In a similar way, the well-known Iberian fine-ware and amphora production site of Fontscaldes (Valls), in the hinterland of Tarragona, may have supplied the larger settlement at El Vilar (Valls).

There are, as yet, too many gaps in our knowledge for us to understand the many complex social, political and economic relationships between these sites and their role within the territories of the different peoples. Nevertheless, the available evidence allows us to construct a working model with which investigation can begin. First of all, one must assume the existence of an élite central authority based at the larger settlements.[15] The existence of monumental defensive walls points to a supply of centrally organized labour. That the central authority was probably an aristocratic élite is suggested by the high concentration of prestigious imported ceramics, foodstuffs, bronze and iron weapons, tools, jewellery and occasional gold and silver work found at the larger settlements. Indeed, this tallies with information provided by Livy, who records the names of local leaders, like Amusicus leader of the Ausetani.[16] The larger well-defended settlements allowed the élites to dominate the better, low-lying, agricultural land and metal sources within recognized territories.

The basis of control was the élite of the larger settlements monopolizing regional exchange networks, and ensuring the virtual exclusivity of foreign imports and their re-distribution. In return for imports, the larger settlements supplied grain, other cereals, vegetables, fruits, metals and ceramics to Emporion.[17] The mechanism by which larger settlements ensured the continued flow of these goods from their territories is not known, although some form of tributary relationship with the lesser settlements probably existed. On a wider canvass, it is doubtful whether a single centralized authority exercised sustained control over the peoples of the north-east. The classical sources make it clear that only exceptionally, as in the rebellion of 197-195 BC (infra) did the tribes of the north-east draw together, and then it was to confront a common enemy.

In conclusion, then, the working model for Iberian settlement in the north east could be summarized in the following way. Evidence for Iberian élites and settlement hierarchies underpinned by status and prestige, being:

1.   The situation, size and degree of sophisticated planning of settlements;
2.   A regular, monopoly, of imports.

However, the whole edifice relied upon a limited supply of imports directly to larger, high status settlements whilst the loyalty of lesser settlements was ensured by the monopoly and re-distribution of these and the force of arms. Such suzerainty was perhaps expressed in the form of tribute paid in agricultural goods and primary resources exacted from the lesser settlements.

The Roman Conquest and consolidation of the Roman presence in north-eastern Spain

The Roman conquest in this part of Iberia was brief and, rather than a blow-by-blow account of military campaigns, its immediate effects are our concern here. It should be stated at the outset that the presence of the Romans in Iberia was not simply aggressive Roman

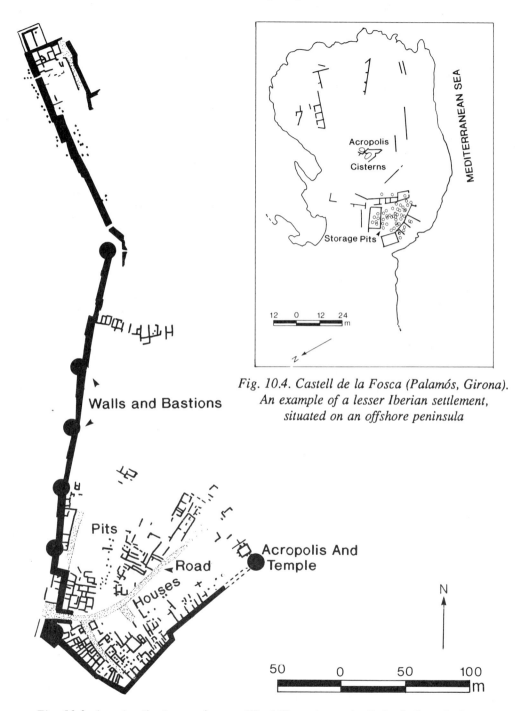

Fig. 10.4. Castell de la Fosca (Palamós, Girona).
*An example of a lesser Iberian settlement,
situated on an offshore peninsula*

Fig. 10.3. A major Iberian settlement. The hilltop site at the Puig de Sant Andreu
(Ullastret, Girona)

expansionism, rather a measured response to Carthaginian expansion in Iberia. The conquest should be understood in the context of Roman strategy in the Second Punic War.[18]

The initial conquest of the north-east was the work of Cnaeus Cornelius Scipio in 218-217 BC at the head of two legions, Roman citizen cavalry, 14,000 allied infantry and 1,600 allied cavalry. After using diplomacy to build Roman influence in the area, Scipio defeated the Carthaginian general Hasdrubal in a battle near Cissis, which may perhaps be identified with the Iberian settlement at Tarragona.[19] Hasdrubal attempted a counter-attack against Roman troops in the vicinity of Cissis, after which Scipio established an important military base called Tarraco in its immediate vicinity. Shortly afterwards, Scipio attacked and defeated the Ausetani and Laietani, killing some 12,000 of the latter. There were further struggles between the Romans (led by Fonteius and Marcius) and Carthaginians to the north of the Ebro, folllowing the catastrophic defeat of Cnaeus and Publius Scipio in southern Spain during 212 BC.[20] In the initial conquest of the north-east, therefore, the Romans blatantly pursued their own strategic interests at the expense of traditional Iberian social networks.

The historical evidence makes it clear that after the Romans had driven the Carthaginians out of the peninsula in 206 BC, the Iberians realized that they intended to retain their military presence and broke into open revolt in 206 and 205 BC.[21] The Roman decision to stay in Iberia was probably coloured by the continued war against Hannibal in Italy, and the determination that this strategically vital area should not fall back into Carthaginian hands.[22] The revolts were instigated by the Ilergetes, and rapidly drew in the Lacetani and Ausetani, but were soon put down. In 197 BC, a revolt broke out against the Romans in southern Spain, rapidly spreading to the peoples of the north-east and becoming serious enough to merit the intervention of M. Porcius Cato as supreme commander in Spain. Cato was involved in battles against the Indiketes, the Bergistani and the Lacetani. Furthermore, he demolished their wall-circuits and disarmed all communities north of the Ebro.[23] The rebellion was finally quelled by 195 BC.

Between 218 and 195 BC, therefore, the Iberian communities of the north-east came firmly under the military control of the Romans in Spain. Indeed, in 197 BC, Roman possessions in Iberia had been formalized into two separate commands, or *provinciae*, each under the command of a praetor specially elected at Rome each year. The northern province, Hispania Citerior, consisted of the coastal strip from the Pyrenees to the south side of the modern province of Murcia.[24] There is no firm evidence as to which, if any, single centre was chosen as the capital of Citerior at this early date, although modern scholars usually assume that it was either Tarraco or Carthago-Nova (Cartagena).

The effect of these 23 tumultuous years was to generate social stresses on an unparalleled scale and to upset the traditional relationships between Iberian communities. In the first instance, as Cnaeus Cornelius Scipio selected Cissis-Tarraco (Tarragona) as his military bridgehead, this settlement gained great regional importance. In 211, for instance, it played host to representatives and delegations from the Iberian peoples allied to Rome who were attending upon Scipio Africanus.[25] The archaeological evidence, of course, is reflected principally in the abandonment of major settlements between the later third and early second centuries BC. Amongst the Indiketes, for example, the greater part of the Puig de Sant Andreu was abandoned, as were the Castellet de Banyoles (Tivissa) and El Vilar (Valls) amongst the Ilercaones and Cessetani.[26]

Archaeology is also starting to reveal some of the military measures taken by Rome to ensure the stability of the area this time. In the territory of the Indiketes, a garrison-building has been identified on the large hill immediately behind the Greek port of Emporion. Its salient features consist of a cyclopean stone wall enclosing a rectangular area, and several large water cisterns.[27] Moreover a monumental Roman wall, running southwards from the town, was built at the same time.[28] These structures are best understood in the context of an attempt by Rome to ensure the security of her faithful ally after the rebellion of 197-195. Emporion at this stage was still vital to Rome as a staging post for supplies coming along the southern Gaulish coast from Italy, en route to Tarraco and Carthago-Nova. The measures taken to ensure the security of Scipio's bridge-head at Tarraco were even more impressive. The great limestone hill overlooking the Iberian settlement of Cissis was seized by the Romans and fortified with at least two stretches of monumental defensive wall and three adjoining towers.[29] These defences were on a huge scale and underlined the great strategic importance of Tarraco to the Romans (Fig. 10.5). It was the most convenient point along the coast for the disembarkation of men and supplies from Italy. During the Second Punic War, it was the ideal springboard for strikes against Carthaginian forces south of the Ebro, while for the greater part of the second century BC, its proximity to the Ebro meant that it was the ideal depôt for Roman forces campaigning in Celtiberia.

Early to Late second century BC

The development of Tarraco

The most important regional development in the north-east, took place in the territory of the Cessetani, as a result of the military considerations discussed above. At Tarraco, towards the middle of the second century BC, the defensive walls of the garrison were extended to run at least 1400 metres around three sides of the hill,[30] and then extended to the south-west to enclose the Iberian settlement below (Fig. 10.5). It was probably provided with towers at 50 metre intervals. It is unlikely that this represents a truly urban development, marking the emergence of a Hispano-Roman town. Recent excavations within the Iberian settlement have shown that Roman-style building techniques (mortar-joined walls with stucco decoration) did not appear until the last quarter of the second century BC.[31] However, it is important to see the enlargement of the walled area in the context of Tarraco's military role as springboard for armies involved in the Celtiberian Wars of the 150's-130's BC. In 180-178 BC, for example, Tarraco is clearly mentioned as the place where Tiberius Sempronius Gracchus reorganized his army.[32] At the outbreak of the Celtiberian War in 153, Appian tells us that Nobilior marched (from Tarraco) against Segeda with an army of nearly 30,000 men.[33] A good many of these could have been bivouacked within Tarraco's newly enlarged enclosure prior to the campaign.

A corollary of the presence of large numbers of Roman and Italian troops at Tarraco over the years, is the development of a steady supply of Italian imports. Excavations in different parts of the town have revealed large quantities of Greco-Italic and Dressel 1A wine amphorae, a wide variety of Black Glaze A wares and a selection of central Italian coarse wares. Comparable goods were not available locally and the imports were probably destined, in the first instance, for the soldiers and resident officials at Tarraco. These people were probably present in some strength and may have been sufficiently influential to form a *Conventus Civium Romanorum*.[34] In the absence of any municipal authority, this body may have played an important role in the running of the community.[35]

The mid-second century BC, therefore, saw Tarraco developing as an exceptional centre for the amassing and re-distribution of foreign imports. There is also evidence that by the later second century BC Tarraco had become the focus of an important road network, which linked it to the lower Ebro valley, the Vallès, the Maresme and such settlements as Auso (Vic). However there is no evidence that it had yet assumed any of the formal juridical or architectural characteristics of a Roman town. The same is true for Emporion, even though it appears that the Greek port underwent some important urban reconstruction around 175 BC.[36]

The beginnings of taxation

As far as this paper is concerned, the importance of centres like Tarraco and Emporion is their rôle as depots for the re-distribution of Italian wine, fine ceramics and other prestigious goods to Iberian settlements of all classes. Before attempting to establish the effect that these imports were to have on the Iberian settlement hierarchy, one has to understand the mechanism which enabled the Iberians to purchase them. If one accepts that there was no single centralized authority in the north-east prior to 218 BC on the one hand, and the importance of taxation in stimulating the generation of a surplus sufficiently large for the purchase of luxuries on the other,[37] then the date of the introduction of regular taxation in Hispania Citerior is of critical importance.

Many scholars believe that the regular collection of a fixed tax (*stipendium*) payable in silver coins issued by Iberian stipendiary communities, and a 5% corn levy (*vicensima*) commutable to payment in Iberian coinage, may have begun in 197 BC.[38] However, Richardson[39] has argued that prior to 179/178 BC at the earliest, ad-hoc levies were the only demands made upon Iberian communities and that the *stipendium* was merely a cash payment for the upkeep of the Roman legions in Iberia. Indeed, this was paid in bronze coinage which was usually brought across from Rome itself.[40] Grain was collected locally by army commanders when the need arose. Indeed the only regular tax prior to 179/178 was instituted by Cato, who "organized the collection of large revenues from the iron and silver mines" north of the Ebro in 195 BC.[41] Richardson argues convincingly that the institution of the *stipendium* and *vicensima* in Citerior was the work of the governor T.Sempronius Gracchus in 179/178.[42] Henceforth, the collection of grain from subject communities was regularized at 1/20th of the crop, whilst the *stipendium* became a fixed payment.

These arrangements seem to have coincided with the appearance of silver and bronze coinage issued by various communities in Citerior.[43] The first silver issues were minted at KESE (probably to be identified with the Iberian settlement at Cissis-Tarraco), at AUSEKESKEN (in the territory of the Ausetani), at ILTIRTA (amongst the Ilergetes), and amongst subject communities in Celtiberia.[44] The coins were minted at Roman behest at a time when Roman regular coinage effectively did not arrive in Iberia. They were on a similar weight standard to Roman denarii and most bore the standard iconography of a male head on the obverse and a horseman on the reverse.

There exists, therefore, a strong possibility that some of the goods and commodities raised from the Iberian communities was converted into this coinage, which was then used to pay for the maintenance (*stipendium*) of Roman troops in the Celtiberian and later wars in Iberia. Towards the middle of the second century, therefore, Tarraco and possibly Auso (Vic) stand out as major centres for the collection of goods received in taxation and their conversion into coinage. During the later second and earlier first centuries BC, the use of coinage in this way spread to communities throughout the north-east. Amongst the Laietani, bronze coinage was

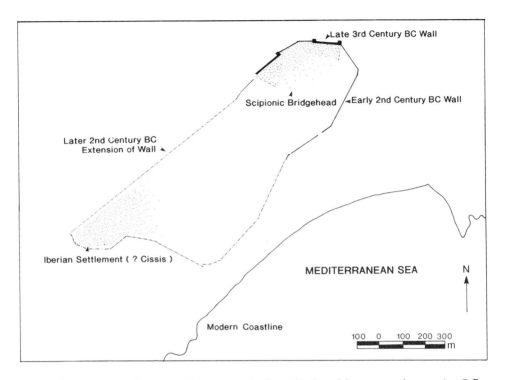

Fig. 10.5. Tarraco (Tarragona) between the late third and late second centuries BC.

issued at ILTURO,[45] and later at LAIESKEN,[46] LAURO,[47] and BAITOLO;[48] UNTIKESSEN[49] was the only issuing authority amongst the Indiketes; EUSTIBAIKULA[50] was probably situated in the territory of the Ausetani. Most of these mints persisted until some time during the first century BC, issuing coinage with a predominately local currency.[51]

It can be argued, therefore, that it was only from some time towards the middle of the second century BC that taxation was regular enough to stimulate an agricultural surplus amongst the communities of Hispania Citerior that was large enough to allow them to sustain a regular silver and bronze coinage and pay for imported luxuries. It would follow that one could only talk in terms of a viable and growing market for Italian merchants from around the middle of the second century BC. The size and quality of the market would have depended, in the first instance, upon the level of taxation imposed by Rome. Iberian complaints of extortion against the governors of Citerior for 176 and 174 were made to the Roman Senate in 171 BC,[52] suggesting that this was high. The quality of the market, no doubt, would have improved as the Iberian small change paid out to soldiers was spent in the areas where they were stationed. In this way, coinage trickled away from centres like Tarraco and Emporion into the Iberian communities, leading to a gradual monetization of the north-east during the later second and first centuries BC.

The Impact of the Changes
This thesis is supported by the sharp increase in the quantity of Italian ceramic imports

(especially Dressel 1A wine amphorae) at all classes of Iberian settlement, from the middle of the second century BC onwards. Nowhere is this clearer than on sites in the Ager Tarraconensis. Survey work is revealing large quantities of imports on lowland sites of small-middling size (probably to be identified as farms) which were either newly founded or yielded traces of earlier occupation. By contrast, imports are absent from the hill-top sites characteristic of the pre-Roman period, which were gradually abandoned. This suggests that towards the middle of the second century BC, Iberian farmers began to participate in local and regional exchange with the Romans for goods imported to Tarraco from overseas. Moreover it suggests that there was a growing intensification in farming, as farmers produced cash crops in an attempt to meet the burdens of taxation and rents.[53]

Other work suggests that these processes soon gave rise to the appearance of small, solidly built, Roman farms. At the site of El Moro (Torredembarra), towards the eastern edge of the Ager Tarraconensis, excavations have uncovered two rooms of a villa with mosaic tesserae decorating pink mortar floors, and evidence of a colonnade. This dated to between the later second and early first century BC.[54] At the site of L'Argilera, to the north-east,[55] the evidence is even more explicit. A small and unsophisticated Roman farm was built at about the same time, coinciding with the abandonment of the important Iberian hill-top settlement of Alorda Park close-by.[56]

The strategic and administrative role played by Emporion was considerably less than that enjoyed by Tarraco. However, it was still an important centre of Roman influence. Prior to the end of the second century BC, it was a major importer of Italian, African and Ebussitanian foodstuffs and ceramics. Moreover, the appearance of appreciable quantities of regular Roman coinage towards the later second century may indicate the presence of a considerable body of Roman and Italian settlers.[57] However, the impact of Emporion upon its hinterland seems to have been correspondingly less than that of Tarraco. Although important Indiketan settlements like Mas Castellà (Pontós) were abandoned in the course of the second century BC, new Roman farms are not documented until the end of the second and beginning of the first centuries BC.

Acculturation and the Romanization of coastal Citerior
up to the mid-first century BC

The first century BC sees an acceleration in the spread of Ibero-Roman acculturation in the north-east and the gradual breaking-down of the Iberian settlement pattern. One of the principal catalysts in this was the construction of a totally Roman town at Emporion. The garrison overlooking the Greek port was demolished and the entire plateau covered by a 21 hectare double-settlement (Fig. 10.6). It has been conjectured that the northern half may have been settled by Indiketes.[58] The southern sector forms an elongated rectangle surrounded by a monumental stone and concrete wall and subdivided by a regular street grid. At the heart of this was a capitolium, cryptoporticus and forum (Fig. 10.7), whose plan and construction are startlingly similar to contemporary monumental centres in central Italy.[59] The archaeological evidence suggests a date of *circa* 100 BC and suggests that that this is the earliest known example of true Roman urban planning in Iberia. Moreover, the discovery of an inscription at the site has given rise to the hypothesis that the new town may have been a *colonia Latina*, founded by Marcus Iunius Silanus the governor of Citerior in 113 BC.[60]

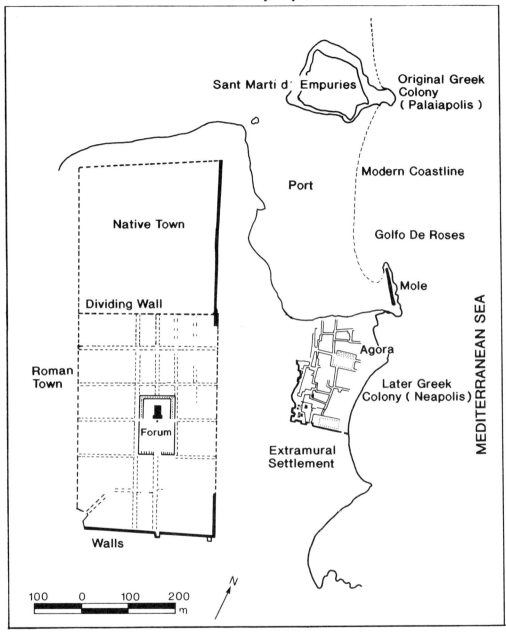

Fig. 10.6. Emporion (Empúries) at the end of the second century BC.

If the Roman town at Emporion was indeed a *colonia Latina*, then one might expect some evidence for a break in the pre-existing pattern of landholding, as the Italian colonists received their plots of land within its territory. This might perhaps explain the first appearance of new Roman farms in the Empordà at this time, appreciably later than those in the Ager Tarraconensis. At the Olivet d'en Pujol (Viladamat), a few kilometres to the west of Emporion,

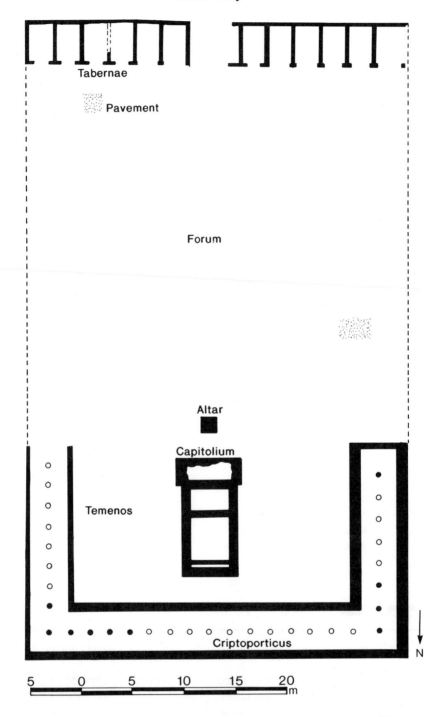

Fig. 10.7. *Late second century BC forum complex at the Roman town of Emporion (after Aquilué et al. 1984)*

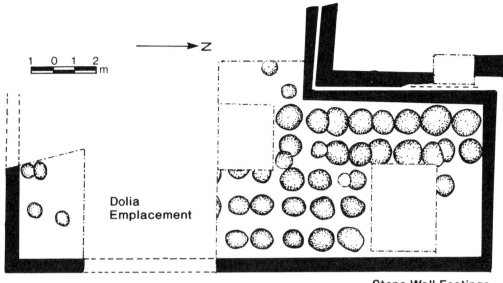

Dolia Emplacement

Stone Wall Footings

Fig. 10.8. Late second century BC Roman farm at the Olivet d'en Pujol (Viladamat, Girona)

excavations have uncovered a rectangular walled enclosure housing a large number of storage dolia (Fig. 10.8), dating to some time after the later second century BC.[61] A similar site was discovered some distance to the south at Puig Rodon (Corçà),[62] and at the Camp Del Bosquet (Camallera).[63] These new farms were functional units dedicated to the processing and storage of agricultural staples in the hinterland of Emporion. As such, it is possible that they represent an intensification in the production of agricultural surplus by the colonists or their tenant-farmers. Such a surplus had a ready market at Emporion, where the goods could be converted for coin in its increasingly monetized economy[64] and used in the payment of rents and taxes, or exchanged for imported luxuries.

There seems little doubt, therefore, that the foundation of the Roman town at Emporion as an important market and centre of Roman influence had a local impact similar to that of Tarraco, over fifty years earlier.[65] There was also an important regional impact. This is reflected in changes in settlement dynamics amongst the Indiketes, Ausetani and Laietani, as the foci of Iberian settlements moved into the lowlands. This allowed local élites to profit from a more active involvement in the networks of exchange which spread out from Emporion and Tarraco.

Between the late second and early first centuries BC there was a major realignment of the settlement pattern of the Indiketes/Ausetani to the south-west of Emporion. A number of important hill-top sites like the Puig d'En Carrerica (Canet d'Adri), Camp de la Vinya (Flaça), Sant Grau (Sant Gregori), Puig de Can Cendra (Bescano) and Les Serres (Sant Martí de Llemena) were abandoned, together with lowland storage depots like Bobila de Can Rafael Ginesta (Cornella de Terri) and Can Figa (Cornella de Terri). The new centre of settlement, Gerunda (Girona), was founded on a rocky knoll on a tributary of the river Ter where it cuts through the Gavarres hills. It also lay astride the Via Hercula (the later Via Augusta), which ran from Narbo (modern Narbonne) to the north, to Gades in southern Spain. It was planned

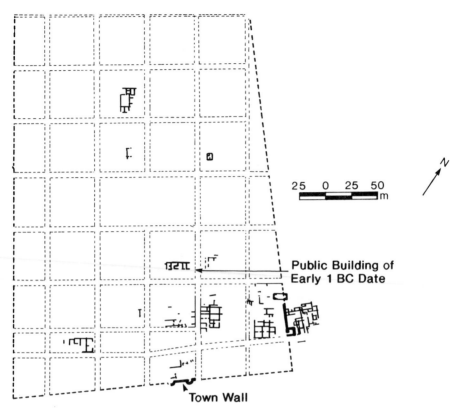

Fig. 10.9. The Ibero-Roman town of Baetulo (Badalona)

as a prestigious centre, whose high status was underlined by the construction of monumental town walls, between 100 and 75 BC.[66] Little is known about its internal layout. However, its geographical location ensured that it soon became a secondary centre for the re-distribution of Italian imports from Emporion, as well as local products. The striking success of this Iberian sponsored town can be measured by the appearance of new farms within its territory, as at the Pla d'en Horta (Sarria de Ter), possibly Vilauba (Camós) and Can Pau Birol (Bell Lloc), during the first century BC.[67]

The early first century BC also sees the foundation of three towns similar to Gerunda along the coast to the south of Emporion, in the territory of the Laietani. Baetulo (Badalona), Iluro (Mataró) and to a lesser extent Blandae (Blanes), appear to be successors to dense Iberian settlement in the coastal mountain chain. Burriac (Cabrera de Mar), in the uplands to the west of Iluro, and Turó d'en Boscà (Badalona), to the north of Baetulo, were amongst the most important settlements.[68] They may have been the mint-sites for the ILTURO and BAITOLO coins, and were both abandoned in the early first century BC. The successor town of Baetulo had a rectangular plan (10 hectares) enclosed within a stone wall similar to that at Gerunda (Fig. 10.9). There is evidence of internal planning, consisting of a large strip-building (c. 30 x 10m) with stone footings. This was built in the second quarter of the first century BC.[69] Otherwise there is no evidence for public or private buildings prior to the early first century AD.[70] The evidence for the successor towns of Iluro[71] and Blandae[72] is not

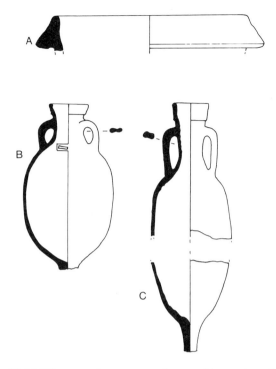

Fig. 10.10 Wine amphorae manufactured in eastern Spain
during the second and first centuries BC.
A. Rim belonging to a local imitation Greco-Italic/Dressel 1A amphora (Ager Tarraconensis)
B. Tarraconense 1/Laietania 1 amphora (Empúries) C. Pascual 1 (Aderrò)

as clear, but suggests that, essentially, they were similar to Baetulo. A similar succession from diffuse Iberian settlements to a centralized Roman town may also account for the appearance of Roman Dertosa (see note 110).

From the moment of their foundation, all three coastal towns imported a large quantity of Italian luxury imports, probably secondary exchange re-directed from Emporion. The towns themselves acted as markets for neighbouring Iberian communities in the coastal uplands. As at Gerunda, the distribution of Italian imports on hinterland sites[73] reflects their success. Moreover, the appearance of new farms, or villas, shows that the intensification of agricultural production was not limited to the territories of Tarraco and Emporion. At Cal Ros de les Cabres (Masnou), a new farm with stone and mortar footings and decorated with mosaic tesserae set into pink mortar floors was built between the later second and early first century BC.[74]

During the first half of the first century BC, the commercialization of agricultural surplus centred at sites had begun to acheive a degree of sophistication. Estates in the vicinity of Baetulo were producing wine of a sufficiently good quality to be marketed at Baetulo[75] (Fig. 10.10).

These developments show that the foundation of Emporion had a major regional impact. Although the diffusion of Italian imports had begun to destabilize the Iberian settlement hierarchy during the second century BC, it was not until the foundation of the Roman town

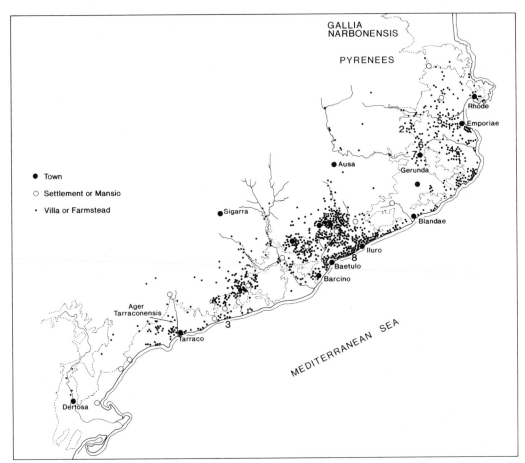

Fig. 10.11. The density of Roman settlement in north-eastern Hispania Citerior/Tarraconensis during the Late Republic and Empire. Based upon published sites and largely compiled before 1983.

Numbers refer to villas/farms mentioned in the text: 1. Olivet d'en Pujol 2. Vilauba 3. L'Argilera 4. Puig Rodon 5. Camp del Bosquet 6. Pla d'en Horta 7. Can Pau Birol 8. Cal Ros de les Cabres

at the end of the century that it actually started to break down. Local élites refounded their settlements in the lowlands at points where they stood to profit from the control of growing commercial networks focused at Emporion.[76]

The Romanization of coastal Citerior from the mid to later first century BC

The further disintegration of the Iberian settlement pattern and the Romanization of Iberian communities during the later first century BC was hastened by the development of a coherent regional administrative system (Fig. 10.11). This was based upon a hierarchy of Roman and Iberian inspired towns, linked together by a network of roads, all of which focused upon Tarraco.

The development of Roman towns

It was the pre-eminent strategic role of Tarraco which ensured that this town not only became the major regional centre of the north-east, but capital of the province of Hispania Citerior, later Tarraconensis, as well. During the Civil War of 49-44 BC, its inhabitants had supported Pompey's cause until Caesar's victory at the battle of Ilerda in 49 BC. Thereafter they lost no time in switching their alliance to Caesar, paying him tribute and supplying his army. Shortly afterwards, Caesar chose Tarraco as the venue for a meeting between himself and his supporters throughout Citerior.[77] This mark of regional pre-eminence was consolidated by the grant of colonial status to the town between 45 and 27 BC.[78] Unlike Emporion, this does not seem to have involved either a settlement of Roman citizens or a replanning of the layout of the town. In the years 26-24 BC, Tarraco rose to even greater prominence. It was Augustus' temporary residence away from Rome while he planned the military conquest of north-western Spain. For these three years, and perhaps again in 15-14 BC, Tarraco was the de-facto centre of power in the Roman Empire.[79] This exceptional role, and the prestige in which Augustus was held, was symbolised by the dedication of an altar to the joint veneration of Rome and Augustus at the town.[80] This may have been located in the Augustan forum built in the heart of what had been the Iberian settlement.[81] Finally, in the provincial reorganization of 16-13 BC, Tarraco was appointed the administrative capital of the Imperial province of Hispania Tarraconensis.[82] As such, it was now the official seat of the Roman governor, his attendant officials and a garrison seconded from the legions stationed in north-west Tarraconensis.[83]

By the end of the first century BC, therefore, Tarraco had become the focus of political and religious loyalties for communities throughout much of the Iberian peninsula. From at least the middle of the second century BC, it had been linked to Emporion, Saguntum, Carthago-Nova by the Via Herculea which went from Italy through Gaul to Gades in Hispania Ulterior.[84] As the Via Augusta this road was upgraded between 12 and 6 BC and formed the basis of a wider network of secondary roads which reached communities throughout the region[85] (Fig. 10.12).

Curiously, however, these very important changes are not reflected in the distribution or density of rural settlement in the Ager Tarraconensis. Analysis of survey data suggests that the pattern of settlement which had developed in response to the mid-second century BC changes, continued largely unchanged into the first and second centuries AD. By contrast, the commercialization of agricultural surplus on estates in the eastern sector of the Ager was growing very rapidly. Fine quality wine was sealed in new varieties of amphora from the earlier first century BC onwards.[86] These are very common on rural sites in the area and at Tarraco itself, helping to undercut the import of Italian wine.

By the side of Tarraco's pre-eminent political importance, Emporion remained primarily a commercial centre. The literary evidence[87] suggests that Caesar installed a contingent of veterans here. This seems to have precipitated a wholesale reorganization of all the communities at the site, and is reflected in the numismatic and archaeological evidence. The local coinage issued between 44 and 27 BC suggests that Emporion became a *municipium*.[88] It has been suggested that, in a juridical sense, this signals the fusion of all the different communities at Emporion: the Greeks in the port area, the Romans in the Roman town, the adjacent Indiketes and the Caesarian veterans.[89] Indeed, the existence of these different communities may have been perpetuated in the plural name Emporiae, by which the town was known under the early Empire. By the Augustan period, the *municipium* of Emporiae was distinguished by the construction of a basilica within the forum of the Roman town.[90] There is also evidence for important building programmes throughout the town: large private houses in the port area,[91] huge mansions at the Roman town,[92] renovation of the street grid in the Roman town and the construction of a gymnasium and wooden amphitheatre to the south.[93] Much, if not all, of this building activity was probably motivated by social competition amongst the élite of Emporiae. Towards the end of the first century BC, for example, an inscription records one of the town magistrates paying for the construction of a small market place (*campus*).[94]

Emporiae, therefore, yields early evidence of the socially motivated building-activity which, through the first and second centuries AD was largely responsible for many of the public and private buildings in towns throughout coastal Tarraconensis. In economic terms the town continued to act as a major market for the region. Indeed, this cycle was sufficiently intense that, by the later first century BC, good quality wine was produced on a large enough scale to be bottled in amphorae manufactured at local estates.[95] However, the growing importance of Narbo (Narbonne) as a major port to the north and the foundation of a *colonia* at Barcino (Barcelona) to the south, meant that Emporiae was to become a secondary centre of only regional importance. By the later first century AD, it had entered upon a cycle of slow decline.[96]

The most spectacular change to the urban network of the north-east, came with the foundation of a *colonia* at Barcino between 15 and 13 BC. This lay on the coastal plain between Tarraco and Emporiae, and was adjacent to a Laietanian hillfort at Montjuic.[97] This was a planned Roman urban settlement which had a regular layout (10 hectares), and which was enclosed by prestigious stone walls and towers (Fig. 10.13). The colonia may have been settled with discharged veterans from the Cantabrian wars. It was situated close to the Besós and Llobregat rivers, which ensured rapid communication with the great pre-littoral depression and the foot hills of the Pyrenees. It must also have played a part in the protection of the coast between Tarraco and Blandae, by virtue of the the forces at the disposal of the *praefectus orae maritimae*.[98]

It is difficult to gauge the impact of the foundation of Barcino on the local settlement pattern, since much has been obscured by the sprawl of modern Barcelona. However several hillforts are known on the Collserola,[99] of which the Turó de la Rovira and the Turó de Can Olivé were abandoned in the course of the first century BC. Moreover new farm buildings with stone and mortar walls and concrete floors of similar date are known from the Llobregat valley.[100] Moreover, from the first century AD, the market offered by Barcino was strong enough to generate strong local wine production, and amphora kilns have been discovered in the region.[101]

The development of Ibero-Roman towns

There is little doubt then, that the foundation of Barcino had an important effect on the settlement pattern in the Plà de Barcelona and the lower Llobregat valley. The presence of colonists and others at the town also constituted an important new market for those farms and estates which had already become established in the territories of Baetulo, Iluro and other neighbouring areas. The integration of the colonia into this regional framework was assisted by the construction of a detour from the Via Augusta in 8-7 BC. This ran through Iluro and Baetulo, linking them closely to the administrative centre at Barcino.[102] Thus, from the later first century BC, there was an intensification in the commercialization of agricultural surplus

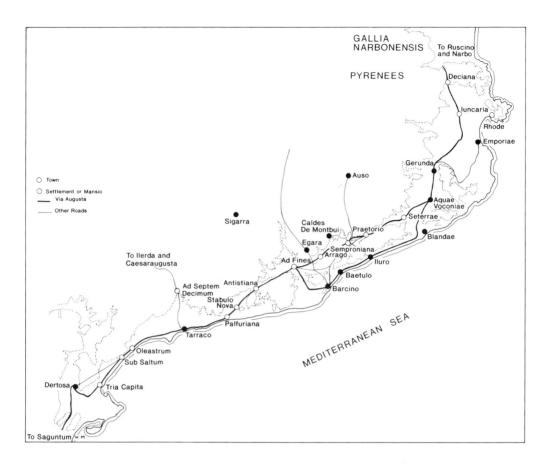

Fig. 10.12. The road network in north-eastern Hispania Citerior/Tarraconensis during the late Republic and early Empire. Rivers have been omitted to ease congestion (see however Figs. 10.2 and 10.11).

in the territories of Baetulo and Iluro.[103] Similarly at the Laietanian spa-town beneath modern Caldes de Montbui which, too, became a focus for wine production. It benefitted from the river Caldes, a tributary of the Besós, which offered seasonal access to Barcino.[104]

A similar process was at work in the hinterland of Gerunda. Thus, excavations at Vilauba (Camós), at the western edge of its territory, reveal the appearance of a sophisticated Roman-style farm. Further west, a kiln producing wine amphorae of first century AD date was discovered at Ermedás (Cornella de Terri).[105]

By the beginning of the first century AD, therefore, wine from estates in different parts of the north-east was sealed in amphorae and marketed at centres like Caldes, Barcino, Baetulo, Iluro and Gerunda. It was also produced near modern Tivissa, in the hinterland of Dertosa (modern Tortosa). The wine was either consumed in the towns, found its way back to local estates, or was bought by merchants acting for buyers in different parts of the Western Empire.[106]

The development of this flourishing local wine production is evidence of the success of the élites of Ibero-Roman towns in dominating the growing commercial networks which focused primarily upon Emporiae, Tarraco and, later, Barcino. The same is true of the large quantities of fine pottery and amphorae from Italy, Southern Gaul, the Eastern Mediterranean, North Africa and Southern Spain which were imported to towns and re-distributed to farms and rural sites throughout the north east. The towns began to develop as centres of wealth, power and prestige. The pressures of living-space at Baetulo, for example, were sufficiently strong for the eastern wall of the town to be demolished and for commercial and residential buildings to spread eastwards.[107] Before the end of the first century BC, social competition within the towns and inter-urban rivalry had given rise to the appearance of public and private buildings that were were essentially Roman. Urban developments at Tarraco probably provided the model for the opus signinum floors decorated with patterns executed in white mosaic tesserae, at Baetulo and Iluro.[108] In view of this and their later development, it comes as little surprise to find that by the early first century AD, Baetulo, Iluro, Blandae and Gerunda may all have achieved municipal status.[109] This meant that although the towns retained their own constitutions and magistrates, those who were elected to magistracies gained the prestigious status of Roman citizenship.

Conclusion

After just over two-hundred years of Roman involvement in north-eastern Spain, the indigenous settlement pattern had finally disintegrated. By the late first century BC, it was dominated by the Roman towns of Tarraco, Barcino and Emporiae and complemented by lower-status Ibero-Roman towns like Gerunda, Baetulo, Iluro, Blandae, Caldes de Montbui, Gerunda and Dertosa. Settlements like Egara (Terrassa), and Auso (Vic) were also of Iberian origin, as perhaps were Sigarra (Prats del Rei) and Aquae Calidae (Caldes de Malavella).[110] In any event, available evidence suggests that these developed later, gaining important regional status. Dertosa, for instance, was a Caesarian *municipium* whilst Egara became a *municipium* during the Flavian period.[111] At the same time, most of the surviving Ibereian hillforts and other settlements were finally abandoned.[112]

The persistence of Iberian settlements until this late date is not so remarkable when it is remembered that tribal consciousness was still strong enough for Caesar to refer to individual peoples of the north east by name.[113] This period also witnessed the disappearance of the last of the traditional Iberian ceramic products, like the hole-mouthed amphorae and fine wares.[114] These had evolved in response to the needs and pattern of the Iberian settlement system. Faced with its disintegration and the appearance of the new urban network dominated by Roman towns, they disappeared.

There were also a number of lowland settlements whose existence has been revealed to us by Roman road itineraries of the second century AD.[115] Seterrae (Hostalrich), Iuncaria (nr. Figueres), Deciana (? San Julian), Praetorio (Llinas del Vallès), Semproniana (Granollers), Antistiana (? Vilafranca del Penedès), Ad Fines (Martorell), Palfuriana (? Calafell), Oleastrum (Ametlla de Mar), Ad Tria Capita (?) and Ad Septimum Decimum (nr. Valls) were all located on the Via Augusta or branch roads. Thus it is more likely that they represented road stations than a development of pre-existing Iberian settlements.

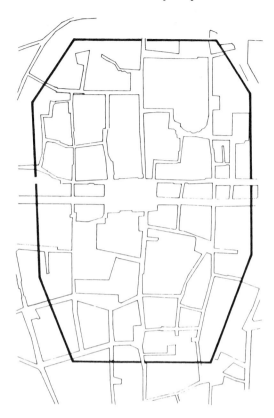

Fig. 10.13. Plan of the Augustan walls of Barcino superimposed upon the modern street plan of Barcelona (after Granados 1984).

By the late first century BC, all these communities were integrated within the newly organized administrative framework of Tarraconensis and focused on the seat of the provincial governor at Tarraco. The Augustan period also witnessed a reorganization of the system of taxation.[116] This involved the progressive regularisation of a coinage in bronze, brass, gold and silver, issued centrally at Rome and Lyons, between 23 BC and the end of the first century AD. This new coinage formed the principal means of tax assessment and payment and gradually obviated local Iberian mints. By the mid-first century BC, bronze coins with Iberian lettering were still issued at UNTIKESKEN, KESE, BAITOLO and ILTURO, whilst by the Augustan period, these had dwindled to Latin inscribed issues from the *colonia* of Tarraco, and the *municipia* of Emporiae and Ilergavonia Dertosa. By the reign of Caius, in the earlier first century AD, these had disappeared altogether.[117]

This article is presented as a working model for our understanding of the processes at work in the development of the coastal communities of Hispania Citerior between the early second and later first centuries BC. Returning to the five themes, or variables, outlined at the start, it is important to note that:

    1.   There is no evidence of any administrative rationale or framework applied by Rome to the communities of the north-east prior to the second quarter of the second century BC.

Subsequently, Rome used selected major Iberian settlements at focal points for collecting together the dues of newly introduced taxes. The settlements were then responsible for converting this into coinage. It was only with the designation of Tarraco as provincial capital in the late first century BC, and the foundation of Barcino, that any coherent administrative structure emerges.

    2.   The introduction of a system of regular taxation in the earlier second century BC does seem to have stimulated an agricultural surplus large enough for Iberian communities to import prestigious luxuries and foodstuffs on a wider scale and in greater volume than hitherto.

    3.   This was an important factor in the abandonment of Iberian settlements and the breakdown of the existing settlement pattern. The ubiquity of imports to settlements of every kind helped to undermine the prestigious monopoly that had been enjoyed by the élite of the larger settlements.

    4.   It was essentially wider Roman strategic interests in the Iberian peninsula which promoted Emporion, Tarraco and Barcino as administrative centres of the first order in north-eastern Citerior.

    5.   From the first century BC, important Ibero-Roman centres like Gerunda, Baetulo, Caldes de Montbui and Dertosa emerge as new high status towns which by the later first century BC/early first century AD are the scene of building activity motivated by social competition and inter-urban rivalry.

It is clear, therefore, that the Romanization of the coastal communities of north-eastern Citerior was a unique blend of Roman strategic expediency and Iberian response and adaptation. Moreover, rather than starting with a preconceived model, the key to understanding the processes of Romanization in the Hispaniae is to define local variables and to incorporate these into regional models. The sheer complexity of the social processes and the stresses of change demand nothing less.

Notes

It should be noted that the research for this article was completed in 1987 and it has not been possible to incorporate most of the more recent works into the text, notes or bibliography. These do not, however, alter the substance or significant details of the work presented here.

1   Especially the Urnfield culture from south-eastern France: Martín 1977, 187ff

2   For Phoenician imports, see Arteaga, Padrò and Sanmartí 1986, 303ff

3   Junyent 1981, 39; Ruiz de Arbulo 1984, 124ff

4   Following the definition of Rathje and Sabloff 1973-1974, 222

5   Villaronga 1981, 42ff

6   Crawford 1985, 86ff; for Emporitan silver, see Amoros 1933 and 1934

7   Sanmartí and Padrò 1977, 157ff

8   García y Bellido 1948

9   For example, Strabo's Geography 3.4.6-10

10   The sites of Puig de Serra (Serra de Daró) and Els Socors (Canapost: Nolla and Casas 1984, nos. 209 and 188) may have been satellites of the Puig de Sant Andreu (Martín 1985, 10ff). A general account of Iberian settlement and society is to be found in Jordá, Pellicer, Acosta and Almagro Gorbea 1986, 481-509

11   Barberà 1982-1983, 146-150 (Burriac); Martín 1985, 21 (Puig de Sant Andreu)
12   Castro 1976; 1980
13   The Iberian pottery kilns of Fontscaldes (Colomines and Puig y Cadafalch 1915-1920, 602-605), for example, are only a few kilometres to the north of the Iberian settlement at El Vilar (Valls)
14   Sanmartí, J, Santacana and Serra 1984
15   One lacks, for example, the thorough and systematic research into Iberian settlement patterns currently being undertaken in Jaen province: Ruiz Rodríguez *et al.* 1985; Ruiz Rodríguez and Molinos Molinos 1981; a general survey of Iberian settlements is to be found in Jordá, Pellicer, Acosta and Almagro Gorbea 1986, 485ff
16   Livy XXI 61
17   Livy XXXIV 9; Ruiz de Arbulo 1984, 121ff (metals); Almagro 1953, 398 illustrates Iberian amphorae which carried foodstuffs produced by Iberian communities
18   Richardson 1986, 20ff; Keay 1988, 25ff for a general account
19   Livy XXI 60-61; Aquilué and Dupré 1986, 14ff and Miró M. 1987, discuss the Iberian predecessor of Tarraco
20   Livy XXV 37-39
21   Livy XXVIII 24-34; XXIX 1-3
22   Richardson 1986, 62ff discusses the reasons for the Roman presence in Iberia after 206 BC
23   Livy XXXIV 8-21
24   Discussed by Richardson 1986, 75ff; Albertini 1923
25   Livy XXVI 19
26   Fabra and Burguete 1986 (El Vilar); Pallarès R. 1982, 218-219; 1984 (Castellet de Banyoles)
27   Aquilué *et al.* 1984, 36ff
28   Sanmartí, Nolla and Aquilué 1983-1984, 125ff
29   Hauschild 1976-1977
30   Following the hypothesis of Aquilué and Dupré 1986, 16ff
31   Miró, M., 1987
32   Livy XL 39
33   Appian VI 45
34   An inscription from Tarraco (Alföldy 1975, nr. 5) may refer to the Magister of such a community: (...) L(ib) EPHES(ius...) S MAG (istri)
35   Wilson 1966, 13-18 discusses these communities
36   Mayer and Rodà 1986, 345 (road network); Nolla 1987a, 292-3 (Emporion)
37   Hopkins 1980, 101ff on this point
38   See, for example, Muñiz Coello 1982, 50ff
39   Richardson 1976
40   Crawford 1985, 95
41   Livy XXXIV 21; some of these mines may have been located in the vicinity of Bellmunt del Priorat (Tarragona)
42   Richardson 1976 and 1986, 114
43   If one accepts the arguments of Crawford 1985, 95ff. By contrast, Villaronga 1979, 119-122 suggests a much earlier date for the introduction of the Iberian bronze coinage. Knapp 1987, 19ff, 21-22, looks at other interpretations of the significance of Iberian coinage.
44   Crawford 1985 101, Fig. 18; Villaronga 1979 and Guadán 1980 for analyses of individual mints
45   Perhaps to be located in the vicinity of Cabrera de Mar (Mataró, Barcelona): it issued bronze coinage
46   Perhaps to be located within the Comarcas of Bages and Baix Llobregat (Barcelona): it issued bronze coinage
47   Probably located near Llerona del Vallès (Barcelona): it issued bronze coinage

48	Possibly located in the uplands immediately to the north west of Badalona (Barcelona); it issued bronze coinage
49	Villaronga 1977, 5; it issued bronze coinage
50	Perhaps to be located in the vicinity of modern Vic; it issued bronze coinage
51	For example see Ripollés 1982, 367, for the limited distribution of known coins from the mint of Baitolo
52	Livy XLIII 2
53	Indeed, the survey work (conducted by the writer and M. Millett) has revealed limited quantities of Greco-Italic and Dressel 1A amphorae being manufactured on local sites (Fig. 10.10), as farmers sought Tarraco as a regular market for their wine
54	Terré 1987, 221
55	Calafell, Barcelona: Sanmartí, J., Santacana and Serra 1984, 16ff
56	Miret, Sanmartí and Santacana 1984, 178ff
57	Crawford 1985, 99; the volume of Roman regular coinage at the site can be appreciated in Ripoll, Nuix and Villaronga 1979
58	Ruiz de Arbulo 1987, 313ff
59	Aquilué *et al.* 1984 48-77
60	Aquilué *et al.* 1984 128-132, and Aquilué *et al.* 1986; the inscription has been expanded to read: M.IUN(io d.f.silano)/PRO (praetori.hisp.cit *or* hc *or* p.h.c.) CO(loni coloniae-*or*-loni et incolae)
61	Nolla and Casas 1984, 114-116
62	Puig Rodon (Corçà, Girona): Nolla and Casas 1984, 127-131
63	Camallera (Girona): Casas 1980
64	Ripollés 1982, 333-357, analyses the volume of coinage in circulation at Emporion and demonstrates the rise in the proportion of coins issued at Rome between 195/133BC-72/27BC, from 7.86% to 23.07%
65	The Roman population at Emporion and, perhaps, Tarraco may have been further augmented by Marian exiles from central Italy in the late 80's, who fought in Sertorius' armies and later formed the basis of Pompey's clientele in Citerior. The evidence, however (presented in Wilson 1966, 29-32) does not specifically mention such settlement at those towns, although it is known that Tarraco probably remained loyal to Sertorius down to his final defeat by Pompey in 72BC (Alföldy 1978, IV 1.b)
66	Nolla 1979-1980
67	Respectively: Oliva 1970 and Nolla and Casas 1984, 181ff; Roure and Keay 1985, 16ff; Serra Ràfols 1942, 40ff
68	Burriac: Barberà and Pascual 1979-1980; Turó d'en Boscà: Junyent and Baldellou 1972
69	Padrós 1985, 43-45, Fig. 13; Aquilué and Subias 1984, 358ff suggest that the architects may have been of Italian origin
70	Guitart 1976, 243; Padrós 1985, 96ff
71	Clariana 1984
72	Del Vilà M. *et al.* 1977-1978
73	For example, see Mapa 3 in Prevosti 1981a, which illustrates the density of the distribution of Black Glaze B wares in the hinterland of Baetulo
74	Prevosti 1981, site nr. 102; other apparently new foundations of this date have been discovered at Vinya del Sr.Mas (Prevosti 1981, 100), Riera de Teià (Prevosti 1981, 104), and at the Veinat del Sant Crist (Prevosti 1981, 164)
75	The latest Iberian inhabitants at Burriac, and those at Baetulo, began producing amphorae imitating the Italian types Dressel 1A and B in the first half of the first century BC (Comas *et al.* 1987)
76	The foundation of Gerunda, Baetulo and Iluro have been interpreted in a different light by Spanish scholars. Guitart (1976) and Prevosti (1981, 1981a) see the foundation of Baetulo and Iluro and the appearance of local villas as a result of settlement by Marian exiles from Rome in the 80's

BC. Nolla 1978-1980, conversely, sees Gerunda as a strategic foundation undertaken during the Sertorian wars (82-72BC). In none of these cases is the historical, epigraphic or archaeological evidence explicit enough to support such hypotheses: see also note 65

77 Caesar Civil War II 21.5

78 Alföldy 1978, V.1.a

79 Suetonius, Augustus 26, 3 (first visit); Cassius Dio 54, 23,7, records Augustus' second visit to Hispania, although he does not explicitly mention a visit to Tarraco

80 Fishwick 1982

81 Fishwick 1982, 229-230 suggests a possible location in the vicinity of the "forum" excavated and identified by Serra Vilaró (1932). This large building has been re-examined (Mar and Ruiz de Arbulo 1986) and plausibly re-identified as the basilica of the municipal forum

82 Albertini 1923

83 Alföldy 1978, VII 1.b; Mackie 1983, 190 note 4

84 Pallí 1985, 29ff

85 Dated by an Augustan milestone discovered in the immediate vicinity of the town: Alföldy 1975, nr. 934 (12 BC)

86 The earlier form, the Tarraconense 1/Laietana 1, was manufactured at some time prior to 30 BC onwards (Fig. 10.10). Examples have been found at the theatre of Tarraco (Nolla 1987, 219) and on sites in the Ager Tarraconensis. The later form, Pascual 1 (Fig. 10.10), is common in the town and in the surrounding country. Kiln sites for local amphorae of Late Republican and Early Imperial amphorae have been discovered in the hinterland of Tarragona, near Reus (Baix Camp) at La Boada and El Vilar (Massó 1978), and other sites

87 Literally, the text speaks of "Roman colonists" installed after the final defeat of Pompey's sons in the Civil War: Livy XXXIV 9

88 Villaronga 1977, 6ff

89 Ruiz de Arbulo 1987, 314ff

90 Aquilué *et al.* 1984, 87ff and Fig. 52

91 Aquilué, Mar and Ruiz de Arbulo 1983

92 Nieto 1979-1980, 281ff and 313ff

93 Almagro 1956

94 Peña 1981 nr. 6

95 As in the hinterland of first century BC Tarraco, the sequence of amphora types carrying the wine seems to have begun with the Tarraconense 1/Laietana 1, followed by the Pascual 1 and Dressel 2-4 at later dates (cf. note 86). Amphora kilns producing some of these and other forms, have been discovered at Llafranch (Palafrugell: Nolla, Canes and Rocas 1982) and at Palamós (Tremoleda 1987), to the south of Emporiae

96 For the later decline of Emporiae, see Keay 1981, 458 and Nieto 1983

97 Granados 1984

98 An official based at Tarraco: Mackie 1983, 184, 190 note 5

99 Gimeno 1984

100 At sites like Ca N'Esplugues (Pallejà: Granados and Solias 1982) and Nuestra Senyora de Sales (Vi ladecans: Solias 1983). Biajot *et al.* 1984, 95ff provide general (and uncritical) background data

101 Pascual 1 wine amphorae were manufactured at Sant Boi de Llobregat, and Dressel 2-4 amphorae at Can Tintorer and Santa María de les Feixes: Pascual 1977. For other kilns in this area, see Granados and Rovira 1987

102   Pallarès F. 1975
103   This is reflected in the bottling of local wine amphorae, produced on kiln sites in the territories of both towns (Pascual 1977), on a much larger scale than hitherto. As at Tarraco and Emporiae, the Tarraconense 1/Laietana 1 seems to have been the earliest type to have been produced in the first century BC (Comas 1985, 65ff), with the Pascual 1 and Dressel 2-4 following later
104   Pascual 1977, 54ff
105   Roure, Castanyer, Nolla, Keay and Tarrús 1988 (Vilauba); Jones, Millett and Keay 1983, 31ff (Ermedás)
106   Nolla *et al.* 1980 and Revilla 1982-1983 (Tivissa); for distribution see Tchernia 1971 and Miró, J., 1987 (Gaul) and Williams 1981 (Britain)
107   Guitart 1976, 243ff
108   For example, in the Calle de Fluvia: Guitart 1976 114, Lam.XXX 1 (Baetulo); Clariana 1984, 94, and Ribas 1980 (Iluro)
109   The probable significance of Pliny's statement (NH.III 4.22), that all four towns were "oppida civium Romanorum". See discussions by Guitart 1976, 19ff and Nolla 1979-1980, 46ff
110   The origins of Dertosa are unclear (Genera and Arbeloa 1987). Recent excavations suggest that the Roman town did not appear before the Augustan period and that its predecessor lay in various neighbouring Iberian settlements. On the other hand it is clear that Dertosa gained the status of *municipium* under Caesar. Evidence for the Iberian predecessor of Egara (Terrassa) is discussed briefly in Almagro *et al.* 1945, and that for Auso (Vic) in Molas 1979. The little available archaeological evidence for Aquae Calidae is discussed by Serra Ràfols 1941
111   CIL II 4494; discussed in IRC 100 nr. 66
112   A similar process whereby a diffuse pattern of Iberian/Celtiberian settlement in the Ebro valley gradually gives way to one dominated by Roman towns in the Late Republic and Early Empire is discussed in Burillo 1986
113   Caesar *Civil War* I 60, refers to the tribes of the Ilergaones and Ausetani, amongst others
114   These are rarely found in site contexts dating to after the end of the first century BC
115   Summarised in Roldán 1975, Appendix II, 209-279
116   Discussed in detail by Muñiz Coello 1982, 143ff
117   Villaronga 1979, 223-306

Bibliography

Albertini E. 1923, *Les Divisions Administratives d'Espagne Romaine.* Paris
Alföldy G.1975, *Die römischen Inschriften von Tarraco* (2 vols). Berlin
Alföldy G. 1978, "Tarraco", in, *Pauly-Wissowa Real Encyklopädie der Klassischen Altertumswissenschaften* Sup.XIV 570-644
Almagro M. 1953, *Las Necrópolis de Ampurias I. Barcelona*
Almagro M. 1955, *Las Necrópolis de Ampurias II. Barcelona*
Almagro M. 1956, El anfiteatro y la palestra de Ampurias. *Ampurias* 27-28, 1-20
Almagro M. *et al.* 1945, *Carta Arqueológica de España: Barcelona.* Barcelona
Amoros J. 1933, *Les drachmes emporitanes.* Barcelona.
Amoros J. 1934, *Les monedes emporitanes anteriors a les drachmes.* Barcelona.
Aquilué J. and Dupré X. 1986, Reflexions entorn de Tarraco en época tardo republicana. *Forum I*, Tarragona
Aquilué J. Mar R. and Ruiz de Arbulo J. 1983, Arquitectura de la Neápolis ampuritana. *Informació Arqueológica* 40, 127- 137

Aquilué X. and Subias E. 1984, Sobre la fundació de la ciutat romana de Baetulo (Badalona). In, *Protohistoria Catalana. 6 Colloqui Internacional D'Arqueologia de Puigcerda*, Institut D'Estudis Ceretans, 353-359, Puigcerda.

Aquilué *et al.* 1984 =Aquilué X. Mar R. Nolla J. Ruiz de Arbulo J. and Sanmartí E. 1984, *El Forum Romà d' Empúries*. Barcelona

Aquilué X. *et al.* 1986, Una lapida dedicada a M.Iunius Silanus aparecida en el foro Romano de Ampurias. *Reunión sobre epigrafia Hispanica de Epoca Romano Republicana. Actas*, 151-156

Arteaga O. Padrò J. and Sanmartí E. 1986, La expansión fenicia per las costas de Cataluña y del Languedoc. In, Del Olmo G. and Aubet M. (eds), *Los Fenicios en la Peninsula Ibérica*, Vol.2, 303-314. Sabadell

Barberà J. 1982-1983, Un paral.lel remot de l'edifici public de Burriac (Cabrera de Mar), *Laietania* 2, 146-150

Barberà J. and Pascual R. 1979-1980, Burriac, un yacimiento protohistórico de la costa catalana (Cabrera de Mar, Barcelona), *Ampurias* 41-42, 203-242

Biajot *et al.* 1984, El poblamiento de la zona sur de la Layetania litoral en época Ibérica y Romana, *Arqueología Espacial* 2, 93-110

Burillo F. 1986, *Aproximación diacronica a las ciudades antiguas del valle medio del Ebro. Seminario de Arqueologia y Etnologia Turolense*. Colegio Universitario de Teruel

Casas J. 1980, L'Estaciò Romana del "Camp del Bosquet" (Camallera, Alt Empordà) I. L'Aljub. *Revista de Girona* 93, 275-284

Castro Z. 1976, Piezas discoidales en yacimientos del N.E. de Cataluña, *Cypsela* I, 173-195

Castro Z. 1980, Fusayolas Ibéricas, antecedentes y empleo. *Cypsela* III, 127-146

Clariana J. 1984, Notes sobre l'estructura urbana d'Iluro. *Faventia* 6/1, 89-112

Colomines J. and Puig y Cadafalch J. 1915-1920, El forn Ibèric de Fontscaldes. *Anuari Del Institut D'Estudis Catalans* VI, 602-605. Barcelona

Comas M. 1985, *Baetulo. Les Amfores*. Monografies Badalonines num.8

Comas M. Martín A. Matamoro D. and Miró J. 1987, Un tipus d'ámfora Dr. 1 de producció Laietana. *De les Estructures Indígenes a l'Organització Provincial Romana de la Hispania Citerior. Jornades Internacionals d'Arqueologia Romana*, 372- 378 Granollers

Crawford M. 1985, *Coinage and Money under the Roman Republic. Italy and the Mediterranean Economy*. London.

Del Vilà M. Genera M. Huntingford E. and Dolors Molas M. 1977, Aportaciones al Conocimiento de la Antigua Blandae. *Pyrenae* 13-14, 211-251

Fabra M. and Burguete S. 1986, Introduccio a l'estudi del jaciment Ibèric de "El Vilar". *Quaderns de Vilaniu* 9, 55-78

Fishwick D. 1982, The Altar of Augustus and the Municipal Cult of Tarraco. *Madrider Mitteilungen* 23, 222-233

García y Bellido A. 1948, *Hispania Graeca* (3 vols), Barcelona

Genera M. and Arbeloa J.M.V. 1987, La Dertosa Romana i la seva influencia. *Tribuna d'Arqueologia 1986-1987*. Departament de Cultura, Generalitat de Catalunya, 81-90

Gimeno X. 1984, Noves consideracions sobre el poblament Ibèric del Pla de Barcelona. *Faventia* 6/1, 113-136

Granados O. 1984, La Primera Fortificacion de la Colònia Barcino. *Papers in Iberian Archaeology* (Eds. Blagg T. Jones R. and Keay S.), BAR International Series 193, 267-319

Granados O. and Rovira C. 1987, Tres Nous Centres de Producció d'Amfores a l'Ager de la Colònia Barcino. *El Vi A L'Antiguitat. Economia Producció i Comerç al Mediterrani Occidental. I. Colloqui d'Arqueologia Romana*, 126-132, Badalona

Granados O. and Solias J.M. 1982, Ca N'Esplugues, Pallejà. In, *Les Excavacions Arqueológiques a Catalunya en els darrers anys*. Departament de Cultura de la Generalitat de Catalunya, 285-286, Barcelona

Guadán de A.M. 1980, *La Moneda Ibérica*. Madrid

Guitart J. 1976, *Baetulo. Topografia Arqueológica, Urbanismo e Historia*. Badalona

Hauschild T. 1976-1977, Torre de Minerva (Sant Magí). Una torre de la muralla Romana de Tarragona. *Boletín Arqueológico de Tarragona* 133-140, 49-73

Hopkins K. 1980, Taxes and Trade in the Roman Empire (200BC-AD 400), *Journal of Roman Studies* 70, 101-125

IRC=Fabre G. Mayer M. and Rodà I. 1984, *Inscriptions Romaines de Catalogne. I. Barcelone (sauf Barcino)* Paris

Jordá F. Pellicer M. Acosta M. and Almagro Gorbea M. 1986, *Historia de España I. Prehistoria*. Madrid

Jones R. Millett M. and Keay S. 1983, Fieldwork and Excavation in the Banyoles Area of Spain, 1982. *University of Durham and University of Newcastle-Upon-Tyne. Archaeological Reports for 1982*, 31-35, Durham

Junyent E. 1981, Empòrion i la Iberització de Catalunya. *L'Avenç* 38, 36-41

Junyent E. and Baldellou V. 1972, Estudio de una casa Ibérica en el poblado de Mas Boscà, Badalona. *Principe De Viana*, 5-67

Keay S. 1981, The Conventus Tarraconensis in the Third Century AD: Crisis or Change? *The Roman West in the Third Century. Contributions from Archaeology and History* (King A. and Henig M. eds.), BAR International Series 109, 451-486, Oxford

Keay S. 1988, *Roman Spain*. London

Knapp R. 1987, Spain. In Burnett A. and Crawford M. (eds.), *The Coinage of the Roman World in the Late Republic*. BAR International Series 326, 19-41

Mackie N. 1983, *Local Administration in Roman Spain AD 14-212*. BAR International Series 172

Mar R. and Ruiz de Arbulo J. 1986, La Basílica de la Colònia Tarraco. *Forum* 3, Tarragona

Martín A. 1977, Los origenes de la Iberización en la zona costera del nordeste de Cataluña. *Simposi Internacional: Els Origens Del Mon Ibèric. Ampurias* 38-40, 187-196

Martín A. 1985, *Ullastret, Poblat Ibèric. Guies de jaciments arqueològics*. Generalitat de Catalunya, Departament de Cultura, Barcelona

Massó J. 1978, *Reus Prehistoria I Antiguitat*. Reus

Mayer M. and Rodà I. 1986, La romanització de Catalunya. Algunes questions. *Protohistoria Catalana. 6e Colloqui Internacional de Puigcerda*. Puigcerda 1984, 339-351

Mayer M. and Rodà I. 1986a, La epigrafía Republicana en Cataluña. Su reflejo en la red viaria. *Epigrafía Hispanica de época Romano Republicana*. Zaragoza, 157-165

Miret M. Sanmartí J. and Santacana J. 1984, Distribución espacial de núcleos ibéricos: un ejemplo en el litoral catalan. *Arqueologia Espacial* 4, 173-186

Miró J. 1987, Ví Català a França (Segle 1 a.c.-1 d.c), Una Síntesi Preliminar. *El Vi a l'Antiguitat. Economia Producció i Comerç al Mediterrani Occidental. I Colloqui d'Arqueologia Romana*, 249-268, Badalona

Miró M. 1987, El Nucli Ibèric de Tarraco: dels seus inicis a la integracio dins la ciutat Romana. *De les Estructures Indígenes a l'Organització Provincial Romana de la Hispania Citerior. Jornades Internacionals d'Arqueologia Romana* 284-290, Granollers

Molas Ma D. 1979, Acerca de la Urbe Ausetanorum y la Ciudad Romana de Ausa. *Boletín del Seminario de Arte y Arqueología*, 189-202

Muñiz Coello J. 1982, El Sistema Fiscal en la España Romana (Republica y Alto-Imperio). Zaragoza

Nieto F.J. 1979-1980, Repertorio de la pintura mural Romana de Ampurias. *Ampurias* 41-42, 279-342

Nieto F.J. 1983, Acerca del progresivo despoblamiento de Ampurias. *Rivista di Studi Liguri* XLVII, 35-41

Nolla J.M. 1987, Una Nova Amfora Catalana: La Tarraconense I. *El Vi a l'Antiguitat: Economia Producció i Comerç al Mediterrani Occidental. I. Colloqui d'Arqueologia Romana*, 217-223, Badalona

Nolla J.M. 1987a, Empúries, creixement, crisis i Adaptació. Algunes consideracions. *De les estructures indígenes a l'organització provincial romana de la Hispania Citerior. Jornades Internacionals d'Arqueologia Romana*, 291-297, Granollers

Nolla J.M. Canes J.M. and Rocas X. 1982, Un forn romà de terrissa a Llafranc (Palafrugell, Baix Empordà). Excavacions de 1980-1981. *Ampurias 44*, 147-183

Nolla J.M. and Casas J. 1984, *Carta Arqueológica de les Comarques de Girona. El poblament d'època romana al N.E. de Catalunya.* Girona

Nolla J.M. Padró J. and Sanmartí E. 1980, Exploració preliminar del forn d'àmfores de Tivissa (Ribera d'Ebre). *Cypsela III*, 193-218

Oliva M. 1970, Descubrimiento de una villa romana con mosaicos en Sarria de Dalt (Gerona). *Revista de Gerona 50*, 19-27

Padrós P.1985, *Baetulo. Arqueologia urbana 1975-1985.* Museu de Badalona

Pallarès F. 1975, la Topografia i Els Origens de la Barcelona Romana. *Cuadernos de Arqueologia e Historia de la Ciudad 16*, 5-48

Pallarès R. 1982, El Castellet de Banyoles, Tivissa. *Les excavacions Arqueològiques a Catalunya en els darrers anys. Excavacions Arqueológiques a Catalunya 1*, 218-219, Barcelona

Pallarès R. 1984, El sistema defensivo frontal del Castellet de Banyoles, Tivissa Ribera d'Ebre. *Pyrenae 19-20*, 113-125

Pallí F. 1985, *La Via Augusta en Cataluña.* Barcelona

Pascual R. 1977, Las Anforas de la Layetania. *Méthodes Classiques et Méthodes Formelles dans l'Etude des Amphores.* Collection de l'Ecole Française de Rome 32, 47-96, Rome

Peña M.J. 1981, Epigrafía Ampuritana (1953-1980). *Quaderns de Treball 4.* Barcelona

Prevosti M. 1981, *Cronologia i poblament a l'area rural d'Iluro (2 Vols).* Mataró

Prevosti M. 1981a, *Cronologia i poblament a l'area rural de Baetulo.* Badalona

Rathje W. and Sabloff J. 1973-1974, Ancient Maya Commercial Systems: a Research Design for the Island of Cozumel. *World Archaeology 5*

Revilla V. 1982-1983, Hornos Romanos en Tivissa (Ribera d'Ebre). *Butlletí Arqueològic 4-5*, 187-196

Ribas M. 1980, Trobailes de restes romanes en una casa de la Plaça Gran de Mataró. *Quaderns d'Arqueologia i Prehistoria del Maresme 11-12*, 372-376

Richardson J. 1976, The Spanish Mines and the Development of Provincial Taxation in the Second Century BC. *Journal of Roman Studies 66*, 139-152

Richardson J. 1986, *Hispaniae. Spain and the Development of Roman Imperialism 218-82 BC.* Cambridge University Press

Ripoll E. Nuix J.M. and Villaronga L. 1979, La Circulacion monetaria en Emporion. *Symposium Numismatico de Barcelona I*, 45-55. Barcelona

Ripollés P. 1982, *La Circulacion Monetaria en la Tarraconense Mediterranea.* Servicio de Investigacion Prehistorica. Serie de Trabajos Varios Num. 77. Valencia

Roldán J. 1975, *Itineraria Hispana.* Valladolid/Granada

Roure A. and Keay S. 1985, Excavaciones a la Vil.la Romana de Vilauba (Camós, Girona) 1979-1983. *Tribuna d'Arqueologia 1983-1984.* Departament de Cultura de la Generalitat de Catalunya, 15-18, Barcelona

Roure A. Castanyer P. Nolla J.M. Keay S. and Tarrus J. 1988, *La Vil.la Romana de Vilauba (Camós,).* Centre d'Investigacions Arqueológiques de Girona. Sèrie Monogràfica Nr.8

Ruiz de Arbulo J. 1984, Emporion y Rhode. Dos Asentamientos Portuarios en el Golfo de Rosas. *Arqueología Espacial 4*, 140-140

Ruiz de Arbulo J. 1987, La Evolución Urbana de Emporion en Epoca Republicana. La Complejidad de una Tradición. *De les Estructures Indígenes a l'Organització Provincial Romana de la Hispania Citerior. Jornades Internacionals d'Arqueologia Romana*. 311-319 Granollers

Ruiz Rodríguez A. *et al.* 1985, El poblamiento Ibérico en el alto Guadalquivir. *Iberos. Actas de las 1 Jornadas sobre el mundo Ibérico*, Jaen, 239-256

Ruiz Rodríguez A. and Molinos Molinos M. 1981, Poblamiento Ibérico de la campiña de Jaen. Análisis de una ordenacion del territorio. *Primeras Jornadas de Metodologia de Investigacion Prehistorica de Soria*, 421-429

Sanmartí E. and Padrò J. 1977, Ensayo de aproximación al fenomeno de la iberización en las comarcas meridionales de Cataluña. *Simposi Internacional: Els Origens del Mon Ibèric, Ampurias* 38-40, 157-176

Sanmartí J. Santacana J. and Serra R. 1984, El Jaciment Ibèric de l'Argilera i el poblament protohistoric al Baix Penedès. *Quaderns de Treball* 6. Barcelona

Sanmartí E. Nolla J.M. and Aquilué X. 1983-1984, Les excavacions a l'àrea del pàrking al sud de la Neàpolis d'Empúries (Informe Preliminar). *Empúries* 45-46, 110-153

Serra Vilaró J. 1932, Excavaciones en Tarragona. *Memorias de la Junta Superior de Excavaciones y Antigüedades* 116 (1930 nr.5)

Serra Ràfols J. 1942, Excavaciones en Gerona. *Memorias de los Museos Arqueológicos Provinciales 1941* II. Madrid

Serra Ràfols J. 1941, Las Termas Romanas de Caldas de Malavella. *Archivo Español de Arqueologia*, 304-314

Solias J.M. 1983, Excavacions a l'ermita de Ntra. Sra. de Sales, Viladecans. *Excavacions Arqueológiques a Catalunya nr.3.* Departament de Cultura de la Generalitat de Catalunya

Tchernia A. 1971, Les amphores vinaires de Tarraconaise et leur exportation au début de l'Empire. *Archivo Español de Arqueologia* 44, 38-85

Terré E. 1987, La Vil.la Romana de "El Moro": Un exemple de poblament rural al camp de Tarragona. *De les Estructures Indígenes a l'Organització Provincial Romana de la Hispania Citerior. Jornades Internacionals d'Arqueologia Romana*, 219- 224

Tremoleda J. 1987, La Producció del Forn de Palamós (Baix Empordà). *El Vi a l'Antiguitat. Economia Producció i Comerç al Mediterrani Occidental. I. Colloqui d'Arqueologia Romana*, 210-216, Badalona

Villaronga L. 1977, *The Aes Coinage of Emporion.* BAR Supplementary Series 23. Oxford

Villaronga L. 1979, *Numismatica Antigua de Hispania. Iniciación a su Estudio.* Barcelona

Villaronga L. 1981, Evolució de les Monedes. *L'Avenç* 38, 42-48

Williams D. 1981, The Roman Amphora Trade with Late Iron Age Britain. *Production and Distribution: a ceramic viewpoint* (Eds. Howard H. and Morris E.), BAR International Series Nr.120, 123-132

Wilson A.J.N. 1966, *Emigration from Italy in the Republican Age of Rome* Manchester Age Of Rome.

11. Romanization and Urban Development in Lusitania

by Jonathan C. Edmondson

Perhaps the most eloquent testimony to Roman rule over the provinces of the West is provided by the remains of the theatres, amphitheatres, circuses, temples, forums and aqueducts that still survive in many formerly Roman cities. These buildings, and the cities in which they stand, represent in physical terms the impact of Rome on the provincial landscape. In some cases it was the Roman conquerors who oversaw the creation and construction of these cities *ex nihilo*, while in many cases towns which had formed part of the settlement pattern of the late Iron Age received Roman settlers and/or status. Thus towns, and the monumentalization of towns, are a potentially revealing index to the spread of Romanization in a particular area of the Roman Empire. Towns must not, however, be seen in isolation; the success of a town depended upon the successful exploitation of the surrounding countryside, and the countryside in turn depended on the town as a focal point for social, economic, political and religious purposes. Thus a preference for an urbanized society, deriving its livelihood, wealth and prestige from settled agriculture carried on in the hinterland of the towns was central to Greco-Roman ideology (Finley 1977; Février and Leveau 1982).

The Greek geographer Strabo, writing under Augustus and Tiberius, represented Rome as bringing civilization to the barbarian Celtic world in these very terms. Strabo equates civilization with the adoption of a 'polis' system, so familiar to him from the heartland of Greco-Roman culture. Thus in his account of the Iberian peninsula in Book Three Strabo considered the agricultural fertility of Turdetania (roughly equivalent to the Roman province of Baetica) a major determining factor in the high degree of urbanization – and civilization – to be found there (3.2.15). Conversely, in the interior the Celtiberians, for example, are held not to lead a civilized life because their natural environment was unconducive to the development of towns (3.4.13). Indeed Strabo's whole account polarizes Roman Spain into two very distinct regions, defined by their accessibility to the Mediterranean world: on the one hand, the southern and coastal area; on the other, the northern and the interior. The former was marked by towns, settled agriculture, a cereal-based diet, supplemented by wine and olive-oil (3.2.15; 3.4.16). Significantly, it was in contact and communication with the central Mediterranean, which led not only to flourishing maritime commerce (3.2.1; 3.2.4-6), but also to the introduction of Greco-Roman culture, which included the use of the Latin alphabet and language, and Roman dress (3.1.6; 3.4.20). On the other hand, the northern, interior zone was marked by a rugged terrain and inhospitable climate (3.1.2); this, as well as the indifference of the inhabitants (3.3.5), meant that cereals, vines and olives were not widely cultivated (3.3.7; 3.4.16). This exiguous economic base held back the development of towns and so allowed settlement only in villages (3.2.15) and a concomitant lack of the outward marks of culture: no coinage, some most outlandish languages and an equally outlandish mode of dress (3.3.7).[1] In short, the south and coastal zone represented for Strabo everything that was 'hemeron' (gentle, civilized), the north and interior the very opposite – 'dushemeron'; the former is blessed with peace, the latter with war, or at best 'brigandage' (3.3.8).

A recurring theme in Strabo's work as a whole is the antithesis between the 'civilized' pattern of an urban lifestyle combined with settled agriculture on the one hand and the 'barbarian' (or marginal) practice of a migratory, pastoralist existence on the other (Shaw 1982-83, 29-30). It is not surprising to find a classic formulation of this latter ethnographic pattern in Roman descriptions of the most famous Lusitanian opponent of Rome, Viriathus. Among others Livy outlines the stock character type succinctly:

> "Viriathus in Spain first from being a shepherd became a hunter, then from a hunter became a brigand, and soon from a brigand became the leader of a veritable army also." (Livy, *Per.* 52)

It is the Romans in Strabo's account who most virulently opposed and eventually transformed native societies where pastoralism/brigandage prevailed. The case of the tribes living in the hinterland of Massilia (modern Marseilles) may be taken as typical:[2]

> "Instead of brigandage they had already turned towards an urbanized life and settled farming because of Roman sovereignty over them." *(4.1.5)*

The major question, therefore, that I would like to pose here is the extent to which Rome can be shown to have encouraged the processes of urbanization in the province of Lusitania, and whether there was any regional variation in the intensity of urbanization within the province. Although the 'polis' system of settlement was widespread from Scotland to the Sahara under the Roman Empire, and although there were many common features between towns of one region of the Empire and another, there were, nevertheless, significant local variations both in the intensity of urbanization, and in its nature (Drinkwater 1987). Urbanization can, therefore, be a useful index to the extent to which the various parts of the province were affected by Romanization.

Ideally this discussion of urbanization should form only part of a much more wide ranging discussion of Romanization in Lusitania. For this a consideration of the following topics would be crucial:

(a) rural development and the interaction between town and country. The highest concentration of Roman villa sites occurs in the hinterland of two Roman colonies of the province: the capital, Augusta Emerita (Gorges 1982 and 1986) and the centre of the judicial *conventus Pacensis*, Pax Iulia (Alarcão, Etienne and Mayet forthcoming). There have to date been few discoveries of villas in the Celtic interior north of the Tagus (Gorges 1979, 454-62, 467-71), where, as we shall see, a different pattern of nucleated rural settlement prevailed;

(b) the preservation of elements of indigenous social relationships – especially extended kinship groupings. Inscriptions suggest that Celtic patterns of kinship groupings survived into the second and third centuries AD – essentially in the north of the province (most dramatically in the modern provinces of Salamanca and Avila) (Albertos Firmat 1975 and 1981);

(c) the persistence of native languages. Although the urban bricklayers of Conimbriga scratched their graffiti in Latin (Fabre 1974), in more rural areas an Indo-European language (?Lusitanian) has survived on inscriptions and was presumably spoken (*CIL* II 415, 738, 739; Tovar 1966-67; in general Untermann 1980);

(d) the continued worship of indigenous deities. Again in the north of the province inscriptions reveal many native deities still being worshipped – especially in the countryside (d'Encarnação 1975); in the cities dedications to Roman deities predominate. Rural sanctuaries of native deities continued to operate under the Roman Empire: for example, the shrines to Endovellicus at São Miguel de Motes, Vila Viçosa (Vasconcelos 1905, 111-46; d'Encarnação 1984, 561-629, nos. 482-565; for new text *Ficheiro Epigráfico* 64 = *AE* 1985, 503) and at the Iron Age site of Candeleda (Avila) (Fernandez Gomez 1986, 882-905).

These 'negative' features, as it were, allow us to attempt a definition of the complex term 'Romanization'. 'Romanization' may be defined as a gradual change affecting provincial society, caused by the adoption (at least at an élite level) of the main strands of Roman practices of government, law, language, dress and culture. It does not imply a mere imitation of Roman customs and values, but rather a fusion of Roman and native elements to form a new and dynamic cultural identity. Although Roman and/or Italian soldiers, traders, administrators were important vehicles of cultural change, the main impetus came from the periphery (that is, from the provincial élite) rather than from the imperial capital. Romanization should not be seen as a cultural matrix imposed on a native society by Rome.[3]

The Physical and Human Geography of Lusitania
Ever since Nero sent Otho to be governor of the province (Tac. *Hist.* 1.21; cfr. 1.13), Lusitania has had something of a reputation as a backwater of the Empire. It suffers constantly from comparison with its neighbour, the highly Romanized, and exceptional, province of Baetica. In Pliny the Elder's list of Spanish towns of privileged status (*NH* 4.22.117), Lusitania can boast only a small fraction of the number of towns in Baetica. But this does not necessarily mean that Lusitania was a backwater throughout the Roman period. The source of Pliny's information may well be the map of the Roman Empire prepared for Agrippa; if so, his information may well be Augustan in date. As we shall see, it is only in the Augustan period that the foundations of urban development in Lusitania are laid. There were two important factors that affected the development of cities in Lusitania, as in other provinces of the western Empire: (a) the nature of the local environment and (b) the extent of Iron Age urban development. That is, local ecological and climatic conditions had to be favourable for successful agriculture, to provide the economic base for an urban community and, secondly, Roman towns are more likely to have flourished in areas that had already seen some form of urban development in the pre-Augustan period. It is the purpose of this section to assess briefly where the environmental and cultural conditions were conducive to urban development, and hence Romanization, in Lusitania.

The Physical Background
First, the physical background. The Iberian peninsula is renowned for the diversity of its physical conditions, and the area that comprised the province of Lusitania is no exception. For discussion, it will be convenient to divide the province into its three Roman administrative subdivisions: the *conventus Pacensis*, the *conventus Emeritensis* and *the conventus Scallabitanus* (Fig. 11.1).

(a) The Conventus Pacensis
Much of this *conventus* consists of an extensive plateau or tableland between two rivers, the Tagus and the Guadiana – now called the Alentejo. For the most part it is covered with tough

maquis or scrub, which supports some olive groves and plantations of evergreen oak, especially the cork oak. Pigs are well suited to this environment and can often be seen foddering on the acorns. Two fertile zones for cereal culture occur around modern Beja and Evora, in medieval times two very important wheat producing areas of Portugal (Oliveira Marques 1978, 77-80). Beja (the Roman colony of Pax Iulia) is surrounded by a high density of Roman villas, which suggests that this was an agriculturally fertile region also in the Roman period (Gorges 1979, 471-477; Alarcão, Etienne and Mayet forthcoming). The territory of Evora (the Roman *municipium* of Ebora) has so far revealed fewer traces of Roman rural settlement, but this is one area of the province in which Lusitanian senators are known to have owned land (Etienne 1982). The southerly part of the plateau is crossed by the important Iberian Pyrites Belt and many Roman copper and silver mines are known from the area, including the major mine of Vipasca (Aljustrel) (Edmondson 1987, 25-99, 208-221). The coastal strip, the Algarve, although narrow, is relatively fertile, especially now for fruit crops, and has easy access to the sea, which led to the development of many fish-processing centres along the coast for the production of *garum, liquamen* and other fish-sauces (Edmondson 1987, 100-198, 255-269 and Edmondson forthcoming a).

(b) The Conventus Emeritensis

This *conventus* covered much of Extremadura, one of the most desolate areas of Spain. But there are pockets of fertility: most notably, the Tierra de Barros, which formed part of the territory of the provincial capital, Augusta Emerita, and which has revealed traces of Roman centuriation (Rodriguez Diaz 1986; Gorges 1982; Sillières 1982). Conditions are also reasonably favourable in the Tagus valley around Caesarobriga (modern Talavera de la Reina) and in the valley of the Tormes around Salmantica (modern Salamanca). But although soil conditions may be promising, the climate is less so, consisting of "tres meses de invierno, nueve de infierno" ("three months of winter and nine of Hell") according to a local proverb of Extremadura. Apart from these areas the tableland between the Guadiana and the Tagus consists of mainly rocky soils which can support little but heathland, while to the north of the Tagus rise the central Sierras (the Sierra de Gredos, de Gata and de Francia), areas of the peninsula remote and for much of their history cut off from the civilizations based in the plain. The terrain levels out again into the Castilian plateau either side of the river Duero.

Much then of this *conventus* could support little productive agriculture; stock-raising has always been more dominant: in the Middle Ages there was widespread, state- controlled transhumance between the upland, summer pastures of the sierras and the lowland, winter pastures in the plains (Klein 1920).

(c) The Conventus Scallabitanus

The central Meseta does not extend this far west, and so the landscape of this *conventus* is much more fragmented, cut east-west by a series of river valleys and intervening mountain ranges. However, favourable conditions prevail in the fluvial plain of the Tagus between Olisipo (modern Lisbon) and Scallabis (modern Santarém) for agriculture, as well as for vines and olives; in the Middle Ages this area was known as the 'granary' of Portugal (Oliveira Marques 1978, 72-77). In the valleys of the Mondego and Vouga agriculture is practised along terraces and is favoured by the more temperate Atlantic climate. Furthermore, many of these river valleys were also rich in metals and many Roman mining sites have been located. However, in the interior the higher ground provides little prospect of successful agriculture,

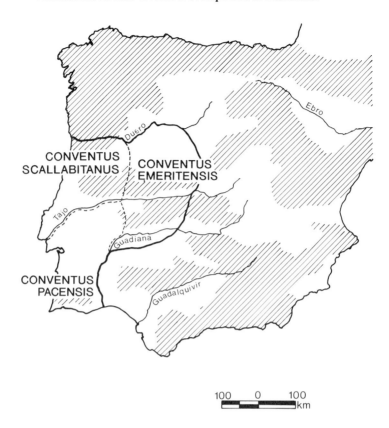

Fig. 11.1 Map of the Iberian Peninsula, showing the terrain, the limits of Lusitania and the Conventus boundaries.

but does contain some Roman gold and tin mines (Edmondson 1987, 231-243). Even now these regions support very low densities of settlement.

Cities then required favourable agricultural conditions to flourish, and these are only forthcoming in certain areas, notably in the river valleys with their richer alluvial soils. The open plateaux, with their poor soils and harsh climate, or still more the more mountainous zones could not support large cities. Furthermore, mountainous areas would have presented problems of communication between urban centre and rural hinterland; thus the classical Roman settlement pattern was not suited to this environment.

The Human Background

Rome was faced not only with a mosaic of differing physical regions when she came to organize the province, but also with very differing degrees of indigenous urbanization. (Fig. 11.2) Furthermore, Roman penetration came only in stages, which in turn led to further regional imbalance in cultural development. Ethnically the province was composed of a variety of peoples (Alarcão 1983, 17-21). The Algarve and southern Alentejo had been inhabited by the Conii, or Cynetes, who had developed not only proto-urbanized communities (e.g.

Conistorgis), but also their own alphabet and script, before they were overwhelmed by Celtic invaders from the central Spanish Meseta in the fifth or fourth century BC (Almagro Basch 1966, 210-11; Coelho 1971). These Celts came to occupy the whole of the Alentejo; they settled in characteristic hill-forts (or 'castros'), and introduced a distinctive form of pottery akin to that found in Celtiberian settlements of the central Meseta (Maia 1980; Arnaud and Gamito 1974-77). But in this zone there were also immigrants from Turdetania (part of Roman Baetica), Turduli, who, by contrast, established communities that may be described as 'proto-urban' at, for example, Balsa (Tavira), Ossonoba (Faro), Myrtilis (Mértola), Pax Iulia (Beja), Salacia (Alcácer do Sal) and Caetobriga (Setúbal) (Maia 1980). Some of these communities had minted their own copper coinage in the pre-Augustan period, a mark of their relatively advanced society (Vives 1924, 81 (Baesuris), 114 (Ossonoba), 85 (Silves), 24-27 (Salacia), 90-91 (Myrtilis)). Strabo comments (3.2.15) that the Celtici were influenced in Hellenistic ways by the proximity of the Turduli, but crucially were not persuaded to adopt an urbanized way of life.

The area to the north of the Tagus in modern Portugal was occupied by the Lusitani, probably a generic term covering a multiplicity of smaller peoples (*populi*), who also settled in hill-top enclosures, each one forming the central place for a kinship grouping. The river valleys and coastal areas, however, being more open to cultural influences from outside, saw a greater development of proto-urban communities in the pre-Augustan age: for example, Talabriga (? Marnel), Aeminium (Coimbra), Conimbriga (Condeixa-a-Velha), Collippo (S. Sebastião do Freixo), Eburobrittium (Amoreira de Obidos) and Olisipo (Lisbon). On a smaller scale, the Iron Age settlement at Olaia (near Figueira da Foz: Fig. 11.3) has revealed signs of a primitive kind of proto-urban layout, as well as imported Phoenico-Punic glass and ceramics (dos Santos Rocha 1905-08). Similarly Greek and Punic artefacts have been found in some abundance at Salacia (Alcácer do Sal) on the Sado, the major entrepot for the exchange of metals for imported goods (Tavares da Silva et al. 1980-81). But such contact with Greeks or Phoenico-Punic traders (whose origin was probably the Phoenician colonies in southern Spain rather than Phoenicia proper) was not totally restricted to coastal regions (Harrison 1988). Occasionally finds have also been made well in the interior: for example, at Medellín (Badajoz) (Almagro Gorbea 1970) or at hill-forts at Botija or Berzocana (both in Cáceres: Fig. 11.3) (Soria Sanchez 1985, 490). The explanation for this presumably lies in the significant mineral wealth of the interior. Phoenico-Punic traders sailed up the Atlantic coast to exchange their luxury goods for such metals extracted by native labour. Some of these goods found their way inland and served as prestige items for the native élites in their local centres of power.

The land north of the Tagus in Spain was occupied by the Vettones, whose material culture was essentially Celtic and who also settled in hill- forts: for example, Las Cogotas, Cardeñosa (Avila: Fig. 11.3) (Cabré Aguilo 1930 and 1932). Again 'Vettones' is probably a generic term, possibly invented by their Roman conquerors. Their territory is neatly defined by the distribution of zoomorphic sculptures of pigs, wild boars and sheep (Roldán Hervas 1968-69; Lopez Monteagudo 1982; Salinas de Frías 1986).

There was, therefore, in broad terms a distinct contrast between the Celticized interior of the province, marked by a 'castro culture' and those regions more accessible to external influences from more developed societies. It is no coincidence that all the communities of Lusitania that received municipal status in the Augustan organization of the province (Ebora, Myrtilis, Olisipo and Salacia) had their origins as proto-urban settlements in the later Iron

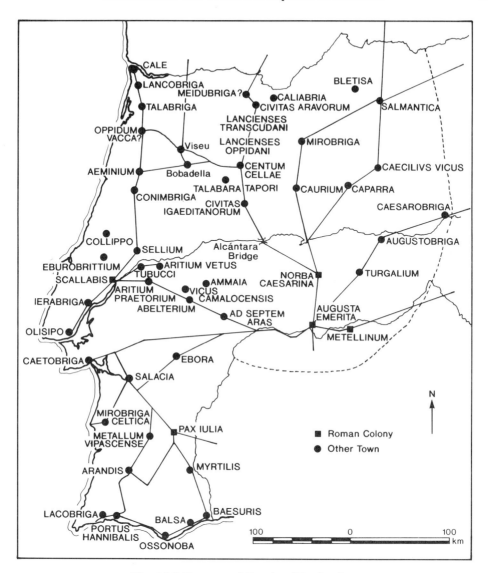

Fig. 11.2 Towns and Roads of Lusitania.

Age under the influence of immigrant peoples and cultural ideas (Plin. *NH* 4.22.117; with Galsterer 1971).

Hill Forts and Iron-Age Proto-Urbanization

A rough guide to the spread of Iron Age hill-forts in shown in Fig. 11.4. Few of these sites have been excavated thoroughly, while intensive field-survey would undoubtedly reveal many more. These hill-forts can hardly be described as 'cities' and Strabo (3.4.13) is right to criticize Polybius for claiming that Ti. Sempronius Gracchus destroyed 300 Celtiberian 'cities'; historians and generals, he reports, often made this false claim, to enhance the general's chance of a triumph. But there is growing archaeological evidence to suggest that they represent an essential first phase of 'proto-urbanization'. It might be thought that these 'castros' were merely places of refuge for use in times of military insecurity. But what is becoming clear is that there was a definite hierarchy of settlements; some of the larger 'castros' had much more permanent economic, religious and political functions, as suggested by their extra-mural burial grounds, stone-built houses, religious sanctuaries and mill-stones for rotary grain mills (as well as carbonized cereal seeds).[4] Even occasionally there is trace of social stratification within the hill-fort: so at Serra da Segovia, near Elvas there was clear differentiation in the style of buildings (Gamito 1982); or at Berzocana (Cáceres) the collections of precious jewellery must have served as status symbols for members of the indigenous élite (Soria Sanchez 1985).

Although isolated finds of Phoenico-Punic or Greek pottery have already been noted, more significant are the cultural ideas that these Mediterranean peoples may have transmitted to this Celtic area. Acculturation is visible in two distinct spheres: (a) religion and (b) urban layout. First, the metaphysical: cult and religious practice. A large votive deposit has recently been excavated at Garvão, Ourique (in the territory of the Celtici); native incised wares of the fourth century BC were found alongside Attic finewares, Punic glassware, two representations of the Punic deity Tanit and various silvered and gilt discs representing eyes. These discs suggest that the hoard was deposited as part of rituals associated with a local healing god, akin to the Greco-Roman Aesculapius (Mello Beirão et al., 1985).[5] Furthermore, the whole ritual practice of 'bothros' (or ritual depositing of cult objects) is familiar from Greco-Roman chthonic cults (Burkert 1985, 199-200).

But more dramatic are two sanctuary sites dated to the later Iron Age. First, the large, mud-brick complex at Cancho Roano, near Zalamea de la Serena (Badajoz). Alongside Iberian banded and painted wares, hundreds of Attic black-glazed pots have been discovered, which would suggest contact with the East Mediterranean world. Furthermore, the style of the building is reminiscent of buildings from the Greek site at Al-Mina on the Orontes. Its exact function is, however, extremely controversial: it has been interpreted as a large ash-altar (Blanco Freijeiro 1981), or, more plausibly, a sanctuary, possibly of the indigenous goddess Ataecina, which was later reused as a cremation site for the Lusitanian élite (Maluquer de Motes 1983; cf. Harrison 1988, 132-4). What is clear that this imposing structure must have made a striking impact on the local landscape and the local society. In its scale and in its two distinctive, successive phases and functions of operation, it bears some similarities with the Toumba complex at Lefkandi (Euboea). Might Cancho Roano not then have been the residence of a local aristocrat, on whose death the house was transformed into a cult place for the dead hero ? In other words, the monument may attest the introduction of not only Greek pottery, but also the Greek custom of hero-cult into this region (see Harrison 1988, 113-21 for some Iberian parallels). Secondly, an Iron Age temple has been discovered at the Celtic hill-fort at Santiago do Cacém, which was later developed into the Roman *municipium* of Mirobriga Celtica, its name preserving trace of its native origin. The form of the temple is hybrid:h it had a Hellenized *pronaos* and *cella*, but was squarish in shape in the Celtic tradition (Slade et al. 1983, 56-58). Its cultic importance is stressed by the fact that it was not destroyed when the forum of the *municipium* was being laid out; rather, it was integrated into the monumental centre and flanked by two Roman temples.

The second sphere of acculturation is more physical, i.e., urban layout. Houses of rectangular plan appear with some frequency in 'castros' of the second and first centuries BC. This style of building would again seem to owe its origin to cultural ideas introduced

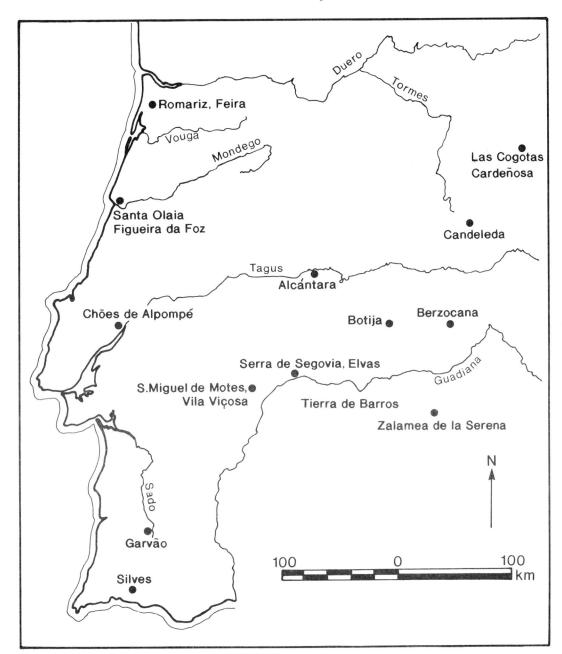

Fig. 11.3 Map showing the smaller sites discussed.

from the East Mediterranean world; significantly, it does not occur north of the river Vouga, where houses of circular plan (for example, at Romariz, Feira: de Almeida 1975, 492) mark the 'castros' in this region as being much more akin to the cultural world of Galicia (on which

Tranoy 1981; Pereira Menaut 1984). But even more eloquent testimony to cultural development than just the appearance of houses of rectangular plan is the occasional organization of these houses into something approaching an urban layout. So at the Vettonian site of Berzocana (Cáceres) rectangular houses were arranged in parallel streets (Soria Sanchez 1985, 490); while at Lusitanian Conimbriga a primitive form of grid system was layed down in the later Iron Age: the two main streets intersected at an angle of 75 degrees, thus grouping the houses into trapezoidal *insulae* (Alarcão and Etienne 1977, 17-25).

But perhaps the most revealing of all recent archaeological discoveries for the development of urban structures is the bronze surrender pact dated precisely to 104 BC found in a (?Vettonian) hill-fort at Villavieja, near Alcántara (Meleno, Sanchez Abal et al, 1984; *AE* 1984, 495; Richardson 1986, 199-201). It records the surrender of a *populus* to the Roman general L. Caesius; the Romans agree to return intact to the *populus* their "buildings, their laws and everything else that was theirs on the day before the surrender". At first sight it might appear that here is a native community that had already acquired a permanent centre, with (? public) buildings and had developed some kind of legal code. But those senatorial decrees concerning settlements after Roman victories in the Greek East (e.g. the decree re. Thisbae of 170 BC: *FIRA* I 31, esp. ll. 25-31; or decree re. Koroneia of 171/70 BC: *SEG* XIX 374; and cf. Polybius 36.4.1-3) show that the Alcántara text may merely be reproducing a standard Roman administrative formula and thus does not necessarily provide distinctive information about its local context. However, the arrival of the Romans in the area and the imposition of such regulations, couched in Roman terms, helped to introduce more advanced cultural ideas. Native *legati* are mentioned in our document, which suggests the existence, or imposition by the Romans, of some form of political hierarchy. It is unclear if the entire *populus* resided within the walls of the 'castro' at Villavieja, or whether Villavieja was established as the 'chief-place' of the *populus* with more dispersed settlement throughout its territory; for there were other smaller 'castros' in the neighbourhood (Meleno et al. 1984, 308-310), perhaps subordinated politically to Villavieja. Finally, the engraving and display of the bronze plaque in the civic centre of the *populus* suggests at least that the familiar Greco-Roman practice of the setting up of inscriptions in the civic centre was being transmitted to this part of the Celtic world (see further Edmondson forthcoming b).

Thus, such archaeological data suggest that there had been some cultural development even in interior, Celticised parts of the later Roman province of Lusitania in the pre- Augustan period. They lead one to reject as unreliable Strabo's picture of a barbarian world that only received civilization (which to Strabo was essentially urbanocentric) at the hands of Rome. Cultural influences from the eastern Mediterranean had reached the area well before the Romans.

The Contribution of Augustus

The province of Lusitania was created when Augustus divided the Republican *provincia* of Hispania Ulterior into Baetica and Lusitania at an uncertain date (Albertini 1932; cf. *Cambridge Ancient History* X 345). One of Augustus' first concerns was to hold a provincial census throughout the Empire (*RG* 8.2). The efficient way to conduct such a project was by dealing with city + territory units (*civitates*); the local magistrates were then responsible for their own *civitates* (Brunt 1981). There is no doubt that a provincial census was held in Lusitania under Augustus, since an inscription preserves the name of an equestrian official

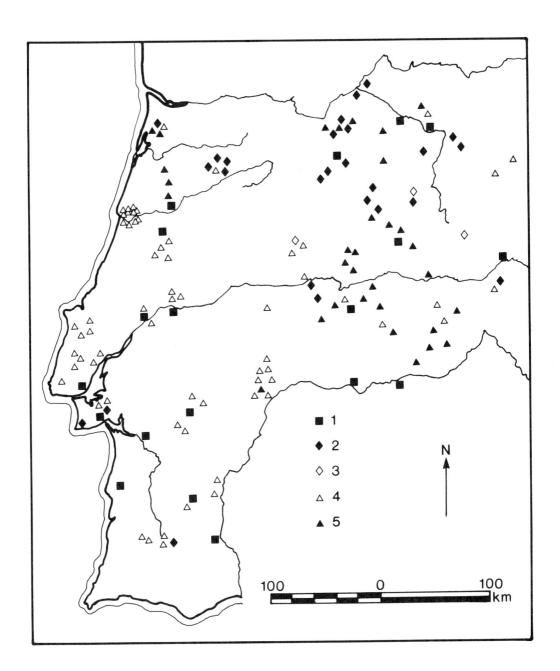

Fig. 11.4 Map showing the hill-forts of Lusitania.

Legend: 1. site that developed into colonia or municipium; 2. site that continued as a vicus under the Roman Empire; 3. site shifted to form a Roman settlement; 4. site abandoned with no Roman occupation; 5. site without information about abandonment or continuity.

sent to the province 'pro censore' (*CIL* X 680). It, therefore, follows that some attention must already have been paid to the internal subdivision of the province into city + territory units. Few problems existed in the *conventus Pacensis*, for example, where cities with fixed territories had already developed in the pre-imperial period. But in other parts of the province substantial efforts had still to be made. The first step was to ensure that endemic brigandage was stopped and the *pax romana* established. The Romans then had to ensure that the peoples that made up the province were settled within fixed limits, with an urban centre established as the focal point for administrative purposes. As far as possible, the Romans would have been keen to use already existing tribal boundaries, but more commonly had to divide the peoples into *civitates* and define their territories more clearly than had previously been the case.The efforts of the early provincial governors can in part be gauged from those inscribed boundary markers (*termini Augustales*) that have survived (Fig. 11.5). Most of them can be dated to AD 4-6, although the example from Goujoim, Armamar (Viseu) dates either to AD 46-7 or to AD 59, depending on which emperor's name is restored to the text (Vaz 1979). This shows that the settlement of all such boundaries was not necessarily effected immediately; there was certainly an initial phase of organization under Augustus, but further action or modification was necessary well into the first century AD. It would be surprising if there were no disputes between neighbouring peoples over these boundaries and this later marker may well reflect the settlement of a controversy. However, in all cases it was the responsibility of the provincial governor to arrange the limits of each *civitas*. The geographical spread is shown in Fig. 11.5. With the exception of the three markers relating to the territory of Augusta Emerita,[6] all have been found north of the Tagus in Vettonian or Lusitanian territory, i.e., in areas where pastoralism had been the dominant element in the local economy in the Iron Age. Here cities with clearly defined territories had not been the rule. The lack of finds of such markers in more urbanized areas seems not to be coincidental.

For the creation of new urban centres the Romans preferred to promote an already existing proto-urbanized settlement to be the capital of the *civitas*; thus, Mediolanum in Cisalpine Gaul was developed from being a mere village to be the *civitas* capital of the Insubres (Strabo 5.1.6), while Vienna in Transalpine Gaul became the capital of the Allobroges (Strabo 4.1.11). If I was correct to argue that some *populi* in Lusitania had already developed central places, then much of the groundwork had already been done. Together with the promotion of an existing settlement, the Romans seem also to have allowed the tribal aristocracy of the original settlement to remain as the élite of the new urban centre. Thus the local aristocracy would be willing to support the interests of Rome to ensure hthat they maintained their dominant positions within their local societies (see Goudineau 1979, 308 for the same process in southern Gaul).

Just as Cn. Iulius Agricola as governor of Roman Britain was seen by Tacitus to "privately encourage and publicly assist" the processes of urbanization in Britain (Tac. *Agr.* 21), so the provincial governors of Lusitania would have given similar encouragement and assistance. The town of Idanha-a-Velha (Roman name unknown) was set up as the *civitas* capital of the Igaeditani. The earliest phase of its urbanization can be dated to the Augustan period (de Almeida 1977, 41). Furthermore, a sun-dial was donated to the community in 16 BC by a citizen of the provincial capital, Augusta Emerita (*AE* 1967, 144). The provincial capital would have been especially important in providing the lead and encouraging urbanization in native communities, a point to which we shall return. The names of the *magistri* of the

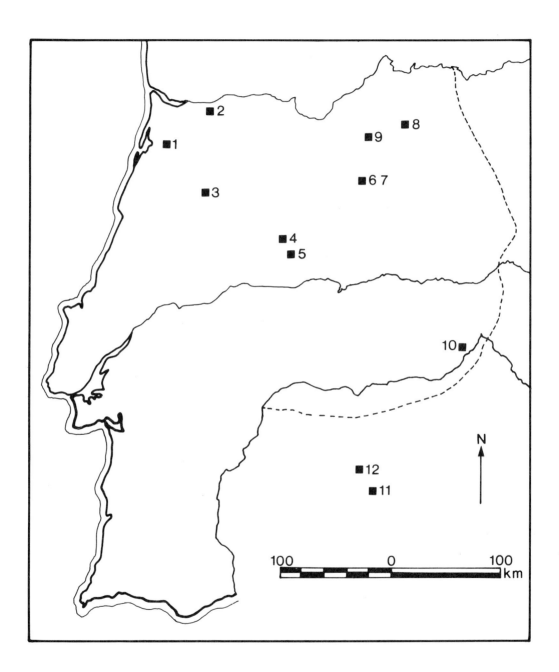

Fig. 11.5 Map showing the geographical spread of Termini Augustales in Lusitania.
For sites see Table 11.1

Igaeditani reflect the heavily Celticised nature of the local society: Toutonus Arci f., Malgeinus Manli f., Celtus Arantoni f. and Amminus Ati f.. The presence of magistrates at this early date again illustrates that Rome had to provide political models for the *civitas* capitals to adopt. Furthermore, the Roman provincial governor needed to operate through the local élite and so political structures had to be established immediately in such new communities. The establishment of the urban centre should be viewed in the wider regional context: it was accompanied by the fixing of boundaries between the Igaeditani and the Lancienses in AD 4-5 (cf. *AE* 1976, 273) and the construction of the road which linked the town with Norba Caesarina (modern Cáceres), a Roman colony, and thence the provincial capital, Emerita.

Abandonment and Continuity of Iron Age Settlements under Roman Rule

The Roman habit of resettling hostile mountain-dwellers on flatter ground is a leitmotif of the ancient accounts of Roman expansion, first, within Italy and, later, throughout the Mediterranean world (e.g. Polyb. 1.65, Liv. *Per.* 19). As for Lusitania, Strabo (3.1.6) talks of

No.	Location	Date (AD)	Tribes	Reference
1.	Oliveira de Azemeis, Arouca	4-5	? Talabrigenses ? Lancienses	*HAEp* 1442; *AP*, 1953, 209
2.	Goujoim, Armamar	46-7 or 59	Coilarni ? Arabrigenses	*Conimbriga*, 1979, 135-158
3.	Guardão-Caramulo, Tondela	4-5	[...]ienses	*AE* 1954, 88
4.	Peroviseu, Fundão	4-5	Lancienses Igaeditani	*AE* 1976, 273 *Conimbriga*, 1977, 27-8
5.	Monsanto Valverde, near Idanha	5-6	Lancienses Oppidani Igaeditani	*CIL* II 460
6.	MIROBRIGA	5-6	Salmanticenses Mirobrigenses	*CIL* II 857
7.	MIROBRIGA	5-6	Mirobrigenses Bletisenses	*CIL* II 858
8.	Ledesma	6	Bletisenses Mirobrigenses Salmanticenses	*CIL* II 859
9.	Traguntia, Virlanga, SE of Yecla de Yeltes	6	[Mi]robrigenses [...]polibedenses	*CIL* II 5033
10.	Valdecaballeros	?	pratores col. Aug. Emer.	*BRAH* 1918, 152
11.	Montemolin	Domitian	Ucubi Augusta Emerita	*CIL* II 656
12.	Valencia del Ventosa	?		Alvárez Martinez 1986, 105

Table 11.1 The geographical spread of Termini Augustales

Roman name	modern	reference
(a) AUGUSTAN *MUNICIPIA* (cf. PLIN. *NH* 4.22.117)		
1. EBORA LIBERALITAS IULIA	Évora	García y Bellido 1971, 87
2. MYRTILIS	Mértola	Alves 1956, 41-45
3. SALACIA URBS IMPERATORIA	Alcácer do Salal.	Tavares da Silva *et al,* 1980-81, 181-7
4. OLISIPO FELICITAS IULIA	Lisbon	Vieira da Silva 1944, 40-41
(b) ROMAN COLONIES (cf. PLIN. *NH* 4.22.117)		
1. AUGUSTA EMERITA	Mérida	Alvárez Martinez 1984
2. METELLINUM	Medellín	Almagro Gorbea 1971
3. NORBA CAESARINA	Cáceres	Callejo Serrano 1968, 121
4. PAX IULIA	Beja	Ribeiro 1960
5. SCALLABIS PRAESIDIUM IULIUM	Santarém	Arruda & Catarino 1982; Arruda 1983-84

*Table 11.2 Iron Age sites in Lusitania which developed
into Augustan Municipia and Roman Colonies*

mountain-dwellers being transplanted by the Romans from their lairs in the north of the province to the Tagus-Anas mesopotamia, while Cassius Dio claims (37.52.3-4) that the professed reason for Caesar's campaigns of 61 BC against the inhabitants of the Mons Herminius (the Serra da Estrêla) was to resettle them on lower ground. He talks of 'cities' being abandoned to Caesar, but must mean hill-top settlements. Such literary anecdotes have led scholars to make some rather sweeping statements: for example, that "the native population was displaced very frequently under Roman rule" (Blázquez 1975, 26). However, a consideration of the archaeological material provides a substantial corrective, since it demonstrates that the Iron Age hill-top sites experienced a variety of different fates under the Roman Empire. Some were abandoned, but many continued to function as rural *vici*, while some were even developed into *civitas* capitals, *municipia* or Roman *coloniae*.

First, Roman colonies and Augustan *municipia* in Lusitania. By definition, the four towns that were granted municipal status under Augustus must have all been flourishing urban centres in the first century BC and this is indeed confirmed by archaeological evidence (see Table 11.2a). More interestingly, all five Roman colonies were also founded on sites that had already seen some settlement in the later Iron Age (see Table 11.2b). However, with the exception of Metellinum they seem not to have undergone substantial urban development before the establishment of the Roman colonies. The published evidence for Iron Age settlement at these cities is cited in Table 11.2.

Secondly, many native settlements had not developed to a sufficient extent by the Augustan period to warrant municipal status, but they had been promoted to be the urban centres of the

Roman name	modern	reference
(a) Conventus Emeritensis		
MIROBRIGA	Ciudad Rodrigo	Martín Valls 1976, 373
CAESAROBRIGA	Talavera de la Reina	Jiménez de Gregorio 1952, 157;
		Alföldy 1987, 58-9
CAPERA	Ventas de Capara	Beltrán Lloris 1973, 3
BLETISA	Las Merchanas,	Maluquer de Motes
	Lumbrales	1956, 74-87
(b) Conventus Pacensis		
OSSONOBA	Faro	cf. Strabo 3.2.5
BALSA	Tavira	cf. lead coins from first century B.C.:
		Casariego *et al.* 1987, 79, 121-2
MIROBRIGA CELTICA	Santiago do Cacém	Slade *et al.* 1983, 54-9
? CAETOBRIGA	Setúbal	Soares & Tavares da Silva 1986
(c) Conventus Scallabitanus		
SELLIUM	Tomar	da Ponte 1985a; 1985b
CONIMBRIGA	Condeixa-a-Velha	Alarcão & Étienne 1977, 17-25
AEMINIUM	Coimbra	Alarcão 1979

Table 11.3 Iron Age sites granted municipal status under the Flavians

new *civitates* for the purposes of the Roman administration of the province. Some of these were granted municipal status under the Flavians (Galsterer 1971). The archaeological evidence for their occupation in the later Iron Age is set out in Table 11.3.

Thirdly, many Iron Age hill-forts failed to develop into fully urbanised communities, but continued to function as smaller centres – most often as rural *vici*. Two areas illustrate this particularly. First, the modern Portuguese *distrito* of Viseu, a mountainous zone and one of scant Romanization: very few Roman villas sites have to date been discovered here (for example, the villa at Quinta do Costa, Chãs de Tavares, Mangualde: *Informação Arqueológica* 5 (1982-83), 144-45), but many hill- forts continued in existence under the Roman Empire.[7] Secondly, the Spanish province of Salamanca, where urban centres only developed along the major Emerita to Asturica road, with some villas appearing in the later Empire (Gorges 1979, 344-46; Pinel 1981). Off this route, no villas are found and inscriptions reveal the scant adoption of Roman names and the widespread survival of native extended kinship groupings and native deities (Maluquer de Motes 1956, passim).[8]

However, exact continuity in the nucleus of the settlement was not always the rule; in some areas there were slight shifts to lower ground. Cerro de Berrueco, Béjar provides a good example: the Iron Age nucleus was situated in the foothills of the Sierra de Gredos; at the end of the first century BC a shift to lower ground took place, with settlement thereafter at two distinct nuclei (El Tejado and Los Tejares) (Cesar Moran 1924-25, 22-24; Maluquer de Motes 1956, 117). Similarly at Salmantica the Roman town was developed in the vicinity of, but not on the exact site of the Iron Age hill-fort (Maluquer de Motes 1951, 72). Again, some hill-forts were abandoned as settlements, but continued in use as religious sanctuaries: for example, El Raso de Candeleda, Avila, where the main settlement and its connected cemetery were abandoned at the end of the first century BC for a new settlement at Candeleda itself on the left bank of the Tiétar, but a connected sanctuary to Endovellicus continued to function under the Roman Empire (Fernandez Gomez 1986, 882-905).

This evidence for whole or partial continuity should not obscure the fact that in some cases the Iron Age hill-forts were abandoned – often, it seems, during Roman military activity in the region, as, for example, at Las Cogotas, Cardeñosa (Avila), abandoned in the early second century BC (Cabré Aguilo 1930 and 1932). However, many hill-forts were abandoned not as a result of Roman military action, but on the initiative of the native population itself. The Lisbon peninsula, for example, had been an area of fairly intense hill-top settlement in the Bronze Age and early Iron Age, but none of these sites remained in occupation into the Roman period. The reasons for this change may well be connected with the lack of warfare in the area and the increased contact with Phoenicians, Carthaginians and Romans. The eventual presence of the Roman army and their use of Olisipo (Lisbon) and Moron (possibly Chões de Alpompé: Kalb and Höck 1984) as bases (Strabo 3.3.1) will have encouraged the intensification of settled agriculture, since the Roman army constituted a ready market for local food supplies. The natives will then have preferred to locate themselves closer to this new Roman military market.

The evidence from Lusitania, therefore, does not suggest that the abandonment of, or the shifts in the main nucleus of, hill-top settlements should be explained merely as a result of Roman military activity. The hill-fort at Villavieja, Alcántara, where the surrender document of the local *populus* to the Roman army in 104 BC was inscribed and set up in its civic centre, (see above, p. 160), clearly remained in occupation long after its surrender to Rome, as the coins (of Augustus, Tiberius, Trajan, Constantine and Theodosius) found here also suggest (Meleno et al. 1984, 315-323). Perhaps a key to explaining the cases where Iron Age settlements were abandoned, or shifted, is provided by an inscription from Sabora in Baetica (*CIL* II 1433 = *ILS* 6092). The people of Sabora made a special request of the emperor Vespasian in AD 78 to be allowed to move their *oppidum* down from its hill-top location to the plain below. From the emperor's reply it is clear that the move was desirable, if not essential, on economic, not political grounds. The siting of their *oppidum* on high ground had led to great economic difficulties, perhaps caused by a combination of unsatisfactory agrarian conditions in the vicinity of their settlement and inaccessibility to the Roman road network and hence other urban centres in the region and especially their markets. The occupants of Lusitanian hill-forts may similarly have desired to locate themselves in closer proximity to the roads and towns of the Roman province and so abandoned their hill-forts of their own accord. It would seem unwarranted and over-generalised to say that all such changes in settlement in Lusitania were effected as a result of Roman military actions and for Roman administrative convenience.

Monumentalization and Urban Development

We have been taught, from Tacitus onwards, to see public monuments as the principal criterion of urban development in the Roman Empire (Tac. *Agr.* 21). The evidence for the nature of the monumental centres of Lusitania is not abundant, but is increasing all the time as a result of excavation and topographical detective work. For, first, urban centres were much fewer in number than in Baetica; and, secondly, most of the Roman towns of Lusitania have remained in occupation, thus removing much of the evidence for their Roman centres. In addition, relatively few building inscriptions are to hand from the province. But what is clear from the available evidence is that Roman-style buildings were erected even in towns located in remoter parts of the province. Thus Bobadella (to the north of the Serra da Estrêla) had a monumental centre with a forum equipped with entrance arches, an amphitheatre, a temple of Neptune and one dedicated to the 'Genius Municipi' (Maia do Amaral 1983; *Informação Arqueológica* 5

(1982-83), 72). Furthermore, stylistic similarities are often discernible between buildings in different towns of the province; the temple at Ebora, for example, was closely modelled on the so-called 'Temple of Diana' (but most likely a temple for the imperial cult) at Emerita (Hauschild 1982), while the bridges at Alter do Chão, at Capera, at Salmantica and over the Aljucen are all similar in design and fabric to that over the Guadiana at Emerita (Alvárez Martinez and Diaz Pintiado 1982, 100). Similarly, the theatres at Metellinum and at Olisipo are clearly modelled on that at Emerita, dedicated in 16 BC (del Amo 1982, 324 on Metellinum; Alarcão 1982, 288 on Olisipo; *CIL* II 474 for date of Emerita theatre). The role of the provincial capital is especially important here; as a Roman colony with its distinctively Roman style of buildings, as we shall see, Emerita provided an ideal model for the other towns of the province when they came to lay out their urban monumental centres. We have already seen how a citizen of Emerita helped in setting up the urban centre of the Igaeditani (see above, p. 162).

But to examine in greater detail the ways in which the urban centres of Lusitania developed under Roman rule, I shall concentrate in this final section on the monumental centres of two towns: Augusta Emerita and Conimbriga, the former as an example of a provincial capital, developed by the Roman authorities as an eloquent symbol of Roman power over the province, the latter a good example of how an Iron Age *oppidum* developed its urban centre in response to being part of the Roman Empire. Emerita provides a striking example of how urban monumentalization was planned from the centre, Rome, while Conimbriga allows us to look at monumentalization from a peripheral perspective.

Augusta Emerita

In 25 BC P. Carisius, *legatus propraetore* of Augustus, destroyed the town of Lancia in north-west Spain and for the settlement of his veterans founded the colony of Augusta Emerita at the confluence of the Guadiana and the Albarregas rivers, at a point where the major north-south land route in the west of the peninsula crossed the Guadiana on its way to Hispalis (Dio 53.26.1). From the start an ambitious programme of monumentalization was undertaken. For colonies served not only as garrison posts to keep the local population in check, but also as models, or even 'mirror images' of what a Roman town should look like for the benefit of the locals, as Cicero observed of Narbo (Cic. *Pro Font.* 13). The basis for the new urban layout was a rectangular grid of streets crossing at right angles along Hippodamean lines. The Roman sewer system can be reconstructed, and this provides the key to the colony's initial layout (Richmond 1930, 99, 102, 106). On the basis of recent topographical work, Emerita, like Tarraco, had two forums: one (near the modern calle Sagasta and calle de Baños) as the forum of the colony, the other (near the modern plaza del Parador Nacional de Turismo) as the forum of the province and of major significance for the provincial cult of the emperors (Alvárez Martinez 1982; 1985, 41-42).

As a vital part of the initial layout of the colony, bridges were built across the Guadiana and the Albarregas, while the Guadiana was dyked to prevent its flooding (Alvárez Martinez 1983). The water supply was assured from an early date, with the three aqueduct systems all probably dating to the Augustan monumentalization (so Canto 1982; *AE* 1984, 493; Alvárez Martinez 1985, 42-43). Two sets of public baths have been discovered in connexion with these aqueducts, one in the aptly named calle de Baños (Alvárez Martinez 1985, 41). Public recreation buildings were also constructed in the very earliest years of the colony. The theatre was dedicated in 16 BC (*CIL* II 474; Melida 1915; Saenz de Buruaga 1982), the amphitheatre in 8 BC (Menendez Pidal 1957), while the circus seems to have been built in the reign of Tiberius (Saenz de Buruaga and Alvárez Martinez 1977; Humphrey 1986, 362-376). Temples also formed a major element of the initial monumentalization. A coin type of the colony issued under Tiberius depicts a temple with the legend 'Aeternitati Augustae' (Beltrán 1976, 97, 102-3, and PL. XXXII F). Parts of a temple of Mars can still be seen, built into the Church of Santa Eulalia (León Alonso 1970). The so-called 'temple of Diana' (but better seen as a temple for the Imperial cult) was built in the Julio-Claudian period on a podium, hexastyle and peripteral, of local granite and decorated with stucco, and probably formed part of the colonial forum (Alvárez Martinez 1976; 1985, 41); while traces of a massive temple revetted with marble plaques came to light in 1983 in the calle Holguín; it probably provided the focus for the provincial forum (Alvárez Martinez 1985, 41-42; 1986, 156).

But more importantly, these two temples seem to derive stylistically from temples in Rome itself: the 'temple of Diana' bears close similarities to the late Republican temples in the Largo Argentina (Alvárez Martinez 1976, 50), while the calle Holguín temple was possibly modelled on the Temple of Concord (Alvárez Martinez 1986, 156). The circus at Emerita is closely modelled on the Circus Maximus at Rome.[9] But even more stunning similarities with the architecture of Rome itself occur in the forum of the colony. For elements from the decoration of the surrounding portico have come to light. They consist of not only roundels (*clipei*) incorporating heads of Jupiter Ammon and Medusa, but also Caryatids, all of a high standard of craftsmanship (Squarciapino 1976 and 1982). But what is most important is that they show that this portico was modelled very closely on that in the Forum of Augustus at Rome (on which Zanker 1968; Ganzert and Kockel 1988). A high-quality marble relief – possibly of Agrippa sacrificing (Trillmich 1986) – also demonstrates the consistently metropolitan nature of the art and architecture of this new colony.

The date of these elements – and that for the monumentalization of the two forums – is uncertain, but the late Augustan or especially the Julio-Claudian period seems more likely than the early Augustan. Given the logistical problems of creating a new monumental centre from nothing (planning, designing, recruiting of architects, sculptors, artists, obtaining the necessary raw materials), it is unlikely that the whole monumental centre of Emerita could have been put up overnight. But what is clear is that Rome (especially through the agency of Agrippa) planned Emerita as a 'mirror-image' of Rome itself (cf. Kienast 1982, 336-365 for the Augustan building programme and Agrippa's role in them). Emerita was designed as a symbol of Roman power on the periphery of the Empire. The local population could now see for themselves what Roman civilization was all about and, in time, they could use Emerita as a model for urban projects elsewhere in the province.

Conimbriga

The response of an indigenous urban centre to Roman rule in Lusitania can best be gauged from the originally Celtic settlement of Conimbriga. After some proto-urban development in the later Iron Age (see above, p. 160), Conimbriga became a *civitas stipendiaria* in the Augustan organization of the province (Plin. *NH* 4.22.117) and it was in this period that Conimbriga undertook its first major phase of monumentalization along Greco-Roman lines. A forum (50m x 60m at its widest and longest points: Fig. 11.6A) was constructed in an area of Iron Age habitations (Alarcão and Etienne 1977, 28-38). It served four functions: religious, political, judicial and commercial. As for the religious, at the north end a temple was built with a skirting portico on both sides and at the rear; as for the political, on the east side a small building has been identified as a local senate-house (*curia*); as for the judicial, alongside this small senate-house was a *basilica*, while on the west side nine shops (*tabernae*) were erected, to enhance the commercial function of the forum. Furthermore, a *cryptoporticus* was constructed beneath the temple portico; this not only served to raise the level of the temple into a dominating position not allowed by the natural topography, but required in Roman town planning (Vitruv. *de Arch.* 1.7.1), but also assured communication between the new forum and the older Iron Age habitation quarter, situated on a lower level to the north of the forum. The open square of the forum was decorated with honorific statues. To the south of the forum a set of public baths were designed in the Augustan period again in a sector of Iron Age dwellings. They were supplied with water by an aqueduct system that led to a source near the modern village of Alcabideque, some 3443 metres from the cold-room of the baths (Alarcão and Etienne 1977, 41-64).

Under the Julio-Claudians typically Roman *atrium*-style houses were built to the west of the forum, while near the public baths more humble dwellings were established (Alarcão and Etienne 1977, 66-81). Thus as the town developed, greater social stratification was manifested in these differentiated habitation zones, some for the richer citizens, others for the poorer. Thus, Conimbriga provides very vivid evidence of an indigenous, Celtic community instituting an ambitious monumentalization along Greco-Roman lines immediately after its integration within the Roman Empire. The local aristocracy were thereby demonstrating their loyalty to Rome and their swift assimilation of Greco-Roman ideals of urban life.

Under Vespasian Latin rights were granted to the communities of the Iberian peninsula, under the terms of which those who held chief magistracies in the municipalities were eligible to become full Roman citizens (Plin. *NH* 3.3.30). The community of Conimbriga once again responded to this upgrading in status by remodelling its monumental centre on a conspicuous scale. First, this may have been the period when Conimbriga's extra- mural amphitheatre was constructed, but since this has not yet been excavated, its date is by no means certain (Alarcão, Mayet and Nolen 1986, 61). But most significantly, the Augustan forum was radically redesigned: it was not only enlarged, but also aligned on a new axis (Fig. 11.6B). The political and commercial buildings were removed (presumably to another, as yet unexplored site), as happened elsewhere in the Iberian peninsula in the later first century AD: for example, at Belo, where the commercial functions of the old forum were taken over by a newly constructed market-building (Didierjean et al. 1986, 94, 264-266). As a result at Conimbriga the forum became an enclosure devoted wholly to the cult of the Emperor. A still larger temple, built on a podium and with a monumental stairway, was constructed at the northern end and enclosed once again at the back and down its sides with a new portico. The expansion of the forum at the north end demanded the demolition of the Iron Age quarters and also the construction of a new *cryptoporticus*. The entrance to the forum at the south was given a monumental arch – perhaps a tetrapylon, as at Capera (Alarcão and Etienne 1977, 87-111; cf. García y Bellido 1972-74 for Capera). The public baths were substantially extended and redesigned, causing some dislocation of private housing in the vicinity in the Trajanic period (Alarcão and Etienne 1977, 113-133). There may be some significance in this date too, since Trajan of course was the first Roman Emperor to be born in Spain. But on balance I would prefer to see this as the natural completion of the Flavian monumentalization. Thereafter, there was no major redevelopment of the monumental centre, but there were frequent alterations and embellishments to the private houses.   The town was fortified in the third century, the

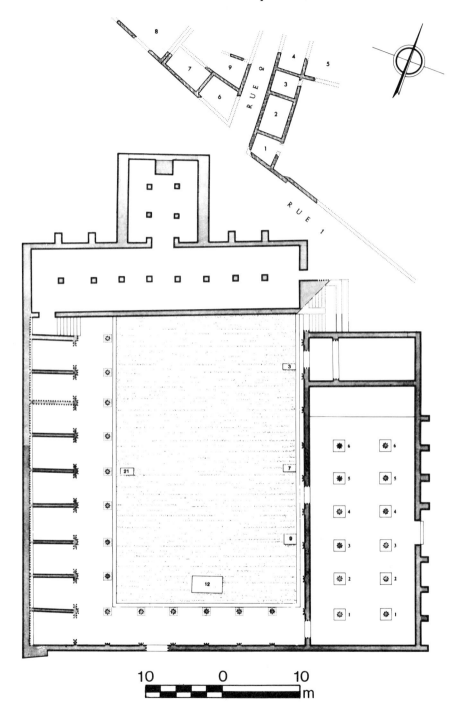

Fig. 11.6A The Augustan forum at Conimbriga (reproduced from Alarcão and Etienne 1977, by kind permission of the publishers).

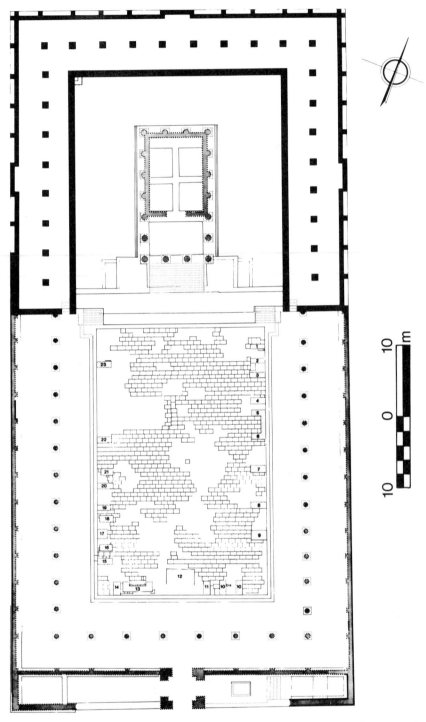

Fig. 11.6B The Flavian forum at Conimbriga (reproduced from Alarcão and Etienne 1977, by kind permission of the publishers).

wall cutting through a zone of luxurious, private dwellings (Alarcão and Etienne 1977, 135-163).

The successive phases of monumentalization of Conimbriga graphically illustrate the possible response of an indigenous community to the impact of Roman provincial rule. It is the timings of Conimbriga's adjustments that are of especial interest; for the local élite chose to upgrade the quality of the urban centre in Roman style at just those moments when the status of the community was upgraded first to *civitas stipendiaria* and subsequently to the Latin rights of citizenship. Conimbriga was not the only Lusitanian town to upgrade its urban centre, when its status was upgraded: recent excavations at Mirobriga Celtica (modern Santiago do Cacém) have revealed that the forum there was also considerably embellished in the Flavian period (Biers et al. 1984, 110; *Informação Arqueológica* 5 (1982-83), 129).

Conclusion

Towns, though not great in density, still formed a major feature of the Roman landscape of Lusitania. Some were created anew to assist the Roman administrative machinery, but most developed naturally out of Iron Age centres of habitation. What is clear is that towns were not a Roman importation; there had been considerable urban development before the arrival of the Romans even in Celticised areas, where hill-forts represented the characteristic form of settlement. The archaeological evidence provides a substantial corrective to the account of Strabo, who perhaps reproduces something of the rhetoric of Roman conquest in his willingness to depict Lusitania as a barbarian zone, outside the cultural orbit of civilization. This very rhetoric that painted Lusitania as a barbarous zone would have helped the Romans to justify their military aggression and subsequent regulation of the area. Contrary to Strabo's view, Rome preferred, wherever possible, to maintain the status quo and not to cause widespread dislocation in areas that Rome wanted subsequently to exploit. If urban development had already taken place, that formed the ideal basis for the Roman organization of that territory. It was only in those areas of less well-defined territories that she had to impose a new urban matrix. Finally, the development of Roman towns or *vici* on sites of Iron Age settlement raises the possibility that Rome also maintained the existing indigenous élite in their positions of authority. In all provinces Roman bureaucracy was minimal; she preferred to rely in great part on the indigenous élite. By maintaining them in their existing positions of influence, and by giving them access sooner or later to Roman status, Rome created for herself not only natural allies, but also the necessary social underpinning for the process of imperial rule. In response, it was this native élite who took over the outward forms of Roman culture – not only for themselves, but also for their own native communities.

Acknowledgements

I am most grateful to Professors Michael Crawford and John Crook and to audiences in Canterbury and Toronto for their comments on versions of this paper. The written version was completed in the summer of 1987; since then it has been possible only to make some bibliographical updates.

Notes

1   The Lusitanians, for example, are berated for their use of beer and butter and flour made from acorns: 3.3.7; 3.4.16; at 3.3.7 Strabo refuses to list all the tribes of the interior "because their names are so unpleasant on the ear".

2   For similar formulations in Strabo's work see 17.3.15 (Numidia), 4.1.11 (the Allobroges), 4.1.14
     (Tolosa in Gallia Narbonensis).

3   For some stimulating ideas on 'Romanization' in a neighbouring, but more remote area of the
     Empire, Gallaecia, see Pereira Menaut 1984.

4   Mill-stones have been found for example at Castro de São Miguel, Amêndoa, Mação (Pereira
     1970, 245-6); seeds and acorns at Castro da Senhora da Guia, Baiões, S. Pedro do Sul (Tavares
     da Silva 1980, 176).

5   Cf. the votive terracottas of parts of the body found in sanctuaries of Aesculapius: for example,
     at Fregellae, Italy: Coarelli et al. 1986.

6   Note the recent find of a 'terminus Augustalis finis Emeritensium' from the *finca* Altos de
     Soloparza, Valencia del Ventoso (now in the Museo Provincial, Badajoz): referred to by Alvárez
     Martinez 1986, 105. It would suggest an enclave of territory belonging to Emerita between the
     territories of the Baetican cities of Curiga to the south, Nertobriga and Seria Fama Iulia.

7   For example, in the *concelho* of São Pedro do Sul: sites at Castro de Carcoda (Carvalhais),
     Rompecilha and Monte de Santa Maria/Monte Redondo (Fiães, Vila de Feira); to date, only one
     can be shown to have been abandoned possibly during the Roman conquest of the region: Senhora
     da Guia, Baiões: Tavares 1970, 665-666; de Almeida 1975.

8   The following Iron Age sites continued in occupation: Yecla de Yeltes, Saldeana, Vitigudino,
     Iruena, Fuenteguinaldo, Lerilla, Picon del Rey, Sandanuela, Ermita de la Virgen del Castillo,
     Villarino de los Aires, Carrascal del Obispo, Teso de Utrera, Alba de Tormes, Castillo Viejo
     (Valero), Navagallega, Cabeza del Castillo (Lagunilla), Béjar: Maluquer de Motes 1956, sv. sites.

9   I am grateful to Prof. J. Humphrey for pointing this out in discussion.

Bibliography

Alarcão, A.M., Mayet, F. and Nolen, J. Smit 1986 *Ruínas de Conimbriga* (Roteiro da Arqueologia
     Portuguesa, 2), Lisbon.

Alarcão, J. de, 1979 'As origens de Coimbra' in *Actas das I Jornadas do grupo de arqueologia e arte
     do Centro (GAAC)*, Coimbra, 23-40.

Alarcão, J. de, 1982 'O teatro romano de Olisipo' in *El teatro en la Hispania romana (simposio, Mérida,
     1980)*, Badajoz, 286-316.

Alarcão, J. de, 1983 *Portugal romano* (3rd ed.), Lisbon.

Alarcão, J. de and Etienne, R. 1977 *Fouilles de Conimbriga. I. L'Architecture*, Paris.

Alarcão, J. de, Etienne, R. and Mayet, F. forthcoming *Les villas romaines de São Cucufate (Portugal)*,
     Paris.

Albertini, E. 1932 *Les divisions administratives de l'Espagne romaine*, Paris.

Albertos Firmat, M.L. 1975 *Organizaciones suprafamiliares en la Hispania antigua* (Studia
     Archaeologica, 37), Valladolid.

Albertos Firmat, M.L. 1981 'Organizaciones suprafamiliares en la Hispania antigua (II)', *BSEAA* 47:
     208-214.

Alföldy, G. 1987 *Römisches Städtewesen auf der neukastilischen Hochbene: ein Testfull für die
     Romanisierung*, (Abhandlungen der Heidelberger Akad. der Wissenschaften, 1987 no. 3),
     Heidelberg.

Almagro Basch, M. 1966 *Las estelas decoradas del suroeste peninsular* (Bibliotheca Praehistorica
     Hispana, VIII), Madrid.

Almagro Gorbea M. 1970 'Hallazgo de un kylix ático en Medellín (Badajoz)', *XI Congreso Nacional
     de Arqueología, Mérida, 1968*, Zaragoza, 437-448.

Almagro Gorbea M. 1971 'La necropolis de Medellín (Badajoz). Aportaciones al estudio de la penetración del influyo orientalizante en Extremadura' *Noticiario Arqueológico Hispánico: Arqueología*, 16: 161-202.

Almeida, C.A.F. de, 1975 'Influenças meridinais na cultura castreja' in *XIII Congreso Nacional de Arqueología, Huelva, 1973*, Zaragoza, 491-498.

Almeida, D.F. de, 1977 'Civitas Igaeditanorum et Egitânia: municipium romain, ville épiscopale wisigotique' in P.M. Duval and E. Frezouls (ed.), *Thèmes de recherches sur les villes antiques d'Occident (colloque, Strasbourg, 1972)*, Paris, 39-53.

Alvárez Martinez, J.M. 1976 'El templo de Diana' in *Augusta Emerita: actas del bimilenario de Mérida*, Madrid, 43-53.

Alvárez Martinez, J.M. 1982 'El foro de Augusta Emerita' in *Homenaje a Saenz de Buruaga*, Badajoz, 53-68.

Alvárez Martinez, J.M. 1983 *El puente romana de Mérida* (Monografías Emeritenses, 1), Badajoz.

Alvárez Martinez, J.M. 1984 'Consideraciones sobre la Mérida prerromana' *Revista de Estudios Extremeños* 40: 101-109.

Alvárez Martinez, J.M. 1985 'Excavaciones en Augusta Emerita' in *Arqueología de las ciudades modernas superpuestas a las antiguas (Zaragoza, 1983)*, Madrid, 35-53.

Alvárez Martinez, J.M. 1986 'Epoca romana' in M. Terrón Albarrán (ed.), *Historia de la Baja Extremadura*, Badajoz, Part II.

Alvárez Martinez, J.M. and Diaz Pintiado, J.A. 1982 'El puente romano de Aljucen' in *Homenaje a D. J. Canovas Pesini*, Badajoz, 95-100.

Alves, L.F. Delgado 1956 'Aspectos de arqueologia em Myrtilis', *Arquivo de Beja*, 13: 21-104.

Amo, M. del 1982 'El teatro romano de Medellín' in *El teatro en la Hispania romana (simposio, Mérida, 1980)*, Badajoz, 317-336.

Arnaud, J.M. and Gamito, T.J. 1974-77 'Cerâmicas estampilhadas da idade do ferro do sul de Portugal. I', *O Arqueólogo Português*, série iii, 7-9: 165-202.

Arruda, A.M. 1983-84 'Alcáçova de Santarém. Relatório dos trabalhos arqueológicos de 1984', *Clio: Arqueologia*, 1: 217-224.

Arruda, A.M. and Catarino, H. 1982 'Cerâmica da Idade do Ferro da Alcáçova de Santarém', *Clio* Lisbon, 4: 35-39.

Augusto Tavares, A. 1970 'A romanização dos castros do concelho de S. Pedro do Sul', *XI Congreso Nacional de Arqueología, Mérida, 1968*, Zaragoza, 665-666.

Beltrán, A. 1976 'Las monedas romanas de Mérida: su interpretación histórica' in *Augusta Emerita: actas del bimilenario de Mérida*, Madrid, 93-105.

Beltrán Lloris, M. 1973 *Estudios de Arqueología cáchereña* (Monografías arqueológicas, XV), Zaragoza.

Biers, W., Caeiro, J., Leonard Jr., A. and Soren, D. 1984 'Investigações em Mirobriga (Santiago do Cacém), Portugal, 1981', *Arquivo de Beja*, série ii, 1: 107-114.

Blanco Freijeiro, A. 1981 'Cancho Roano: un monumento proto-histórico en los confines de la antigua Lusitania', *Boletín de la Real Academía de Historia* 178: 225-241.

Blázquez, J.M. 1975 *La Romanización. II. La sociedad y la economia en la Hispania romana* (= Ciclos y temas de la historia de España), Madrid.

Brunt, P.A. 1981 'The revenues of Rome', *Journal of Roman Studies* 71: 161-72.

Burkert, W. 1985 *Greek Religion* (tr. J. Raffan), Oxford.

Cabré Aguilo, J. 1930 *Excavaciones de las Cogotas, Cardeñosa (Avila). I. El Castro* (Memorias de la Junta Superior de Excavaciones Arqueológicas, 110), Madrid.

Cabré Aguilo, J. 1932 *Excavaciones de las Cogotas, Cardeñosa (Avila). II. La necropolis* (MemJSEA, 120), Madrid.

Callejo Serrano, C. 1968 'La arqueología de Norba Caesarina', *Archivo español de Arqueología* 41: 121-49.

Canto, A.M. 1982 'Sobre la cronología augustea del acueducto de los Milagros de Mérida' in *Homenaje a Saenz de Buruaga*, Badajoz, 157-176.

Casariego, A., Cores, G. and Pliego, F. 1987 *Catálogo de plomos monetiformes de la Hispania antigua* (Serie numismática, 1), Madrid.

Cesar Moran, P. 1924-25 *Excavaciones en el Cerro de Berrueco* (MemJSEA, 65), Madrid.

Coarelli, F. et al. 1986 *Fregellae. 2. Il santuario di Esculapio*, Rome.

Coelho, L. 1986 'Inscrições da necrópole proto-histórica da herdade do Pêgo – Ourique', *O Arqueólogo Português*, série iii, 5: 167-180.

Didierjean, F., Ney, C. and Paillet, J.-L. 1986 *Belo III. Le Macellum* (Publ. de la Casa de Velázquez, série archéologique, fasc. V), Madrid.

Drinkwater, J.F. 1987 'Urbanization in Italy and the western Empire' in J. Wacher (ed.), *The Roman World*, London, I, 345-387.

d'Encarnação, J. 1975 *Divindades indígenas sob o domínio romano em Portugal: subsídios para o seu estudo*, Lisbon.

d'Encarnação, J. 1984 *Inscrições romanas do Conventus Pacensis: subsídios para o estudo da romanização*, Coimbra.

Edmondson, J.C. 1987 *Two Industries in Roman Lusitania: Mining and Garum Production* (B.A.R. International Series, 362), Oxford.

Edmondson, J.C., forthcoming a 'Le *garum* en Lusitanie urbaine et rurale: hiérarchies de demande et de production' in J.-G. Gorges (ed.), *Les villes de la Lusitanie romaine: hiérarchie et territoires*.

Edmondson, J.C., forthcoming b 'Instrumenta Imperii: law and imperialism in Republican Rome' in B. Halpern and D. Hobson (ed.), *Law in its Social Setting in the Ancient Mediterranean World*.

Etienne, R. 1982 'Les sénateurs originaires de Lusitanie' in *Epigrafia e ordine senatorio* (Tituli, 5), Rome, 521-29.

Fabre, G. 1974 'A propos d'une inscription sur brique inédite de Conimbriga' *Actas do III Congreso Nacional de Arqueologia, Porto, 1973*, Oporto, 191-200.

Fernandez Gomez, F. 1986 *Excavaciones arqueológicas en El Raso de Candeleda*, Avila.

Février, P.A. and Leveau, P. (eds.) 1982 *Villes et campagnes dans l'Empire romain: actes du colloque à Aix-en-Provence, 1980*, Aix-en-Provence.

Finley M.I. 1977 'The ancient city: from Fustel de Coulanges to Max Weber and beyond', *Comparative Studies in Society and History* 19: 305-327.

Galsterer. H. 1971 *Untersuchungen zum römischen Städtewesen auf der iberischen Halbinsel* (Madrider Forschungen, 8), Berlin.

Gamito, T.J. 1982 'A idade do ferro no sul de Portugal: problemas e perspectivas', *Arqueologia (Porto)* 6: 65-78.

Ganzert, J. and Kockel, V. 1988 'Augustusforum und Mars-Ultor-Tempel' in W.-D. Heilmeyer, E. la Rocca and H.G. Martin (ed.), *Kaiser Augustus und der verlorene Republik*, Mainz, 149-199.

García y Bellido, A. 1971 'El recinto mural romano de Evora', *Conimbriga* 10: 85-92.

García y Bellido, A. 1972-74 'El tetrapylon de Capera (Capera, Cáceres)', *Archivo español de Arqueología* 45-47: 45-90.

Gorges, J.-G. 1979 *Les villas hispano-romaines: inventaire et problématique archéologiques* (Publ. du Centre Pierre Paris, 4), Paris.

Gorges, J.-G. 1982 'Centuriation et organisation du territoire: notes préliminaires sur l'exemple de Mérida' in Février and Leveau 1982, 101-110.

Gorges, J.-G. 1986 'Prospections archéologiques autour d'Emerita Augusta. Soixante-dix sites ruraux en quête de signification', *REA* 88 (= *Hommage à R. Etienne*): 215-236.

Goudineau, C. 1979 *Les fouilles de la Maison au Dauphin: recherches sur la romanisation de Vaison-la-Romaine* (Gallia, Suppl. XXXVII), Paris.

Harrison, R.J. 1988 *Spain at the Dawn of History: Iberians, Phoenicians and Greeks*, London.

Hauschild, T. 1982 'Zur Typologie der römischen Tempel auf den iberischen Halbinsel: peripterale Anlagen in Barcelona, Mérida und Evora' in *Homenaje a Saenz de Buruaga*, Badajoz, 145-156.

Humphrey, J.H. 1986 *Roman circuses: arenas for chariot racing*, London.

Jiménez de Gregorio, F. 1952 'Hallazgos arqueológicas en la Jara. V', *Archivo español de Arqueología* 25: 150-160.

Kalb, P. and Höck, M. 1984 'Moron – historisch und archäologisch', *Madrider Mitteilungen* 25: 92-102.

Kienast, D. 1982 *Augustus: Prinzeps und Monark*, Darmstadt.

Klein, J. 1920 *The Mesta: a study in Spanish economic history 1273-1836*, Cambridge (Mass.).

León Alonso, M. del Pilar, 1970 'Los relieves del templo de Marte en Mérida', *Habis* 1: 181-197.

Lopez Monteagudo, G. 1982 'Las esculturas zoomorfas 'Celticas' de la peninsula ibérica y sus paralelos polácos', *Archivo español de Arqueología* 55: 3-30.

Maia, M. 1980 'Povos do sul de Portugal nas fontes clássicas – Celtici e Turduli', *Clio* (Lisbon) 2: 67-70.

Maia do Amaral, A.E. 1983 *Considerações préliminares acerca do Forum II de Bobadela*, Coimbra (first published in *Munda* 4 (1982), 33-39; 5 (1983), 3-14).

Maluquer de Motes, J. 1951 'De la Salamanca primitiva', *Zephyrus* 2: 61-72.

Maluquer de Motes, J. 1956 *Carta arqueológica de España: Salamanca*, Salamanca.

Maluquer de Motes, J. 1983 *El sanctuario protohistórico de Zalamea de la Serena, Badajoz. II. 1981-82* (= Programa de investigaciones protohistóricas, 5), Barcelona.

Martín Valls, R. 1976 'Nuevos hallazgos arqueológicas en Ciudad Rodrigo' *Zephyrus* 26-27: 373-388.

Meleno, R.L. et al. 1984 'El bronce de Alcántara. Una *deditio* del 104 a.C.', *Gerión* 2: 265-323.

Melida, J.R. 1915 'El teatro romano de Mérida', *Revista de Archivos, Bibliotecas y Museos* 32: 1-38.

Mello Beirão, C. et al. 1985 'Depósito votivo da II idade do ferro de Garvão: notícia da primeira campanha de escavações', *O Arqueólogo Português*, série iv, 3: 45-136.

Menendez Pidal y Alvarez, J.R. 1957 'Restitución del texto y dimensiones de las inscripciones históricas del anfiteatro de Mérida', *Archivo español de Arqueología* 30: 205-217.

Oliveira Marques, A.H. de 1978 *Introdução a história de agricultura em Portugal: a questão cerealífera durante a Idade Média* (3rd ed.), Lisbon.

Pereira, M.A. 1970 *Monumentos históricos do concelho de Mação*, Mação.

Pereira Menaut, G. 1984 'La formación histórica de los pueblos del norte de Hispania. El caso de Gallaecia como paradigma', *Veleia* 1: 271-287.

Pinel, C. 1981 'El yacimiento tardorromano de 'El Soto', Calvarrasa de Abajo (Salamanca)', *Zephyrus* 32-33: 217-225.

Ponte, S. da 1985a 'Estação arqueológica na Rua Carlos Campeão: relatório préliminar de 1982/3', *Arqueologia na região de Tomar (da préhistoria a actualidade)* 1: 89-101.

Ponte, S. da 1985b 'Tomar – antiga Sellium', *Arqueologia (Porto)* 11: 112-114.

Ribeiro, F. Nunes 1960 'Pré-história e a origem de Beja', *Arquivo de Beja*, 17: 3-113.

Richardson, J.S. 1986 *Hispaniae: Spain and the development of Roman Imperialism 218-82 BC*, Cambridge.

Richmond, I.A. 1930 'The first years of Emerita Augusta', *Archaeological Journal* 87: 98-116.

Rodriguez Diaz, A. 1986 *Arqueología de Tierra de Barros*, Badajoz.

Roldán Hervas, J.M. 1968-69 'Fuentes antiguas para el estudio de los Vettones', *Zephyrus* 19-20: 73-106.

Saenz de Buruaga, J.A. 1982 'Observaciones sobre el teatro romano de Mérida' in *El Teatro en la Hispania romana (simposio, Mérida, 1980)*, Badajoz, 303-316.

Saenz de Buruaga, J.A. and Alvárez Martinez, J.M. 1977 'Informe sobre los trabajos realizados en el circo romano de Mérida', *Noticiario arqueológico hispánico: Arqueología* 5: 97-103.

Salinas de Frías, M. 1986 *La organización tribal de los Vettones (pueblos prerromanos de Salamanca* (2nd. ed.), Salamanca.

Santos Rocha, A. dos 1905-08 'Estações préromanas da idade do ferro nas vizinhanças da Figueira da Foz em Portugal', *Portugalia* 2, fasc. 3: 301-359.

Shaw, B.D. 1982-83 '"Eaters of flesh, drinkers of milk": the ancient Mediterranean ideology of the pastoral nomad', *Ancient Society* 13-14: 5-31.

Sillières, P. 1982 'Centuriation et voie romaine au sud de Mérida: contribution à la délimination de la Bétique et de la Lusitanie', *Mélanges de la Casa de Velázquez* 18: 437-448.

Slade, K.W., Biers, W.R., Biers, J.C. and Soren, D. 1983 'Mirobriga: the 1983 season', *Muse* 17: 38-63.

Soares, J. and Tavares da Silva, C. 1986 'Ocupação pré-romana de Setúbal: escavações arqueológicas na Travessa dos Apóstoles' in *I Encontro Nacional de Arqueologia Urbana (Setúbal 1985)*, Lisbon, 1986.

Soria Sanchez, V. 1985 'Descubrimientos arqueológicos en Extremadura', *XVII Congreso Nacional de Arqueología, Logroño, 1983*, Zaragoza, 483-499.

Squarciapino, M.F. 1976 'Ipotesi di lavoro sul gruppo di sculture da Pan Caliente' in *Augusta Emerita: actas del bimilenario de Mérida*, Madrid, 55-62.

Squarciapino, M.F. 1982 'Cultura artistica di Mérida romana' in *Homenaje a Saenz de Buruaga*, Badajoz, 33-52.

Tavares da Silva, C. 1980 'Contribuição para o estudo da cultura castreja na Beira Alta', *Actas do Seminario de Arqueologia do noroeste peninsular*, Guimarães, 1980, II, 171-181.

Tavares da Silva, C. et al. 1980-1981 'Escavações arqueológicas no Castelo de Alcácer do Sal (campanha de 1979)', *Setúbal Arqueológica*, 6-7: 149-218.

Tovar, A. 1966-67 'L'inscription du Cabeço das Fraguas et la langue des Lusitaniens', *Etudes Celtiques* 11: 237-268.

Tranoy, A. 1981 *La Galice romaine: recherches sur le nord-ouest de la péninsule ibérique dans l'antiquité* (Publ. du Centre Pierre Paris, 7), Paris.

Trillmich, W. 1986 'Ein historisches Relief in Mérida mit Darstellung des M. Agrippa beim Opfer: ein Rekonstruktionsversuch', *Madrider Mitteilungen* 27: 279-304.

Untermann, J. 1980 'Hispania' in G. Neumann and J. Untermann (ed.), *Die Sprachen im römischen Reich der Kaiserzeit* (Beihefte der Bonner Jahrbücher, 40), Bonn, 1-17.

Vasconcelos, J. Leite de 1905 *Religiões da Lusitânia*, II, Lisbon.

Vaz, J.L. 1979 'Termino augustal de Goujoim (Armamar)', *Conimbriga* 18: 133-138.

Vieira da Silva, A. 1944 *Epigrafia de Olisipo: subsídios para a história de Lisboa romana*, Lisbon.

Vives y Escudero, A. 1924 *La moneda hispánica*, III, Madrid.

Zanker, P. 1968 *Forum Augustum*, Tübingen.

12. Urban munificence and the growth of urban consciousness in Roman Spain[1]

by Nicola Mackie

Introduction

My first quotation comes from a Roman lawyer writing at the end of the second century AD:

> ...If anyone has promised to embellish with marble a building constructed by someone else, or to add to it any other way in accordance with the people's wish, inscribing his own name on it: the senate resolved that this should be done, provided that the inscriptions of the previous builders remained intact. But if private individuals have contributed some money of their own to buildings constructed at public expense, it is provided in the same (imperial) mandates that they should inscribe their own names only to record the amount of money they contributed to the work. (Callistratus in *Digest* 50, 10, 7. 1)

Although this quotation comes from a Roman (not a local Spanish) source, and belongs to a date in the history of the Roman Empire when Spanish 'urban consciousness' could be said to have reached maturity, it concerns precisely the type of evidence which I mean to discuss: that is, inscriptions recording expenditure by individuals on public buildings and other amenities in the towns of Roman Spain. Such inscriptions, as is well known, are to be found widely distributed over the Romanized (and Hellenized) areas of the Roman Empire. They reflect a pattern of communal life which has sometimes been equated with 'Romanization' itself; a life centred around urban buildings, and urban activities, which were frequently paid for out of the pockets of wealthy individuals. Our quotation shows some of the legal industry which was generated as a by-product of this lifestyle: the writer addresses himself to the question who, in what circumstances, was entitled to inscribe his (or her) name on a public building, and exactly what such an inscription ought (explicitly or implicitly) to claim. Had the individual in question paid the whole cost of the building, or only a part; was it a case of an entirely new building, or just some addition or embellishment to an existing one?

The purpose of this paper is to investigate how and why the practice of urban munificence gained ground in the Spanish provinces of the Roman Empire; and how it was related to the more general phenomenon which we call 'Romanization', a term which I take to mean (among other things) the assimilation of the Latin language, of Roman political, legal, social and economic practices, of Roman architecture, artefacts, and technological skills. I am more interested in Romanization as a process than as a state (felicitously?) achieved. The fact that this paper spans, not the first two centuries of Roman control in Spain, but the two centuries after that (beginning, roughly, with the reign of Augustus), will I hope serve to emphasize that the process of Romanization was complicated and long-drawn-out, without any clear starting-point (or conclusion). Whatever we adopt as our starting-point, we are rarely confronted with a simple dichotomy of things 'Roman' supervening on what was 'native', 'indigenous', 'barbarian' and so on; for however early we go into the history of a province, and however minimally we define 'Romanization', we continue to find that what there is resembles what went before.

It has been said that, in the provinces of the Roman Empire, 'romaniser c'est municipaliser en même temps qu'urbaniser' – to Romanize was to municipalize and to urbanize at the same time – (Gagé 1964, 153-4). ('Urbanization', in this context, refers to the habit of treating a single settlement as the political centre for a territory, as well as to the social, economic, and architectural development of the settlement itself). The statement perhaps over-simplifies, not just because it diverts attention from the private, non-urban, aspects of cultural change. We are left with the impression that Romanization was a sort of package whose elements all came in a single wrapper, and a package which someone – whether the provincials themselves, or the Roman government – quite consciously and deliberately set out to get, or to impose. Whatever the ambitions on either side, we should not expect the process to have been so straightforward.

This simple view is one into which we are led both by our own hindsight, and by the perspective of the ancient literary sources. (This is not to find fault, except perhaps on ideological grounds, with the ancient sources: they were not composed with our particular requirements in mind). 'It is less a province than a part of Italy,' said Pliny approvingly of Southern Gaul (Natural History 3, 31); and about Southern Spain Strabo, writing in the early Principate, made a similar judgement: 'they have changed over completely to the Roman lifestyle, and do not even remember their own language any more' (3, 2, 15). We find the poet Calpurnius Siculus using Andalusia ('exposed to the savage Moors') as a romantic image of exile at the world's end (4, 37-49); and Martial in Bilbilis (Calatayúd) being stifled by his 'provincial desert' but also luxuriating in the freedom of not having to dress up in his toga (*Epigrams* 12 pr., 18, 17-18). Rome and Italy are the centre, and the norm; the cultural magnetism they exercise is simple and inevitable, because what lies beyond is savage, uncultivated, and ultimately invisible.

This same perspective, as well, tends to make us think of the striking uniformity of monumental architecture, inscriptions, and local government throughout the Western Empire as (frankly) rather dull. Roman was what the natives wanted (or should have wanted) to be, and, allowing for their limitations, they achieved it (more or less). But, unexciting though uniformity may seem in itself, the fact of uniformity may be surprising and remarkable. The result conceals from us the complexity of its causes. I shall argue that the practice of urban munificence in Spain was not just part of a Romanization 'package', but had its own logic and its own dynamics, which not only help to explain the growth of the practice itself, but also indicate how urban munificence made a creative contribution to the process of Romanization in the Spanish provinces.

The cultural background

By the beginning of our era, the Romans had had a foothold in Spain for over two hundred years; their control spread gradually from the east coast and the south until, by the middle of Augustus' reign, it covered the whole peninsula. Phoenicians, Greeks, and Carthaginians, earlier than the Romans, had visited and occupied the accessible coastal areas. The Mediterranean fringes of Spain, at least, were identified with a long history of Mediterranean civilizations in rise and decline. If foundation-legends are (as Wiseman 1983 has suggested in the case of Italian towns) to be taken as markers of cultural development, parts of Spain were, well in advance of the fall of the Roman Republic, embedded in a Greco-Roman cultural tradition. Odysseus had visited Andalusia: there was a city of Odysseia named after him, and a temple of Athene containing shields and ships' prows commemorating his wanderings (Strabo, 3, 4, 3, citing Posidonius, Artemidorus, and Asclepiades of Myrleia). And before

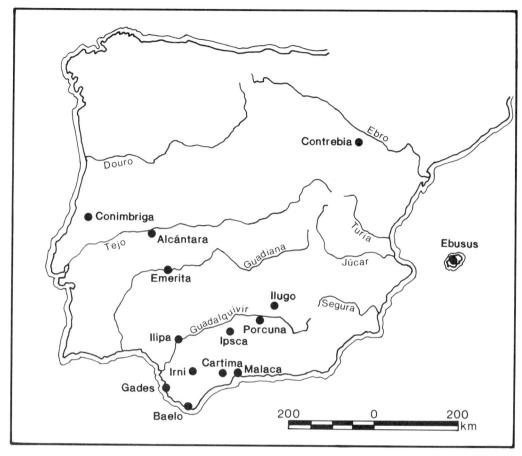

Fig. 12.1. Map of Spain showing the findspots of the inscriptions mentioned in the text.

Odysseus there was Heracles, whose 'Pillars' the people of Gades (Cádiz) claimed as the site of their town, and who had adopted as his own the Punic temple of Melkart in Gades (Strabo 3, 5, 5; García y Bellido 1967a, 152-66). As for acquaintance with the Latin language, and with Roman law, the recently-discovered inscriptions from Alcántara and Contrebia (Botorrita) prove that this existed, in inland Spain, as early as the beginning of the first century BC (Richardson 1986, 164-5; 199-201). Contrebia had, by the same date, a large, rectangular, two-storey building which was not exactly 'Greek' or 'Roman' in style, but which represented a good step along the way towards the urban architecture of Imperial Spain (Richardson 1986, 172-3; Beltrán and Tovar 1982, 22-33). The earliest known villas in the peninsula, in Catalonia, the Levant, and Andalusia, date from the late second century BC (Gorges 1979, 23-9). Already in the Republican period there were Roman settlers; trade with Italy and the eastern Mediterranean; and Iberian coinages reaching back to the third century (Richardson 1986, 172-5; Villaronga 1973; 1984).

As all this shows, the roots of 'Romanization' in Spain were by no means exclusively Roman. But, by the early Empire, it was the Roman version of Mediterranean culture that was winning. Heracles of Gadeira became Hercules Gaditanus (*CIL II*, 3409; García y Bellido

1967a, 164); Greek, Punic and Iberian had by Augustus' reign virtually disappeared from inscriptions, and from coins as well (Mackie 1983, 13 note 8; cf. Alföldy 1975, nos. 4, 9, 18). And here one might raise a question about the cultural implications of learning, and using, a foreign language. Of all the aspects of Roman culture, the Latin language itself was perhaps most easily and readily absorbed by the Spaniards. (On the learning and use of Latin in Spain, see García y Bellido 1967b). But, through its implications for all areas of life – social, economic, legal, and political – may it not have contributed more than any other single aspect of cultural change?

Inscriptions and their uses

The usefulness of inscriptions for our present project lies first of all in the fact that they have survived, while the activities, and frequently even the buildings, to which they refer have disappeared from sight. But it is not simply a matter of using inscriptions as evidence, *faute de mieux*, because they happen to have survived. On the contrary, inscriptions are an unparalleled repository of answers to such questions as 'Who paid for public building and entertainments?', 'How much money did individuals commonly spend?', 'What did they gain by doing so?' (cf. Duncan-Jones 1982; 1985; Frere 1985). Without an inscription to inform us, we should not know that it was Marcus Agrippa who built the famous theatre at Emerita (Mérida –*CIL II* 474 = *ILS* 130); and at well-excavated sites which are relatively poor in inscriptions, for example Baelo (Bolonia) and Conimbriga (Condeixa-a-Velha), archaeology in itself leaves numerous questions of this type unanswered (see Domergue 1973; Alarcao and Etienne 1977-9).

This is not to deny that, as evidence, inscriptions have some serious pitfalls. Using inscriptions as evidence is not unlike running a film backwards towards an initial scene (the context in which the stones were inscribed) without which we cannot make sense of the ending (the inscriptions we find ourselves studying now). And the film as it runs may jar, or slip off the reel altogether. The inscriptions we study may mislead us as to the incidence (absolute or relative) of a certain activity, in a certain place, at a certain time, for a variety of reasons: accidents of survival, availability or non-availability of suitable stone, the presence or absence of the 'epigraphic habit' (or 'epigraphic consciousness') among the people concerned. (On these problems see MacMullen 1982; Mann 1985). The 'epigraphic habit', if it is found to have been present at all, may in turn be unpacked into an habitual bias towards recording on stone some events rather than others: for example, deaths rather than business contracts, mature deaths rather than infant ones (cf. MacMullen 1982, 239), private benefactions rather than expenditure from a community's public funds, and so on. Such bias will not always be predictable from the outside, but may instead derive from cultural attitudes which we look to our (biased sample of) inscriptions to elucidate. And so, in using the evidence of inscriptions (as here) to study the practice of urban munificence in Roman Spain, we must constantly be asking ourselves about the inscriptions we do *not* have, and why we do not have them: from accidents of survival to habitual bias, there is a whole series of possible alternatives to the easy answer 'Such happenings were rare, or no-existent'.

Let us return, warned of these pitfalls, to the nature of the present project, and to the more positive aspects of the epigraphic evidence. Through the answers which they provide to such questions as 'Who paid?' and 'Why?', the inscriptions can be used to map out a *specific* practice of urban munificence in Roman Spain consisting both of certain patterns of behaviour and also (I would hold) of certain beliefs, shared between donors and their communities, about the appropriate forms, occasions, motives, and rewards, of munificence. And this in turn will help to explain how and why the practice gained ground, and how it was related to other developing phenomena which commonly appear alongside urban munificence in the 'package' vision of Romanization alluded to in my introduction.

The reason why it is important to map out a specific practice is not that urban munificence in Roman Spain was necessarily different from urban munificence elsewhere (although it may have been), but that terms like 'urban munificence' and 'civic pride' are on their own too vague. Unless we know the details, we shall literally not know what was going on, nor shall we know how it was related to anything else. To refer to 'beliefs' as constituting part of the practice is neither to deny individuality to ancient perceptions of a particular case of munificence, nor to be naive about the (conscious and unconscious) motives of benefactors. It is merely to imply that, in any society, there are certain common modes of thought which influence the ways in which actions are perceived, and the sorts of aspirations peoples have. For example (as will be seen in the following sections) the concept of *honor* as a motive and reward for benefactions appears to have been fundamental to the practice of urban munificence in Spain; and the language of the inscriptions is particularly helpful in drawing attention to the varied aspects of the concept. But this does not preclude the presence of other, indeed idiosyncratic, motives and reactions, some of which can themselves be deduced, directly or indirectly, from the epigraphic evidence.

Finally, it is perhaps appropriate to draw attention to a certain bias in the *selection* of material for this paper. Records of urban munificence are in fact (for reasons which I hope to make clear) one of the most common types of inscription we have from Spain. But to concentrate almost exclusively on these records may be to give a false impression that urban munificence was the only sort of communal benefaction there was in Roman Spain, and public building the only sort of building. In reality, people gave money for the celebration of religious cults – such as the cult of Isis (*CIL II*, 3386) – which were not official urban cults; they built substantial private houses for themselves, in town and countryside, at the same time as public building in the towns was expanding thanks to private munificence (Gorges 1979; Knapp 1983, 66). But it is private giving for official urban purposes which constitutes our theme.

Urban munificence in early Imperial Spain

Urban munificence did not begin or persist in a vacuum: it had a cultural, social, and economic background. The cultural background to the development of urban munificence in Spain has briefly been described (above, p. 180ff). Here I should like to point out some necessary (social and economic) conditions for the practice, and to run through some suggestions about donor's motives, before going on to discuss the inscriptions in detail.

It was necessary, first of all, that there should be rich people within reach of a community (usually, but not always, citizens or residents), possessing the sheer ability to spend money on public munificence. (For donors from outside the community, see Mackie 1983, chapter 8). It was also necessary that the community, or individuals within it, should have (or have access to) the relevant architectural awareness and technological skills; and that a great deal of hard work should be put in (by donors, or their heirs, or a community's own officials) to seeing that building programmes, public feasts, entertainments and the like were adequately organized. Urban munificence involved effort (for someone), as well as skills and money: it was not something one embarked upon in a spirit of nonchalance, because one might as well do this with one's money as anything else.

Some motives that have been suggested for munificence are: regard for fellow-citizens, pride in one's town, religious sentiment, desire for power, for posthumous prestige or memory; and of course *philotimia* and its Latin variant *honor* – the competitive pursuit of prestige, esteem, a public reputation (eg. Mackie 1983, chapter 7; Johnston 1985, 105-6; Frere 1985; Brown 1978, chapter 2). These are all understandable, and plausible, enough as motives: the question is, how can we see them fitting into a specific practice of urban munificence?

The earliest inscriptions recording urban munificence in Spain belong to the last years of the Republic, and the first years of the Principate. This does not of course mean that there was no urban munificence before then, unrecorded or its records now lost. But certainly the earliest building inscriptions we have record *supervision of* building by local magistrates rather than munificence (eg. *CIL II*, 3425-6 = *ILS* 5332-4; *HAE* 798 with Granados 1984, 270-4 for the date); or else tend to refer to private expenditure on fairly basic sorts of public amenity: perhaps a temple (*CIL II*, 5943, AD 21), gates and accompanying archways built and paid for by an individual at Ilipa (Alcalá del Río) in Southern Spain with a Carthaginian name (*CIL II*, 1087 = *ILS* 5573). From Ipsca (Castro del Río) in the same region (a town which was peregrine until the Flavian period) we have what reads like a self-conscious declaration by the local senate of its own rôle as recipient and guardian of gifts made to the community. It was inscribed on a statue-base; the year was AD 46:

> In the reign of Tiberius Claudius Caesar Augustus Germanicus, *pontifes maximus*, in his fifth year of tribunician power, hailed imperator for the tenth time, *pater patriae*, designated consul for the fourth time, Optatus son of Reburrus was the first to give at his own cost a statue of Caesar Augustus, *pater patriae*, and he dedicated it in company with his sons Optatus and Reburrus. The senate decreed that it should be among the public possessions (*bona publica*) in perpetuity.   (*CIL II*, 1569)

But there was much more to come. In Spain, as elsewhere in the Empire, urban munificence seems eventually to have reached a peak, in quantity and in complexity, during the second century AD. (For caution about inferring a date directly from the quantity of inscriptions, see MacMullen 1982, 242-5). Further, in Spain, epigraphic evidence, in parallel with archaeology, indicates an upsurge in public building and public activity of all kinds as a result of the emperor Vespasian's grant of the Latin right to the peninsula in the seventies AD (Mackie 1983, 125-7 with appendix 3 for Vespasian' grant).

One inscription which may date from soon after the grant comes from the Flavian municipality (*municipium*) of Cartima (Cártama), near Málaga on the south coast:

1)   Junia Rustica, daughter of Decimus, first and perpetual priestess in the *municipium* of Cartima, repaired public porticoes which had deteriorated through age, gave land for a bath, restored public revenues, placed a bronze statue of Mars in the forum, and at her own cost gave and dedicated porticoes next to the bath on her own land, with a reservoir and a statue of Cupid, giving a feast and public shows; the statues voted to herself and her son Caius Fabius Junianus by the council of Cartima she made and gave at her own cost, remitting the expense, also a statue to her husband Caius Fabius Fabianus.   (*CIL II*, 1956 = *ILS* 5512)

The next (slightly damaged) inscription probably belongs to the late second century AD, and comes from Porcuna, a town which lay just off the via Augusta leading from the southern province of Baetica northwards into Tarraconensis:

2)   (Quintus?) Quintius, son of Quintus, grandson of Quintus, great-grandson of Quntius, great-great-grandson of Quintus, of the tribe Galeria, Hispanus...aedile, *flamen, duovir* and *pontifex* of the *municipium*...procurator of the river Baetis (a list of other posts in the imperial administration follows) diffusely honoured with numerous immunities and benefits...by emperors, gave as a gift at his own cost shops and a granary on land which he bought from the community.   (*CIL II,* 2129 = *ILS* 1404)

Less ostentatious is the following, from Ilugo (Santisteban del Puerto) across the border in the province of Tarraconensis, near the mining district of Cástulo (Linares):

3)   Annia Victorina, daughter of Lucius, in memory of her husband Marcus Fulvius Moderatus and her son Marcus Fulvius Victorinus, built a water-supply entirely at her own cost, constructing bridges and pipes and pools with ornaments attached, and dedicated it, giving a feast.   (*CIL II*, 3240 = *ILS* 5764)

These three inscriptions might have been chosen virtually at random: they serve here to illustrate several points about urban munificence. In the first place, the inscriptions show a range of individuals as benefactors: two women, one an official priestess of the community, one with no official position, so far as one can tell; and a man who was at one point a councillor, magistrate, and priest of the community which receives his benefaction, but has since that time risen high in the financial branches of the imperial administration. Secondly, we can see the scope and scale of munificence: although no figures are stated, none of these gifts will have been inexpensive, and from Junia Rustica's repairs to public porticoes through to the feast mentioned at the end of the last inscription, these donors have been responsible for an immense range of public amenities and activities. Munificence could change the face of a town. (For further details of munificence and its costs in Spain, see Curchin 1983).

Thirdly, the inscriptions show, or suggest, a number of different motives at work, even within each individual case of munificence. It may be observed to begin with that the gifts described were variously pleasant, useful, and profitable to the communities concerned. For example, shops brought in money, in the form of rent, to the public funds; a water-supply need not be purely functional, but could have agreeably decorative features too (as was evidently the case with that built by Annia Victorina). (It is perhaps significant that baths and systems of water-supply were one of the most popular forms of urban benefaction in Spain. For functional and aesthetic aspects of Roman water-supply systems, see Frontinus 1982). Were the donors, then, guided solely by the knowledge that they were making local residents' lives easier and more pleasant?

This is a genuine question, not a rhetorical one. The reason why it cannot be answered in the affirmative is not so much that there must have been 'something in it' for the donors (although naturally there was, if it was only self-satisfaction), as that 'making local residents' lives easier and more pleasant' is an explanation which fails to do justice to the complexities of the problem. For example, why should donors have chosen to make life easier and more pleasant for *these* people (why not spend money on a village, or a particular social class, or members of one's own family)? Why should money have been spent in this style, and on this scale, in Spain during the early Roman Empire, and not in all societies with a similar distribution of wealth, and comparable technological skills? Why did Spanish donors have to write down what they were doing: why could they not just do it?

If one wants to understand people's behaviour, it seems logical to look, not just at their behaviour in isolation, but also at the response. The first of the three inscriptions, recording the munificence of Junia Rustica, priestess of Cartima, at the same time records a response: the town council voted statues to herself and her son, which in the event she set up at her own cost. These may be termed 'honorific' statues; the practice whereby the council voted a statue, and the person thus honoured paid for it, was so common as to warrant a special abbreviated formula in inscriptions: 'h(onore) a(ccepto) i(mpensam) r(emisit)' ('s/he accepted the honour, and remitted the expense') (*CIL II*, Index, p.1176). Other ways of conferring *honor* on public benefactors were the acclamation 'patron' (*patronus* – *CIL II*, 1054), and appointment to public magistracies or (especially) priesthoods. Consider this statue-base:

> Augustan Fortune. ...daughter of Lucius, Celerina, having twice previously feasted the public, on account of the *honor* of her priesthood, gave and dedicated this from 100 pounds of silver, giving a feast.   (*CIL II*, 1278)

Evidently what is described here is not a fixed or standard charge (cf. Duncan-Jones 1962; Mackie 1983, 93). How 'voluntary' the payment really was, in the circumstances, is not here at issue: the point to notice is that public authority, a public position, was itself conceived of as a variety of *honor*, and it was this that made appointment to public office an appropriate exchange for munificence. (One might compare the epigraphic formula, 'having discharged all *honores* in his community', where *honores* refers to public magistracies, and probably priesthoods as well (*CIL II*, Index, p. 1167; Mackie 1983, 50 note 8).

The language of the inscriptions can help us to map out the varied aspects of the Spaniards' concept of *honor* (similar, but not identical to our own concept of 'honour'), and its place in the practice of urban munificence. The appearance of the term in these (Latin) inscriptions gives rise to a suspicion that regard for honour, in the particular shape in question, was imported to Spain along with the language in which the inscriptions were written. This is not to deny that Roman *honor* may have corresponded, to some degree, with pre-existing social values (cf. Drinkwater 1983, 142). At any rate, the Roman concept appears, in strikingly recognizable form, in this altar-dedication, from northern Portugal, to the native spring-god Bormanicus (on whom see Blázquez 1970, 67): '...you who pursue *honor*, whoever you are, may your glory keep you; and tell your child not to scribble on this stone' (*CIL II*, 2403 = *ILS* 4514b).

Once one has identified the presence of *honor* as a response to munificence, regard for *honor* emerges clearly from what the donors in inscriptions (1)-(3) say about their activities, and the use they make of the inscriptional mode of communication. All three donors give what is in effect an itemized account of their munificence, and place emphasis on 'giving at their own cost'. This reflects, not just a feeling that it is a shame to be generous and not get the credit for it, but also the conception of *honor* as attached to the sheer ability to spend large sums of money which appears in the emperor Augustus' own *Res Gestae*. In (1) and (2), the inscriptions recording the gifts function as a vehicle for advertising the donors' *other* claims to *honor*. Junia Rustica is 'first and perpetual priestess in the *municipium* of Cartima'; Quintius Hispanus is a local citizen who has made good in the imperial service, and spells out his success in the process of recording the gifts which are concrete symbols of his achievement. Finally, all three donors went to the trouble of cutting an inscription: why?

Cutting an inscription, in these three cases, implies a desire for contemporary esteem and/or a memorial: the donors had an (indefinite) audience in mind. In (3), Annia Victorina explicitly refers to commemoration as a motive for the gift ('...in memory of her husband..'). This leads us to the question whether the inscriptions we have are in fact representative of urban munificence as it was practised in Roman Spain. It is possible that the donors we know about constitute only a select type: the ones who cared especially about esteem and commemoration. Other people may have made the same sort of gifts, equally lavishly, to Spanish communities, but have failed to record the fact because their motives and preoccupations differed from those of the donors we have discussed.

There are, from Spain, very few inscriptions which explicitly refer to altruistic care for the community as a motive for munificence; and none (to my knowledge) which refers to such a motive on its own. This inscription, from the island of Ebusus (Ibiza), is remarkable for its other-regarding tone:

> ...he left 90,000 sesterces to the community of Ebusus so that, from this sum, taxes should be paid annually to the Romans and the citizens not be obliged to pay taxes in difficult times, the remaining 6,000 to be lent out and the interest used for annual games, with lights (?), on his birthday, the fifth...   (*CIL II*, 3664 = *ILS* 6960)

Notice that the man is anxious to have his own birthday commemorated, as well as to relieve the citizens of financial pressures; also that there was a special point in recording the phrase about paying taxes 'in difficult times' (on which see Duncan-Jones 1964, 201-3), that is, in order to ensure that the testator's wishes were carried out.

I would infer, neither that there was large-scale, and silent, giving from people who cared nothing for esteem or commemoration; nor that the impression the inscriptions give us as to the donors' motives is the whole story. Cutting an inscription is not the same thing as making a gift, and that the inscriptions should give undue emphasis to the pursuit of public esteem rather than to more altruistic motives is just what we would expect. On the other hand, the communities' own reactions to munificence reveal a close association between munificence and *honor*; an association which donors could not have escaped even if they wanted to, and which was fundamental to the *practice* of urban munificence (if not necessarily central to each individual case of it). In early imperial Spain, public esteem was habitually bestowed on people who spent large sums of money, visibly and personally, on urban amenities; and (as the tone of the extant inscriptions shows) openly to pursue public esteem by such expenditure was considered unexceptionable. In these respects, the evidence from Spain echoes evidence for other areas of the Roman Empire, East and West (eg. Brown 1978, chapter 2; Johnston 1985); and this association between *honor* and munificence goes some way towards defining and explaining what was going on. Giving to the community, and receiving *honor* in return, was something that one did; and it was also a practice that supplied donors in general with powerful motivation. As to the *origins* of the practice in Spain: we could call urban munificence simply a cultural accretion, or, more subtly, locate its origins in the arrival of a new language and a new conceptual scheme. But neither explanation on its own can explain why *this* (alien) practice should have gained ground and flourished. It is to a more specific explantion that we shall turn in the next section.

The dynamics of honour and power

Urban munificence, at its height, pervaded the life of the towns, in permanent and temporary, visible and invisible, forms. For us, it is the physical relics of the practice – the inscriptions and remains of buildings – which appear as its foremost manifestations. We tend to give less than full weight to the feasts, the entertainments, the distributions of money about which the inscriptions tell us. We forget that council-chambers, temples, theatres, circuses, baths, a water-supply, were not just built to be used, in that order: in many cases, these constructions must have been a secondary response to a felt need for the relevant activities. From the donor's point of view, the practice accommodated, and was sustained by, many different motives: the motives of *honor*, of commemoration for oneself and others, the pleasantness, usefulness, and religious significance of the objects of expenditure themselves. There was also, perhaps, a question of pride in one's community, a community that was becoming, not merely agreeable to live in, but Roman. (For pride in the *Romanitas* of one's community, see for example *CIL II*, 1955, where a man's friends have arranged for a statue to be set up of him, 'the first Roman *eques* from the community of Cartima'). The common factor, in all cases, was personal expenditure, of which the community was the beneficiary, the channel, and the focus.

If one wants to understand urban munificence in Spain, not just as the mature and established practice it eventually became, but also as an embryonic practice progressively taking hold from the beginning of our era onwards, the key perhaps lies in the particular processes by which the exchange of *honor* and munificence was managed. The *honor* which accrued to donors was both generalized (esteem, gratitude, in the community) and specific (*honor* in the shape of a public statue, appointment to a public position, and so on). In its specific forms, *honor* lay largely in the gift, not of citizens or residents in general, but of the local council, the *senatus* or *ordo*. Making appointments, voting public statues, permitting others to set up statues in public places, conferring the title *patronus*, granting public funerals, the local council appears in inscriptions as the dominant source and controlling body for specific *honores* of all kinds (Mackie 1983, chapter 5; *CIL II*, Index, pp. 1162-5).

The actual money which local councils had at their disposal was limited. The convention whereby individuals repaid the cost of public statues (and public funerals) voted by the council indicates a system of public administration fundamentally geared to private contributions (*CIL II*, Index, p. 1176). Public funds in Spain relied on scattered and sometimes unpredictable sources of revenue, for example rents and fines; standard cash payments for office (*summae honorariae*) are barely attested; power to raise local taxes was restricted by the Roman government (Mackie 1983, chapter 7). The fact that Spanish inscriptions overwhelmingly report private rather than public expenditure probably reflects something more than a bias in the epigraphic record. (For substantial buildings, recorded in inscriptions, from public funds in Africa, see Duncan-Jones 1985). The council's own currency can be seen as *honor* rather than cash: *honor* which tempted, and duly rewarded, the munificence of those who could afford to pay for public amenities.

Just as examination of the specific forms and sources of *honor* leads us to the local council's powers and responsibilities, so examination of the process of giving points in the same direction. Urban munificence benefited everyone (more or less) in the community; the honour that rewarded it, generalized or specific, was public honour, its theoretical source being the community as a whole. But, as a public practice centred on the community, urban munificence was beset with practical, legal, and political complications. Specific public honours to benefactors had to be assigned and controlled. And, on the other side of the balance, someone had to accept a gift on behalf of the community; to see to (or be responsible for neglecting) the maintenance of buildings; to administer funds left to a community for perpetual benefactions. The right of towns throughout the Empire to accept legacies had to be established in law (cf. Johnston 1985). In all of this, the figure of the council looms large; and behind it the figure of the Roman government itself, regulating, extending, and clarifying the respective rights of communities and their benefactors.

'If anyone has promised to embellish with marble a building constructed by someone else...' We revert at last to the situation with which this paper began. When the senate of the peregrine Ipsca accepted a statue of the emperor Claudius, and declared that it should be 'among the public possessions in perpetuity' (above, p. 184), it was setting the community on a path towards a situation where local munificence would be exhaustively and meticulously circumscribed by Roman lawyers, in treatises applying Empire-wide. In gifts of land for building to communities – such as the land given to Cartima by the priestess Junia Rustica for a bath (above, p. 184) – we can see the responsibilities of communities, and so of local councils, literally expanding before our eyes.

As a final clue to why it all happened, I should like to appeal to the evidence of the Spanish town charters: in particular the charters of the Flavian period, which appear ever more compellingly to have come as a routine follow-up to the Latin right granted by Vespasian (see Mackie 1983, appendix 4; and for recent developments González 1986). The powers and activities of local councils, as prescribed in the charters, were no less pervasive than the practice of urban munificence itself. The following are excerpts (not all directly related to urban munificence) from the Flavian charters of Irni and Malaca (quoted at length by González 1986):

§19 (The aediles) are to have the right and power of managing the corn-supply, the sacred buildings, the sacred and holy places, the town, the roads, the districts, the drains, the baths and the market...and of seeing to and doing whatever else the council decides is to be done by the aediles...

§62 No one in the town of the *municipium*... or where buildings are continuous with the town, is to unroof or destroy or see to the demolition of a building, except by resolution of the council...

§73 The scribes who are to write and prepare the common records, books and accounts in that *municipium*, whom the majority of the council of that *municipium* have approved...

§76 A *duovir* of the *municipium*... each in his year, is to raise with the council of that *municipium*, when not less than two-thirds are present, whether it is to be decided that the territories and fields and sources of revenue of that *municipium* are to be visited and inspected that year...

The practice of urban munificence in Spain required that local councils have wide-ranging powers and responsibilities: the power to confer *honor*, the power to accept and manage benefactions, and all the administrative responsibilies that these powers brought in their train. It required, in short, that councils have the sort of rôle in the community that the charters prescribe. The upsurge in urban munificence in Spain from Vespasian's reign onwards can be seen as having had some precise legal and practical causes. It was not just a self-conscious reaction, by the towns and their citizens, to a new 'Romanized' status; it was also facilitated and stimulated by contemporary definitions of governmental authority.

But the development of urban munificence was a two-way process, in which the initiatives and ambitions of benefactors, as well as definitions of authority, played a part. Private giving, and public responsibility, went hand in hand: the one depended on the other, and stimulated the other. Already, before Vespasian's reign, gifts such as the one at Ipsca had been encouraging local councils to extend their responsibilities; from the Flavian period onwards, benefactors continued to exploit, and to stretch, the authority of the institutions which acted on the community's behalf. Munificence helped to create its own market; the reward of honour was inflated by the council's expanding power.

Conclusion

'Romaniser c'est municipaliser en même temps qu'urbaniser'. Among the surviving Romano-Spanish inscriptions, the two most numerous types are epitaphs, on the one hand, and records of urban activity, especially urban munificence, on the other. This is no accident. People inscribed things on stone to be noticed, and to be remembered. If the evidence of inscriptions is treated without caution, the proportion of records of munificence can (like the proportion of epitaphs) be misleading: people did a great many other things as well, about which the stones, for the best and most logical of reasons, fail to inform us. But records of munificence do at least bear witness to a widespread practice which contributed both to urban development, and (because of the cultural implications of munificence) to the spread of a 'Roman' lifestyle as a broader phenomenon. This practice consisted essentially in private expenditure for the sake of honour, which was directed towards the local community, and which – through the administrative strength of the community's institutions – was welcomed and rewarded with formal public esteem. The practice had many conditions and causes, among which can be numbered familiarity with Roman technology, architectural styles, and amusements; the presence of economic élites anxious to pursue *Romanitas*; and the Roman government's idea of provincial order, which led it to recognize and (at least) protect local government on the urban model. But, of the structural causes of urban munificence, the most significant appears to have been the dynamic coherence that existed between this practice and the model of local government prevailing in the Roman provinces.

'It is as if the whole world were celebrating a festival', wrote the Greek Aelius Aristides in the second century AD. 'Everywhere is full of gymnasia, fountains, monumental gateways, temples, workshops, schools; and one can say with full knowledge that the world, which has been in distress since the beginning, has been brought to health' (*Panegyric on Rome*, 97-8). Spain itself participated in this communal festival of East and West. It was – if occasionally idealized, then and now – a remarkable state of affairs, and it did not come about because 'native' succumbed to a package called 'Romanization'.

This paper has not been concerned, except peripherally, with the issue of Roman imperialism: how much, and how consciously, the Romans wanted an empire, and why; and to what lengths it occurred to them to go in order to secure one. But whatever the motives of imperialists, considered in isolation, it is at least true that there are some imperial structures which are better geared to survival than others. I would suspect that –in contrast to modern empires where the idea of self-government has been at war with imperialism, the idea of assimilation with the maintenance of a central power (Hargreaves 1979, 3-23) – the Roman Empire owed much of its astonishing durability to a constructive collaboration, over time, among its various social, political, and administrative ideals and practices. Urban munificence in Roman Spain is a small but relevant part of the story.

Notes

1   Editorial note: Nicola Mackie died in tragic circumstances on 9th August 1988. We publish here her paper as submitted soon after the Canterbury Conference. It is a fine tribute to an outstanding scholar who is much missed.

References

Alarcao, J. and Etienne, R. 1977-9 *Fouilles de Conimbriga*, 7 volumes, Paris: de Boccard

Alföldy, G. 1975 *Die römischen Inschriften von Tarraco*, 2 volumes, Berlin: de Gruyter

Beltrán, A. and Tovar, A. 1982 *Contrebia Belaisca I*, Zaragoza: Universidad de Zaragoza

Blázquez, J. M. 1970 'Las religiones indígenas del área noroeste de la península ibérica en relación con Roma', in *Legio VII Gemina*, 63-77. León: Diputación Provincial

Brown, P. 1978 *The Making of Late Antiquity*, Cambridge Ma.: Harvard University Press

CIL II = Hübner, E. (ed.) 1869-92 *Corpus Inscriptionum Latinarum* Vol. II with supplement, Berlin: Reimer

Curchin, L. A. 1983 'Personal wealth in Roman Spain', *Historia* 32, 227-44

Domergue, C. 1973 *Baelo I*, (Publications de la Casa de Velazquez, Série Archéologie Fasc. 1). Paris: de Boccard

Drinkwater, J. F. 1983 *Roman Gaul*, London: Croom Helm

Duncan-Jones, R. P. 1962 'Costs, Outlays and *Summae honorariae* from Roman Africa' *Papers of the British School at Rome* ns 17, 47-115

Duncan-Jones, R. P. 1964 'Human numbers in towns and town-organizations of the Roman Empire: the evidence of gifts' *Historia* 13, 199-208

Duncan-Jones, R. P. 1982 *The Economy of the Roman Empire: Quantitative Studies*, second edition, Cambridge: Cambridge University Press

Duncan-Jones, R. P. 1985 'Who paid for public buildings in Roman cities?' in Grew, F. and Hobley, B. (eds.) *Roman urban topography in Britain and the western Empire*, 28-33. London: Council for British Archaeology

Frere, S. S. 1985 'Civic pride: a factor in Roman town planning' in Grew, F. and Hobley, B. (eds.) *Roman urban topography in Britain and the western Empire*, 34-6. London: Council for British Archaeology

Frontinus 1982 Frontinus-Gesellschaft e.v. (ed.) *Wasserversorgung im antiken Rom*. Munich: Oldenbourg

Gagé, J. 1964 *Les classes sociales dans l'Empire romain*, Paris: Payot

García y Bellido, A. 1967a *Les religions orientales dans l'Espagne romaine*, Leiden: Brill

García y Bellido, A. 1967b 'La Latinización de Hispania' *Archivo Español de Arqueología* 40, 3-29

González, J. 1986 'The Lex Irnitana: a new copy of the Flavian Municipal Law', *J. Roman Stud.* 76, 147-243

Gorges, J.-G. 1979 *Les villas hispano-romaines*, Paris: de Boccard

Granados, J. O. 1984 'La primera fortification de la colonia Barcino' in Blagg, T. F. C., Jones, R. F. J. and Keay, S. J. (eds.). *Papers in Iberian Archaeology*, 267-319. Oxford: B.A.R.

HAE 1950- *Hispania antiqua epigráphica: Suplemento anual de Archivo Español de Arqueología* Madrid: C. S. I. C.

Hargreaves, J. D. 1979 *The End of Colonial Rule in West Africa* London: Macmillan

ILS Dessau, H. (ed.) 1892-1916 *Inscriptiones Latinae Selectae* 3 vols. Berlin: Weidmann

Johnston, D. 1985 'Munificence and *Municipia*: bequests to towns in classical Roman Law', *J. Roman Stud.* 75, 105-25

Knapp, R. C. 1983 *Roman Córdoba*, Berkeley: University of California Press

Mackie, N. 1983 *Local Administration in Roman Spain AD* 14-212, Oxford: B.A.R.

MacMullen, R. 1982 'The Epigraphic Habit in the Roman Empire' *American J. of Philology* 103, 233-46

Mann, J. C. 1985 'Epigraphic Consciousness' *J. Roman Stud.* 75, 204-6

Richardson, J. S. 1986 *Hispaniae: Spain and the development of Roman imperialism* 218-82 BC. Cambridge: Cambridge University Press

Villaronga, L. 1973 *Las monedas hispano-cartaginesas* Barcelona: Círculo Filatélico y Numismático

Villaronga, L. 1984 'Las primeras emisiones de monedas de bronce en Hispania', in Blagg, T. F. C., Jones, R. F. J. and Keay, S. J. (eds.) *Papers in Iberian Archaeology*, 205-215. Oxford: B.A.R.

Wiseman, T. P. 1983 '*Domi nobiles* and the cultural élite', in *Les 'bourgeoisies' municipales italiennes aux IIe et Ier siècles avant J.-C.*, 299-307. Paris: C.N.R.S.

Section IV
Cultural and Social Change

Whilst there has been a widespread acknowledgement of the social and cultural changes which characterize Romanization, until recently there has been little detailed exploration of how religion, art and architecture were used as active ingredients in the processes rather than simply as passive reflections of them. The three papers in this section examine ways in which different aspects of social and cultural change in Gaul and Britain are illuminated by these data.

Blagg looks at housing, which provides a wealth of information about patterns of social change. He argues that houses provide a more valuable barometer than contemporary public buildings since they had to satisfy the living needs of their inhabitants as well as displaying their *Romanitas*. Roman architectural forms allow valuable comparisons to be made between town and country, and between different regions, whilst the morphology of the buildings may be a key to social structure. Romanized buildings appeared first in the countryside where, besides the major villas which, with their Mediterranean-type layouts, allowed public ceremonial display, there are also more basic corridor houses together with larger linear buildings apparently for multiple occupancy. The towns show a less elaborate development of housing before the second century AD with the buildings more appropriate to urban artisans rather than a social élite. When the towns are provided with more elaborate houses, their forms are similar to those of the villas, implying occupation by the same social group who were new to the towns.

Drinkwater sets out to examine whether or not the Gauls benefitted from incorporation into the Empire, bearing in mind the losses of both freedom and indigenous culture that this involved. He outlines the economic benefits and the opportunities for social advancement which accrued from the *Pax Romana*, but contrasts this with the subjugation of the natives. To illustrate this, he takes Vertet's argument that Central Gaulish pipe-clay figurines of goddesses symbolized native powerlessness and resignation to Roman rule. Drinkwater proposes an alternative view of their iconography as suggesting more positive and beneficial aspects of Rome's new order in Gaul.

King's paper is concerned more directly with the nature of Romano-Celtic religion. He sees religion as a vital and active ingredient in the processes of social and cultural change, rejecting its separation from other aspects of Romanization. Since archaeological evidence all pertains to ceremonial rather than belief, he examines the emergence of the related phenomena of Romano-Celtic temples, cult images and dedicatory inscriptions in relation to the core-periphery models some use to explain cultural change. It is shown that there were differing patterns of regional development resulting from the varying histories of cultural contact, particularly with the Greeks, although there were also common La Tène III precursors. Only dedicatory inscriptions can be seen as an essentially Roman introduction. The evidence of Roman policy to the Druids is used to question the extent to which their attitudes to native religion were truly laissez-faire. He concludes that there was a deliberate policy over religion which included associating the Imperial Cult with the worship of Celtic deities. In the synthesis resulting from Romanization, Celtic cults lost the separate identity of their ceremonial forms, though not necessarily their beliefs. The resulting regional patterns are shown to provide a valuable index of Romanization and useful insights into the processes of cultural change.

13. First-century Roman houses in Gaul and Britain

by T.F.C. Blagg

An examination of the earliest Roman houses in the north-western provinces is not straightforward. For one thing, many 1st-century AD Roman sites, both urban and rural, continued to be occupied in later centuries. Consequently, few 1st-century houses have survived without being much altered by later buildings, and the archaeological evidence for them is more fragmentary and difficult to use. Those who have made general studies of Roman houses in the provinces have naturally tended to concentrate on the more fully developed and better preserved examples, mainly of the 2nd century and later (McKay 1975; Percival 1976; Ward-Perkins 1981). This tendency has allowed earlier buildings to be seen mainly as simpler and less evolved manifestations of Roman provincial building methods, representing the initial stages in rectilinear planning, whether of timber beam or mortared stone construction, and of furnishing with *opus signinum* or mosaic floors, hypocaust heating and painted wall-plaster. In this, they may constitute the beginning, either of the particular evolution of a structure (e.g. the villa at Gorhambury: Neal 1978), or of the general evolution of a site (e.g. that of Verulamium from the timber structures of the pre-Boudiccan town to the courtyard houses of the late-3rd and 4th-century 'first-class classical city': Frere 1983, 7-23). Buildings which were large and ambitious from the start, like the Fishbourne houses, do not of course fit into this pattern, except with the hindsight which can regard them as anticipating later developments. If, however, we consider types of housing not just in architectural terms, but also as reflecting the social institutions of those who lived in them, then those of the 1st century should be of particular interest for what might be deduced from them about the variety of social response to the Roman conquest, in a period when alternative directions and changes of direction may be observed. This will involve a comparison between urban and rural sites from a standpoint rather different from the studies of the later relationship between town and country, in the period after the towns had become fully established (*cf.* Fulford 1982; Millett 1982).

Although it has long been noticed that among the main types of Romano-British house, those with corridors and courtyards as parts of their plan, 'no special type of town-house occurs' (Haverfield 1923, 40), studies of Roman domestic architecture in Britain, and in other provinces too, have tended to observe in practice a distinction between houses in the country (i.e. villas) and houses in the towns. Villas have been considered in regional groups, as those of a whole province, or a part of it. Town houses however have not usually been so grouped, but have normally been treated as one aspect of the architectural remains of the individual town to which they belonged. Villas seem to have been regarded as the more interesting, if the number of books or conferences on them is anything to go by (e.g. Rivet 1969, Percival 1976, Todd 1978). In part, this may be because it has been more fashionable in recent years to concentrate on socio-economic functions, i.e. villas as farms, rather than on their morphology and their domestic (and also social) function as houses (*cf.* Slofstra 1983, 84). One exception to these generalisations is the paper by Walthew (1975) on the town house and the villa house in Britain, in which he drew attention to the similarities which suggested that the *developed* form of town houses appeared to derive from the planning of villas. Very little of the evidence which he used was earlier then the 2nd century, and for the 1st century, rather a different picture may be suggested.

It was, in the first place, a period of striking innovation in domestic architecture. In Britain, the main difference between houses in the late pre-Roman Iron Age and those typical of the Roman period is not merely formal, in that the former were mainly circular and the latter rectangular in plan (though *cf.* Rodwell 1978), and that in Roman housing a different range of constructional methods and building materials was employed. There is also a fundamental difference between them in their organization of interior space. With the increase in knowledge of Iron Age houses from the excavations of hill forts and farmstead sites during the past twenty years, and with the insight derived from experimental reconstructions, notably at Butser (Reynolds 1979), it is now more widely accepted that Iron Age houses could be large and impressive structures, the product of accomplished skills in construction, and representing some elaboration in social organization. Nevertheless, there is as yet little sign of systematic internal divisions within these houses of the kind which would reflect a hierarchy in social custom or a differentiation in domestic function. That is, in the design of the house, separate parts are not set in compartments aside from the rest in order to accommodate individuals or groups of different status within the household, or for such particular activities as cooking, eating, entertaining guests or sleeping. Some rectangular late Iron Age houses on continental sites, e.g. the oppida of Manching, Mont Beuvray and Villeneuve-Saint-Germain (Collis 1984, 109-17 and 130) and the farmstead at Verberie (Agache 1978, 92 and 180), have lines of internal posts which might have represented partitions. Although some of the British rectangular buildings had similar internal posts (Rodwell 1978, 29-33, Figs. 2.15, 2.19, 3.3, 3.4b), it is not certain that they functioned as houses. Even in circular houses, it is possible that parts of the peripheral area, between the walls and the roof posts, might have been screened off. All this, however, is not more than slight or hypothetical evidence that British Iron-Age houses had the systematic divisions which are characteristic of even relatively modest-sized Roman-style houses. Even if we are usually unable to identify the functions of the rooms of an excavated Roman house, their number and variety may be significant in themselves.

In his contribution to this volume, Trow makes the point that in Britain in the immediate post-conquest period architecture was an obvious new medium in which to express the status and the favourable relations with the occupying power held by those members of the native élite whose authority had survived the transition to Roman rule. He also notes that luxurious romanized structures began to appear more rapidly on rural sites than in towns. Both points are relevant to the evidence which will be examined in this chapter. In relation to the first, there was conspicuous display in public architecture, in forums, basilicas, temples and theatres, of a kind which was identical with the munificence of the élite of Roman Italy during the late Republic. The benefaction of public building in return for *honor* could be sheer ostentation, but it is less credible that private domestic architecture in the Roman manner should have been nothing more than display. However splendid and luxurious, a house is still, in le Corbusier's phrase, a machine for living; even when Nero remarked of his extravagant Golden House in Rome, 'that he was at last beginning to live in human conditions' (Suetonius, *Nero* VI.2), the exaggeration has point only because of its core of truth, that Nero did live there.

The proposal that architecture was selected after the conquest as a medium for expressing the status of the Romanized élite is as relevant to Gaul as it is to Britain, as King also observes (this volume, 231) with reference to temples. For Gaul we have a little more historical information than we do for Britain about the native aristocrats concerned. References to villas in Tacitus' accounts of the revolts of Julius Sacrovir in AD 21 and Julius Civilis in AD 69 provide evidence of a circumstantial kind. Sacrovir, an Aeduan nobleman, after his defeat in battle fled first to Autun and then to a nearby villa, where he killed himself, after which the house was set on fire (Tacitus, *Annals* III, 46). Civilis, who also had Roman citizen status and was an auxiliary cohort commander as well as being a Batavian of royal lineage, is said to have had his lands and villas spared from the ravaging of Batavian territory by order of the opposing Roman general Petillius Cerealis (Tacitus, *Histories* V, 23). The term used is *villa*, contrasting with Caesar's description of the properties which he saw in the British countryside simply as buildings: 'creberrimaque aedificia fere Gallicis consimilia' (*De Bello Gallico* V, 12, 3). From his use of the word, Tacitus, as an educated metropolitan Roman, evidently knew, or if not could plausibly assume, that these Romanized Gauls lived in country houses of the kind appropriate to Roman landowners. So far as concerns the Batavians, there is little archaeological sign of rural Romanization, but this may not be surprising, considering the probably rather exclusive nature of the tribe's military élite. (*cf.* Bloemers, this volume, 74ff.).

Wightman has suggested (1985, 105) that roughly one half of the villas in Belgica were built in the second half of the first century AD (see also Haselgrove, this volume, 52ff.). The archaeological evidence for first-century villas is varied, however, and can be complex to interpret. This may first be illustrated by the Belgian site of Haccourt (de Boe 1974). Initially there were two phases of timber post-hole construction, the first of which was late Iron Age, possibly immediately post-conquest, the second approximately mid-1st century AD. After that date, and probably towards the 70s AD, according to the pottery evidence, the first masonry villa was built. A column capital found in the destruction debris suggests a house of some quality, but all that remained of the structure was a cellar, aligned slightly differently from the Period II house, the terracing for which had removed the rest of the earlier structure, some time before the end of the 1st century. The period II house consisted of a range of a dozen rooms, several of them very long and narrow (1.6 – 2.6m), with a corridor along the north side (Fig. 13.1). The bath suite was later converted to residential use, replaced by smaller baths, and a south corridor was added, before the whole building was demolished and an enormous new villa was built over it in the first half of the 2nd century. The furnishings of the late 1st century house were relatively simple, with earth floors and little evidence of wall-plaster, except in the baths. The linear arrangement of rooms, lacking a central architectural focus, suggests a fairly egalitarian household, not one which needed a reception room for *clientes*, for example.

In relation to the overall development of the villa, de Boe (1974, 41) has commented that, given the relatively uniform distribution of villas in the region (62 sites are known in an area of 95 km^2 west of the Meuse), there was little to indicate Haccourt's future great development. He inferred that the distribution implied a degree of social uniformity and exploitation of what had previously been public or communal land, rather than a clustering of tenants on the estate of a great landed proprietor. Nevertheless, it should be noted that there is no evidence of centuriation, the site is not close to a Roman *colonia*, and there is no particular reason to suppose the imposition of a Roman superstructure on the pattern of occupation, rather than a native adaptation. On the other hand, Haccourt was presumably in the territory of Tongeren (Tongres), and Bloemers (this volume, 83) notes the difference between the sleeper-beam construction of Claudian buildings there and the typical groundplans of native farmsteads, as

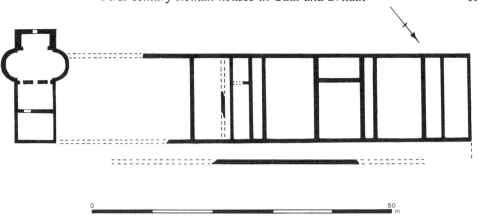

Fig. 13.1. Haccourt, the Period II villa.

well as the dislocation of the proto-urban settlement which Tongeren's development involved. One problem of interpretation is not knowing how many of the 62 villa sites were in contemporary occupation, especially in the century prior to Haccourt's Period IV large-scale rebuilding.

The same problem applies to understanding the villas in the Somme region, where Agache's work (1978) has added enormously to our knowledge of Roman rural occupation in the area. Although few of the sites have been explored by excavation, an appreciable number of those excavated originate in the 1st century. Few, however, have a demonstrable relationship to pre-Roman occupation. Port-le-Grand, near to an Iron Age farmstead enclosure, is the only example in Agache's survey of such a juxtaposition (1978, 368). Allowing for the possibility of selectivity in the conditions for the aerial detection of different types of site, there still seems to be a substantial change in the preferred location of sites, with native-type farmsteads along the valleys or on the heights overlooking them, and villas on the plateaux. Agache reminds us that some at least of the native farms continued to be occupied into the 2nd century (1978, 368). Nevertheless, there is the phenomenon of grand villas build on rich if heavy land previously unoccupied. At the large villa of Estrées-sur-Noye, for example, the excavations have produced no pottery earlier than Roman (Fig. 13.2).

Wightman (1985, 111) has drawn attention to the important point that there were some villas which did not grow from simple comfort to luxury, as Haccourt did, but which were luxurious from the start. Echternach is an early example, dated to Nero's reign, a palatial establishment with marble-veneered central room, baths, and wings flanking an ornamental pool. A striking feature of these houses is the elaboration of their layout and particularly, as at Estrées-sur-Noye, the symmetrical relationship of the villa and its subsidiary buildings along a central axis. This is not a very notable feature of Italian villas, though somewhat reminiscent of the seaside villas in Pompeian wall-paintings. It is, however, a dominant feature of the layout of Gallo-Roman religious sanctuaries, e.g. Ribemont-sur-Ancre (Somme) (Cadoux 1984), where the ancillary buildings form an avenue and the theatre and the baths lie on the central axis leading up to the temple on its hill. This symmetry of arrangement grandly imposed on a rural setting is also characteristic of some of the late Republican religious sanctuaries of central Italy. Walthew (1982, 229) has suggested that in northern Gaul, the religious sanctuaries rather than the towns were the formative sites for public monumental architecture (though *cf.* Drinkwater 1983, 190-1). In Picard's view (1983) these *conciliabula* were the product of the patronage and benefactions of the great Gallo-Roman landowners (see also Drinkwater, this volume, 217). Luxury 1st-century villas may reflect the same planning concepts as the sanctuaries, as Agache has already suggested (1978, 410), representing a particular choice of what architecture in the Roman manner was supposed to look like; in Picard's words (1983, 421) 'une romanisation mitigée'. The orthogonal layout of some late Iron age settlements in the Aisne valley, e.g. Condé and Beaurieux (Haselgrove, this volume, 48) may be relevant to the sort of choice which was made.

In Britain, this axially symmetrical planning is not a marked feature of religious sanctuaries (Blagg 1986). Nor would it seem clearly demonstrable on early villa sites. It has been claimed for the villa at Rivenhall (Rodwell 1985, 41-5), but the case depends on a geometry in which several of the constituent features are conjectural, and there are doubts about the 1st century 'proto-villa' which in any case was not necessarily on the same alignment (Millett 1987). While this type of axial planning might have influenced the layout of some more modest sites (e.g. Gorhambury), it is much less obvious than in Gaul. By contrast, some of the earliest villas in Britain follow a different model of regular Roman planning, the square courtyard.

The finest known so far is the so-called proto-palace at Fishbourne, dated to AD 65-70 (Fig. 13.3: Cunliffe, 61-69). The excavated part consists of three main elements: a courtyard, surrounded on its north, east and west sides by corridors of between 2 and 3 metres in width; a bath suite comprising at least eight rooms; and a range of rooms at least 52 metres in extent along the east side of both the courtyard and the baths. The walls of the baths are likely to have been of masonry, but the superstructure of the northern part of the house appears to have been clay, rendered in painted plaster. Little is known about the arrangement of the residential rooms, but is clear that the house was magnificently decorated. It had Corinthian columns of a size indicating probable use in an atrium or entrance porch, and smaller columns either round the courtyard or on the facade. Two rooms in the baths had black and white mosaic floors, and there were *opus sectile* and wall veneers of Purbeck and imported marbles and other stones, wall-plaster painted with geometric, floral and marine designs, and stucco ornament. In addition to the architectural design, the construction techniques in masonry, tile hypocausts, ornamental stonework, flooring, painted plaster and other decorative features all required skilled craftsmen who initially had to be brought in from other provinces. Their employment advertised the extent of the patron's influential connexions in securing such rare commodities (Blagg 1980; Trow, this volume p. 112-3).

The Fishbourne proto-palace was not unique in these respects. At Angmering, 16 miles to the east, a bath suite built about AD 65-75 had an arrangement of rooms very similar to that at Fishbourne, and also had floors of *opus sectile*. It stood separate from the villa building, of which little is known, save that it was at least 24 metres long and had walls with masonry foundations (Scott 1938). Another masonry house at Fishbourne, 100 metres north-west of the proto-palace, had at least two ranges of rooms joining at right angles, and was still unfinished when the period 2 Flavian palace was built *c.* AD 75 (Cunliffe 1971, 69-72). Black (1987, 84-6) would postpone the palace's date to the last decade of the 1st century, on the basis of the tile used; the argument may need more supporting evidence, though it is a reminder that the excavator's interpretation of the stratigraphy associated with the construction is not the only one possible.

For Roman Britain, the palace was exceptional in its size and amenities, and clearly it must have been built for someone equally exceptional, whether or not it was the Romans'

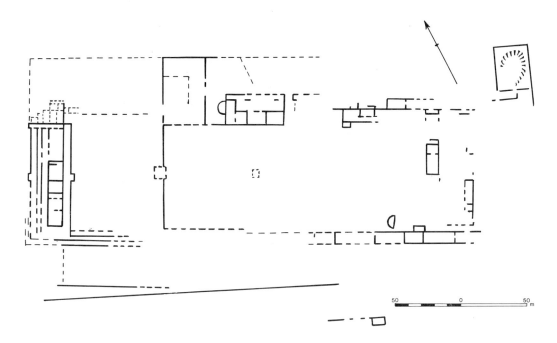

Fig. 13.2. Estrées-sur-Noye, villa and ancillary buildings.

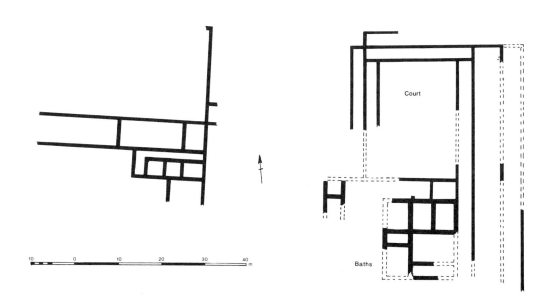

Fig. 13.3. Fishbourne, Period I houses.

allied British king Ti. Claudius Cogidubnus. In its courtyard plan and its furnishings, however, it was not so different in concept from its predecessor, except in being on a far vaster scale. It was built round a colonnaded garden 100 metres wide, across which an avenue of hedges and fountains led from the monumental entrance hall to the apsidal vaulted room in the centre of the west range, which may have been an audience hall or a formal dining room. Cunliffe (1971, 151-3) was impressed by the resemblance of this arrangement to that of the Palace of Domitian in Rome, which is indeed striking. There are two major points of difference, however. The entrance hall and apsidal room at Fishbourne are considerably smaller than the corresponding rooms in Domitian's Palace, but its courtyard garden is twice as large; the greater space would have reduced the dominating effect of the architecture. That would have been appropriate, given the second point of difference, that the Fishbourne palace courtyard layout included the residential quarters which in the Rome palace formed a separately planned complex adjacent to the ceremonial and state rooms. The residential quarters at Fishbourne were arranged in suites around subsidiary courtyards on the north and east sides of the main garden courtyard.

Black (1987, 102-4) has argued that the courtyard plan house at Southwick, also in Sussex, can be seen as a small-scale version of Fishbourne's (Fig. 13.4). In particular, the entrance and an apsidal room are placed centrally on opposite sides of the courtyard, and the rooms in the north wing are arranged in a manner very similar to the suites built around the enclosed courtyards in the north wing at Fishbourne. Applying J.T. Smith's suggestion (1978, 162) that 'multiple-unit' houses, i.e. those which appear to comprise several units of accommodation, might be designed for an extended family or kindred, Black proposed (1987, 28) that Fishbourne and Southwick could have been occupied by more than one family of similar status.

The earliest stage of the villa at Eccles in Kent is very different from these Sussex houses (Fig. 13.5), except for the bath-house which, as at Angmering, was a separate building, constructed c. AD 65. The house consisted of a range of twelve rooms, 75 metres long overall, fronted by a corridor. The five rooms at the north-west end had tesselated floors; those of the remainder did not survive, though there were indications that some were tiled. The corridor had a wooden floor, and it is thought that its roof was supported at the front by timber posts placed upon a low sill wall. In front of the house, and parallel with it, at a distance of 11.6 metres, there was a long narrow rectangular structure measuring 51.1 x 5 metres, rendered internally with *opus signinum* and with a drain in one corner, which has been interpreted as an ornamental pool (Detsicas 1983, 120).

The plan of the house is unusual in the combination of its length with a very simple linear arrangement of rooms. As J.T. Smith (1978, 160) has pointed out, the plan can be analysed in terms of there being three identical groups of three rooms, of which two were square with a narrower room between them. Three other rooms were placed, one between two of the groups of three, and one at each end of the building. There is no cross-axis of symmetry. Apart from the insertion of cross-walls in two of the rooms, this range of rooms remained essentially unaltered in plan, though about AD 180 further rooms were added at the north end, and an east corridor, itself later divided into a series of rooms. Initially, however, the villa must have had a rather barrack-like appearance, and in the relative simplicity both of its planning and of its decoration it resembles the period II house at Haccourt.

The house built at Mileoak, Northamptonshire, c. AD 65-75, is barrack-like in a different sense, in having several pairs of large and small rooms (Fig. 13.6). It was 39.6 metres long,

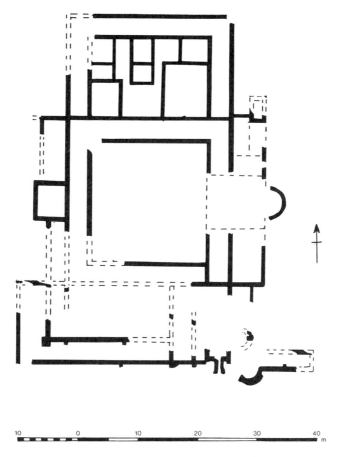

Fig. 13.4. Southwick, courtyard villa.

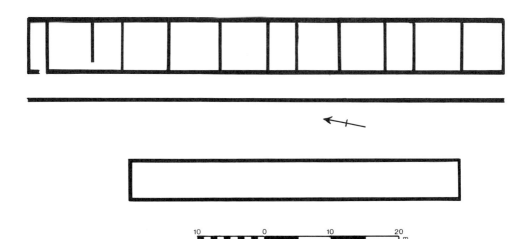

Fig. 13.5. Eccles, the Period I building.

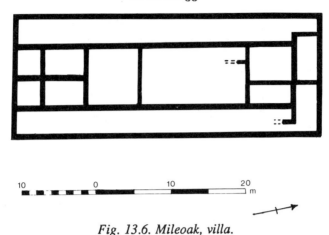

10   0   10   20
                                m

Fig. 13.6. Mileoak, villa.

and had a corridor along each side of the central range. In that sense it does not so much resemble the aisled houses to which the excavators likened it (Green and Draper 1978, 64), but rather a wingless corridor villa. It had clay floors and a tiled roof. The walls had footings of coursed rubble, but at least part of the superstructure was of timber and clay daub. The internal walls had plaster painted with panelled designs, and the outer walls of the building were rendered externally in maroon-coloured plaster (Green and Draper 1978, 34-41).

It was not until the last years of the first century that the form of villa most characteristic of northern Gaul and Britain, the winged corridor type, was introduced into Britain, and it did not become fully established until well into the following century. In many cases, the plan can be seen as a straight-forward evolution from a rectangular block of five or six rooms arranged side-by-side, sometimes with a corridor or portico of timber posts along the front. Richmond (1969, 52-3) described such villas as the 'cottage' type, but that epithet gives too modest an impression of their probable social status, size and comfort. The next stage, formally, was the addition to the front of a projecting room or wing of rooms at each end, with a corridor between them or along the entire facade, in some cases around the back as well.

There are, of course, individual variations from this generalised sequence. At Gorhambury, 1 km north-west of Verulamium, Iron Age circular houses were succeeded by a rectangular structure of timber, forming a block of at least three rooms with puddled chalk and clay floors. The sleeper beam construction was similar to that used in 1st century buildings at Verulamium. In the late 1st or early 2nd century a masonry house was built, with five rooms, a corridor with one wing room at the north-east corner, and a cellar at the south end (Fig. 13.7). It was decorated with moulded and painted stucco. Extensions to each end were built in the early 2nd century. It was replaced by a larger winged double corridor house built alongside in the mid-2nd century (Neal 1978, 37; Selkirk 1983). At Boxmoor, 9 km west of Verulamium, the earliest structure was a relatively small (21.6 metres long) late 1st century winged corridor house with an all round corridor. It was built of timber, with sleeper beams, wattle and daub walls, one room with painted plaster, and mortar floors. It was destroyed by fire, and replaced by a Hadrianic/Antonine winged corridor house of more than double the floor area with cob walls on masonry foundations (Neal 1974-6, 57-9).

It is striking how frequently a rectangular block of five or six rooms, 25 to 30 metres in length overall, forms the earliest phase of a villa, as at Park Street and Lockleys (Richmond

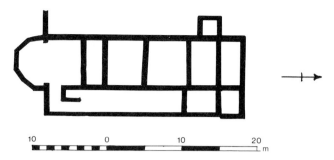

Fig. 13.7. Gorhambury, first century masonry house.

1969, 54, fig. 2.1), and continues as its nucleus. The regular repetition of certain groups of rooms within such nuclear blocks has also been noticed (Drury 1982, 295-99). Since the precise uses of the rooms are uncertain, the significance of the repetition cannot be closely defined, but it might be deduced that the nuclear block represents a plan evolved to meet the basic housing requirements of the Romano-British or Gallo-Roman landed family. It was to provide the main model for urban housing, as well as the unit from which most later and larger villas developed. The grander 1st century courtyard houses were not influential in the same way. They may, however, in combination perhaps with the similarly planned officers' houses in military forts, have been the model for one particular type of urban house, the *mansio*.

The evolution of early town houses in Britain follows a rather different pattern from what can be observed in Gaul. In the south of Gaul, the 1st century BC peristyle courtyard houses at Glanum and Vaison follow Hellenistic precedents which could well have been derived from such nearby Greek colonies as Marseille. Goudineau (1979, 239-48), however, in observing that Hellenistic peristyles were also common in Campanian houses, prefers to see their presence in the Gaulish cities as the result of Romanizing influence, introducing a feature which had already been assimilated in central and southern Italy.

Outside Provence, there is little evidence for Roman town housing until late in the 1st century BC. At Lyon, for example, excavations which began in 1974 adjoining the Rue des Farges on the Fourvière hill uncovered an area of housing, terraced into the hillside, and laid out at the end of the century. This included a series of shops on one side of the street, and a large house with a peristyle courtyard, the columns being composed of brick faced in stucco (Desbat *et al.* 1976). The greater element of luxury seen in the 1st century AD houses at Vaison (Goudineau 1979) is also illustrated in Autun (Fig. 13.8), where two courtyard houses built beside the Cardo Maximus, on the site of earlier similarly aligned buildings, date 'from the Flavian period, probably towards the beginning of the 2nd century' (Blanchard-Lemée *et al.* 1986). That of Balbius Iassus (named from the dedication of an altar to Dea Tutela which was found in it) had two floors of *opus sectile*, one being of marble, a room with marble wall veneers, and a garden fountain. The other house also had *opus sectile* floors, and two of black mosaic with sporadic white tesserae, comparable with those of southern Gaul.

Knowledge of 1st century AD town houses further north in Gaul, however, is inhibited by problems of dating and the absence of detailed plans for comparison, though there are indications of buildings of quality. Beauvais, at least, has produced part of the plan of a rich house with peristyle courtyard and *impluvium* on the Rue Biot (Frézouls 1982, 168). In Metz, the stratified evidence for several fires allows the early development of housing to be indicated in some detail. J.-J. Hatt's identification (1958, 324-5) of these fires with the events of AD 21 and 68-70 should be viewed with caution, however; little has been published of the evidence, other than reference to some Arretine potters' stamps. Two areas of 1st century housing have been explored. At the north end of the city, in the Sainte-Croix quarter, native-type houses of wood were destroyed in an early 1st century fire, rebuilt in wood, but with painted plaster walls, and after a fire attributed to the year 68 they were rebuilt in stone, again with painted plaster walls. In the Esplanade and Citadelle area to the south the development seems to have been of higher quality to begin with, the houses being built of *petit appareil* masonry and decorated with black-ground frescoes in the Third Pompeian style. After their destruction *c*. AD 68-70, their successors included houses with coloured marble wall veneers, Fourth-style wall paintings and hypocaust heating.

At Trier, by contrast, such evidence as there is for 1st century houses is for modest timber and wattle-and-daub structures, but nothing approaching a complete house-plan has been recovered. The second half of the century saw the building of some rather more substantial structures, with stone foundations and black and white geometric mosaics, found in Insula H 10 and in H 4, G 5 and G 6, beside and below the Aula Palatina. In Insula H 8 excavations discovered the stone-built cellars of 1st century houses (Wightman 1970, 73). In comparison with the spacious and well-furnished houses of the second century and later, this suggests relatively modest beginnings of domestic architecture in the city (as was also true of its public buildings). This contrasts both with the evidence from Autun and Lyon in central Gaul, and with that from the more luxurious villas in Gallia Belgica. It is not too surprising, however, in view of Walthew's observation (1982) of a slowing down of urban development in Gallia Belgica in the second half of the 1st century.

Domestic architecture in the British towns has equally modest beginnings. The best evidence comes from those damaged by fire at the time of Boudicca's rebellion, since ironically the destruction deposits have preserved the remains of timber and clay structures to a greater than usual extent. At Colchester, after the foundation of the *colonia c*. AD 47, some of the timber-framed barracks of the legionary fortress were adapted by alteration of internal partition walls. New buildings were constructed in places where the streets had been realigned, but in most cases little of their plans has survived. At the Lion Walk site, however, Building 8 was found to have ranges of rooms on three sides of a rectangular gravelled yard which opened on to the street (Fig. 13.9). These ranges may in fact have formed more than one building, since two types of superstructure were found. One was of wattle-and-daub set between squared uprights, the other type, in three walls in the western half of the site, was of clay blocks only; both types of wall were built on sill-beams resting on the ground (Crummy 1984, 40). One room contained the burned remains of two mattresses in one corner, and was presumably a bedroom; the wall at the head of the bed was plastered and painted on both sides to imitate marble.

The period I building on Insula XIV at Verulamium is one of the best-preserved timber buildings of this date. It stood at a street corner, and had a continuous portico along both frontages with rooms of regular size opening on to it. The height of the roof implied by the width of the building indicates that there would have been ample space for accommodation above the ground floor. The manner of construction, with sleeper beams and uprights of oak carrying an infill of wattle-and-daub, and the estimated quantity of timber required (over 3000 metres) suggested to the excavator that military craftsmen and stockpiles had been made

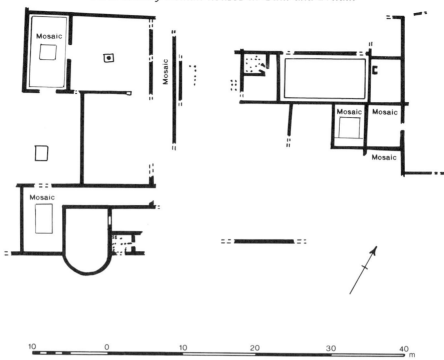

Fig. 13.8. Autun, Flavian courtyard houses.

available (Frere 1972, 11). Frere found analogy for the construction in the fort at Valkenburg in the Netherlands, but its similarity to the techniques used in Building 8 at Colchester, excavated after the report on Insula XIV was written, might suggest that the military affinities were at one remove, with the veteran *colonia* as the intermediary for its introduction into civilian contexts. Moreover, as Perring has pointed out (1987, 147), the technique was used in civilian buildings outside Britain, for instance at Lyon. Perring has also noted (1987, 149-50) that the materials used for these 1st century buildings indicate that they 'were built as simply and cheaply as possible', with a structure based on earth-fast posts or sleeper beams, and walls of wattle-and-daub, planks or unbaked clay bricks. In Insula XIV at Verulamium and the Newgate Street site in London (Perring 1987, 150-1) later 1st century shops were built end-on to the street, and their more complex plan of rooms perhaps indicates more provision for domestic comfort. House D at Watling Court, London, with mortar and mosaic floors, painted wall-plaster and rooms occupying a street frontage of at least 30 metres, is a rare example of a 1st century Romano-British house comparable with some of the villas described above (Fig. 13.10), if not in the same class as the marble-furnished houses of Autun and Metz. Not until the mid-2nd century do substantial town houses become at all common in Britain (Walthew 1975, 204; see also Trow, this volume, 113).

Conclusions
One point made in the introductory paragraphs to this paper related to what might be deduced from 1st century houses about the variety of social response to the Roman conquest. Considering first the large courtyard villas, e.g. Echternach and Fishbourne: their formal

Street

Yard

0   10
                        m

Fig. 13.9. Colchester, Lion Walk, Building 8.

symmetrical layout reflects Mediterranean tastes; the courtyards and multiplicity of rooms could accommodate a large household retinue and numerous guests; and they have a large reception room as a main feature on the central axis. All these features suggest a choice of design intended for the display of ceremonial public life. There are really only two social categories for whom such arrangements would be appropriate: either wealthy Roman officials or settlers; or the Romanized descendants of native noble and royal families, such Gaulish and British Julii and Claudii as Florus, Sacrovir, Vindex, Civilis and Cogidubnus. The grand 1st century villas could represent the latter category in a way appropriate to their actual or equivalent equestrian status as commanders of Roman auxiliary regiments. If the patronage of early religious sanctuaries, e.g. Ribemont and Hayling Island, was also due to these aristocrats, such a nurturing of their traditional rural power base might explain why urban development was initially so much slower. Conversely, the fact that grand courtyard houses were something of an early exception to the norm of rural housing, superseded by the more gradual development of other types of house, might suggest that these grandees did not long maintain their exceptional position (*cf.* Picard 1983, 420). The Gaulish rebellions were one of the ways in which they overreached themselves.

Among the other types which show the growth of a more broadly based Romanized rural society, two may be chosen for further comment. First, the appearance of the five- or six-roomed corridor house, often much elaborated later with wings and additional rooms. In their basic form, they show the adoption of Roman building standards. In relation to Iron Age houses, the more specialised plan implies the adoption of Roman manners of living, but it does not suggest the frequent entertainment of visiting guests or clients. It seems to have needed two or three generations after the conquest for the assimilation of ideas or the accumulation of resources to build in this manner. Such houses might be seen as the properties of Romanized native gentry, and their increasing frequency as an indication of the greater significance which that class acquired at the expense of the magnates who had been the traditional leaders of pre-Boudiccan and pre-Civilis days. These developments may also reflect the broader changes in the nature of social control over land and forms of land tenure which Gregson (1988) has discussed.

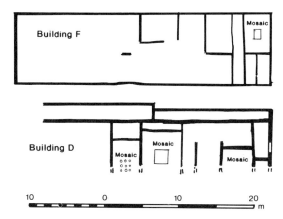

Fig. 13.10. London, Watling Court, House D.

In the second case, exemplified by Haccourt II and Eccles, the linear arrangement and repetition of small suites of rooms might suggest joint occupation by two or more nuclear families, rather reminiscent of the Italian *fattoria*, housing dependent peasants or tenants rather than landowners. The large-scale 2nd century rebuilding of Haccourt is of such different character that a radical change in the type of occupant is indicated.

Only rarely are 1st century town houses similar to those in the country in detail, and the differences indicate a radically different social structure, one which seems to become much more assimilated in the course of the 2nd century. One of the main questions in considering the process of Romanization has been the extent to which the native provincials adopted an urban way of life. Part of the answer must depend on the quality of that urban life. Its quality in Gallia Belgica and Britain, to judge from housing, was in general rather poor until well into the 2nd century, whatever may have been invested in public building. That makes the exceptional finer houses, as in Beauvais and Watling Court, London, the more striking. Also, when in the 2nd century town houses in Britain are built on the model of villas (Walthew 1975), it might be deduced that they were being built for the same social group, rather than for the upwardly mobile shopkeepers of Newgate Street, London and Insula XIV, Verulamium (*cf.* the 'self-assured artisans' of Gaul: Drinkwater, this volume, 212). This might indicate that a new generation now saw an advantage – perhaps in controlling markets and the raising of taxation – to be gained by adopting the bourgeois style of living from among the available Roman options. We do not know, of course, whether those who prospered sufficiently to patronise the construction of public buildings and to build large town houses, adapting the architecture of the villa to that purpose, were also landed gentry moving to the town; or whether the gentry remained rurally apart from an urban mercantile class whose houses showed that they aspired to the gentry's standards, if indeed it is not too anachronistic to make such a distinction.

Some distinction must be made, however, in judging the significance of Roman building materials. It is evident, from Lion Walk, Colchester and from the early Boxmoor villa, that quite modest houses might have painted wall-plaster and mortar floors. Mosaics and stucco mouldings show greater aspirations. Marble floor and wall veneers and columns of stone (particularly if also imported from a distance, as Fishbourne's were) needed a wider network of social connexions both for supply and for installation.

Architecturally, these are some of the varied levels of social response to what Rome had to offer. It is as well also to remember what Pliny (*NH* XXXVI, 7, 49) said of the house of M. Aemilius Lepidus at Rome, the finest of its time when built, but thirty-five years later, not to be counted among the top hundred. As Roman building methods and standards became increasingly widespread in Gaul and Britain, expectations of comfort and of architectural prestige increased also; and as wealth accumulated during the Pax Romana, so did the means to satisfy those expectations. That, however, is beyond the concern of this volume.

References

Agache, R. 1978 *La Somme préromaine et romaine*. Amiens.

Black, E.W. 1987 *The Roman Villas of South-east England* (Brit. Archaeol. Rep. 171). Oxford.

Blagg, T.F.C. 1980 Roman civil and military architecture in the province of Britain: aspects of patronage, influence and craft organization, *World Archaeol.* 12 (1), 27-42.

Blagg, T.F.C. 1986 Roman religious sites in the British landscape, *Landscape History* 8, 15-25.

Blanchard-Lemée, M., Olivier, A. and Rebourg, A. 1986 Deux maisons à pavements d'*Augustodunum* (Autun, Saône et Loire), *Gallia* 44, 120-49.

Boe, G. de 1974 Haccourt I, *Archaeol. Belgica* 168, 5-52.

Cadoux, J.-L. 1984 Le sanctuaire gallo-romain de Ribemont-sur-Ancre (Somme): état de recherches en 1983, *Rev. du Nord* 66, no. 260, 125-45.

Collis, J. 1984 *Oppida: earliest towns north of the Alps*. Sheffield.

Cunliffe, B. 1971 *Excavations at Fishbourne 1961-1969, I: The Site* (Soc. Antiq. London Res. Rep. 26). Leeds.

Crummy, P. 1984 *Excavations at Lion Walk, Balkerne Lane and Middleborough, Colchester, Essex* (Colchester Archaeol. Rep. 3). Colchester.

Desbat, A., Helly, B. and Tavernier, D. 1976 Lyon retrouve ses origines, *Archéologia* 92, 8-19.

Detsicas, A.P. 1983 *The Cantiaci*. Gloucester.

Drinkwater, J.F. 1983 *Roman Gaul*. London and Canberra.

Drury, P.J. 1982 Form, function and the interpretation of the excavated plans of some large secular Romano-British buildings. In P.J. Drury (ed), *Structural Reconstructions* (Brit. Archaeol. Rep. 110: Oxford), 289-308.

Frere, S.S. 1972 *Verulamium Excavations I* (Soc. Antiq. London Res. Rep. 28). Oxford.

Frere, S.S. 1983 *Verulamium Excavations II* (Soc. Antiq. London Res. Rep. 41). London.

Frézouls, E. 1982 *Les Villes Antiques de la France I. Belgique*. Strasbourg.

Fulford, M.G. 1982 Town and country in Roman Britain – a parasitical relationship?, in Miles 1982, 403-19.

Goudineau, C. 1979 *Les Fouilles de la Maison au Dauphin*. (37 suppl. à *Gallia*) Paris.

Green, C. and Draper, J. 1978 The Mileoak Roman villa, Handley, Towcester, Northamptonshire. Report on the excavations of 1955 and 1956, *Northants. Archaeol.* 13, 28-66.

Gregson, M. 1988 The villa as private property. In K. Branigan and D. Miles (eds), *The Economies of Romano-British Villas* (Sheffield), 21-33.

Hatt, J.-J. 1958 Informations archéologiques: antiquités historiques, circonscription de Strasbourg, *Gallia* 16, 322-42.

Haverfield, F. 1923 *The Romanization of Roman Britain* (4th ed). Oxford.

McKay, A.G. 1975 *Houses, Villas and Palaces in the Roman World*. London.

Miles, D. (ed) 1982 *The Romano-British Countryside: studies in rural settlement and economy* (Brit. Archaeol. Rep. 103) Oxford.

Millett, M. 1982 Town and country: a review of some material evidence, in Miles 1982, 421-31.

Millett, M. 1987 The question of continuity: Rivenhall reviewed, *Archaeol. J.* 144, 434-8.

Neal, D.S. 1974-6 Northchurch, Boxmoor and Hemel Hempstead station: the excavation of three Roman buildings in the Bulbourne valley, *Herts. Archaeol.* 4, 1-135.

Neal, D.S. 1978 The growth and decline of villas in the Verulamium area, in Todd 1978, 33-58.

Percival, J. 1976 *The Roman Villa: an historical introduction.* London.

Perring, D. 1987 Domestic buildings in Romano-British towns, in J. Schofield and R. Leech (eds), *Urban Archaeology in Britain* (CBA Res. Rep. 61: London), 147-55.

Picard, G.-C. 1983 Les centres civiques ruraux dans l'Italie et la Gaule romaine. In *Architecture et Société* (Coll. de l'Ecole Française de Rome 66: Paris and Rome), 415-23.

Reynolds, P. 1979 *Iron Age Farm: the Butser experiment.* London.

Richmond, I.A. 1969 The plans of Roman villas in Britain, in Rivet 1969, 49-70.

Rivet, A.L.F. (ed) 1969 *The Roman Villa in Britain.* London.

Rodwell, W.J. 1978 Buildings and settlements in SE Britain in the Iron Age. In B. Cunliffe and T. Rowley (eds), *Lowland Iron-Age Communities in Europe* (Brit. Archaeol. Rep. S 48: Oxford), 25-41.

Rodwell, W.J. and K.A. 1985 *Rivenhall: Investigations of a Villa, Church and Village 1950-1977* (Chelmsford Archaeol. Trust Rep. 4, CBA Res. Rep. 55). London.

Scott, L. 1938 The Roman villa at Angmering, *Sussex Archaeol. Coll.* 79, 3-44.

Selkirk, A. and W. 1983 Gorhambury, *Current Archaeol.* 87, 115-21.

Slofstra, J. 1983 An anthropological approach to the study of Romanization processes. In R. Brandt and J. Slofstra (eds), *Roman and Native in the Low Countries: spheres of interaction* (Brit. Archaeol. Rep. S 184: Oxford), 71-104.

Smith, J.T. 1978 Villas as a key to social structure. In Todd 1978, 149-85.

Todd, M. (ed) 1978 *Studies in the Romano-British Villa.* Leicester.

Walthew, C.V. 1975 The town house and the villa house in Roman Britain, *Britannia* 6, 189-205.

Walthew, C.V. 1982 Early Roman town development in Gallia Belgica: a review of some problems, *Oxford J. Archaeol.* 1 (2), 225-35.

Ward-Perkins, J.B. 1981 *Roman Imperial Architecture.* Harmondsworth.

Wightman, E. 1970 *Roman Trier and the Treveri.* London.

Wightman, E. 1985 *Gallia Belgica.* London.

14. For Better or Worse? Towards an Assessment of the Economic and Social Consequences of the Roman Conquest of Gaul

by J. F. Drinkwater

Julius Caesar conquered Gaul beyond the Republican *Provincia* between 58 and 51 BC. His campaigns, motivated more by personal political ambition than by the needs of the Roman state, resulted in confiscation of property, enslavement, mutilation and death on a massive scale, and will have brought great misery to the indigenous population. Yet, in the course of a recent survey of the events of this period, I justified the forced integration of northern Gauls into the Roman Empire as follows:

> This is the debit side of the account. On the other hand there is an important credit side. For example, it may be argued that the very disruption and destruction which resulted from the Conquest-period, and the military activity which followed, served to remove those Gauls least susceptible to the acceptance of Romanization (Drinkwater 1983: 123)

This statement amounts to an acceptance of political and cultural imperialism quite out of keeping with contemporary regard for the virtues of a liberal and pluralistic society; it has caused me considerable unease. On the other hand, I would suggest that in expressing it I was merely, albeit somewhat crassly, putting into words a sentiment shared by many who interest themselves in Roman imperial history: that the Roman Empire was a "good thing" (*cf.* Millett above, p. 37). In English-speaking scholarship, at least, this pre-supposition is seldom acknowledged and even less explained; it surely deserves closer investigation.

The case that the Roman Empire served in some way or other to advance the human condition may be argued in two ways. On the one hand, there is the Marxist interpretation, according to which the Empire should be seen as providing the political and social framework for a process of class-conflict that eventually led to the slave-owning society of classical antiquity's being replaced by the feudal society of the Middle Ages. The transformation improved the lot of mankind because it brought it one stage closer to communism, albeit at the sometimes considerable suffering of those caught up in the change (Marx and Engels 1888: 7ff; *cf.* de Ste. Croix 1981: 226-55, 267ff. – preferring 'serfdom' to 'feudalism'). On the other hand, there is what may be characterised as the 'vulgar positivism' of western 'bourgeois' historiography. This thinking is founded on the conviction that, despite the immediate distress involved, the Roman conquest and the process of Romanization that followed fairly quickly (in a matter of a generation or so) led to a general amelioration in the lives of the subject peoples. It does not directly concern itself with the contribution of the Roman Empire to long-term historical development. It is not the aim of this paper to contrast and decide between the Marxist and positivist views. While I accept that there is much to be learned from Marxist analysis, it will be clear from my opening quotation that I belong firmly in the positivist camp. Rather, my purpose here is to test the validity of the positivist interpretation on its own terms, with particular reference to the experience of the Three Gauls: were the northern Gauls better or worse off under Roman rule than they had been before?

It seems appropriate to give separate consideration to the material and cultural consequences of the Roman conquest of northern Gaul. Of these, the material side is by far the easier to deal with. Those who share the view that Roman rule had a beneficial effect would argue that, from the late-first century BC to the middle of the third century AD, Gaul became much more prosperous than ever before. In simple terms, the improvement may be explained as resulting from the Roman Peace. The blessings of the *Pax Romana* are nowhere better expressed than in what in my opinion remains the most perceptive historical novel about Caesar's Gallic War. Naomi Mitchison pictures how, after 51 BC the Gauls began to settle down, and those few who continued to oppose Rome were increasingly seen as rebels, not freedom-fighters:

> ...everywhere the Roman was the good comer. Men were glad to be able to
> sow winter wheat and be certain that there would be no war to snatch them
> off before it was ripe; women knew there would be no more running from
> burning towns with a baby clutched to the breast, their husbands safe now.
> Maybe it was the quiet after a great storm; there still would be gusts from
> time to time; but the chiefs were beginning to look towards Rome, to be
> dazzled by that great name   (Mitchison 1923: 305)

More recently, however, archaeologists and historians have begun to explain the growth of Gallic prosperity more closely, and with more allowance made for the complexities of this development. It is, for example, now generally accepted that the quickening of Gallic artisanal and commercial life, which led to increased if aristocratically monopolised wealth, began long before Roman intervention in the west: in the Celtic Iron Age, and perhaps even earlier (Daubigney 1984; Drinkwater 1987a). In favour of the Roman occupation it can be said: first, that it did not destroy the basis of this prosperity; and second: that it provided conditions that accelerated economic growth. Indeed, as far as the latter is concerned, over the last few years archaeologists and historians, inspired to a large extent (though by no means wholly) by the work of Hopkins, have begun to relate the growth in Gallic wealth directly to the great Roman military presence on the Rhine. On such an interpretation, the emergence of the 'German' frontier-provinces (for the most part, in fact, created out of Caesar's 'Belgica' and 'Celtica') acted as an important, though unplanned, stimulus to the economy of Gaul as a whole: taxes raised in Gaul, and beyond, to supply and pay the troops were spent in Gaul and, increasingly, on Gallic products (Hopkins 1978, 1980; Drinkwater 1983: 128f; *cf.* Drinkwater 1977/78). Although certain details of this model have been criticised (e.g. Millett 1984: 67), it seems well on the way to becoming the new orthodoxy . For example, it has been adopted, virtually in its entirety, by no less an authority than Wightman: "There can be no doubt that incentive to improve agricultural output came from the twin sources of taxation and army-supply" (Wightman 1985: 148; *cf.* Drinkwater 1987b).

In any event, whatever explanation one adopts, it seems reasonable to accept that in the years following the Roman conquest northern Gaul became significantly richer in material terms. The boom in Gallic agriculture is represented by the mushroom-growth of the Somme villas, and the invention of the Gallic harvesting-machine (Agache 1975, 1978; White 1969). The vitality of Gallic commerce and industry may be seen in the emergence of a network of urban settlements, above all the *vici* ('townships'/'villages') which, unlike the *civitas*-capitals ('cities'), cannot be dismissed as parasitic administrative centres. To these will have been conveyed the products of the surrounding countryside for further processing, and sale both

Fig. 14.1 "Venus and children" after Vertet

at a local level and beyond. The income thus generated will also, of course, have enabled those involved in this trade in their turn to purchase goods from other areas, and so have caused each township to act as a centre for the distribution of 'imports' (Drinkwater 1983: 129f.). It comes as no surprise, therefore, that the main townships eventually produced a well-to-do and self assured class of artisans and shopkeepers, the most enterprising of whom may even have risen to become, as *nautae* ('river-shippers'), members of the Gallic mercantile élite (Drinkwater 1978: 846). Some scholars would, indeed, argue that the most successful *nautae* even intermarried with the landowning aristocracy (Picard 1981: 890). This was a world unlike that of Caesar's Gallic warlords: different people had become wealthy; and wealth was more evenly spread.

The latter point is surely borne out by the richness of western continental museum collections, in which the relative frequency of bronze and iron objects of the Roman period is especially striking (Drinkwater 1983: 186: *cf.* Ladurie 1987: 90f., for the poverty in metal tools etc. of the fourteenth-century French peasant). It must also be supported by the continuing identification of settlement-sites of the high imperial period, the frequency of which suggests a density of population (at *c.* 20 persons per square kilometre: a total of *c.* 11,000,000 for the Three Gauls as a whole) that was not to be exceeded until the high-medieval and early-modern periods (Wightman 1985: 121; *cf.* Ladurie 1987: 22f., 42). The rising population must have resulted from, and may itself have further increased, the strength of the Gallic economy (Drinkwater 1982: 124).

Thus Gaul, and the Gauls, grew richer under Roman rule. However, it requires little historical imagination to picture that the transformation will have been far from instantaneous and untraumatic. The early years will have witnessed an odd mixing of Gallic and Roman ways; in particular, the removal of direct military rule, and the spread of the engine of Romanization, the planned Greco-Roman city, with its street-grid and wide range of public buildings, are likely to have occurred much more slowly and irregularly in Gaul than they did, for example, in Britain at a later date (Drinkwater 1985: 52f.; *cf.* Millett above, p. 41). It is arguable that such delay both contributed to the hybrid look of the country and substantially increased the overall cost of change, since it would have encouraged early, uncoordinated construction of Romanized buildings that, only a generation or so later, were abandoned or levelled in favour of the new cities. Certainly, the Gallic notables caught up in the rebellion of AD 21 were involved in serious overspending of some sort (Drinkwater 1983: 28). The increase in prosperity was not without its difficulties. This point takes us to consideration of an even greater price to be paid for relative peace and material good fortune: the social and cultural consequences of Roman rule.

Here again it is instructive to turn to the historical novel, and to Mitchison's imagined exchange between a young Roman and a young Gaul:

> "...our rule's not hard; we treat a people better than its own kings do. And the things we bring with us: trade and peace and prosperity, goods roads and good laws; they ought to weigh a little."
> "There's liberty in the other scale: it's heavy."
> "But what is liberty? Liberty to be oppressed. But you don't care as long as it's your own chiefs! We don't interfere with you, we leave you your religion and your customs and your councils; it makes no difference to a poor man where he pays his taxes. And if you want to fight, we can give you good fighting and good pay all over the world: in Asia and Africa, along thousands of miles of frontier! Isn't that good enough?"
> "Not for a free man!"   (Mitchison 1923: 224)

A major cost of becoming part of the Roman Empire, over and above the immediate agonies of military defeat, was indeed the loss of political freedom. The particular interests of the hitherto turbulent and volatile Gallic *civitates* were now to be fully subordinated to those of Rome (Drinkwater 1983: 7). Mitchison's Gallic hero eventually escapes from the comfortable cage of Roman protection by magically joining the creatures of the Celtic wildwood. His metamorphosis also signifies his recognition that a further cost would have to be paid by those who were content to suffer Roman rule: loss of cultural identity. Despite the Roman's claims to the contrary, it is arguable that Rome did not leave her subjects' "religion...customs and...councils" intact. She demanded not just their bodies, but also their souls. Her success in imposing her will in this respect can be seen most dramatically in the disappearance of the Gallic language as an intellectual medium. As far as the upper classes are concerned, Gaul went Greco-Roman: there was no independent Gallo-Celtic culture. The *locus classicus* of the extinction of indigenous tradition is to be found in the request of a late-fourth century Gallic nobleman to Symmachus, a leading Italian aristocrat, for suggestions as to source-material for a planned history of Gaul. Symmachus recommended Livy, Caesar and the elder Pliny: all, of course, Roman writers (Wightman 1975).

The two main causes of the overwhelming victory of the Latin language and Greco-Roman civilisation are, in my opinion, not hard to identify. On the one hand there was Rome's deliberate destruction of druidism, and thus of the uncompromisingly oral tradition for which the religion had acted as guardian (Drinkwater 1983: 38f.; Vertet 1984: 88). On the other, there was a spontaneous and enthusiastic willingness to Romanize on the part of the leaders of Gallic society, confirmed in their positions and ready to be used as an unpaid imperial civil service by the ruling power (*cf.* Millett, above, p. 38). The replacement of druidical by classical education was an essential element in both processes, and may be discerned at a remarkable early date, for example in the origins of the university of Autun (Tacitus, *Annales* 3.43.1; *cf.* Millett, above, p. 38-9). In the absence of any alternative rallying-point or leadership for the defence of the old ways, the remainder of the population will have followed in the aristocrats' train. There is no evidence to suggest that the Gallic upper classes ever repented of their abandonment of their heritage. On the contrary, as the centuries progressed they became ever more Roman in outlook. However, there remains the important question as to how the disruption of indigenous culture was experienced further down the social scale, by the majority of the Gallic population.

At this point we encounter a serious problem: evidence for the cultural life and world-view of the common people of Roman Gaul under the early Empire is virtually non-existent. It is possible to glean something from much later literary sources, such as Ausonius, Sulpicius Severus and Sidonius Apollinaris, but what is wanting is significant contemporary intelligence. However, the problem may now have been eased a little if, as Vertet proposes, archaeological material, in the form of small, religious statuettes, produced among the Arverni and sold widely throughout the north-western provinces, may be admitted in evidence.

In a recent bold and very stimulating article, Vertet puts forward the thesis that these terracotta statuettes represent a fourth element in Romano-Gallic religious activity, to be set alongside the 'official', 'oriental' and 'Romano-Celtic' cults conventionally accepted by scholars; as such, they may be regarded as a statement by those who made and bought them about the Empire in which they lived (Vertet 1984: 82-88, 90f.). Vertet argues that the deities comprised in the conventional groups were predominantly aristocratic and urban in their appeal, as is shown by the high quality of the temples, inscriptions and statuary dedicated to them. They were, therefore, very much part of the wider, blander, Greco-Roman culture of the upper classes of Gallic society. Such Celtic divinities as continued to be worshipped within this cultural environment lost many of their indigenous characteristics, above all, their aggression: their personalities and functions were re-fashioned to suit the prevailing political climate (Vertet 1984: 86ff.). The Arvernian statuettes, however, should be regarded as something quite different – beyond the classicizing influences of Roman officials and Gallic villa-owners and townsmen. They were manufactured in small, poor, rural potteries by Celtic-speaking craftsmen who, evidently, well understood their market: cheap to produce and, presumably, cheap to buy, the statuettes are found throughout Gaul and Britain, and as far east as Raetia. In fact, their distribution pattern closely resembles that of central Gallic ('Lezoux') samian ware (Vertet 1984: 95ff., 97ff.). It used to be thought that these statuettes

Fig. 14.2 "Wet nurses" after Vertet

dated to the third and fourth centuries; now, however, it seems clear that they were at their most popular in the second century, the high point of the Roman Peace in the west (Vertet 1984: 81, 87).

The Arvernian statuettes are usually taken as depicting Greco-Roman or classicised Celtic gods (Vertet 1984: 89, *cf.* 85f.). As Vertet has pointed out, while some indeed appear to represent classical deities, many do not; they should not be forced to fit a preconceived frame of reference (Vertet 1984: 89ff., 95). The strikingly common 'Venus' and *matres* figures are, for example, quite unlike their supposed classical or Rhenish models (Fig. 14.1 and 14.2): 'Venus' is frequently accompanied by other, smaller, figures; and the *matres* appear alone, suckling one or two babies (Vertet 1984: 92). The identity of 'Venus' eludes us; she and her companions were perhaps concerned with a fertility cult (Vertet 1984: 95). The 'wet nurse' may, however, with more confidence be interpreted as a powerful, protecting, earth- or mother-goddess (Vertet 1984: 105). The phrase 'mother-goddess' provokes the thought that this divinity may have been a survival from the pre-Roman past, uncontaminated by assimilation with the Greco-Roman pantheon because she lacked educated worshippers to make the association. Vertet, however, denies such a straightforward origin, preferring to see the statuettes at issue as reflecting a new type of religious thinking, born of a fusion of ancient Celtic and contemporary classical elements, and serving to help people come to terms with (by articulating their reaction to) changed conditions brought about by the Roman conquest (Vertet 1984: 97-102). On this view, the 'mother-goddess' should be interpreted as no less than an image of Rome, the all-powerful guardian and provider (Vertet 1984: 107).

In Vertet's eyes, the statuettes tell a depressing story regarding the relationship between the imperial mother and her children. She is distant, stiff and cold. She grasps, rather than supports, her infants, who are tightly swaddled and totally unregarded by her. Her breasts are small and oddly positioned: she gives milk, but does so grudgingly and meanly (Vertet 1984: 106f., 109: "allaitant peu et mal"). In Vertet's view, the statuettes express people's feelings of powerlessness and resignation before the imperial power; resistance is useless:

> Les dirigeants et les représentants de Roma Aeterna sont puissants et sages.
> Toute résistance à leur égard, preuve d'ingratitude devant ses bienfaits
> méconnus, est toujours châtiée. Elle a les droits du paterfamilias sur un empire
> aux provinces infantilisées.   (Vertet 1984: 107)

Thus Gallic peasants live in peace, but without esteem or even prosperity: they have no share in the new-found wealth of the aristocrats and urban dwellers; and they have no cause to hope for any improvement in their lot (Vertet 1984: 109ff., 117f.). The manufacture, purchase and worship of the statuettes Vertet would see as suggesting their acceptance of the situation; on the other hand, the iconography of the 'wet nurse' figure might well also reflect some unconscious reaction against it as people, unable to act for themselves as adults, reverted to the dependency of childhood, and associated Rome with an image from a much older and more primitive religion than that of the Homeric pantheon (Vertet 1984: 113f., 119). In any event, they were not at ease with the world as they found it; for them, certainly, both materially and culturally, the Roman Empire was not a "good thing".

If we accept Vertet's contention that the Arvernian statuettes are acceptable in evidence for the "univers mental" (Vertet 1984: 107) of the bulk of the Romano-Gallic population, and his analysis of what they have to say, it would seem, despite the positivist argument proposed above, that for most people the Roman conquest was in both the short and long terms very much for the worse. In my opinion, Vertet's ideas should be given serious consideration. However, I believe that the statuettes may be interpreted more favourably than he suggests. For reasons I outlined at the beginning of this paper, I believe that Vertet has overstated his case for the material poverty of the Gallic peasantry. As far as the cultural side is concerned, despite my earlier acceptance of the victory of the Roman educational tradition over the Gallic, I would emphasise that not everything was swept away. It is a commonplace among archaeologists and historians that Rome was temperamentally inclined to respect *mos maiorum*, the ancestral tradition, as it applied both to her own society and even to those of her subjects. The provincial upper classes were expected to conform to the norms of Greco-Roman civilization; but this expectation was not to be taken by them as a directive totally to destroy their indigenous heritage. Rome's cultural imperialism was aggressive, but not ruthless: throughout the Empire much was changed, but much survived (*cf.* Millett above, p. 39). It may, indeed, be argued that native traditions enjoyed a higher than average chance of survival in the Three Gauls since, under the high Empire, the behaviour of the local Gallic aristocracy was even less damaging to the fabric of provincial society than that of their peers elsewhere. In brief, northern Gallic aristocrats remained close to home: as far as can be judged, from the late-first century, at least, they were not anxious to involve themselves in imperial senatorial or equestrian careers; they confined their activities to Gallic or *civitas*-affairs (Drinkwater 1983: 202). Furthermore, the relatively small number of Gallic *civitates* must have helped to prevent excessive spending by them on the embellishment of *civitas*-capitals, after the usual Greco-Roman fashion (Drinkwater 1983: 108f.; *cf.* Drinkwater 1984: 360); on

*Fig. 14.3 Coin of Hadrian of the PIETAS AUG type showing
a female figure and children (after Robertson).*

the contrary, they can be seen concerning themselves with the administration and development
of the subordinate tribal districts (*pagi*) and their *vici* (Drinkwater 1983: 108f.). Perhaps most
interesting in this respect is the construction, very likely at the encouragement and expense
of local aristocrats, of great rural shrines (*conciliabula*), surrounded by urban-style amenities
(theatres, baths etc.), in many parts of Gaul (Drinkwater 1983: 181). The religious aspects of
such patronage are particularly important in the context of this paper, the more so when there
is other evidence to suggest that the Gallic aristocracy conscientiously maintained local cults
(Drinkwater 1979: 94). The druids may have disappeared, but the main Gallo-Celtic deities,
however Romanized and 'sanitized' they may have become, were kept firmly in the public
eye. Aristocratic funding did not preclude, indeed (as a means of winning acclaim) it
presupposed, active popular participation in their worship. As Vertet himself remarks,
evangelising Christians were to discover this to their cost when they attempted to convert the
Gallic country-dwellers (*pagani*) from the late-fourth century onwards (Vertet 1984: 86f.). It
was, therefore, possible for the peasantry to enjoy the peace and prosperity of Roman rule
without totally losing its old beliefs and customs.

On this view, the Arvernian statuettes may be taken as a set of devotional objects that
demonstrates a positive appreciation of Rome and her Empire. To our eyes the 'nursing
mother' appears cold and stiff, but we must bear in mind the relatively low level of artistry
involved in the production of such pieces (*cf.* Vertet 1984: 106). We should do better to
establish the models of such pieces: the images that both potter and customer had in mind
when they made and bought these wares, and that allowed them to overlook their technical
shortcomings. In fact, as Vertet is at pains to point out, the iconography of the Arvernian
statuettes is strongly reminiscent of certain coin-types of the second century (in particular, as
far as the 'Venus' figures are concerned, I would note the Hadrianic *Pietas Augusti* type (Fig.
14.3): *RIC* 2, p. 477, nos. 1030/1), that attempt to project a very positive and benign picture
of the Empire and its rulers (Vertet 1984: 98-105, esp. 99). There is, however, an even more
dramatic possible source of inspiration for the 'nursing mother' statuettes, apparently

Fig. 14.4 The Augustan 'Ara Pacis'

unnoticed by Vertet, namely the Augustan *Ara Pacis*, dedicated in 19 BC (Fig. 14.4). A sculptured panel on the east face of the outer wall of this monument depicts the promise of the New Order: a full-breasted young female, usually identified as Tellus/Italia, clasping two chubby babies (whom she seems about to suckle) in a scene of rural plenty. As far as the population of Gaul is concerned, I would argue that, at least down to the mid-third century, this was a promise that was fulfilled.

References

Agache, R. 1975 'La campagne à l'époque romaine dans les grands plaines du Nord de la France', in H. Temporini (ed.), *Aufstieg und Niedergang der Antiken Welt* II.4, Berlin/New York, 658-713

Agache, R. 1978 *La Somme préromaine et romaine* (Mémoires de la Société des Antiquaires de Picardie 24), Amiens

Daubigney, A. (ed.) 1984 *Archéologie et rapports sociaux en Gaule*, Paris

de Ste. Croix, G. E. M. 1981 *The Class Struggle in the Ancient Greek World*, London

Drinkwater, J. F. 1977/8 'Die Sekundinier von Igel und die Woll- und Textilindustrie in Gallia Belgica', *Trierer Zeitschrift* 40/1, 107-25

Drinkwater, J. F. 1978 'The rise and fall of the Gallic Iulii', *Latomus* 37, 817-50

Drinkwater, J. F. 1979 'Local careers in the Three Gauls under the early Empire', *Britannia* 10, 89-100

Drinkwater, J. F. 1982 'The wool textile industry of Gallia Belgica', *Textile History* 13, 111-28

Drinkwater, J. F. 1983 *Roman Gaul: the Three Provinces, 58BC-AD260*, London

Drinkwater, J. F. 1984 'Peasants and Bagaudae in Roman Gaul', *Classical Views* N.S. 3, 349-71

Drinkwater, J. F. 1985 'Urbanization in the Three Gauls: some observations', in F. Grew and B. Hobley (eds.), *Roman Urban Topography in Britain and the Western Empire* (C.B.A. Research Report 59), London, 49-55

Drinkwater, J. F. 1987a Review of Daubigney 1984, *Trierer Zeitschrift* 50, 472-4

Drinkwater, J. F. 1987b Review of Wightman 1985, *Classical Views* N.S. 6, 383-9

Hopkins, K. 1978 'Economic growth and towns in classical antiquity', in P. Abrams and E. A. Wrigley (eds.), *Towns and Societies*, Cambridge, 35-77

Hopkins, K. 1980 'Taxes and trade in the Roman Empire', *Journal of Roman Studies* 70, 101-25

Ladurie, E. Le Roy 1987 *The French Peasantry 1450-1660* (trans. A. Sheridan), London

Marx, K. and Engels, F. 1888 *Manifesto of the Communist Party*, London

Millett, M. 1984 'Forts and the origins of towns: cause or effect?', in T. F. C. Blagg and A. C. King (eds.), *Military and Civilian in Roman Britain* (BAR British Series 136), Oxford, 65-74

Mitchison, N. 1923 *The Conquered*, London

Picard, G. C. 1981 'Ostie et la Gaule de l'Ouest', *Mémoires de l'Ecole Française à Rome* 93, 883-915

Vertet, H. 1984 'Religion populaire et rapport au pouvoir d'après les statuettes d'argile sous l'empire romain', in Daubigney (1984), 72-122

White, K. D. 1969 'The economics of the Gallo-Roman harvesting machines', in J. Bibauw (ed.), *Hommages à M. Renard* (Collection Latomus 101-3), Brussels, 804-9

Wightman, E. M. 1975 'Priscae Gallorum memoriae', in B. Levick (ed.), *The Ancient Historian and his Sources: Essays in Honour of C. E. Stevens*, Farnborough, 93-107

Wightman, E. M. 1985 *Gallia Belgica*, London

15. The Emergence of Romano-Celtic Religion

by Anthony King

A diffident approach to religious archaeology is manifest in the study of Iron Age and Roman Britain. The majority of archaeologists of these periods have little to do with religious material, which is considered a specialist preserve. Indeed, many are extremely wary of analysing the religious component of the material cultures they are working on, to the extent that in some studies the reader could be forgiven for thinking that ancient society was almost entirely secular. This type of approach to the subject has even been used for religious buildings and objects themselves, so that analysis is conducted purely in architectural or typological terms. As a consequence, the majority of sites and objects, unless displaying 'odd' characteristics, are presented as devoid of religious significance.

An example of this is the well/shaft problem, in which most deep holes in the ground are given a prosaic water-provision function unless their fill contains groups of objects that appear to be of religious or funerary origin. In these cases, there has in the past been the temptation to drop the well interpretation altogether, in favour of a ritualistic one, particularly if there are human remains which justify calling the hole a 'puits funéraire'. Specialists in religion have tended to make separate studies of these 'odd' deposits, with the result that many holes that quite obviously were wells or cess-pits before being filled have been deemed ritual shafts or the like. It is only fairly recently that archaeologists have started to recognize that a great many of the pits and wells that they excavate have deposits in them, e.g. of animal bones, that mark the ritual 'closure' of the hole at the time it was filled in. In other words, the past unwillingness to entertain the possibility of rituals affecting many apparently secular activities has created a false dichotomy, only now starting to disappear, between 'ordinary' archaeology and religious archaeology.

In the wider realm of synthesis of archaeological findings, the dichotomy still exists, to a great extent. Ideas of social change and political development in the Late Iron Age and early Roman periods have undergone several transformations in the last few decades, but religious ideas of change have not, still being discussed, for the most part, in terms of Roman toleration of native cults (with the notable exception of the druids) and of individual freedom of choice in the matter of religious belief. The aim of this paper is to make a brief and speculative contribution towards the understanding of religious change in the social and political context of the period.

Religion and the Iron Age/Roman core-periphery system

Currently, a view of the period's political and social framework that has become widely discussed, is that of Iron Age Europe as a core-periphery system, or rather, a series of such systems (Haselgrove 1984; Bradley 1984; Cunliffe 1984a). The Mediterranean cultures, Greek, Etruscan and Roman, according to this view in its simplest form, were powerful enough to have a marked effect on their neighbours, particularly in Gaul, Spain and the Alpine region. Economic links, principally in the form of raw materials being traded from periphery to centre, and luxury goods being traded in the other direction, paved the way for more extensive contacts, of craftsmen travelling to peripheral areas to execute commissions, for instance, or the gradual introduction of core-area cultural traits such as scripts and loan-words for the peripheral languages. A great many of the developments in pre-Roman Gaul and Britain in particular can be explained in core-periphery terms:

the development of an 'archaic state' political formation in southern Gaul (Nash 1978),

the acquisition of luxuries such as wine,

the introduction of a coinage that was firstly sub-Greek and later more recognizably Roman in spirit,

the use of Greek writing for local languages in southern Gaul, and later Latin script further north as Roman influence supplanted that of the western Greek colonies,

the introduction of Greek-style urbanization in the oppida of southern Gaul.

In other words, before the Roman conquests of Gaul and Britain, there had been extensive infiltration of Graeco-Roman cultural patterns into Celtic society, with greatest effect on the more immediately peripheral societies and their tribal aristocracies. The latter appear to have controlled the flow of goods and ideas, and thus were most exposed to Mediterranean influences.

How does religion fit into this model? At present, it has to be said that virtually no consideration has been given to this matter, as much of the core-periphery model is conceived in economic terms only. However, if we take the operational aspect of religion to be rooted in the general cultural milieu of the society that practises that religion, then it is possible to make an association with the model. It is one that is potentially changeable through time, since significant changes in society, as outlined above, have the potential to transform the functioning of religion, either in reaction to these other changes, or to reinforce the ideological foundations for change.

In order to sustain such a proposition, it is best to follow a definition of religion that is couched in social and also material terms, rather than in terms of individuals and their beliefs (the most common current approach to the religions of the period), although it must be remembered that individuals both condition and are conditioned by the prevailing beliefs of the social group as a whole. Thus, to follow Geertz (1966, 26-9), there is a 'religious perspective' on the world by which sacred symbols are created as a focus for beliefs that serve to give 'reality' to existence. The beliefs themselves are of no absorbing concern here, given the paucity of the written sources for religious matters during the period under consideration, but the sacred symbols, specifically those that have material form, are accessible to archaeological study, given that, 'It is in some sort of ceremonial form...that the moods and motivations which sacred symbols induce in men, and the general conceptions of the order of existence which they formulate for men, meet and reinforce one another' (Geertz 1966, 28). In other words, since the materials available for study are largely the physical remains of rituals, an archaeological definition of religion is, perforce, more concerned with 'ceremonial form' than with 'moods and motivations', and therefore has to use the former effectively as a substitute for the study of beliefs.

'Ceremonial form' in Celtic and Romano-Celtic religion means essentially the shrines themselves, their cult-images and votive offerings. Our immediate problem is how to use the data offered by these categories for the exploration of the theme given above – the integration of religion into current models of interaction between the Iron Age and Mediterranean worlds.

'Celtic' and 'Roman'

A possible approach is to try to define 'Celtitas' as seen in the earliest relevant remains, and assess how far the data from the period of contact between the Graeco-Roman and Celtic cultures differ from this, i.e. whether and how far 'Romanization' of the Celtic religious form took place. Methodologically, this uses the device of an opposition between 'Celtitas' and 'Romanitas', as far as these terms can be applied to religion. It is an approach that owes much to ideas emanating from structural anthropology, as reworked by archaeologists such as Ian Hodder (1982, 185ff.), and put within an historical archaeological framework by Donley (1982) and Small (1987).

The core-periphery model for the north-west European Iron Age would predict that the 'Celtic' element would be partially or completely subsumed by the 'Roman', from which it follows that sacred sites and objects can be placed on a 'Celtic-Roman gradient' according to the extent of 'Roman' influences. This in turn allows for comparison with non-religious sites and material culture, for instance in terms of whether ceremonial form was conservative or progressive in the take-up of 'Roman' ideas. This particular question is of some interest, in that a commonly-held viewpoint on religion in general is that it is conservative in nature, and is used as a means of upholding tradition. This viewpoint has a respectable ancestry going back to the ancient authors themselves (North 1976, 1-2), but we have to question whether it held true for all cultures in all periods, or whether religious change facilitated adaptation to sometimes unpalatable cultural changes.

M.J.T. Lewis, in a famous phrase, characterized Celtic religion as 'essentially aniconic and atectonic' (1966,4). His view was based on the description of cult sites by Livy, Lucan, Pliny and others, who tended to portray Celtic worship in sacred groves, with wooden cult-images, altars dripping with offerings and human sacrifices taking place. This evocative and sometimes spectacular ancient portrayal is, of course, shot through with prejudice, and is probably a literary conceit, but it appears to have a kernel of truth, deriving from observations of the Celts in Italy in the 4th-3rd centuries BC. Early Irish texts provide some confirmation of the Classical evidence, although they are not very specific in describing the material side of Celtic religion, and are distant in time and space from the period under discussion (cf. Chadwick 1970, 141ff. and Ross 1986, 101ff.). It is possible to dispute the aniconic nature of Celtic religion on the basis of the known reverence for the severed head and its portrayal in a variety of media (Ross 1986, 117-9), but it can equally be suggested that the iconic habit was strongest in areas known to be influenced by Mediterranean cultures (see below). Iron Age temples, too, are known both in literary sources and from archaeological discoveries, but are also to be found mainly in the same areas.

In Graeco-Roman religion, by contrast, there is an early attachment to monumental structures built to house deities portrayed in recognizable human guise. Stone was the preferred material for both structures and images, resulting in a highly elaborated architecture and iconography at the time of the main period of contact between these peoples and the Celts (cf. Stambaugh 1978, 568ff.). Another feature of Graeco-Roman religious practice, not found in Celtic religion, is the use of writing and inscriptions to codify and commemorate.

Although distinctive areas of contrast exist, and can be tabulated as oppositions in Table 15.1, many features of religious material culture are the same, notably the use of sacred areas with specific delimitation (Piggott 1978), the practice of sacrifice as the main means of propitiating deities, and the existence of specialized officiants (and their paraphernalia) to carry out rituals and preserve religious knowledge. Since these aspects are common to both systems, they consequently do not need to be considered further in any detail. It is in the areas of temple structures, cult-images and inscriptions that elements of Romanization of Celtic religion

Celtic	Roman	Common to both
open-air shrines	roofed temples	delimited cult areas
partial aniconism	anthropomorphic cult-images	sacrifices and votive offerings
oral teaching	epigraphic tradition	specialised officiants

Table 15.1. Traits of Celtic and Roman Religious practice

	S Gaul	Three Gauls, Germany	Britian
1. purely 'Celtic'	up to C1 BC (literary evidence only)	up to C3 BC	no evidence
2. tectonising & anthropomorphising	C3?-C1 BC	C2-C1 BC	C1BC
3. proto-Romano-Celtic	mid-late C1 BC	late C1 BC -early C1 AD	early C1 AD (little evidence)
4. Romano-Celtic	late C1 BC+ (little evidence)	early C1 AD+	mid-late C1 AD+
5. 'Roman' element dominant	late C1 BC+	late C1 AD+ (limited in scope)	no evidence

Table 15.2. Stages in the emergence of Romano-Celtic religion

are to be found, thus defining the material on which we need to concentrate in order to pursue the theme of this paper.

Temples

Early Iron Age religious structures dating to Hallstatt D and La Tène I in Celtic Europe are rare, but the diverse sample available points to open-air sanctuaries. The most famous site is in Czechoslovakia at Libeniçe (Rybova and Soudsky 1962), where a long rectangular enclosure contained an area of ritual activity at one end, centred upon stones and apparently free-standing posts. This site, unfortunately, has no clear descendants in later La Tène periods, an observation that also applies to the Goloring in the Rhineland (Röder 1948), a circular enclosure *c.* 90m in diameter centred on a large post possibly *c.* 12m in height.

Some scholars (e.g. Schwarz 1962; De Laet 1966; Black 1986, 229) have seen the origins of what was to emerge as the Romano-Celtic temple type, not in these styles of open-air sanctuary, but in the La Tène funerary enclosures of NE France, e.g. Ecury-le-Repos (Brisson and Hatt 1955) or Menil-Annelles (Flouest and Stead 1979), where a square enclosed feature within a cremation cemetery has structural elements which may represent a small central wooden building. It is difficult to see the exact linkage, since the post-hole formations of the funerary monuments are not regular, and are open to several alternative reconstructions (e.g. platforms for the exposure of corpses; Brunaux *et al.* 1985b, 49-50), but there is obviously the possibility that this hypothesis for the development of temples is correct. A salient observation that appears to diminish support for the hypothesis is that temples and cemeteries are not normally found together in either the late Celtic or Roman worlds, although mausolea could take the form of temples (e.g. Lullingstone; Meates 1979, 122ff.). Structures in cemeteries are more likely to have been derived from temples than the other way round.

Evidence for late Iron Age sacred sites is, more often than not, in the form of square or trapezoidal enclosures. These take a variety of forms and modern names (*Viereckschanzen, enclos cultuels,* etc), and have been shown by Schwarz (1962) and more recent work (e.g. Planck 1986; Slofstra and Sanden 1987) to have a distribution from Czechoslovakia to Gaul and southern Britain. Examples that have been dated indicate that a range from third-first century BC is typical, with some sites occuring during the early Roman period as survivals of the type (e.g. in the Low Countries: Slofstra and Sanden 1987). As stated in the previous section of this paper, the concept of an enclosure as sacred delimiter is common to both Celtic and Mediterranean areas, and consequently will not be discussed in any detail here. Of more significance in the present context are the internal features of some of these enclosures, including shafts, settings of wooden posts, and buildings. Post-built wooden buildings of carefully-constructed, apparently basilical, rectangular plan have been excavated at various sites, notably at Holzhausen in southern Germany (Schwarz 1962) and Mšecké Žehrovice in Czechoslovakia (Venclová 1989). Both these instances are of an early enough date (c. third-first century BC) and in regions sufficiently distant from the Mediterranean sphere of influence to be unlikely candidates for the early Romanization (or Hellenization) of their architectural form. Thus, this immediately raises the hypothesis that the tectonizing trend in late Celtic religion was a native, rather than externally-inspired phenomenon.

Paradoxically, despite their high-quality evidence, both the sites just mentioned lay in areas that were to be on the fringes of the more westerly region that developed as the heartland of Romano-Celtic religion. Events at the end of the pre-Roman Iron Age – expansion of Germanic groups southwards, and Roman military operations – caused severe diminution of any possible influence that the eastern Celts might have had on the Celtic world at large. Descendents of the *Viereckschanze* buildings are virtually absent, although possible basilical Romano-Celtic structures exist at one or two sites, such as Pesch in the Rhineland (Horne and King 1980, 447, Pesch B; Follmann-Schulz 1986, 706, Gebaude B). Because of this lack of continuity, in order to pursue the aim of documenting the influence, if any, of the Mediterranean world on Celtic temples, the geographical focus has to be narrowed down to Gaul, where disruption at the end of the Iron Age was less radical, and where Romano-Celtic forms clearly emerged at an early date.

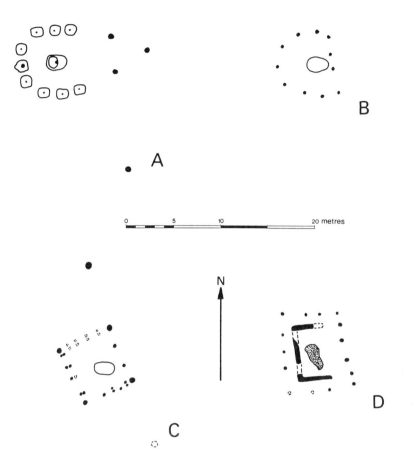

Fig. 15.1. Gournay-sur-Aronde
Legend: A. third century BC, B. second century BC, C. late second-60s/50s BC, D. 40s BC.
(After Brunaux *et al.* 1985b)

A key site for understanding the way in which structures came into being at Gaulish sanctuaries is the recently-excavated Gournay-sur-Aronde temple in Picardy (Fig. 15.1: Brunaux *et al.* 1985b). The earliest phase is third century BC, consisting of a ditched enclosure around a cross-shaped setting of posts, carefully arranged, but too widely-spaced to have been supports for a coherent structure. They were probably free-standing, not unlike the early Iron Age structures mentioned above, and had an intimate relationship with a group of nine pits dug around a central pit. The pits follow the orientation and east-west axis of the post settings, and appear to have been added to the ensemble not long after the posts were put in position. The pits are not considered by the excavator to have held structural elements, although small, probably free-standing posts, *c.* 10 cm in diameter, were carefully positioned in each one. The symmetry of the early phase structures suggests that the individual positions of the posts were important in creating a ritual environment for the sacrifices that were taking place, remains from which were found in profusion in the enclosing ditch.

Succeeding this initial open-air sanctuary was a tectonizing phase. The pits had been largely infilled when new posts were positioned in or very close to them, probably in the second century BC. It is not certain that this irregular D-shaped group of posts in fact supported a roofed building, as put forward in Brunaux's discussion (Brunaux *et al.* 1985b, 85), since the apparent continuity with the system of pits and free-standing posts in the previous phase suggests that this may more easily be interpreted as a reconstitution, on a somewhat less regular basis, of the free-standing arrangement after the original posts had rotted. However, the next structure on the site is much more clearly a building, roughly square (6-6.5 m on each side) with corner posts and smaller post-holes for walling in between. It enclosed the central pit, which was still in use, and opened to the east, on the same general orientation as the earlier phases. The construction date for this building is uncertain, but is in the range late second to early first century BC.

The early temple at Gournay lasted until the 60s or 50s BC, when there was a fire, followed by deliberate demolition, clearing away of the ritual deposits and sealing of the site with a sterile layer. Reconstruction followed after an indeterminate interval of perhaps ten years or more. However, the old temple's site was known, since a new stone-built structure was set up in the same position and on almost the same orientation. The central pit, too, was replaced by a hearth in the same position. The only major difference in the sanctuary as a whole was the abandonment of the enclosure ditch and its replacement by a rectilinear ditch on the same orientation as the temple itself. The inference is that there was continuity of cult, even if the surviving material sequence shows a discontinuity. In this context, it is all the more relevant that the architecture of the new temple can be regarded as proto-Romano-Celtic, taking the form of a stone-footed cob wall for a rectangular *cella* open to the east, surrounded by a wooden ambulatory. Its date, too, is significant, being just post-conquest, perhaps in the late 40s BC, thus making the temple one of the earliest stone-footed structures in the newly-conquered territory.

The technique of cob or mud-brick on stone foundations is known in southern Gaul from a much earlier date, and can be regarded there as a manifestation of Gallo-Greek culture. It subsequently appears in first century BC and Augustan buildings in Roman towns (e.g. Lyon; Desbat 1981), and probably marks one of the elements in the Romanization of architecture, as techniques in use in southern Gaul came into Gallia Comata. The inference for Gournay, therefore, is that this phase is a Romanizing one, concurrent with the material culture facies in northern Gaul that goes under the name of '*gallo-romaine précoce*'. The opportunity for reconstruction of the temple presented by the mid first century BC fire was taken by setting up a building to a new design, not in conservatively maintaining the old features of the sanctuary. The cult itself may not have been affected by this, since the same position for the temple and the continued use of the central pit/hearth demonstrate an essential continuity of certain key features. Nevertheless, the material surroundings and possibly the ceremonial form of the cult did change, with a greater emphasis on the physical structures, and an apparent lessening in the number of sacrificial remains. This new emphasis on structures at Gournay is an early example of a widespread phenomenon in Romano-Celtic religion, to be discussed more fully below.

Gournay is not an isolated instance, since there are other sites in northern Gaul and south-eastern Britain that demonstrate similar sequences, though admittedly less fully or perfectly (e.g. Tremblois: Paris 1960; Vendeuil-Caply: Piton and Dilly 1985; see note 1 for other temple sites with definite pre-Roman traces). Gournay also has an advantage over most of the other sites in having been burnt down in the mid first century BC (for unknown reasons), which allowed for a relatively early rebuilding in proto-Romano-Celtic style. Elsewhere, this stage of development is usually later, and the temples more fully Romano-Celtic in form. We therefore have a privileged glimpse into a vital and fast-moving period of transition, during which the Romano-Celtic type was becoming established as the normal form of sanctuary building in Gaul.

By the late first century BC-early first century AD there were evidently numerous examples of wooden or stone, roofed shrines in Gaul, which were the outcome of a tectonizing trend during the first century BC in Celtic religious architecture. The question inevitably arises as to the impetus which led to this trend being established – was it due to local innovation, or, as suggested by the core-periphery model, a result of Mediterranean influences? To support the latter notion, some elements of the classical temple types would have to be present in the Iron Age precursors to the Romano-Celtic temple, and the immediate contact zones should have the most highly-developed or the earliest examples of such temples. Accordingly, it is from southern Gaul that evidence, if any, will be forthcoming.

There are two striking features about what was later to be called Gallia Narbonensis in the third-first centuries BC; the extent of Greek influence, as manifested in Gallo-Greek culture, and the wide variation between those sites that display a high level of Graeco-Roman culture (e.g. Glanum), and those that remained almost untouched by it right up to the end of the republic, such as the defended sites in the pre-Alps. In religion, this variation is seen in the presence during the first century BC of four different but contemporaneous modes of ceremonial form.

1) Open-air sacred woods with no structures, but with wooden images, as attested in, for instance, Lucan's flamboyant account of Caesar's destruction of a shrine near Massalia in 49 BC (*Phars.* 3, 399-426).

2) Stone versions of the open-air shrines, with details of architecture and sculptural technique that owed much, originally, to Greek (and Etruscan) influence. They had stone lintels, tall *stelae*, free-standing painted stone sculptures and occasionally columns with distinctively-styled capitals. At the same time, there are many severed heads, either of stone, or human skulls placed in niches in the structures. The statues have a distinctive cross-legged pose, and sometimes are depicted holding severed heads. Dating of these sites and associated artefacts is uncertain, but it is accepted that the best-known of them, Entremont (Lantier 1943; Benoit 1981) and Roquepertuse (de Gérin-Ricard 1927), were probably destroyed during the Roman intervention of 125-4 BC. However, the lintel with niches for human heads at Glanum (Rolland 1968) may have been in use later than this, and at La Cloche, Pennes-Mirabeau, cross-legged statues and skulls with metal fitments for display formed part of the assemblage of a site apparently destroyed at the time of Caesar's siege of nearby Massalia (Chabot 1983).

3) Primitive temples, of which three are tolerably well-known (Fig. 15.2): a) Nages hillfort, near Nîmes, has a rectangular stone room with a tiled roof surrounded by a portico that made use of stone column shafts (Py 1978, 88-90). The structure is interpreted by the excavator as a version of the cella/ambulatory temple that becomes the standard Romano-

Celtic type. It is dated 70-30 BC, and stands enclosed by other buildings within the highly-regulated Hellenistic-style *insulae* of the hillfort; b) at Aumes, Hérault, a first century BC temple of square plan had three columns on each side, with possible curtain walling between them. The one surviving capital was in an unusual local style with a Gallo-Greek inscription (Horne and King 1980, 379); c) the third temple at Vieille-Toulouse is the most significant, in that it has a claim to be the earliest known example of a regular cella/ambulatory temple. It was built of brick with columns around the ambulatory, and a curtain or dwarf wall between the columns (Vidal 1973; 1987; *Gallia* 34, 1976, 482-3). This site may be associated with a Latin inscription of 47 BC (*CIL* XII, 5388), and more certain dating evidence comes from pottery of the period 30-10 BC in an apparently overlying destruction layer.

4)   Greek and Roman temples existed, of course, at Massalia, Narbo and other colonies, but there is epigraphic evidence from the Greek temple of Aristea, Iles d'Hyères, for Gauls worshipping there (Coupry and Giffault 1982), and it would seem very likely that Gauls were present at the urban temples, too.

Eventually, the last group became the dominant form in southern Gaul, and largely supplanted the native types as far as the outward, physical manifestation of religion was concerned.

Of more immediate concern, however, are the possible links between the early Romano-Celtic temples in the south and the classical forms of temple. Wheeler (1928, 317), Lewis (1966) and others have pointed out that the Romano-Celtic form had some resemblance to Greek temples, mainly in the peripteral arrangement and the use of columns. Two key features, on the other hand, do not have any known link with Greek temples; the generally square concentric plan, and the tower-like cella (*cf.* Wilson 1980). Indeed, these are the very characteristics that mark out Romano-Celtic temples as a regional type, and it has to be admitted that the present state of knowledge of the earliest examples does not allow us to pinpoint any particular source of origin for these features.

A hypothesis that would account for the distinctiveness of the Romano-Celtic temple, within the context of the Hellenization of late Celtic southern Gaul and the general suppositions of the core-periphery model, is one where the shrine layout is essentially local, answerable to Celtic ceremonial forms, but where the details respond to cultural changes in society as a whole, hence what is effectively a process of accretion of initially Greek and later, Roman stylistic features. A parallel for this comes from the Etruscan world, where shrines of a characteristic local form, with high *podia*, shallow *cellae* and frontal steps (developed from altar platforms), have markedly Hellenized details in the form of columns, terracotta pediments and stone sculpture (Colonna 1985; Strong 1968, 69). These details become crystallized as normal features of the Etruscan temple type, and can be seen as a facet of the deeply pervasive Hellenization of Etruscan culture.

In conclusion, Gaulish temples that can be regarded as antecedents to the Romano-Celtic type can be placed in the period just before the period of the Caesarian conquest or later. In Britain, all could be put into the post-Caesarian period (except possibly Heathrow[2]). However, the evidence from northern Gaul and Germany also suggests that there is a phase prior to the regularization of the antecedent to the Romano-Celtic type. In this earlier phase, probably to be dated to the second-early first centuries BC, there are structures of irregular plan, which seem to indicate the building of shrines before any Graeco-Roman influences could reasonably be said to be a relevant factor. Although it is not certain whether all these irregular structures were roofed, it is best to conclude that the tectonizing trend was not directly influenced by

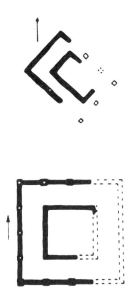

Fig. 15.2. Early temples in southern Gaul
1. Nages (after Py 1978), 2. Vieille-Toulouse (after Vidal 1973 and *Gallia* 34, 1976, 482-3)

knowledge of Mediterranean religious architecture. However, it is much more likely that the regularization of the temple type did in fact come about as a result of such knowledge, firstly in the immediate contact zone on the fringes of Gallia Narbonensis, and later in the rest of Gaul.

Cult-images and Inscriptions
In a similar manner to early Celtic shrines, early iconic representations do not have clear links with what was to emerge in late La Tène. Hallstatt D/La Tène I statuary such as the Hirschlanden figure (Zürn 1964) exist in apparent isolation as far as stone representations are concerned, since most Celtic anthropomorphic figures are late La Tène or even Roman in date. However, it is relevant to point out that Lewis's characterization of Celtic religion as essentially aniconic must be tempered by the existence of the human form, notably the head, in La Tène art (Megaw 1970; Ross 1986). Connections between La Tène art and Celtic religion can not be appropriately discussed here, nor, indeed, can the Greek influences on the emergence of La Tène art styles, but there are three specific points that should be made:

1)   The early free-standing representations, such as Hirschlanden, occur in an area that was notable for its precocious links with the Greek world, within the framework of a prestige-goods economy (Collis 1984, 82 ff.) that acted as a channel for Greek influences into a key region for the development of Celtic culture in the late Hallstatt and early La Tène period. It has often been noticed that the Hirschlanden figure resembles a local version of a Greek *kouros* figure.

2)   By the time late Celtic (and early Roman) religious statuary comes into being, the typical La Tène styles are generally agreed to be in decline in Gaul (but not in Britain).

Fig. 15.3. Glanum: reconstruction drawing of cross-legged statue on pedestal (after Rolland)

3) The area in which specifically religious, free-standing stone sculptures are first commonly met with in the mid-late La Tène period (3rd-1st century BC) was in southern Gaul and the lower Rhône Valley, the main contact zone with the Mediterranean world. However, this area also appears to have been culturally marginal to La Tène civilization as a whole, often being referred to as Celto-Ligurian rather than Celtic. It is not certain how influential its culture was on the Celtic heartlands, unless it was the case that artistic ideas emanating from southern Gaul found favour in the north by being linked with the general flow of goods, services and ideas from the Graeco-Roman world into Gaul.

The sculptural style of the Rhône Valley cross-legged statues, typified by examples from Entremont and Glanum (Fig. 15.3), is curiously reminiscent of archaic Greek sculpture, despite being several centuries later. It is not easy to account for this feature, but the statuary as a whole shows essentially the same characteristic as the temples in having a distinctive local form not found elsewhere (i.e. the cross-legged pose), but depicted and detailed in Greek style.

This iconic form is also known further north (e.g. Argenton-sur-Creuse: Argenton Mus.; Etaules: Espérandieu 1910, no. 2218), but the examples cannot be dated earlier than the Roman period. Indeed, it is difficult to date any of the other stone representations precisely, but those from central and northern Gaul are generally considered to be ultimate La Tène or early Roman period. The wooden anthropomorphic religious sculptures from sites such as Chamalières (Romeuf 1986) and Sources de la Seine (Deyts 1983) are also dated to the early Roman period.

It seems, therefore, that free-standing cult-images in anthropomorphic form are late in date, although the dating is imprecise, and they emerge first in southern Gaul, as a manifestation of Gallo-Greek culture.

Inscriptions are also first encountered within the *milieu* of southern Gallo-Greek culture (Lejeune 1985). The earliest example is on a third century BC column capital from Montagnac, Hérault (Lejeune 1985, G-224)), in Gaulish using Greek script. Most Gallo-Greek inscriptions are second-early first century BC in date and are either funerary *stelae* or graffiti on pottery. In the context of Celtic religion they scarcely figure at all, and it appears that Gallo-Greek inscriptions are a short-lived phenomenon, being almost universally supplanted by Latin inscriptions from the late first century BC onwards. In contrast to the former, Latin inscriptions are used in religious contexts, while Gallo-Latin inscriptions are very rare. This would suggest that the advent of epigraphy into Romano-Celtic religion was late compared with the development of temples and cult-images, for although there was an epigraphic tradition in southern Gaul, this did not really impinge on religious practice. After the Roman conquest of northern Gaul, the epigraphic tradition that developed was a Latin one, using the standard formulae of Latin religious inscriptions within a Romano-Celtic framework.

The emergence of Romano-Celtic religion

The way in which temples, anthropomorphic images and, at a later stage, inscriptions came into use on late Iron Age and early Roman period sacred sites has been presented above, and we have seen that there are a number of features which support the hypothesis that Graeco-Roman influence played an important role.

This role continued and intensified after the conquest of Gaul by Caesar and after the invasion of Britain in AD 43. Romanization across virtually the whole spectrum of cultural life at this time was probably closely connected with the destruction of Celtic 'warrior culture' and the need for tribal élite groups to find new social positions and rituals as a means of maintaining and legitimating their status within the newly-founded provinces. The flowering of Romano-Celtic religion from the Augustan period in Gaul and the Neronian period in Britain was an important manifestation of these changes.

Temples were amongst the earliest stone structures to be erected in northern Gaul and Britain, nearly all of them following the Romano-Celtic pattern (e.g. Elst: Bogaers 1955; Hayling Island: King and Soffe 1990; Colchester-Sheepen: Crummy 1980). At Hayling Island, the transition from a pre-Roman to a Roman shrine can be documented, since the pre-Roman circular wooden temple was removed *c.* AD 60-70, and a large stone temple of similar plan set up in its place (Fig. 15.4). Construction work on the new temple was contemporary with other projects within the tribal territory (e.g. the proto-palace at Fishbourne), and reflects the rapid pace of Romanization in this pro-Roman area. For the worshippers at Hayling, the large new temple, at least twice the volume of the old, and in a different and very new building style, must have decisively altered the ceremonial form of the cult from one that was Celtic to one that was now firmly Romano-Celtic. An important feature is that the change marks an emphasis now on the structure and appearance of the temple rather than on the votive offerings, which decline in variety and status (a development paralleled in Latium in the late Republic: Blagg 1985). Metalwork, for instance, was less common than previously, and the wealthy warrior element almost entirely absent. It seems that the construction of conspicuously Romanized buildings was a new form of status display at this time, and that temples such as Hayling were in the forefront of this trend.

Hayling Island temple may also provide a clue as to why this should have been so. The Roman phase cella can be reconstructed as a tall cylindrical tower, probably higher than the overall diameter of *c.* 13 m., on the basis of surviving examples from south-west Gaul. This reconstruction as a tower *cella*, of course a feature shared by Romano-Celtic temples of more typical form, is of interest when put in juxtaposition with the pre-Roman reconstruction, since the latter seems to have been no more substantial than a typical Iron Age round-house (Fig. 15.5). Superficially, this may suggest that the stone phase in fact reflected a difference in religious approach, despite the continuity of the site and the ground-plan. A possible explanation, however, is that there was some formal element in Celtic religion that made tower-like structures desirable, which could only be properly realized when Roman construction methods became available. This may account for the relatively early stone phases of many Romano-Celtic temples, since there could have been ritualistic as well as social reasons for Romanizing the temples. If this was the case, it can be suggested that Celtic religion only reached its fruition in structural terms in the Roman period, and it can be argued that the Roman element in Romano-Celtic religion is no mere veneer over a conservative Celtic base, but marks a decisive stage in development.

This, in fact, has previously been suggested for religious sculpture, since it was only from the early Roman period that the full variety of Celtic religion began to be revealed and depicted (Green 1986, 35, 102; Henig 1984, 39). Thevenot has commented on this as the exteriorization of Celtic religious feelings in the Roman period (1968, 233). It was an exteriorization, however, that was ambiguous semiotically, since certain signifiers (e.g. sculptural technique, architectural detailing) proclaimed themselves as 'Roman' to worshippers, while others (e.g. iconography, elements of the architectural form) looked back to the pre-Roman 'Celtic' world.

The problem of the druids

At this point it is necessary to consider one of the very few aspects of Celtic religion to be directly affected by Roman official intervention; the suppression of the druids (*cf.* Piggott 1974, 108-11; Zecchini 1984; Clavel-Lévêque 1985; Guyonvarc'h and Le Roux-Guyonvarc'h 1986, 437-42). The bald facts are that Augustus banned Roman citizens from following the *religio druidarum* (Suet., *Claud.* 25, 5), that under Tiberius a decree of the Senate was passed against the druids and related diviners (*vates*) and healers (*medici*) (Pliny, *H.N.* 30, 13), principally on account of their practice of human sacrifice, that Claudius abolished the 'cruel and inhuman religion of the druids in Gaul' (Suet., *Claud.* 25, 5) in AD 54, and that Suetonius Paulinus attacked Anglesey, a centre of druidic power and resistance to Rome, in AD 59-60 (Tac., *Ann.* 14, 30). At face value, this appears to represent an onslaught, apparently for moral but also for political reasons, on both the officiants of Celtic religion and at the same time, certain major facets of the rituals practised, notably human sacrifice.

The implication for the archaeological evidence is that we should expect to find a diminution of traces of Celtic religion during the first half of the first century AD, or at the least major changes in the physical manifestations of ceremonial form, because of the banning of the religion's officiants. For some sites, this may be the case, notably at Ribemont-sur-Ancre, where in La Tène III, a large mound of possibly sacrificial human bones occupied a prominent position in the temple. The mound was burnt and partially destroyed soon after the Roman conquest (Cadoux 1984), to be followed by an Augustan and later, Romano-Celtic temple complex. The excavator of Gournay, too, suggests that the Augustan phase temple was abandoned in the early first century AD due to the anti-druid decrees (Brunaux *et al.* 1985b,

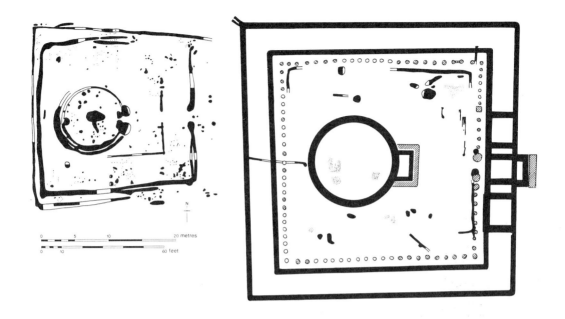

Fig. 15.4. Hayling Island
A. Iron Age, B. early Roman (after King and Soffe 1989)

115-6). However, the great majority of sites record no major changes of this sort during this period, and indeed, many of them go on to establish stone-built Romano-Celtic temples. There is, therefore, an apparent contradiction between the historical evidence, which suggests confrontation and opposition to Rome's influence, and the archaeological evidence, which suggests Romanization.

There are two possibilities for resolving this dilemma, by proposing either that the *religio druidarum* was not in fact the same as mainstream Celtic religion as represented by the temple sites, or that the effect of the Imperial decrees was less than the sources would have us believe. The latter proposition is preferable, since most ancient and modern commentators place the druids in a primary and privileged position as the priests of Celtic religion. Like many other Roman laws, anti-druid decrees were probably unenforceable, while there is the suspicion that they merely acted as a moral gloss on the much more important general changes in society that Romanization was bringing about. If this was the case, therefore, it can be suggested that the Romanization of Celtic religion would eventually have harmonized Celtic and Roman norms of ritual practice, without the specific Imperial intervention that actually occured. Nevertheless, the fact that the decrees were issued at all shows how important the Roman state regarded religion as an arbiter of *mores* and as a focus of power. It is very likely that druidic priesthoods were regarded as similar to Roman priesthoods, with political as well as religious prestige accruing to the holders.

Arguably, the anti-druid decrees can be seen as one side of a concerted bid by the Romans to obtain religious power in Gaul, and thereby sanctify their presence and authority in the province. The other side of this coin was the setting up of an alternative focus of ritual, the

Altar of the Three Gauls at Lyon in 12 BC, and the other provincial altars in Germany and Britain (Fishwick 1972; 1978; *cf.* also Price 1984, ch. 9), which from the mid first century AD were having a marked effect on provincial religion, as attested by the numerous dedications at Romano-Celtic temples that include the divine Augustus (or a similar formula) as well as the local deity (e.g. Allonnes: Térouanne 1960; *cf.* Raepsaet-Charlier 1975). Viewed in this perspective, the measures taken against the druids can be seen as just one aspect of the Romanization of religion, but at the same time they raise another issue, not so far considered, of whether the Romans really took the *laissez-faire* attitude often attributed to them in religious matters. Attempts to do away with a potential source of resistance to Rome (*cf.* Bowersock 1986; Momigliano 1986) and at the same time the provision of an alternative ritualistic focus were clearly officially promoted, and can even be conceived in terms of a 'policy' as far as this concept can be applied to Roman government. Augustus's ban, in particular, can be envisaged as a move to deny indigenous religious power to aspiring Roman citizens in Gaul, and the establishment of the new provincial cult as a controlled and Romanized alternative.

Later Romano-Celtic religion

Such actions by the Roman state probably did not have much immediate effect on the day-to-day veneration of local deities in Romano-Celtic temples, and even in cases where druids in fact ceased to officiate at rituals, a very similar priesthood must have been created to provide the continuity of ritual that is evident at so many temple sites. The long-term effects of official intervention, however, were more subtle, for, as Wightman observes (1985, 186; 1986, 549; *cf.* also Carré 1978, 124-5), relief sculpture of deities at first depicts native gods (e.g. Cernunnos) in original iconographic poses, albeit in a Romanized artistic style, but from the late first century AD, more Romanized attributes appear and the deities are shown as more 'Roman' than before. This would seem to reflect a change from the conscious development of a native iconography during the first century or so after the Roman conquest, to a more general acceptance of classical models as the norm for religious depictions. This also applies to the formulae used in epigraphic dedications (Raepsaet-Charlier 1975; Carré 1978), and there is an element of the same trend in temple architecture, too, since several Romano-Celtic temples are constructed with imposing classical façades at this time (Horne's classicized type; Horne 1986), and there are some instances of Romano-Celtic temples being replaced by classical-style buildings, notably Augst-Schönbühl (Laur-Belart 1978, 79-85) and Faimingen (Weber 1981), but also, unusually, the rural temple sites of Antigny (Richard 1988) and Masamas, Saint-Léomer (de Lavergne *et al.* 1982). These replacements mark the apparent abandonment of Romano-Celtic cults in favour of more classical ones, but Bath may be the unique case of a classical temple constructed *de novo* for a Romano-Celtic cult (Cunliffe and Davenport 1985; Cunliffe 1986).

These developments during the early Empire mark the normalization of provincial religion in the Celtic provinces. What had previously been regarded as a certain level of antagonism between the Roman and Celtic religious worlds evaporated with the political neutralization of the druids, and a synthesis emerged, based mainly on Romanized Celtic models that had been developed in the late first century BC-early first century AD. Iconography, architecture and epigraphy for Romano-Celtic cults were drawn freely but somewhat eclectically from Roman sources to create what is known, rather erroneously, as *interpretatio romana*. At the same time, Celtic cults lost whatever cultural integrity they may have had, as they reflected

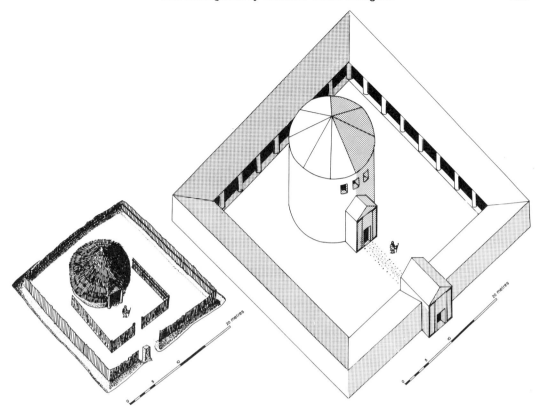

Fig. 15.5. Hayling Island: reconstructions of the Iron Age
and Roman phases given in Fig. 15.4.

more the north-western provinces' version of the Empire-wide religious *koiné*, itself a manifestation of a Roman culture that created conformity but allowed local variation within limited constraints. This could be called cultural or even religious imperialism, operating through the creation of a power structure that encouraged competition for positions and status by emulating Roman ways, in religion as well as more mundane affairs (hence Tacitus's famous remarks in *Agric.* 21).

From this period, therefore, Romano-Celtic temples and material remains become a regional 'type-fossil', characteristic of the civilian regions of the north-west provinces. The semiotic significance of the various 'Roman' and 'Celtic' elements that had contributed to the creation of this type-fossil was probably now unimportant, as new generations of worshippers accepted Romano-Celtic religion for what it was, without dissecting out its contributory elements. Another regional religious characteristic was the re-emergence of the druids in the third and fourth centuries, now without political significance and in a role as philosophers and intellectuals (Clavel-Lévêque 1985, 593; Ausonius, *Comm. Prof. Burd.* 4 and 10). This is not a 'Celtic renaissance' as has been claimed, but more a manifestation of the regionalism seen in the later Empire (*cf.* King 1990, ch. 8). The Celtic side of Romano-Celtic religion continued to decline, as Roman names for deities start to predominate, and as the Celtic language in

Gaul became less widespread, particularly amongst the literate classes (Guyonvarc'h and Le Roux-Guyonvarc'h 1986, 442ff.; Whatmough 1970, proleg., 68-76; Schmidt 1983, 1003-11).

The end of Romano-Celtic religion as a major cultural force came with its derogation as 'paganism' by early Christian writers, who did not, of course, separate it from other non-Christian cults. It was regarded as an aspect of a conservative rural population resistant to religious change – in marked contrast to the role it had played only a few centuries earlier as a potent agent of the cultural transition from Celtic to Roman civilization in the north-west provinces.

Conclusion I: Romano-Celtic religion and the assessment of acculturation

This paper has attempted to bring out the cultural, rather than the purely religious significance of Romano-Celtic religion, on a diachronic basis and with a view to assessing the extent of Romanization of Celtic society. Religious monuments and artefacts are in many ways uniquely suited to this task, since they are a major symbolic focus of rituals that give cultural identity and cohesion to a society (Cohen 1985, 50 ff.). Because of this, there is considerable semiotic significance in the details of the physical remains. A 'Roman' feature such as the use of Corinthian capitals in a Romano-Celtic temple reflects the level of Romanization of the sanctuary, and the distribution of temples with a strong presence of such attributes could be taken as mapping the area where Roman acculturation of the Celtic provinces was greatest. Central and eastern Gaul and the Rhineland would in fact be the areas where this was so; regions to the west and north having a lesser degree of Romanization, and Britain markedly less.

Britain is also different from the continental provinces in having little evidence for the proto-Romano-Celtic stage of development seen at Gaulish sites such as Gournay or Nages. This is probably due to the lesser extent of 'pre-Roman Romanization' (Haselgrove 1984), following the precepts of the core-periphery model. The result is that there is a rapid transition from the tectonizing phase in the late pre-Roman Iron Age to the establishment of fully developed Romano-Celtic types, presumably inspired by Gallic examples, from the Flavian period. The distribution of the Romano-Celtic type was also limited to the lowland areas of Britain. Further north and west, the limited acculturation of local culture results in few, if any, civilian religious sites being known, probably because they were atectonic or ephemeral structures. It would be of the greatest interest to have a well-excavated example of an un-Romanized 'Celtic' sacred site from this region. Of course, temples dedicated to Celtic deities are known in a military context, for instance in the vicinity of Hadrian's Wall. These are Romanized structures, with Romanized ritual appurtenances, and as such, form a distinctive 'military Romano-Celtic' style, quite separate from civilian Romano-Celtic ceremonial forms. The military variant is also found, to a lesser extent, in some of the military *vici* in Germany, and there is a case to be made for these types of temple being a facet of military culture following its own precepts and not drawing on local archetypes.

Another region on the margin of the main area of Romano-Celtic cults, southern Gaul, went by contrast in the direction of almost complete acculturation and absorbtion of Roman styles in religion (*pace* Lavagne 1970). Here, Romanization appears to have penetrated the final bastions of native culture, language and religious belief, to result in a culture almost wholly devoid of Celtic characteristics, to the extent that Pliny could refer to it as more like Italy than a province (*H.N.* 3, 32). The reasons for this are threefold, a) a relatively weak local culture, marginal to the Celtic core area further north, b) long exposure to Hellenization and Mediterranean civilisations generally, and c) a rapid and intense phase of Romanization in the first century BC, which saw the establishment of Roman cities, centuriation systems and of course, classical religion. The phase of Romanization was probably the most important factor, as it is clear that Hellenization resulted not in the ending of native culture but in a Gallo-Greek synthesis. Roman cultural intervention in southern Gaul may have been more deliberate and conscious policy than further north, due perhaps to the deep-seated prejudice of the *terror gallicus*, discussed by Drinkwater (1983, 7 ff). The results were similar in many ways to the intensive Romanization of the Po Valley, where Celtic culture was also weak and effectively extinguished by Rome.

Conclusion II: conservatism and change

A final remark brings us back to the realm of beliefs, a subject deliberately submerged by concentration on ceremonial form. Romanization clearly altered the latter, but it may be questioned how far the belief system itself changed. Conservatism of belief is often considered to be an essential facet of religion, following Malinowski's (1948, 67) conception of religion as a means of enduring situations of emotional stress, through the comfort of a traditional belief system. This is perhaps debatable, since recent commentators would lay more stress on the comfort of ritualistic behaviour than of the underlying belief system itself (Geertz 1966; Cohen 1985). As we have seen, ritualistic behaviour may have changed during the emergence of Romano-Celtic from Celtic religion, thus implying that religion was not being relied upon to provide traditional values during a crucial period of transition, but on the contrary, was being used to promote that transition. The needs and desires of Celtic society, especially in Gaul, almost certainly favoured Romanization; and Romano-Celtic religion, far from inhibiting this trend, actually came to symbolize the new social developments. However, it would have been possible for these changes to have taken place without much alteration of the belief system, for, paradoxically, the Romanization of Celtic religion could have acted as a means of protecting the underlying religious beliefs. Instead of being marginalized or replaced by more classical forms of Roman religion, Celtic cults nearly everywhere survived and became acceptable by having a sufficiently flexible belief system to accommodate Romanized ceremonial forms. During the early Empire, at least, Romano-Celtic religion became culturally Roman while remaining ethnically Celtic.

Notes

1   For sites in Gaul and Germany see Horne and King 1980, s.v. Alise-Sainte-Reine A & C, Allonnes, Ancy-et-Mâlain, Bern-Engehalbinsel A & B, Château-Porcien, Essarois A & B, Eu A, Faye-L'Abbesse, Genainville, Hochscheid, Koblenz A, Mayen-Adenau, Mont-Beuvray, Mouzon A, Offemont, Otrang, Poitiers, Ribemont-sur-Ancre (plus Cadoux 1984), Saint-Bonnet-de-Chirac, Saint-Germain-Sources-Seine, Saint-Léomer, Saint-Marcel (plus Fauduet 1986), Trier, Trougouzel, Vendeuvre. See also Villeneuve-au-Châtelot (Piette 1981), Digeon (Delplace *et al.* 1986), Mirebeau (Brunaux *et al.* 1985a), Baron-sur-Odon (Bertin 1977). For a recent catalogue of German sites see Follmann-Schulz 1986. For British sites see Drury 1980, plus Danebury (Cunliffe 1984), Hayling Island (King and Soffe 1990), Uley (Ellison forthcoming), Witham (Turner 1982).

2   Heathrow has been put forward as the earliest example of the Romano-Celtic temple type, dating as early as the 3rd century BC (Drury 1980, 52-4; Grimes 1948). In view of the evidence from the sites listed above and in the text, such a date is anomalous and seems unlikely. The dating

apparently comes from the immediately adjacent settlement, not from the temple itself, from the area of which came the only sherd of Roman pottery from the site (from an overlying ditch). Therefore the temple could be of some other date than the settlement, and on the analogy of the other sites, is best placed in the late 1st century BC/early 1st century AD. It could be an early example of a religious site existing after the adjacent settlement has been abandoned, as happened at Maiden Castle (Drury 1980). For a recent discussion of the Heathrow site and its regional setting, see Cotton *et al.* 1986, 50-7.

Bibliography

Benoit, F. 1981 *Entremont. Capitale celto-ligure des Salyens de Provence*, Gap: Ophrys

Bertin, D. 1977 'Le sanctuaire celto-romain du Mesnil de Baron-sur-Odon (Calvados)', *Gallia* 35, 75-88

Black, E.W. 1986 'Romano-British burial customs and religious beliefs in south-east England', *Archaeol. J.* 143, 201-39

Blagg, T.F.C. 1985 'Cult practice and its social context in the rural sanctuaries of Latium and southern Etruria', in, Malone, C. and Stoddart, S. (ed), *Papers in Italian Archaeology IV*, Oxford: British Archaeological Reports, 33-50

Bogaers, J. 1955 *De Gallo-Romeinse Tempels te Elst in de Over-Betuwe*, s'Gravenhage: Staatsdrukkerij- en Uitgeverijbedrijf

Bowersock, G.W. 1986 'The mechanics of subversion in the Roman provinces', *Foundation Hardt Entreteins sur l'Antiquité Classique* 33, 291-320

Bradley, R. 1984 *The Social Foundations of Prehistoric Britain*, Harlow: Longman

Brisson, A. and Hatt, J.-J. 1955 'Cimitières gaulois et gallo-romains à enclos en Champagne', *Rev. Archéol. Est Centre-Est* 6, 313-33

Brunaux, J.-L., Goguey, R., Guillaumet, J.-P., Meniel, P. and Rapin, A. 1985a 'Le sanctuaire celtique de Mirebeau (Côte-d'Or)', *Rev. Archéol. Est Centre-Est Supp.* 6, 79-111 (= *Les Ages du Fer dans la Vallée de la Saône*)

Brunaux, J.-L., Meniel, P. and Poplin, F. 1985b *Gournay I: les fouilles sur le sanctuaire et l'oppidum (1975-1984)*, Amiens: Société des Antiquités Historiques de Picardie

Cadoux, J.-L. 1984 'L'ossuaire gaulois de Ribemont-sur-Ancre (Somme). Premières observations, premières questions', *Gallia* 42, 53-78

Carré, R. 1978 'Les cultes voconces', *Dialogues Hist. Anc.* 4, 119-33

Chabot, L. 1983 'L'*oppidum* de la Cloche aux Pennes-Mirabeau (Bouches-du-Rhône)', *Rev. Archéol. Narbonnaise* 16, 39-80

Chadwick, N. 1970 *The Celts*, Harmondsworth: Penguin

Clavel-Lévêque, M. 1985 'Mais ou sont les druides a'antan...? Tradition religieuse et identité culturelle en Gaule', *Dialogues Hist. Anc.* 11, 557-604

Cohen, A.P. 1985 *The Symbolic Construction of Community*, Chichester: Ellis Horwood

Collis, J. 1984 *The European Iron Age*, London: Batsford

Colonna, G. (ed) 1985 *Santuari d'Etruria*, Milan: Electra

Cotton, J., Mills, J. and Clegg, G. 1986 *Archaeology in West Middlesex*, Hillingdon: Hillingdon Borough Libraries

Coupry, J. and Giffault, M. 1982 'La clientèle d'un sanctuaire d'Aristée aux Iles d'Hyères (Ier siècle avant J-C)', *La Parola del Passato* 37, 360-70

Crummy, P. 1980 'The temples of Roman Colchester', in, Rodwell, W. (ed), *Temples, Churches and Religion: recent research in Roman Britain*, Oxford: British Archaeological Reports, 243-83

Cunliffe, B.W. 1984a 'Iron Age Wessex: continuity and change', in, Cunliffe, B. and Miles, D. (ed), *Aspects of the Iron Age in Central Southern Britain*, Oxford University Committee for Archaeology, 12-45

Cunliffe, B.W. 1984b *Danebury: an Iron Age hillfort in Hampshire*, London: Council for British Archaeology Research Report 52

Cunliffe, B.W. 1986 'The sanctuary of Sulis Minerva at Bath: a brief review', in, Henig, M.E. and King, A.C. (ed), *Pagan Gods and Shrines of the Roman Empire*, Oxford: Oxford University Committee for Archaeology, 1-14

Cunliffe, B.W. and Davenport, P. 1985 *The Temple of Sulis Minerva at Bath I, The Site*, Oxford: Oxford University Committee for Archaeology

de Gérin-Ricard, H. 1927 *Le Sanctuaire préromaine de Roquepertuse*, Marseille: Société de Statistique, d'Histoire et d'Archéologie de Marseille et de Provence

de Lavergne, E., de Lavergne, S., Reix, R., Aucher, M.R. and Aucher M. 1982 'Résultats de 17 années de fouilles à Masamas (Saint-Léomer)', *Bull. Soc. Antiq. Ouest* ser. 4, 16, 469-78

De Laet, S.J. 1966 'Van grafmonument tot heiligdom', *Meded. Kon. Vlaamse Acad. Wetensch. Lett. Schone Kunst Belg., klasse Letteren* 28, 2, 17-73

Delplace, C., Jobie, F., Meniel, P. and Rapin, A. 1986 'Le sanctuaire de Digeon', *Rev. Archéol.* Picardie 1986, 3/4, 83-117

Desbat, A. 1981 'L'architecture de terre à Lyon à l'époque romaine', in, Walker, S. (ed), *Récentes Recherches en Archéologie gallo-romaine et paléochrétienne sur Lyon et sa Région*, Oxford: British Archaeological Reports, 55-81

Deyts, S. 1983 *Les Bois sculptés des Sources de la Seine*, Paris: CNRS

Donley, L.W. 1982 'House power: Swahili space and symbolic markers', in, Hodder, I. (ed), *Symbolic and Structural Archaeology*, Cambridge University Press, 63-72

Drinkwater, J.F. 1983 *Roman Gaul*, Beckenham: Croom Helm

Drury, P. 1980 'Non-classical religious buildings in Iron Age and Roman Britain: a review', in, Rodwell, W. (ed), *Temples, Churches and Religion: recent research in Roman Britain*, Oxford: British Archaeological Reports, 45-78

Ellison, A. forthcoming *Excavations at Uley, Gloucestershire*

Espérandieu, E. 1910 *Recueil général des Bas-Reliefs, Statues et Bustes de la Gaule romaine*, III, Paris: Imprimerie Nationale

Fauduet, I. 1986 'Cult and ritual practice at Argentomagus, Indre, France', in, Henig, M.E. and King, A.C. (ed), *Pagan Gods and Shrines of the Roman Empire*, Oxford: Oxford University Committee for Archaeology, 25-8

Fishwick, D. 1972 'The temple of the Three Gauls', *J. Roman Stud.* 62, 46-52

Fishwick, D. 1978 'The development of provincial ruler worship in the western Roman Empire', *Aufstieg und Niedergang der Römischen Welt* II, 16, 2, 1201-53

Flouest, J.-L. and Stead, I. 1979 *Iron Age Cemeteries in Champagne: the third interim report*, London: British Museum

Follmann-Schulz, A.-B. 1986 'Die römischen Tempelanlagen in der Provinz Germania Inferior', *Aufstieg und Niedergang der Römischen Welt* II, 18, 1, 672-793

Geertz, c. 1966 'Religion as a cultural system', in, Banton, M. (ed), *Anthropological Approaches to the Study of Religion*, London: Tavistock Publications, 1-46. Reprinted in shortened form in, Bocock, R and Thompson, K. (ed), 1985, *Religion and Ideology*, Manchester University Press, 66-75

Green, M.J. 1986 *The Gods of the Celts*, Gloucester: Alan Sutton

Grimes, W.F. 1948 'A prehistoric temple at London airport', *Archaeology* 1, 74-8

Guyonvarc'h, C.-J. and Le Roux-Guyonvarc'h, F. 1986 'Remarques sur la religion gallo-romaine: rupture et continuité', *Aufstieg und Niedergang der Römischen Welt* II, 18, 1, 423-55

Haselgrove, c. 1984 '"Romanization" before the conquest: Gaulish precedents and British consequences', in, Blagg, T.F.C. and King, A.C. (ed), *Military and Civilian in Roman Britain: cultural relationships in a frontier province*, Oxford: British Archaeological Reports, 5-63

Henig, M. 1984 *Religion in Roman Britain*, London: Batsford

Hodder, I 1982 *Symbols in Action*, Cambridge University Press

Horne, P.D. 1986 'Roman or Celtic temples? A case study', in, Henig, M. and King, A.C. (ed), *Pagan Gods and Shrines of the Roman Empire*, Oxford: Oxford University Committee for Archaeology, 15-24

Horne, P.D. and King, A.C. 1980 'Romano-Celtic temples in continental Europe: a gazetteer of those with known plans', in, Rodwell, W. (ed), *Temples, Churches and Religion: recent research in Roman Britain*, Oxford: British Archaeological Reports, 369-555

King, A.C. 1990 *Roman Gaul and Germany*, London: British Museum Publications

King, A.C. and Soffe, G. 1990 'Hayling Island', in, Jones, R.F.J. (ed), *Britain in the Roman Period*, Sheffield: Department of Archaeology and Prehistory, forthcoming

Lantier, R. 1943 'Les nouvelles statues d'Antremont', *Fondation Eugène Piot. Monuments et Mémoires* 40, 87-106

Laur-Belart, R. 1978 *Führer durch Augusta Raurica*, Basel: Historischen u. Antiquarischen Gesellschaft zu Basel

Lavagne, H. 1970 'Recherches sur l'interprétation romaine dans les cultes de la Narbonnaise', *Annu. Ecole Pratique Hautes Etudes, IVe Section* 102, 707-14

Lejeune, M. 1985 *Recueil des Inscriptions Gauloises (RIG) I. Textes gallo-grecs*, Paris: CNRS

Lewis, M.J.T. 1966 *Temples in Roman Britain*, Cambridge University Press

Malinowski, B. 1948 *Magic, Science and Religion*, Boston: Beacon Press

Meates, G.W. 1979 *The Lullingstone Roman Villa, I, The Site*, Maidstone: Kent Archaeological Society

Megaw, J.V.S. 1970 *Art of the European Iron Age: a study of the elusive image*, Bath: Adams and Dart

Momigliano, A. 1986 'Some preliminary remarks on the "religious opposition" to the Roman Empire', *Foundation Hardt Entretiens sur l'Antiquité Classique* 33, 103-33

Nash, D. 1978 'Territory and state formation in Central Gaul', in, Green, D. *et al.* (ed), *Social Organization and Settlement*, Oxford: British Archaeological Reports, 455-75

North, J. 1976 'Conservatism and change in Roman religion', *Pap. Brit. School Rome* 44, 1-12

Paris, R. 1960 'Un temple celtique et gallo-romaine en Forêt de Châtillon-sur-Seine (Côte-d'Or)', *Rev. Archéol. Est Centre-Est* 11, 164-75

Piette, J. 1981 'Le fanum de la Villeneuve-au-Châtelot (Aube). Etat de recherches en 1979', *Mém. Soc. Archéol. Champenoise* 2, 367-75 (= *L'Age du Fer en France Septentrionale*)

Piggott, S. 1974 *The Druids*, Harmondsworth: Penguin

Piggott, S. 1978 'Nemeton, temenos, bothros: sanctuaries of the ancient celts', in, Accademia Nazionale dei Lincei (ed), *I Celti e la loro Cultura nell'Epoca pre-romana e romana nella Britannia*, Rome: Accademia Nazionale dei Lincei, 37-54

Piton, D. and Dilly, G. 1985 'La fanum des "Chatelets" de Vendeuil-Caply (Oise)', *Rev. Archéol. Picardie* 1985, 1/2, 25-64

Planck, D. 1986 'Die Viereckschanze von Fellbach-Schmiden', in, Planck, D. *et al.* (ed), *Der Keltenfürst von Hochdorf: Methoden und Ergebnisse der Landesarchäologie* (exhib. cat.), Stuttgart: Landesdenkmalamt Baden-Württemberg, 340-53

Price, S.R.F. 1984 *Rituals and Power. The Roman Imperial Cult in Asia Minor*, Cambridge University Press

Py, M. 1978 *L'Oppidum des Castels à Nages (Gard)*, Paris: CNRS

Raepsaet-Charlier, M.-T. 1975 'La datation des inscriptions latines dans les provinces occidentales de l'Empire romain d'après les formules "IN H(ONOREM) D(OMUS) D(IVINAE)" et "DEO, DEAE"', *Aufsteig und Niedergang der Römischen Welt* II, 3, 232-82

Richard, C. 1988 'Du fanum gaulois au temple classique au vicus du Gué de Sciaux', *Archéologia* 231, 48-53

Röder, J. 1948 'Der Goloring', *Bonner J.* 148, 81-132

Rolland, H. 'Nouvelles fouilles du sanctuaire des Glaniques', *Riv. Stud. Liguri* 34, 7-34

Romeuf, A.-M. 1986 'Ex-voto en bois de Chamalières (Puy-de-Dôme) et des Sources de la Seine. Essai de comparaison', *Gallia* 44, 65-89

Ross, A. 1986 *The Pagan Celts*, London: Batsford

Rybová, A and Soudsky, B. 1962 *Libeniçe. Keltská Svatyne ve Strednich Cechách*, Prague: Ceskoslovenské Akademie Ved

Schmidt, K.H. 1983 'Keltisch-lateinische Sprachkontakte im römischen Gallien der Kaiserzeit', *Aufstieg und Niedergang der Römischen Welt* II, 29, 2, 988-1018

Schwarz, K. 1962 'Zum Stand der Ausgrabungen in der spätkeltischen Viereckschanze von Holzhausen', *Jahresber. Bayerischen Bodendenkmalpflege* 3, 22-77

Slofstra, J. and Sanden, W. van der 1987 'Rurale cultusplaatsen uit de Romeinse tijd in het Maas-Demer-Scheldegebied', *Analecta Praehistorica Leidenensis* 20, 125-68

Small, D.B. 1987 'Towards a competent structuralist archaeology: a contribution from historical studies', *J. Anthro. Archaeol.* 6, 105-21

Stambaugh, J.E. 1978 'The functions of Roman temples', *Aufsteig und Niedergang der Römischen Welt* II, 16, 1, 554-608

Strong, D.E. 1968 *The Early Etruscans*, London: Evans Bros

Térouanne, P. 1960 'Dédicaces à Mars Mullo découvertes à Allonnes (Sarthe)', *Gallia* 18, 185-9

Thevenot, E. 1968 *Divinités et Sanctuaires de la Gaule*, Paris: Fayard

Turner, R. 1982 *Ivy Chimneys, Witham. An interim report*, Chelmsford: Essex County Council Archaeology Section

Venclová, N. 1989 'Mšecké Žehrovice, Bohemia: excavations 1979-88', *Antiquity* 63, 142-6

Vidal, M. 1973 'Vestiges d'un édifice du Ier siècle av. J-C à Vieille-Toulouse', *Pallas* 20, 105-13

Vidal, M. 1987 'L'emporium de Vieille-Toulouse et les puits funéraires du Toulousain', in, *Toulouse et sa Région*, Dijon: Dossiers d'Histoire et d'Archéologie 120, 37-41

Weber, G. 1981 'Neue Ausgrabungen am "Apollo-Grannus-Heiligtum" in Faimingen. Zwischenbericht', *Ber. Rom.-Germ. Komm.* 62, 103-218

Whatmough, J. 1970 *The Dialects of Ancient Gaul*, Cambridge, Mass.: Harvard University Press

Wheeler, R.E.M. 1928 'A "Romano-Celtic" temple near Harlow, Essex, and a note on the type', *Antiq. J.* 8, 300-326

Wightman, E.M. 1985 *Gallia* Belgica, London: Batsford

Wightman, E.M. 1986 'Pagan cults in the province of Belgica', *Aufstieg und Niedergang der Römischen Welt* II, 18, 1, 542-89

Wilson, D.R. 1980 'Romano-Celtic temple architecture: how much do we actually know?', in, Rodwell, W. (ed), *Temples, Churches and Religion: recent research in Roman Britain*, Oxford: British Archaeological Reports, 5-30

Zecchini, G. 1984 *I Druidi e l'opposizione dei Celti a Roma*, Milan

Zürn, H. 1964 'An anthropomorphic Hallstatt stele', *Antiquity* 38, 224-6

Index

Place-names are generally given in the modern language of the country concerned. Where other ancient or modern forms are in common use they are cross-referenced.